MIAMI'S ART BOOM

UNIVERSITY PRESS OF FLORIDA

Florida A&M University, Tallahassee
Florida Atlantic University, Boca Raton
Florida Gulf Coast University, Ft. Myers
Florida International University, Miami
Florida State University, Tallahassee
New College of Florida, Sarasota
University of Central Florida, Orlando
University of Florida, Gainesville
University of North Florida, Jacksonville
University of South Florida, Tampa
University of West Florida, Pensacola

ELISA TURNER   *Foreword by Franklin Sirmans*

FROM LOCAL VISION TO
INTERNATIONAL PRESENCE

MIAMI'S ART BOOM

UNIVERSITY PRESS OF FLORIDA

Gainesville/Tallahassee/Tampa/Boca Raton

Pensacola/Orlando/Miami/Jacksonville/Ft. Myers/Sarasota

Cover: *Re-Collections VIII (rojo y azul)* by Carlos Betancourt

Publication of this work made possible by grants from the John S. and James L. Knight Foundation; Miami-Dade County Board of Commissioners and Mayor Daniella Levine Cava through Miami-Dade County Department of Cultural Affairs; and Oolite Arts.

30 29 28 27 26 25   6 5 4 3 2 1

LIBRARY OF CONGRESS CATALOGING-IN-PUBLICATION DATA

Names: Turner, Elisa, author. | Sirmans, Franklin, author of foreword.

Title: Miami's art boom : from local vision to international presence / Elisa Turner ; foreword
    by Franklin Sirmans

Description: Gainesville : University Press of Florida, 2025. | Includes index. | Summary: "In Miami's
    Art Boom, art critic Elisa Turner captures the evolution of Miami's visual arts community before
    and after the inaugural Art Basel Miami Beach, revealing how local artists, galleries, and museums
    transformed the city into a hub of global artistic exchange"— Provided by publisher.

Identifiers: LCCN 2025019210 (print) | LCCN 2025019211 (ebook) | ISBN 9780813081212 (paperback) |
    ISBN 9780813075051 (ebook)

Subjects: LCSH: Art Basel Miami Beach—History. | Art—Florida—Miami—20th century—Exhibitions.
    | Art fairs—Florida—Miami—Exhibitions. | Art—Florida—Miami Beach—20th century—
    Exhibitions. | BISAC: ART / History / Contemporary (1945-) | ART / American / General | LCGFT:
    Exhibition catalogs.

Classification: LCC N6487.M53 T87 2025 (print) | LCC N6487.M53 (ebook) |
    DDC 709.759/381—dc23/eng/20250618

LC record available at https://lccn.loc.gov/2025019210

LC ebook record available at https://lccn.loc.gov/2025019211

The University Press of Florida is the scholarly publishing agency for the State University
System of Florida, comprising Florida A&M University, Florida Atlantic University,
Florida Gulf Coast University, Florida International University, Florida State University,
New College of Florida, University of Central Florida, University of Florida, University
of North Florida, University of South Florida, and University of West Florida.

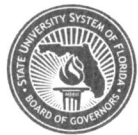

University Press of Florida
2046 NE Waldo Road
Suite 2100
Gainesville, FL 32609
http://upress.ufl.edu

GPSR EU Authorized Representative: Mare Nostrum Group B.V., Mauritskade 21D, 1091 GC Amsterdam, The Netherlands, gpsr@mare-nostrum.co.uk

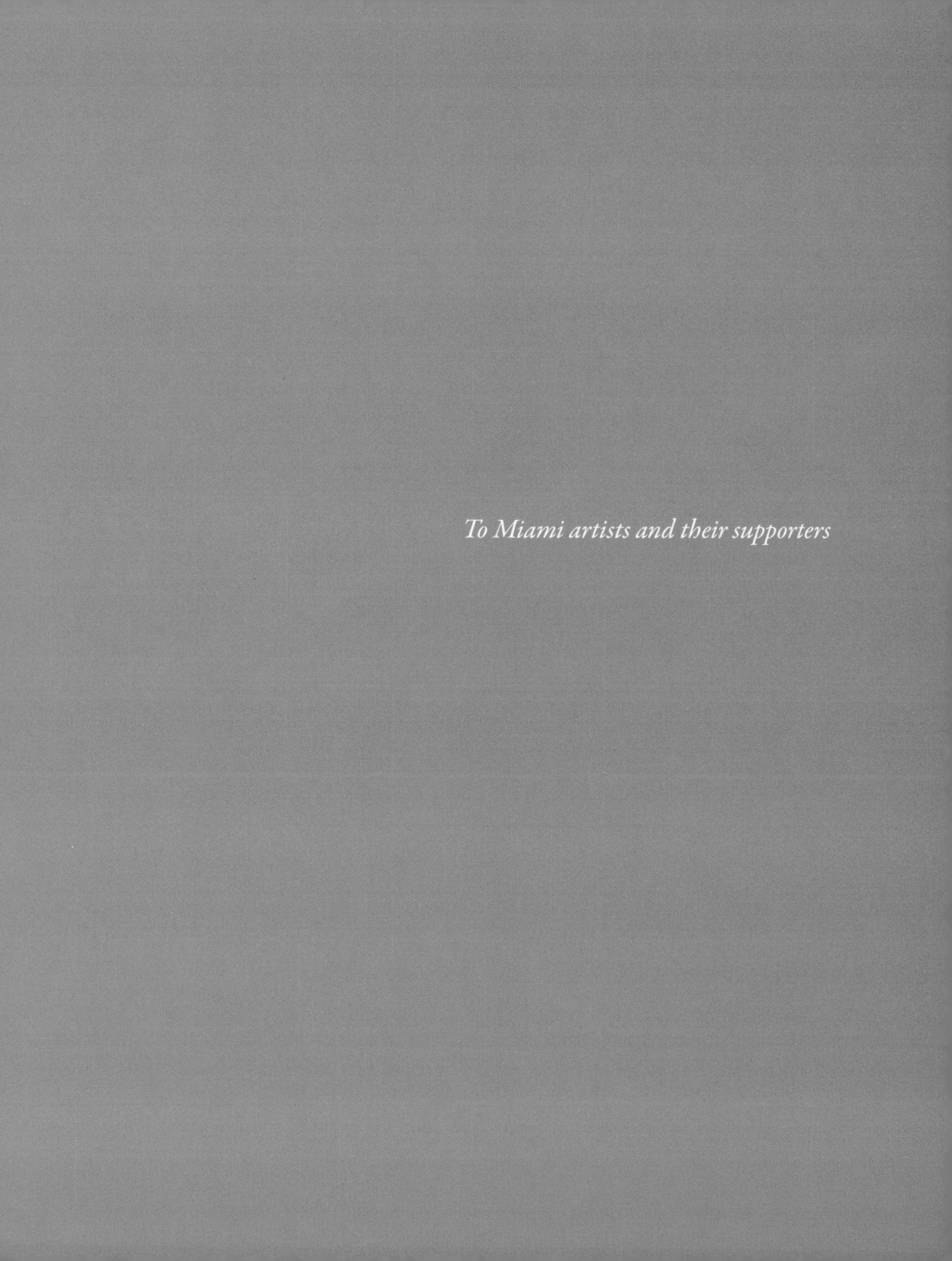

To Miami artists and their supporters

CONTENTS

PART II. VISUALLY ON THE VERGE, 1998–2000

PART III. MIAMI / "A LOT OF FREEDOM TO EXPERIMENT," 2001–2004

PART IV. GLOBAL ART LOCALLY, 2005–2007

FOREWORD

Where would we be without Elisa Turner?

So often we hear the refrain of pundits talking about the world of art as if it comes solely as something to be bought and sold. In the current environment—the proliferation of art fairs—the price tag has become, wrongly, ever more a language to describe artistic value.

Did it happen if it wasn't documented? Thanks to Elisa Turner, not only did it happen, but this book made up of collected and new writings puts it all together in the same place, highlighting Turner's deep commitment to writing, documenting, and showcasing the art that made Miami. The big events are there: Art Basel coming to town and joining Art Miami as global art fairs presenting the best art created from all around the world, seen first in Miami. The new museums and galleries that demonstrated a city committed to the arts year-round, not only the first week in December. And the big-name artists made in Miami, who found their mark in Miami, are all there: Alfonzo, Bedia, Duval-Carrié, Gelfman, González-Torres, Fernández, Bas, Fisher, Gispert, Guerrier, and on to the current generation, which is primed for global greatness on the heels of the history Turner so acutely documents. The gallerists, who helped bridge the gap for artists between starving and making ends meet, from Gloria Luria to Fred Snitzer and newer spaces dedicated to the art of the now, are all there. As are the collectors whose names may be bigger in the popular imagination than the artists, a fact that Turner doesn't shy away from addressing in a town of Pérez, Rubell, Braman, Robins, de la Cruz, Scholl, and Shack.

Documenting Miami's art scene through its denizens, artists, and exhibitions would be more than enough! But Turner has a small axe to grind, or just a proper nudging. The book takes art as the vantage point from which to examine the growth of a city and is in effect an exploration of art as the cornerstone to growth in all facets of Miami's comeuppance. It's a primer for how cities grow and a prime example of the role that art plays in any city's growth. People want to raise families, work, and play in a place that has the best art the world has to offer. It makes people feel at home and creates a sense of community. Shining a light on the artists and innovators who make art for the sake of making art is the gift that Turner has given continuously and consistently like no one else. We should all be thankful. Thank you, Elisa!

Franklin Sirmans

INTRODUCTION

Tapping Local Tenor and
Pulse of the Moment

In 1983, two visionary artists brought an astounding sensation to Miami. Directing a 430-member crew, Christo and Jeanne-Claude surrounded 11 islands in Biscayne Bay with 6.5 million square feet of woven propylene fabric, colored a fabulous hyacinth pink. The artists' *Surrounded Islands* was spread over 7 miles, visible from land, water, and air. After two weeks, their art was dismantled. Its ephemeral beauty is legendary, an audacious Miami moment still reverberating for its celebration of the city's luminous sky and water.

Three years after *Surrounded Islands*, I began writing as an art critic for the *Miami Herald* and continued through 2007. These were pivotal years in Miami's evolution into an international cultural destination, foreshadowed by the daring vision of Christo and Jeanne-Claude. I wrote about adventurous accomplishments by a broad range of artists, curators, galleries, museums, and nonprofit spaces.

This volume looks closely at work by over 50 artists, with more mentioned in stories recounting memorable events. It documents crucial decades from 1987 to 2007, recording how the arrival of Art Basel Miami Beach in 2002 contributed to an already-expanding art scene. It is divided chronologically into parts 1, 2, 3, and 4. Beginning and ending each of the four parts are columns I felt were particularly newsworthy and significant. My goal was to convey the momentum of Miami as it became an internationally known ecosystem for the visual arts.

From the outset of my tenure at the *Miami Herald*, I often heard astonished conversations about *Surrounded Islands* and its galvanizing effects. Still, I was quick to immerse myself in what the local art community was doing then to make its own mark. As a recent arrival learning to find her way among multiple ramps on and off Interstate 95 slicing through this densely populated tip of Florida, I met people passionately attentive to the local art scene. Both artists and art supporters, they weren't content to bask in the glow of famous outsiders' accomplishments.

Long dismissed as sleepy and provincial, Miami's art community in the 1980s percolated with DIY grassroots energy. Lured by low-cost rents, artists refurbished blighted neighborhoods. Forward-thinking artist Ellie Schneiderman founded South Florida Art Center (now Oolite Arts) in 1984 on Lincoln Road in Miami Beach, establishing studio spaces and a cooperative gallery. North of downtown in Wynwood, the Bakehouse Art Complex provided affordable artist studios reconfigured inside a 33,000-square-foot former industrial bakery. It was fully open in 1987.

This book reveals the inner workings of an evolving art community moving toward global prominence. In this chronologically ordered book, readers can witness that growth unfolding through art reviews, profiles, and reported stories. Yes, there were disappointments and faltering moments, which I describe, but this book also records rewarding times and challenges overcome. It unspools a cinematic portrait over time of artists and other players, many still active, who shaped considerable changes transforming Greater Miami in the years leading up to the inaugural Art Basel Miami Beach.

Although the book recounts the momentous effects of the world-renowned fair on the local cultural community through 2007, there is no section devoted to early editions of Art Basel Miami Beach. Rather, my focus is on generally lesser-recognized but no less worthy contributions of creative local individuals and institutions. Their innovations have brought stimulating energy driving cultural offerings today throughout Greater Miami and South Florida.

It must be said that the long-term advantages of hosting "Basel," as the annual December citywide phenomenon of the Swiss fair is sometimes known, are still debated. Does it overshadow ambitious local events staged during the fair, when satellite art fairs and lavish parties attract scores of well-heeled tourists and out-of-town collectors? Yes, to some extent. But the fair has sparked a wider interest in Miami's art community lasting long after the moneyed, at times raucous Basel crowd departs.

There's no denying that cultural opportunities have increased since 2002 even as Miami grapples with urban ills including soaring costs of living, homelessness, systemic racism, and environmental degradation.

Numerous local institutions and artists have gained significantly from the annual presence of this art world juggernaut. As my predecessor at the *Miami Herald* Helen Kohen said, "These days depend on those days."

In the late 20th century, the groundwork for Miami's cultural growth was laid in considerable measure by Miami-Dade County and the John S. and James L. Knight Foundation. One of the country's first public art programs, Miami-Dade Art in Public Places, traces its beginning to 1973.

Playing a critical supporting role to Miami's penchant for nurturing its own creative talent are extensive arts magnet programs in Miami-Dade County Public Schools, first established in 1973 to enable desegregation. These magnet programs now number over 370 in 119 public schools, focused on various disciplines. Amplifying youthful, creative ferment are two highly respected magnet high schools located in downtown Miami. They are Design and Architecture Senior High School (DASH) and New World School of the Arts High School, which offers programs in the visual arts, dance, theater, and music.

Some artists have left Miami to further their education at schools such as Maryland Institute College of Art and Yale University. Others take advantage of local BFA and MFA programs at Barry University, Florida International University, New World School of the Arts, and University of Miami.

Miami Dade College (MDC) offers an associate of arts degree in art or art education. Influential artists in this book who have taught at MDC are Robert Huff and Robert Thiele. (During most of the years covered in this book, MDC was known as Miami-Dade Community College. In 2003, the college began offering four-year degree programs and changed its name to MDC.) Across Miami, university art galleries, exhibiting faculty artists reviewed here, provide opportunities to educate and engage.

To produce this writing, I crisscrossed the vast area of Miami-Dade County, which sprawls over 2,000 square miles. I witnessed how art could both bring positive change and be part of the damaging stress of gentrification in suburban and grittier urban neighborhoods. There were trips to Hollywood and Fort Lauderdale in next-door Broward County, as well as to Boca Raton farther north in Palm Beach County.

My travels in Greater Miami took me north and east of downtown to galleries and institutions in Bay Harbor Islands, North Miami, Miami Beach, and south to Coral Gables. To visit the modestly sized Art Museum at Florida International University (now replaced by the much larger Frost Art Museum on campus), I drove considerably west from downtown. Destinations to galleries, museums, and other art venues in the city of Miami included Edgewater, Miami Design District, Liberty City, and Wynwood neighborhoods.

In the 21st century, Miami's enviable cultural and philanthropic landscape has altered markedly since my time at the *Miami Herald*. In recent years, Miami-Dade County, the Knight Foundation, the Miami Foundation, the Jorge M. Pérez Family Foundation, Fountainhead, Oolite Arts, private collectors, and others have injected millions into the art community. Museums, art centers, studios, and programs to reach multilingual audiences have multiplied.

Why is this support so vital? History shows us that great cities treasure their art. Art can enrich daily life with lasting insights capturing the pulse of our time by holding up an expansive mirror to the surrounding world. Art can draw people together to share experiences, to learn about the richly varied cultures making up Miami. Stories in this book demonstrate the resilience and tenacity of Miami's early art community moving forward without the largesse of current levels of philanthropy.

Even in or especially in divisive periods, art has the potential to enhance a sense of community, to link people together. This happens when visual art offers stimulating objects and stories that capture the local tenor and pulse of the moment. Such vibrant contributions by artists can connect Miami's diverse population by engaging audiences with art redolent of distinctive cultural traditions.

As a writer, perhaps what attracted me most was the opportunity to learn more about the variegated, changing strands of Miami's distinctive culture. Some of those strands radiate passion for Florida's natural history and the lustrous gleam of South Florida vegetation. Now more than ever, artists heighten our awareness of despoiled natural resources and the escalating threat of rising seas.

Other strands are entwined with insights and customs transported to Miami by artists arriving from points encompassing the globe. Many have fled repressive homelands, particularly in the Caribbean and Latin America. Often their art carries thought-provoking reminders of a departure under duress. Its urgent creativity freshens the city with remarkable, even radiant resilience.

There's a special energy of creativity stamped with a Miami postmark. That energy may be wistful and infused with an abiding sense of loss. It is nevertheless invigorated with a restless drive to reinvent, reconfigure, and remake anew daily encounters with the past and present.

A Miami postmark is maddeningly elusive and peripatetic. Above all it is fluid, fitting for a place lapped to the east by the Atlantic Ocean, once prominent for its bloodstained vessels of the Middle Passage, and to the west by the Everglades' vast River of Grass, flowing with reminders of an Indigenous past and scarred by encounters with a tumultuous present. This ever-evolving place named Miami pushes back against the very idea of a permanent residence.

Miami's recent art history needs to be more widely known. Reading national and international press coverage for the 20th anniversary of the inaugural Art Basel Miami Beach in 2022, I recognized there was little understanding of how this art community grew, how it became more sophisticated and self-aware in the years before Art Basel Miami Beach launched its spectacular presence in the art world.

This book tells that history through compelling stories told to me by artists, curators, and others I would meet on this journey encountering the rich, complex rhythms of Miami's creative spirit. It documents the cultural awakening steadily reinventing Greater Miami as it morphed from a glitzy fun-in-the-sun resort town, once considered a backwater, to a metropolitan city with serious cultural vision and accomplishments.

PART I

SETTING THE STAGE, 1987–1997

Part 1 begins with historic events singling out Cuban-born artists Arturo Rodriguez and María Brito. They set the stage for this book's overall focus, showing how Miami's art community was built largely by the inventive drive of many creative thinkers who settled here from other locations, especially from the Caribbean and Latin America. At various times, political and economic turmoil occurring in that region has created dramatic repercussions throughout South Florida's political and economic life. Tumultuous events in nearby Cuba and Haiti particularly reverberate in local immigrant communities.

In 1987, the painting *Exiliados* by Arturo Rodriguez was presented to Pope John Paul II on the occasion of his visit to the Florida International University campus. "It's always going to be with you that you can't go back," said Cuban-born Rodriguez. The young boy in his painting *Exiliados* resembles the artist, who left Cuba with his family in 1970, moving to Spain, then reaching Miami in 1973. About the painting, Florida International University president Modesto "Mitch" Maidique remarked, "We hope that it will help His Holiness to remember Miami and understand more about all of us who chose to settle here."

In 1988, María Brito's first metal sculpture *Introspection: Childhood Memories* was commissioned by the executive committee for the Olympiad of Art of the Seoul Olympics to be permanently installed at the Olympic Sculpture Park in Seoul, South Korea. It shines a light on her background as a Cuban exile.

"I was 13 going on 5," Brito told me in 1988, revealing her childish naïveté upon arriving as a teen in the United States from Cuba in 1961. She and her brother joined other Cuban children at a camp in Miami, waiting for their families to emigrate from Cuba. Bittersweet memories, particularly those of growing up, have been an abiding subject for the artist. Her compelling sculpture describes fragments of houses and furniture left behind, with mysterious doorways and windows.

A 1987 review at the beginning of part 1 highlights paintings of Robert Huff shown at Gloria Luria Gallery. Huff's abstract paintings combine impressionistic patches of pink, blue, and white similar to skies over Miami, with geometric shapes recalling bridges and the built environment characterizing the city's expanding urban landscape. Huff played a widely respected role in Miami's art community as an accomplished artist and mentor to many who studied with him at Miami Dade College, further strengthening the art community as it matured. Gloria Luria was one of a few local dealers who presented Miami artists at the time, part of the region's critical cultural infrastructure.

Another stalwart local dealer was Barbara Gillman. On February 17, 1989, I wrote about Barbara Gillman Gallery's 10th anniversary exhibition. It proved an opportunity to reflect on how the art community had begun to grow but also remained stagnant in the past decade. A common complaint was that Miami museums and collectors paid no attention to art produced locally.

At the *Miami Herald*, Black and Afro-Caribbean culture was part of my art beat. In 1989, a *Miami Herald* editor asked me to explore whether annual art events presented during Black History Month in February actually made a difference. Could these events truly raise awareness of Black artists with attention only one month a year? A dancer, musician, visual artist, curator, and museum director offered their opinions. Despite other events occasionally presented during the year, limiting annual attention to Black History Month amounted to a form of segregation, marginalizing if not erasing Black accomplishments. "The thing that bothers me about Black History Month is that we have to have a Black History Month," said jazz singer Alice Day. "Why is Black history not part of American history? Why is it not part of everyday curriculum [in the schools]?" Her question anticipated protests of the Black Lives Matter movement, begun in 2013 following the acquittal of George Zimmerman for fatally shooting Trayvon Martin, a 17-year-old African American.

The 1992 exhibit *The Golden Age of Black Art* at what is now the Marshall S. Davis Sr. African Heritage Cultural Arts Center was prescient, an early example in this book showing Miami artists of African descent achieving important recognition. Initiating this exhibit was the National Conference of Artists, a nationwide organization of Black visual artists. Among the artists represented were Charles Humes Jr. and Dinizulu Gene Tinnie. Thirty years later, Oolite Arts would make a considerable difference in the careers of both men.

During his career, Humes taught art in Miami-Dade County Public Schools. His first solo exhibition in decades took place after his retirement following the murder of George Floyd. It was *Matters of the Inner City* in 2021–22 at the Marshall S. Davis Sr. African Heritage Cultural Arts Center, produced with support from Oolite Arts.

Tinnie has for years been a consequential figure in Miami, recognized in 2023 as a Social Justice Award winner from Oolite Arts, receiving a $9,000 Ellies Award. Tinnie is praised on the Oolite website for his "local career as a proactive force of historic change," especially when he joined the historic Miami Black Arts Workshop in Coconut Grove in 1974. Oolite notes that he's well known for his long-standing Middle Ship Passage Replica Project.

A profile of Carlos Betancourt was published in June 1994. Betancourt's exuberantly colored multidisciplinary art has earned widespread attention in the years since I interviewed him at his Lincoln Road studio in Miami Beach. In 2024, during events coinciding with Art Basel Miami Beach, Betancourt and architectural designer Alberto Latorre participated in the Reefline, an ambitious, massive collaboration bringing together committed minds of art and science. Reefline partners include the Knight Foundation, the international architectural firm Office of Metropolitan Architecture (OMA), the University of Miami, and Coral Morphologic. Miami's Coral Morphologic combines art and science to study how coral reefs will evolve and can be protected in the 21st century, working with the University of Miami and the National Oceanic and Atmospheric Administration (NOAA). Reefline was conceived as a way to create sculptural, artificial reefs that will conserve marine life severely damaged by the climate crisis. Betancourt and Latorre's contribution is *Miami Reef Star*, a large-scale environmental sculpture that promises to radiate their signature brio. During Miami Art Week 2024, the prototype for *Miami Reef Star* was installed as illuminated 3D-printed stars arranged in the shape of a 60-foot star temporarily positioned near the water's edge of Miami Beach. Plans call for their completed sculpture to be placed in water 15 to 20 feet deep. Initially slated "to break water" by late spring 2025, the Reefline will be a seven-mile underwater sculpture park, snorkel trail, and hybrid reef located just off Miami Beach. It is the brainchild of art curator Ximena Caminos and Colin Foord, a marine biologist and cofounder of

Coral Morphologic. According to the Reefline's website, its goal is to nurture "environmental awareness through art and action-driven conservation."

In 1995, I began my role as the *Miami Herald*'s primary art critic. In August that year, a show at the Main Library downtown branch of Miami-Dade County Public Library System took as its provocative theme the politics of boats. Boats have a particular resonance in South Florida, from pleasure yachts anchored in coastal marinas to rickety vessels delivering—or floundering in the attempt—Cuban and Haitian refugees to South Florida.

Such waterborne vessels present a potent symbol of how the immigrant experience continually reinvents Miami. This review is the first of many documenting an important series of library exhibits curated by Barbara Young and others. They placed artists' vivid takes on arresting topics front and center in the public sphere.

During 1995 and 1997, Barbara Neijna and Mira Lehr produced work inspired by Miami's fragile coastal geography. In the early 21st century, we've become intensely aware of how rising seas adversely affect this cosmopolitan city perched on the edge of the Atlantic. Now an acute timeliness infuses 1990s art by Neijna and Lehr.

In October 1995, the Center for the Fine Arts, renamed Miami Art Museum the following year, presented Neijna's large-scale installation *Interior Landscapes* for the museum's *New Work* series. A strong, Everglades-earthy sense of primeval South Florida imbued her *Interior Landscapes*.

Slightly over a decade later, Neijna completed a resounding, handsomely textured tribute in public art to the Everglades, besieged for years by relentless urban sprawl. The magnificent scale of her *Foreverglades* at Miami International Airport, installed in 2007 on two floors of Concourse J, permits travelers to step across a glossy black terrazzo tile floor stretching 65,000 square feet. It is graced with jewel-like photos of vegetation and bas-relief panels embedded with reminders of South Florida's natural history. Throughout *Foreverglades* are poetic quotes from the 1947 classic *A River of Grass* celebrating the Everglades by Marjory Stoneman Douglas, whose words begin the concourse: "Nothing else is like them, their vast glittering openness, wider than the enormous visible round of the horizon."

Widely exhibited and collected, Lehr has been hailed as an eco-artist for her elegant odes to the endangered natural world, especially to marine life. Her paintings and three-dimensional works lead the eye into labyrinthine clusters inspired by marine life. Lehr's mixed-media paintings, shown at Continuum Gallery in June 1997, anticipated her later, more ambitious pieces.

Bringing vigorous new energy to Miami, the Museum of Contemporary Art (MOCA) in North Miami opened in February 1996 and began acquiring a permanent collection. It was located in a handsome 23,000-square-foot building designed by Gwathmey Siegel & Associates in New York. MOCA's founding executive director was Lou Anne Colodny, who had directed the institution that evolved into MOCA, the nearby and much smaller Center of Contemporary Art (COCA).

Barely a decade earlier, writing about Barbara Gillman Gallery's 10th anniversary exhibit, I had recorded how Miami artists grumbled that local collectors and museums ignored them. Now a sweeping change was beginning in how museums interacted with their own art community. MOCA and the soon-to-be-established Miami Art Museum (MAM), evolving from the Center for the Fine Arts (CFA), both became collecting institutions in 1996. As they grew, they began to acquire and exhibit Miami-based artists.

In 1996, MOCA's inaugural exhibit was *Defining the Nineties: Consensus-Making in New York, Miami, and Los Angeles*, curated by Bonnie Clearwater. Miami artists included in that show were José Bedia, Robert Chambers, Quisqueya Henríquez, Teresita Fernández, and Rubén Torres Llorca. MOCA drew support from prominent Miami collectors Norman and Irma Braman, Carlos and Rosa de la Cruz, Mera and Donald Rubell, and MOCA board chair Richard Shack.

Also in 1996, the Center for the Fine Arts, later that year renamed the Miami Art Museum when it became a collecting institution, exhibited an exquisitely installed presentation of Haitian art and cultural history. That exhibit was *Sacred Arts of Haitian Vodou*. It offered an extra flourish not available to other venues: an altar painting of the dark-skinned, earthy spirit Ezili Dantor by artist Rara Kuyu and an installation by Edouard Duval-Carrié, both Haitian-born South Florida artists.

Sacred Arts traveled from the organizing institution UCLA Fowler Museum of Cultural History. It was designed to speak to the broader Miami community as well as to a significant population of people settled in Miami with Haitian roots.

Other artists were compelled to speak to Miami's exile culture. Photography by Cuban-born Eduardo del Valle and Mirta Gómez has documented the changing vernacular architecture of mud, pole, and thatch huts in Mexico's Yucatán Peninsula. My story in February 1997 was on the occasion of their exhibit *The Mayan Dwelling* at New York City's gallery O. K. Harris. At the time, they were a married couple and artistic collaborators. Visitors to Mexico since the late 1980s, they had watched how these iconic domestic dwellings were displaced, forgotten, or transformed into something rough and new. As immigrants, they could identify with the domestically displaced. Their work is owned by New York's Museum of Modern Art and the San Francisco Museum of Modern Art.

Part 1 concludes with my review of the 1997 *Triumph of the Spirit: Carlos Alfonzo, a Survey, 1975–1991* at Miami Art Museum. This exhibit was guest curated by Olga Viso of the Hirshhorn Museum and Sculpture Garden, where it later traveled.

Woven into my review is a profile of the late Cuban-born artist Carlos Alfonzo, who died in Miami in 1991 at age 41 from complications of AIDS. He did not live to see his paintings exhibited that year in the Whitney Museum of American Art Biennial. Alfonzo's first career survey, *Triumph of the Spirit*, was a coup for the Miami Art Museum and the art community. It was the first traveling museum show organized by MAM under founding director Suzanne Delehanty, who oversaw MAM's transformation into a collecting institution in 1996.

In 2011, Cuban American billionaire and art collector Jorge Pérez donated $40 million to the Miami Art Museum. In homage to that gift, the board of trustees decided to rename the soon-to-be-relocated institution after Pérez. That decision proved controversial, causing four trustees to resign, generating ill will among other potential donors. When in 2013 the museum moved to a stunning new facility overlooking Biscayne Bay, it bore the name Jorge M. Pérez Art Museum (PAMM) of Miami-Dade County.

Franklin Sirmans became PAMM director in 2015. One of the country's few Black museum directors, he grew up in Harlem around African American art collected by his father, studying art history at Wesleyan University, and writing his thesis on Jean-Michel Basquiat, which led to further projects on Basquiat. His far-flung experience as a curator and writer was impressive, but before coming to Miami, he'd never directed a museum. Speaking about leading PAMM, he's been enthusiastic about the unique opportunities Miami affords with its close ties to the Caribbean and Latin America. "We're here," he said, "and we should be able to do 'here' better than anybody else."

Shortly before and after Sirmans arrived in Miami, the museum benefited significantly from an initiative enhancing its permanent collection through purchases of contemporary work by African American artists. In September 2013 when this initiative began, funding for a $1 million seed fund was provided equally by Jorge M. Pérez and the John S. and James L. Knight Foundation. Thus, the ongoing PAMM Fund for African American Art was established. It has gone a long way to mirror the diversity of South Florida, specifically its Black and Afro-Caribbean cultures.

It's worth noting that in fairly recent years, two of PAMM's more provocative shows requiring intricate installations traveled to PAMM from the Museum of Contemporary Art in Chicago. Although it would have been an impressive accomplishment if PAMM had organized these exhibits, they did speak directly to Miami's diverse communities. There was *Doris Salcedo* in 2016, billed as the largest presentation of art by this prominent Latin American artist to date with some 40 works produced over 30 years, tirelessly giving shape to years of brutal conflict in Salcedo's native Colombia. Opening in 2023 for Miami Art Week was *Gary Simmons: Public Enemy*, a trenchant look at racist ideas insidiously embedded and blurred in American history. "It's about the figure, but the figure is always invisible or not there," Sirmans told *Miami New Times*. "You have the boxing ring with no figures in it, but the dance steps are." In both exhibits, these quite different artists powerfully address assaults on the human figure with objects that evoke its absence.

Other exhibits organized by PAMM have been sparked by Miami's multicultural ties to Latin America and the Caribbean as well as by talented Miami-based artists. There was the timely and searing *Antonia Wright: State of Labor* by Miami-based Wright. It launched a passionate protest against the 2022 overturning of *Roe v. Wade*.

In 2023, Sirmans spoke to *Artnet* about dynamic changes in Miami's art scene following his arrival in 2015. "It didn't come out of nowhere, but there has been exponential growth in the last five years. There's an incredibly vibrant community that's happening all the time," he said, noting that the African diaspora is key. "There's this vibrant space that has been continuous among people who find Miami to resonate and to be receptive to their work in ways that other places might not have been until recently. And that's massive. But it continues—you see it in the Bakehouse Art Complex, Locust Projects, the Miami Light Project residency over on the beach."

In February 2025, PAMM announced that philanthropists Sandra and Tony Tamer endowed the position of director with a substantial donation. Both Tamers are major benefactors to YoungArts, among other significant arts institutions. Sirmans is now the Sandra and Tony Tamer Director of PAMM, and as the Tamers said in a statement, "We are thrilled by the growth of Miami's arts community and ecosystem, and PAMM has been at the forefront of making the city a world-class arts destination."

ARTURO RODRIGUEZ

Spirit of Exile Shines in Painting for Pope

September 20, 1987

"It's always going to be with you that you can't go back," says Cuban-born Arturo Rodriguez. Exile has special meaning for this Miami artist, whose painting, *Exiliados*, is returning with Pope John Paul II to the Vatican.

The painting was a gift to the pope commissioned by the Florida International University Foundation in honor of the papal visit to the campus. *Exiliados*, a 62-by-36-inch oil on linen, evokes an exiled family's feeling of loss and displacement. They seem to be stranded near a beach, the father hobbled by two left feet, the mother holding a squirming baby. Everything is bleached by an intense tropical sun; the distant skyline could belong to Miami.

Shortly before the papal mass at Tamiami Park, FIU president Mitch Maidique presented the painting to Pope John Paul II, explaining that the painting "contained some eternal truths about the state of mankind . . . set in Miami."

"We hope," Maidique said later, "that it will help His Holiness to remember Miami and understand more about all of us who chose to settle here."

Rodriguez's personal experience is no doubt a source of his painting. In fact, the young boy in *Exiliados* resembles the artist. After leaving Cuba in 1970, he moved with his family to Spain and came to Miami in 1973. Though proud to call this country home now, he smiles ruefully and says, "It seems to me that I never fit anywhere. I always feel like an outsider."

Rodriguez, born in 1956, is a dedicated artist whose talent is gaining recognition. In 1961, he was awarded a fellowship by the Florida Arts Council and a year later received the CINTAS Fellowship. Last year he, with two New York artists, was invited by the Norton Gallery of Art in Palm Beach to paint the walls surrounding the museum's courtyard. On October 8, a survey of his paintings and works on paper will open at the Frances Wolfson Art Gallery at Miami-Dade Community College.

The human figure, with its capacity for expressing the moody depths

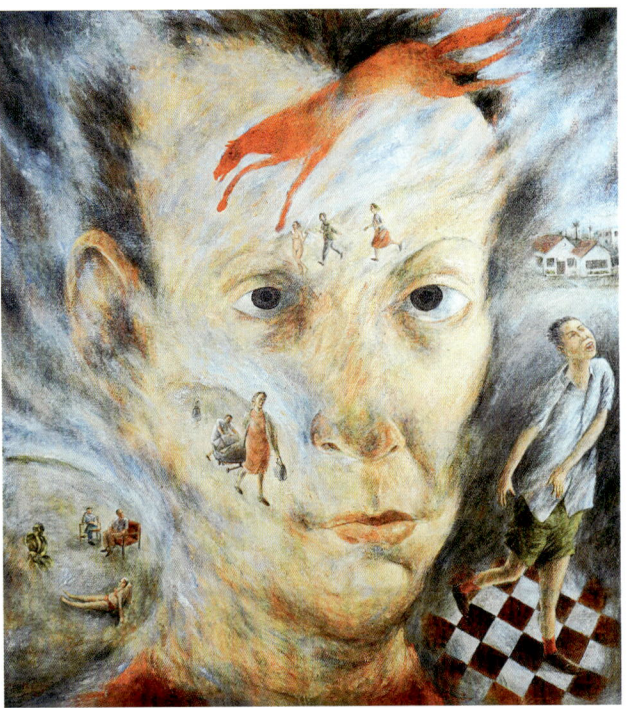

FIGURE 1. Arturo Rodriguez, *Self Portrait with Dreams* (*Autorretrato con Sueños*), 1987. Courtesy of the artist.

of experience, has always fascinated Rodriguez. His paintings are filled with awkward people who exert a peculiar, ghostly presence. These figures often seem to be floating in space, uncomfortable and lost, like restless dreamers unable to stride confidently into the real world. And yet the reality of our emotions, of the way time passing affects us, is an impetus behind Rodriguez's work.

He does not consider himself a particularly religious person. What did he think when FIU asked him to paint for the pope?

"Oh," Rodriguez sighs, "I thought that I wasn't able to do it. I told them, 'If you want something religious I can't do it. I will do just what I've been doing and that's all.'"

Maidique, who believes the painting tells a story of painful change, describes the pope's response: "He looked at me in his inimitable spiritual, warm way and thanked me."

ROBERT HUFF AT GLORIA LURIA GALLERY

September 24, 1987

Growing up in Clearwater, Robert Huff was fascinated by the tools of his father's construction business. As an artist in Miami, he still keeps T squares, rulers, and compasses among the brushes and paint on his studio shelves.

References to construction and architecture abound in Huff's mixed-media paintings, which combine acrylic, pencil, and oil.

This show of recent works reveals Huff working on a big scale, turning out ever more complex variations on familiar themes. In the works on canvas, all composed of two or more panels, penciled grids and architectural elements appear and disappear. They are often eclipsed by broad impressionist patches, brightly flecked with pink, blue, and white. Huff's flat, gray-shaded grids of earlier paintings now curve like cylinders or rows of columns. The architectural elements, also penciled, are bridges fashioned of increasingly intricate arches and supports.

Such compositions set up rhythmic patterns as precisely drawn bridges appear to melt and resurface among shimmering fields of color. Part of what makes Huff's paintings so striking is the way the artist creates layers of color, line, and shape. He has said that he is interested in perception, and in these works, he uses the layers to tease our perceptions

FIGURE 2. Robert Huff, *East West*, 2003. Ceramic tile. Palmetto Metrorail Station. Image Robin Hill, courtesy of Miami-Dade County Department of Cultural Affairs, Art in Public Places Trust.

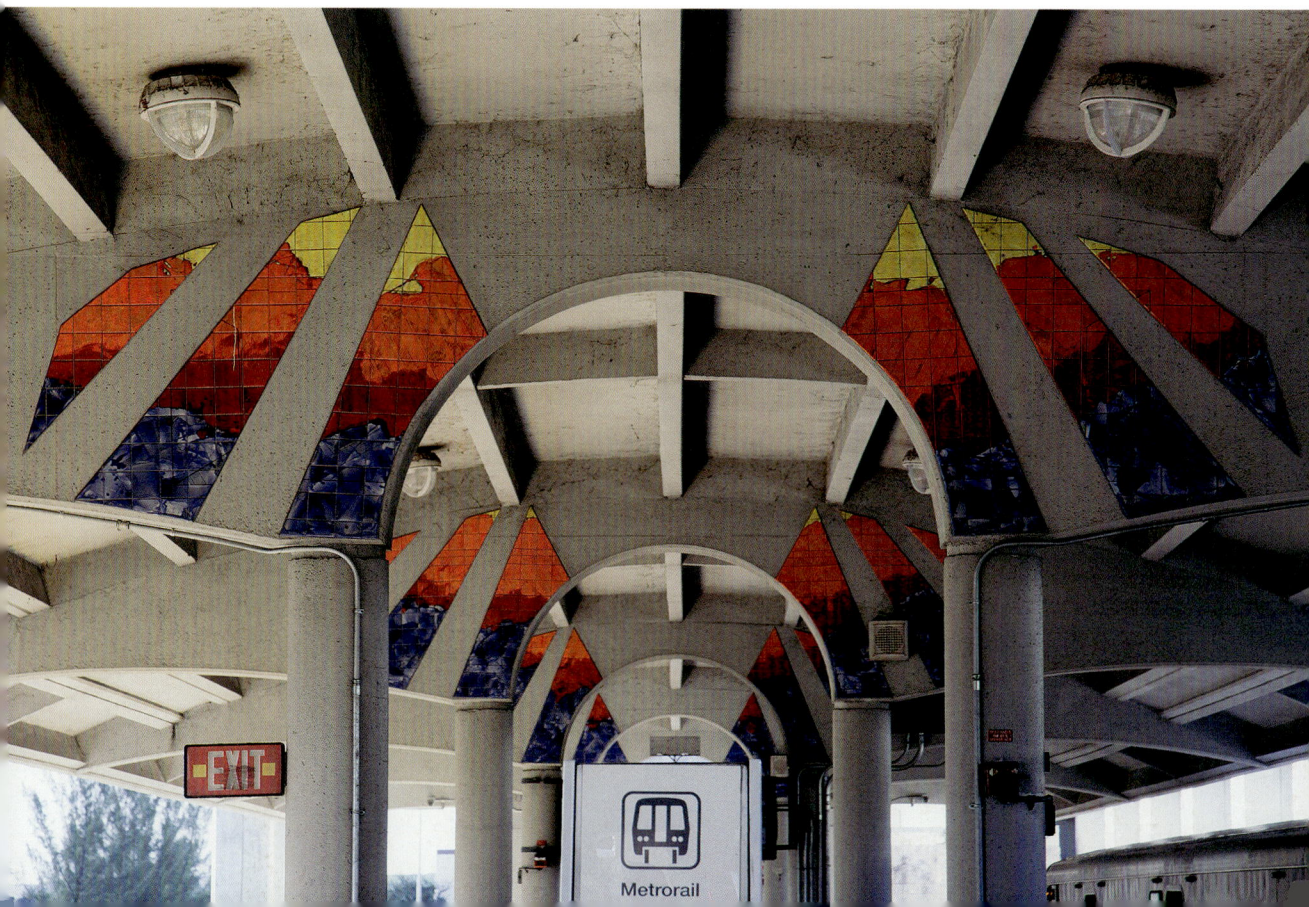

of depth and volume. For instance, the grids, which are usually curving but sometimes drawn to suggest a door pushed open into space, create three-dimensional illusions. That illusion is deliberately violated by pink, blue, or green fields, which often slice through the drawings at disconcerting angles.

"I set up a system and break through it," Huff has said—a remark that neatly sums up these intricate paintings. There may be times when this new body of work is almost too intricate, dazzling us with quick shifts in perspective and color, calling attention to Huff's accomplished draftsmanship. These are paintings executed with lots of technical flash.

That flash is particularly evident in the largest work, *Bay/Point/Vail*, composed of four panels. There is much to look at here, and in this instance, all the complex elements work together, echoing rather than battling each other for attention. Here the penciled bridges are echoed in a broad diagonal area in which Huff's impressionist technique has produced another dense layer of arches and supports. The arches appear to waver and shimmer, as if reflected in water.

Huff plays a dizzy game with viewers, using tightly structured elements to create a shifting world of unstable perspectives. Nearly always, it's a game worth playing.

In memoriam: Robert Huff, 1945–2014
Gloria Luria, 1925–2023

MARÍA BRITO

She Sculpts Out of Memories

May 23, 1988

"I was 13 going on 5," Cuban-born sculptor María Brito confesses to her childish naïveté with a bittersweet laugh, recalling her arrival in the United States in 1961.

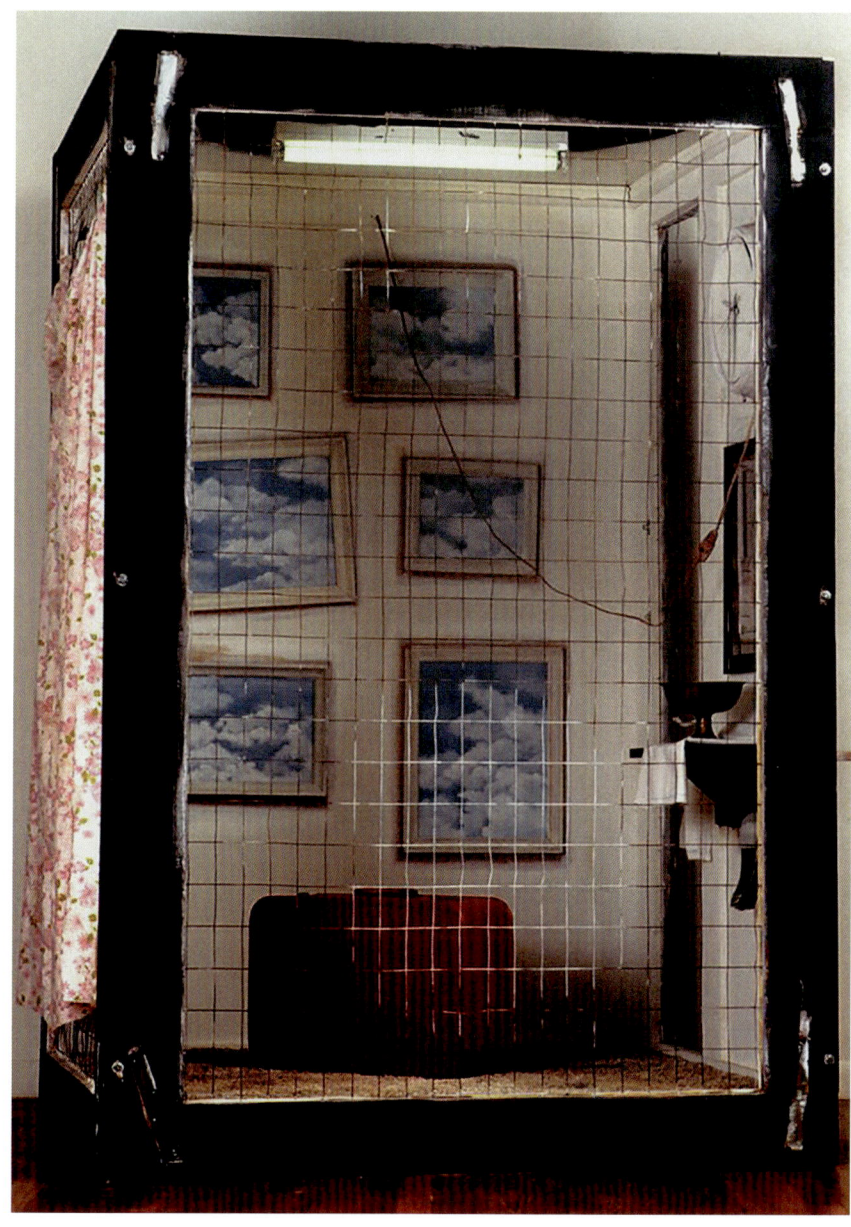

FIGURE 3. María Brito, *Whitewash*, 1990. Mixed media, 83 × 62 × 55. Courtesy of the Collection of Liza and Arturo F. Mosquera.

At that young age, she and her brother joined other Cuban children at a camp in Kendall, where they waited for their families to emigrate from Cuba. The uncertainty and anguish attending such a memory contrast in her artworks with the joyful innocence suffusing her recollection of childhood visits to the beach in Cuba, a family outing never complete without a whimsical menagerie of birds and turtles.

Bittersweet memories, particularly those of growing up, are a favorite subject for Brito, now 40. The artist, whose work has been recognized by CINTAS and National Endowment for the Arts fellowships as well as by one-woman exhibits and several traveling group shows, has recently earned yet another honor. *Introspection: Childhood Memories*, her first metal sculpture, will be installed permanently this summer at the Olympic Sculpture Park in Seoul, South Korea.

SHOWING AT BACARDI GALLERY

Thanks to the initiative of gallery director Juan Espinosa, South Floridians can see the work at the Bacardi Gallery on Biscayne Boulevard for the next few weeks, until it is shipped overseas.

Brito's sculpture was commissioned by the Executive Committee for the Olympiad of Art of the Seoul Olympics through Thomas M. Messer, director of the Solomon R. Guggenheim Museum. According to Jill Snyder, administrative coordinator at the museum, Brito was chosen "through recommendations of New York–based art professionals." Hers will be one of 100 works from 80 countries. Come mid-August, the artist will be on hand for the installation ceremonies in Seoul.

Constructed of iron, steel, and aluminum, this particular piece marks a turning point in the artist's career. First working in clay, Brito has produced sculpture made mostly of wood for a number of years. Everything in her studio, a converted garage at her home in Kendall, is covered with a sandy-colored film of sawdust. She points to a formidable Sears radial saw, proudly describing it as "the main piece of equipment I work with." Nearby are a jigsaw, drill, and sander, other tools used in her efforts to transform the carpenter's craft into art.

FRAGMENTS OF THE PAST

Such a craft has been necessary to build the fragments of houses and pieces of furniture that make up her haunting sculpture. Many works, resting on wooden platforms, create spaces that resemble rooms or stages, with mysterious windows and doorways. Often occupying such "rooms" are chairs, beds, ladders, shelves, and light bulbs—as well as images of the artist herself.

She Never Liked Dolls (1985), for instance, is a rich example of the artist's ability to create intricate spatial relationships as well as stir up profound emotional currents within the viewer. Here, a dismembered baby doll is trapped in a crib-like cage, connected by miniature ladders to a cube that suggests a child's oversized building block. From inside that cube, many tiny doll-like hands reach upward, skewered grotesquely on poles.

After spending the last three months working closely with Gay García to complete *Introspection: Childhood Memories*, Brito is clearly exhilarated by the challenge metal poses. García, a metal sculptor whose work, like Brito's, is now traveling in the exhibit *Outside Cuba*, did all the welding. Brito chose the materials and did the grinding and cutting.

WORKING IN METAL

Since she had only a few months to produce the work for the Summer Olympics and had never worked in a medium suitable for outdoors, the artist decided to make a metal version of a wooden sculpture she had created six years ago. There was not time, she believed, to create an entirely new piece while also learning the intricacies of a new medium. Comparing the new *Introspection* to its earlier form in wood, Brito is excited by the "presence" of metal, by its dramatic impact.

Like many of her larger works, *Introspection: Childhood Memories* resembles a stage, suggesting a tableau in which the viewer is invited to participate. In this work, a wall with a door tantalizingly ajar creates two room-like spaces. In the larger space on the left, a chair is placed several feet from the door, directly facing the viewer. It's a simple chair, vaguely old-fashioned. On the seat is a knob resembling a light switch, which is connected to a metal cord running along the floor of the work, through the wall, and out the other side, finally connected to a crib-like cage, in which a light bulb appears to shine. Inside the cage is a small rocking horse, cast, according to the artist, from one of her children's old toys. Mounted in a niche in the wall near the cage is a battered ribbon of metal resembling a roll of film; another niche contains a mask of the artist's face and fetish-like elements.

It is a more subtle work than *She Never Liked Dolls*. Tension between the lyrical and grotesque, adjectives Brito likes to use when talking about her work, is less pronounced but apparent all the same. The quiet horror engulfing the caged rocking horse—welded in place and literally off its rocker—is ultimately just as powerful as her more freakish imagery.

TWO STATES OF AWARENESS

What's remarkable about this piece is the way it evokes two states of awareness. Those states are linked by a cord charting the perilous, eerie path memory can take. The space with the chair has a veneer of reality, although a set of footprints on the floor in front of the chair suggests a ghostly presence. Objects through the doorway and on the other side of the wall—which would not be visible to anyone sitting in the chair—are magical and symbolic, as if visible only to the mind's eye.

"A wonderful forum for the viewer's mind and eye," is Sheldon Lurie's opinion of Brito's sculpture. Lurie, director of the Frances Wolfson and InterAmerican Art Galleries of Miami-Dade Community College, will be showing the artist's work twice at the InterAmerican Art Gallery.

In June Brito will be represented in a group show, and in February she'll have a one-woman show that will travel to the Museum of Contemporary Hispanic Art in New York City.

IS BLACK HISTORY
MONTH EFFECTIVE?

January 29, 1989

It's like you have a little box of Black History Month things to do.
And you open it up and there's art exhibits, and dance recitals, and films,
and you kind of spread things around, and when the month is over you
kind of gather it together and put it back in its box until next year.
—*Gary Moore, Miami-based artist*

Wednesday, it'll be February again, which means Black History Month.
Around South Florida, the special events will include exhibitions of the
work of Black artists throughout the Miami-Dade County Public Library
System, shows in college galleries, a Black film festival in Fort Lauderdale,
plays about the Black experience, concerts, and lectures.

But does Black History Month also mean that, when it's March, it's time
to forget all about Black history until next year?

A number of Black artists in our community, while appreciative of the
flurry of exposure they receive in February, resent the implications inherent
in the attention that may come just once a year. Some believe that while Black
History Month was intended to foster an awareness of African American contributions to the national culture, it has become a subtle form of segregation.

"It's disturbing," says Ed Love, visual arts dean of the New World School
of the Arts. "You either show then, or you don't show at all. . . . If you either
have February or nothing, then that's an awful choice."

But others find that the month's educational value is very much needed
in an age when, as musician Nicole Yarling notes, some young people think
that Louis Armstrong was the first man to walk on the moon.

Or, as art dealer Caleb Davis, owner of Gallery Antigua on Biscayne Boulevard, laments, "You have young kids out here throwing rocks and bottles,
and they don't even know that there are important people in their history,
their culture, that have made contributions. You ought to be able to roll off

your tongue the major artists, performers, and prominent people of your ethnic background that you take pride in."

A sampling of the artists' comments reveals a story, perhaps, of what can happen when good intentions do not necessarily evolve with the changing times.

"The thing that bothers me about Black History Month is that we have to have a Black History Month," says jazz singer Alice Day, who hosts a radio show on WLRN and recently opened her own jazz club, Alice's Place, in Fort Lauderdale. "Why is Black history not part of American history? Why is it not part of everyday curriculum [in the schools]? I don't understand why this is so . . ."

Choreographer and dancer Freddick Bratcher, who studied ballet and has danced with both the Martha Graham and the Alvin Ailey companies, worries about the type of pigeonholing that could result from focusing attention on African American artists only once a year. It's "like being labeled 'the best Black newscaster' instead of 'one of the top newscasters,'" he says.

"It's sort of like a double-edged sword," comments art dealer Davis. "If there were no exhibits put on during Black History Month, there would be even fewer shows for African American artists. I think Black History Month is a good thing, but I think we shouldn't show the works of African American artists only in February."

Davis would like to see more exhibits throughout the year in such public spaces as the libraries and the Center for the Fine Arts in downtown Miami. Comparing Miami to other cities with a diverse ethnic population, such as Los Angeles, Philadelphia, Atlanta, and New York, he says, "I think Miami is anywhere between two to five years behind these other cities in terms of showing and exhibiting the work of African American and Caribbean artists."

The New World School's Ed Love, a nationally honored sculptor, is showing his work in February at the Coral Gables Branch Library. But Love is so opposed to the way Black History Month is observed, he usually denies requests to exhibit in February, except at institutions that showcase the work of African American artists year-round.

If Black History Month "leads to the next step, where people are exhibited year-round because of the quality of their work, then I think it's fine," he says. "But if we've become satisfied, which I suspect we have, with having these monthly activities so we don't have to do anything the rest of the year, then it's better to not have it. Because then we are settling for too little and assuaging our consciousness and not really expanding it."

Love says he would like to curate a show with his partner, Monifa Atungaye, that would feature African American artists using certain conventions that "would not be considered traditional African American modes, but which we think are." He would include works related to performances based on African mythologies and Eastern rituals and invite nationally known artists such as Martin Puryear, Yvonne Pickering Carter, and Jerome Meadows. Love says he has proposed the show to several museums, including the Center for the Fine Arts, but has had no response.

Heads of some of the major local art institutions say they recognize that Black artists need more exposure throughout the year.

Dahlia Morgan, director of the Art Museum at Florida International University, who says she doesn't curate shows "on the basis of gender and race," points out that FIU has exhibited the work of a number of major contemporary Black artists, including Robert Colescott, Romare Bearden, Lester Johnson, and Richard Hunt.

"It's a dilemma," she says. "Specific exhibitions can raise the consciousness of the community, but many African American artists wouldn't want to be exhibited in ethnic shows."

Ira Licht, director of the Lowe Art Museum, agrees that there are problems with the concept of Black History Month.

"I hate to do Black shows for Black History Month and Latin shows for Hispanic Heritage Month," he says. "I've always tried to break through that kind of grouping so that people could be appreciated on their own."

As to whether Black artists deserve more attention in the community, he says, "I have no idea because I haven't been keeping tabs. I would like to see more attention paid to good artists, from whatever group."

Asked what kind of attention the Lowe has given to Black artists, he points to the 1986 exhibition *Sharing Traditions*, featuring five Black American artists of the 19th century. He says next season, most likely in December or January, the Lowe will offer a show on African art titled *Wild Spirits—Strong Medicine*, which will include artifacts dealing with magic and ritual. He's also planning a show devoted to the works of Black artist Adrian Piper, titled *Reflections, 1967–87*.

Neither the Lowe nor FIU staged art shows for Black History Month. But the Miami-Dade County Public Library System did, and Barbara Young, the library's art services coordinator, says she is well aware of the issues the exhibitions could raise.

"We've tried to be sensitive to the possibilities of exclusion," she says, emphasizing that the library has "incorporated Black artists in group shows we have throughout the year."

"The library's collection, which numbers about 1,500 pieces," she adds, "is very strong in works by Black artists." Pieces from that collection are exhibited year-round throughout the system.

One of the Black artists being showcased at the library in February is Purvis Young, a painter who has had museum, gallery, and library exhibitions year-round. His work is in the library's permanent collection. Young, who considers himself a historian of Overtown, his home for many years, says he isn't interested in talking about Black History Month.

"I'm just an artist . . . I paint what I see," he says. "I paint pictures of people just reaching out, reaching for better things. It's a lot of angry people."

In memoriam: Edward (Ed) Love, 1936–1999
Purvis Young, 1943–2010
Alice Day, 1946–2020
Ira Licht, 1938–2023

BARBARA GILLMAN GALLERY

Artists Survey Scene

February 17, 1989

Recalling how she came to establish her art gallery on Biscayne Boulevard in 1979, Barbara Gillman observes, "There was a real need to champion emerging young artists. . . . The artists here have always been every bit as good as artists anywhere."

On February 24, Barbara Gillman Gallery will celebrate its 10th anniversary with an exhibition of work by about 50 of the South Florida artists who have shown at the gallery at 3886 Biscayne Boulevard.

Some artists in the anniversary show took time out to look at how South Florida's visual arts scene has evolved since 1979. They talked about where South Florida has been, where it is now, and where they think it should be going. Many believe that, despite significant gains, our museums have a lot of growing up to do.

"I do see much more national recognition of local artists," says Carlos Maciá. He credits Gillman with providing more opportunities to show their art outside Miami. "Before [1979], we were totally ignored. I remember when people from up north would not come here to buy art."

Like many, Maciá is disturbed by the absence of a collecting museum with space to exhibit its holdings. "We certainly have enough people here with great collections; with private collections we could get together so we could have our own museum with good art," he asserts. "But people here don't seem to get together."

Roberta Marks, who lives in Key West and travels widely, praises the Latin community and its artists for "introducing different sensibilities, a new vitality into our area. I think because of that we have been forced to become more worldly." Marks believes that having to deal with "all the problems and new issues" South Florida faces gives artists a chance to sharpen their awareness and sensitivity.

As one who moved here from New York 11 years ago, Dina Knapp believes that a steadily growing Miami is "getting a bit more sophisticated—otherwise how could something like New Music America happen here?" But she adds that the "really supportive people" in the arts now are the same as 10 years ago, though she applauds the increased attention local artists receive from commercial galleries.

"A lot of our artists are getting grants and receiving recognition they didn't have 10 years ago," says Rosemarie Chiarlone. "So we are in competition nationally and I think we hold our own. As far as museums are concerned, I think that the FIU museum [the Art Museum] is the best museum. They do the most innovative things."

For Stephen Bird, there have been a lot of changes in the way galleries respond to local artists. "I think a lot of the change has been brought by what Barbara's done, in terms of showing local artists that a lot of people hadn't seen."

He believes that, owing to the area's growth and to the strength of work produced by artists here, South Florida artists have earned greater credibility. "Art seems to be rather international now rather than just focused in one spot, and the creation doesn't have so much to do with where it's being done as with who is doing it and why."

With the exception of the North Miami Center of Contemporary Art, local museums are "much more interested in showing what's hot rather than extolling their own. It's very difficult in that Miami is still a kind of adolescent city," Bird adds.

Sounding a familiar theme, Mario Bencomo says, "The museums are not growing with the city. It's important that we have an institution that collects art here."

While commending the support that the Miami-Dade County Public Libraries, Bacardi Gallery, Miami-Dade County Art in Public Places, and the North Miami Center of Contemporary Art give to local art, Bencomo insists, "We have incredible artists in this community . . . enough here to make the city important in the visual arts. But everything is so divided into the so-called tri-ethnic community that I think it does not do a good service to the one common goal, to advance the culture in general of Miami."

In memoriam: Dina Knapp, 1947–2016
Barbara Gillman, 1937–2023

CARLOS MACIÁ

Remarkable Books Reflect Artist's Rich Journey

November 13, 1991

Carlos Maciá once planned to enter the priesthood. He became an artist instead.

Though years of religious studies would leave their mark on his paintings, drawings, and books, art was always his first vocation.

"I would draw plants in pots and views from my window," Maciá says, recalling his childhood in Cuba during the 1950s. "My grandmother would take my drawings to art school in Havana. They would say, 'Those are wonderful drawings, but we don't take teenagers,' and my grandmother would say, 'My grandson is not a teenager, he's only eight years old.'"

The memory, brought forth modestly, may explain Maciá's ability to render scenes with superb precision.

As he grew up in Miami, his appetite for the visual was enhanced by his fascination with books, especially those about the Middle Ages and the Renaissance, with their ornate religious images.

All those interests are brought together in the current show of Maciá's work at Arregui Hsia Fine Art in Coral Gables. Maciá still draws as well as paints, but now he has bound his work into remarkable books—intricately crafted volumes that are richer in color, line, and texture than in words.

As art objects, his books reveal Maciá's love of religious studies and art history. They also reflect the long journey he made to reach this point.

After graduating from Miami Springs Senior High in 1970, he won a scholarship to study at the San Fernando Royal Academy of Fine Arts in Madrid. As with Picasso, who enrolled there 73 years before, the school failed to keep Maciá's interest. While Picasso returned to Barcelona, Maciá chose to study with Franciscan priests in Navarre, in northern Spain.

He remembers the enchantment of living "in an 11th-century monastery full of frescoes and paintings, of looking out at a 14th-century castle" from the window of his cell. He traveled to other monasteries in Spain to study art history and philosophy, later receiving a bachelor's degree from Barry University and doing missionary work with a religious order in the Dominican Republic.

But in 1980, the intellectual and spiritual appeal of the priesthood dimmed: "I became a little sacrament machine," he says. With only two years of study left before ordination, he returned to Miami and began making art.

Among the first works Maciá exhibited in Miami were prints and paintings of peeling building facades. They echoed the views from his window in Havana, in the Calabazar section, where the architecture ranged "from super-rich to ghetto."

The influence of his travels in Spain and Italy, where he found more stunning views of cathedrals and museums, would become increasingly apparent in his work.

Maciá now calls Barcelona home, and books have become his passion. Many are studded with allusions to his wide reading. Some deal in biblical stories, with references to creation and the apocalypse. Some of the most recent invite personal meditations—intimate encounters with pages of abstract, organic forms, gritty with sand or glinting with color. Still others draw on the artist's fascination with classical mythology, illuminated manuscripts, and the culture of the Middle Ages and the Renaissance.

"I'm an artist who loves Catholic iconography—the whole coloring, the whole sensuality of spiritual images. I like my works to be touched and handled," he says.

Walking through the show at Arregui Hsia, Maciá studies a copper box designed to hold his book about the first chapter of Genesis. He seems both amused and pleased by a friend's comment that this elaborately embossed and hinged box suggests a priest's confession booth.

Another copper construction, mounted on the wall and shaped like an altarpiece, holds the richly colored pages of *The Garden, Genesis Chapter II*. He used a gestural style of painting to record his vision of "the earth being swallowed up by the waters, and all the seeds springing forth with life." Turning to another page, he says, "Here is the creation of man, and I used God in the shape of a woman, breastfeeding—because creation is a form of nurturing."

While Maciá may bring his own twist to these ancient stories, he's primarily concerned with capturing their vivid poetry. That's especially true of *El Apocalipsis*, based on the apocalyptic vision of Daniel in Hebrew scriptures.

Though these powerful images don't always need an explication, Maciá doesn't mind offering one: "This is the end of time. The moon becomes red as blood, the sun becomes black, and the stars roll up like a scroll."

At the end of the book, an inverted triangle of silver leaf bleeds across a two-page spread, flanked by waving rivulets of color. This is the face of God, he explains. According to Daniel, "The face of God was light, fire, water, and the four winds. It's such a beautiful image."

Other books in the exhibit, spanning 1987 to the present, reflect his taste for arcane lore, including astrology, astronomy, and alchemy.

Rife with obscure allusions, layered with Latin quotations, inscribed with unfamiliar symbols, such works can be intimidating. Unfolded from their elaborate boxes and bindings, they raise more questions than they answer. One can get bogged down trying to decipher all the references. Even the artist, in a recent interview, can't remember them all.

"There are multiple layers of meaning that you can never completely grasp," says Dr. Alexander Angelides, a Miami collector who has loaned a book to the show. "I always have the feeling that something great is going on which I have to work hard at to understand."

The sense of intrigue is enhanced by Maciá's consummate craftsmanship in stained glass, wood inlay, and bookbinding.

His most recent art carries less obvious dazzle; the artist compares their flowing, sensual textures to lava. Built up with pigments, dirt, copper shavings, bits of aluminum foil, and modeling paste, the heavy linen pages seem ancient. They are shorn of erudite references, bearing indentations that seem too worn to identify.

"I think these latest works are very spiritual and emotional," says Bernardine Heller-Greenman, a lecturer in art history at the University of Miami. "They leave you with something for a very long time."

A few books fuse these earthy textures with free-flowing drawings, some erotic, inspired again by classical myth and the Bible. But the allusions are looser now. Pages of clear acetate laid over drawings on paper create images

27

Setting the Stage,
1987–1997

that unfurl and recede as one moves through the book. A delicate line is revealed to outline a pelvis; a bull's flank bristles into abstraction.

But one can never see the whole work at once—each page is layered with memories of previous pages. For Maciá, that's the point of his art, to feel and see these layers of experience. "I find no better analogy for life than the book," he says.

In memoriam: Carlos Maciá, 1951–1994

CAROL BROWN

New Work Intriguing

December 11, 1991

"I couldn't lift anything heavier than a loaf of bread. It was an enormous challenge," recalls Miami artist Carol K. Brown of the months she spent recovering from a serious illness. Known for her larger-than-life-size aluminum sculptures of anthropomorphic figures, Brown scaled down her art but not her imagination. She still treads the line between the "frivolous and creepy."

The results of this most recent phase in her career are on view at Gloria Luria—an installation of some 400 mixed-media reliefs, each four inches in diameter. Molded from a clay-like substance and coated with a dark mix of lead and wax, the reliefs echo many of Brown's signature forms. But they are also malleable and wriggly, incised with an array of textures not possible in aluminum.

Here are hairy, scaly, blistery creatures and appendages. These could be young specimens captured from the peculiar world Brown has long been exploring, already straining to outgrow their circular petri dishes. Claws that could also be gaping mouths, phallic forms with tiny eyes, wormy coils with wings or thorns, clumps of pods: they all look both familiar and strange.

While her work has always echoed the many connections between

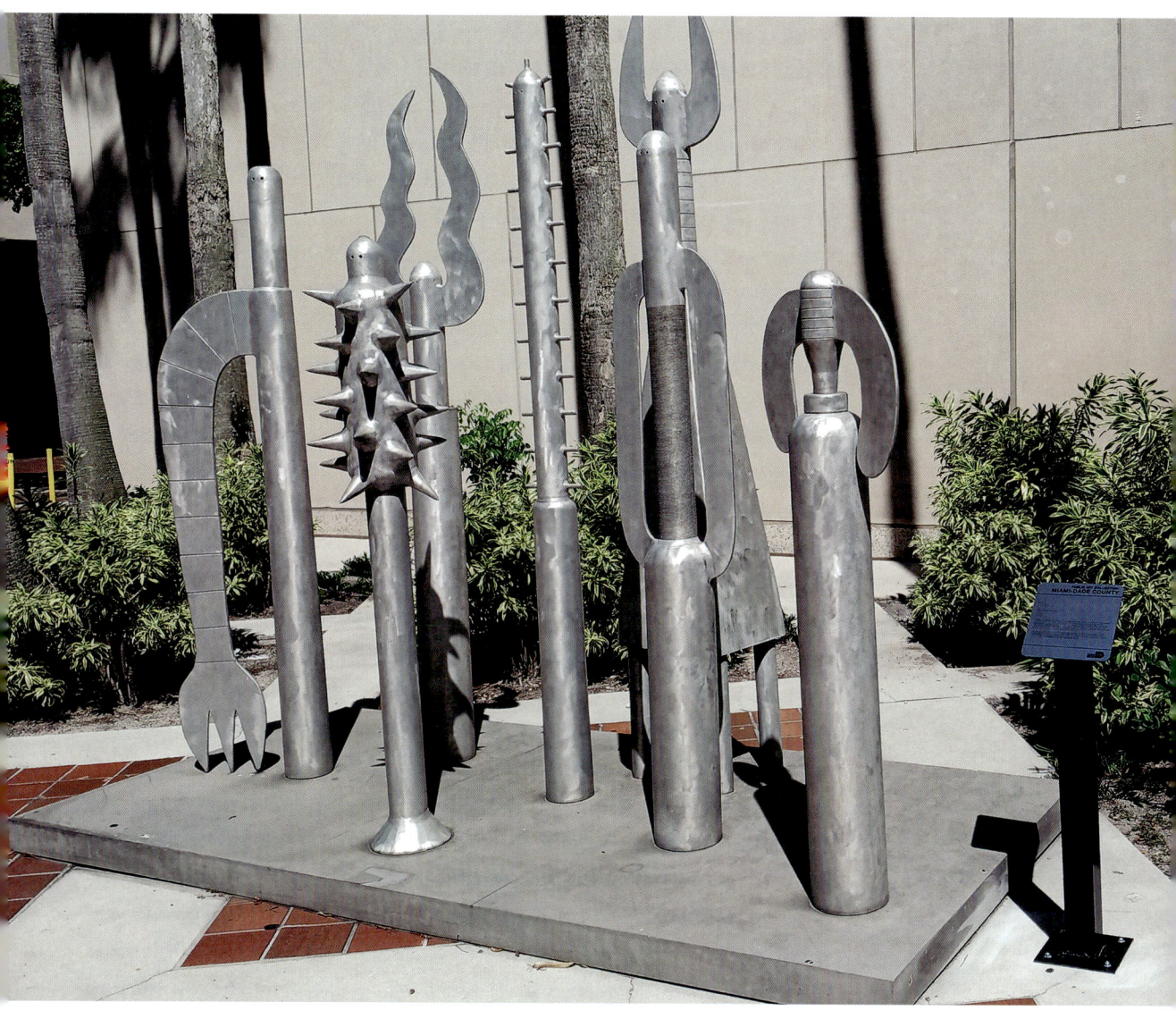

FIGURE 4. Carol Brown, *Seven More of Them*, 1986. Aluminum. Stephen P. Clark Government Center. Image Yusimy Lara, courtesy of Miami-Dade County Department of Cultural Affairs, Art in Public Places Trust.

modernism and a surreal sense of fantasy, with links to Brancusi and Max Ernst, Brown also splices surrealism with her own whimsical sense of humor. She dares to coax something almost cute out of the bizarre.

This installation, which uses small pieces in a big way, is built on connecting grids. Brown not only pokes fun at the rational severity of minimalism but also sets up an odd game board with one surprise move after another. The work may not always be as satisfying as her large sculpture, but it's intriguing.

In the front gallery are paintings and sculpture by Ida Kohlmeyer.

At Opus Gallery are aggressive and visceral oil paintings by recent Cuban defector Tomás Esson Reid. Once a darling of the Cuban arts establishment, Esson Reid exhibited in traveling shows in Europe, Latin America, and Australia. His paintings were also included in *The Nearest Edge of the World*, a group show of contemporary Cuban paintings seen last season at the Bronx Museum and the Massachusetts College of Art in Boston.

The work aims to shock, and it does. Mutilated bodies, phallic imagery, hairy hunks of flesh spewing out streams of blood, even clumps of excrement recur throughout his work. Much of the sexual and scatological posturing stands as a brash metaphor for corrupt political and social systems. Even while he was in Cuba, Esson Reid's work launched criticisms of a moribund revolution; since his defection in April, however, his work has become even bolder.

In earlier pieces, a limb or backside of delicately modeled flesh would deliberately clash with the unsavory content. Now Esson Reid, at 28, seems less interested in such painterly flourishes. His figures have become cartoonish, as in *Jugando al Beisbol* (*Playing baseball*). Here a white figure, apparently a woman, wields a baseball bat over a Black man, who seems to be growing both horns and a pregnant belly. Baseball, as an icon of popular culture here and in Cuba, collides with troubling images of power and control.

Like many artists of his generation, Esson Reid appropriates high and low to critique conventional wisdom. An installation of 28 small canvases offers sardonic send-ups of art by other Cuban exiles and references to the Cuban countryside. *¡Que Calor!* (*How hot!*) is the show's apt title.

BACARDI GALLERY

Griots of South Florida

March 18, 1992

In the Kiswahili (a.k.a. Swahili) language of East Africa, a griot is someone charged with keeping a record of tribal history and culture. *Griots of South Florida*, at Miami's Bacardi Gallery, represents the work of eight artists who "believe strongly in the positive aspects of traditional African American culture," writes curator Caleb Davis. "There is a fundamental relationship between their art and the culture."

Griots of South Florida is a richly diverse show, though uneven in quality. Carl J. Latimore's acrylic abstracts, painted in filmy pastels, for example, don't seem to belong here.

Some artists have made more direct use of African American themes than others. Oscar Thomas's oil portraits may seem more adulatory than insightful, but he doesn't shy away from blunt political references. Included here are portraits of Malcolm X and Martin Luther King Jr., as well as a more complex composition, *We Shall Overcome*, which draws on multiple images—the Statue of Liberty, bullet-shattered glass, and imprisoned African Americans—to retell the battles for civil rights.

(Thomas's mixture of art and politics, however, doesn't possess the same creative power of Ed Love's more ambitious installation, seen four seasons ago at the North Campus gallery of Miami-Dade Community College. *Signs: The Maximum Security Series* incorporated used shooting targets with steel sculptures that described the human figure, mutilated and sacrificed.)

Charles Mills, a former medical and scientific illustrator, has used his knowledge of human anatomy to create portraits of such figures as Alberta Hunter, Billie Holiday, John Coltrane, and James Brown. In his portraits, inspired by photographs, Mills adapts the lighting and composition of the camera's image. Attempts to render the human figure, and the spirit within, are especially striking in Mills' use of colored scratchboard, which offers rich textures and nuances. His portrait of Billie Holiday fuses delicacy and strength.

Donald Neal's paintings are marked by a deft skill at trompe l'oeil, the art of illusionist textures. Droplets of water, the grain of woods, and masking tape seem breathtakingly real. But Neal goes well beyond mastering clever tricks in his thoughtful, compelling work. *World*, painted only in shades of gray, shows a hand squeezing a globe in which Africa is the most visible continent. Most of its surface is featureless, though chunks where South Africa is located seem to be scraped away. The piece evokes direct questions about apartheid and Eurocentrism.

Sculptures by John Andrew Smith and Maria Jeannine Smith, father and daughter, are strong additions to the show. The senior Smith's more architectural pieces contain references to what he calls "the functional art of ancient African and other primitive civilizations." His daughter's work counters hints of the human figure with chunky, angling forms. Both incorporate abstract shapes and rough, drab surfaces, playing tension against balance in fascinating ways.

DOES "LATIN ARTIST" LABEL ENHANCE OR HINDER CAREERS?

June 14, 1992

What does it mean to be called a Latin American artist? Does the label help or hinder a career? Does it promote public understanding of this richly various "new" art? Cuban American artists here are divided on the answers to these questions.

Painter Lydia Rubio and Pablo Cano, sculptor and performance artist, take a positive view. The label, says Rubio, "makes for a group of artists to be identified in the States. It helps establish a market. It is positive at this point." Adds Cano, "Some artists feel a ghettoizing effect. I don't. I feel very fortunate to have an identity as a Latin American. In a world where there are so many images for American artists, you can get lost."

Sculptor María Brito is proud of the increasing attention: "I think it's about time that people are interested in Latin American art not only as a curiosity or as something for tourists. Artists in North America are very concerned with how their work reflects certain trends. I see more individuality in Latin American artists—they are more into following their own voices." Describing a visit two years ago to SoHo galleries in New York, she says, "It was disappointment after disappointment. There were corpses on the walls, pieces with no life to them."

But other local artists express dismay over the stereotypes associated with their art and find the label limiting.

"I hate to be categorized," says painter Arturo Rodriguez. "I try to be the least Latin American as possible," although he cites Latin American as well as North American and European influences on his work. He avoids "strong colors" and imagery that's "primitive, very convoluted" because these are characteristics that often crop up in simplistic attempts to define Latin American art.

"I hear certain comments at my shows, even from curators: 'It's not Latin enough, it's not primitive enough' and 'Why don't you use Afro-Cuban things?' . . ."

Still, he adds, "things are getting better." He praises such traveling exhibitions as *Art of the Fantastic: Latin American Art, 1920–1987*, which came to the Center for the Fine Arts in 1988, for showing the "cross currents" of very different countries. Sculptor Maria Lino, who says her work has more to do with images of women than her Latin heritage, complains that the tendency to associate Latin art with vibrant, so-called tropical colors "is absurd. That always gets me. What about the strong colors of the Fauvists and van Gogh?"

Both Brito and Lino object to the tendency to link the work of Cuban artists with the Afro-Cuban cult of Santería, with its emphasis on altars, deities, and other religious trappings. Brito, more annoyed than amused, recalls how a New York critic misinterpreted one of her figurative sculptures, a "purely political" piece dealing with repression. The critic called it a victim of Santería.

Even museum shows, Brito and Lino say, fall prey to such stereotyping.

"Curators always ask for altars, things that deal in religion," says Lino.

"We're supposed to be more concerned with religion than other cultures. Some artists play into that."

"I have seen a lot of artists take advantage of the political correctness of being Latin American," says César Trasobares. "I have seen the label become as much a ladder as a trap. I'm delighted to see the market evolving, but as an artist I don't aspire to be exclusively a part of this."

He notes that many Miami galleries specializing in Latin American art shy away from the more conceptual work by Latin artists that is gaining attention in Europe and New York. Latin galleries here have yet to show, for example, work like that of Brazilian artist Jac Leirner. Her circular sculpture of thousands of worn bank notes, commenting on the politics of Brazil's hyperinflation, was featured in the October 1991 *ARTnews*, an issue devoted to Latin American art.

Manhattan art critic Robert Mahoney takes a similar view. Much of the art he's seen in Miami, he says, "does still seem to play to popular stereotypes, with lots of colors and flowers. Hardcore real conceptual or minimal art won't sell there." But is Mahoney just voicing the cultural bias of New York? His attitude frustrates artists like Rubio, who believes many North Americans, in thrall to SoHo trends, don't appreciate the formal training many Latin artists receive in mixing colors and in drawing.

While the debates in Miami and elsewhere continue over what is good, hot, or just hype, Trasobares points to another problem: "It is sad that not one major institution (in Miami) has taken a significant interest in collecting Latin American art, given that this is a field that's very rich and powerful." None, he says, has taken "a position of national leadership in that role."

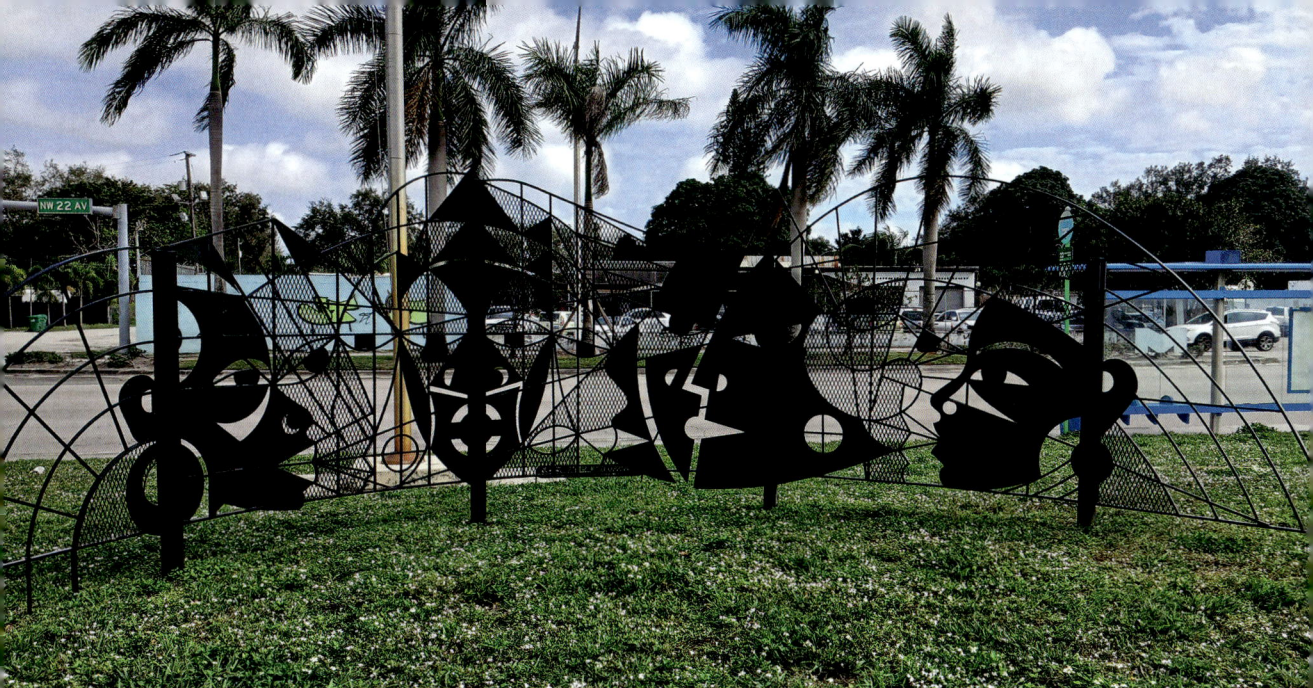

FIGURE 5. Gene Tinnie, *A Gathering of Spirits*, 1996. Painted and welded steel. West Little River Fire Station, exterior southeast corner. Image Yusimy Lara, courtesy of Miami-Dade County Department of Cultural Affairs, Art in Public Places Trust.

AFRICAN HERITAGE CULTURAL ARTS CENTER GALLERY

Diverse Styles Mark Exhibit

December 24, 1992

An eclectic mix of styles, talent, and media joins forces in a group exhibition at the African Heritage Cultural Arts Center Gallery, now known as the Marshall L. Davis Sr. African Heritage Cultural Arts Center. The show features paintings, drawings, photography, sculpture, and ceramics by 13 African American artists who work in Miami but hail from locations including Jamaica, Cuba, Puerto Rico, Haiti, and Ghana, as well as the States.

The show, *The Golden Age of Black Art*, takes its title from a program of the same name. GABA was initiated by the National Conference of Artists, a nationwide organization of Black visual artists, to nurture and promote art by African Americans.

While the selections are uneven—and curiously weak in Haitian art, with no paintings included—works by several artists do stand out in this handsomely designed space. Among the best are the exquisitely shaded etchings and other prints by Charles E. Humes Jr. Working in a palette that runs from velvety charcoals to palest silvery grays, Humes is a master at evoking nuances of character in the social gatherings he describes. *Flashpool*, for example, depicts men hunkered over a bar, evoking the urban isolation found in Edward Hopper's famous painting *Nighthawks*.

The untitled graphite drawing by Antonius Roberts aspires to Humes's fine sense of shading. In a series of self-portraits, Roberts repeats the same image of his face, first drawn almost completely in black, then gradually in lighter shades of gray so that the image seems to disappear into a ghostly blur.

Although the paintings are among the weakest selections, the oil-on-paper portraits by Nelson Franco are noteworthy for their subtle use of texture.

Other strong pieces include the simply designed, smoky-colored pots of Simone Clunie and photographs by Marc-Arthur Jean Louis and Olusegun Ifalase. Louis' *Ti Peyizan* (*Little peasant*), printed in golden-brown tones, shows a small boy in a big hat, dwarfed by adults in a marketplace. It strikes an edgy balance between the rough spontaneity of street photography and the delicacy of an artfully composed shot. Ifalase's *Ceremonies*, with its angry crowd bearing placards and open umbrellas, records the recent controversy over Miami's refusal to welcome South African leader Nelson Mandela.

Taking a more historical look at the many troubling links between this country and Africa, Dinizulu Gene Tinnie drew on his research of the slave trade to create *In the Wake of Columbus*. This elaborate mix of drawings and Xeroxed reproductions of engravings from Abolitionist literature features a harrowing central image—the diagram of a ship carrying slaves, with bodies tightly packed in row after row. Like many of his works, *Wake* refers to the riches of African culture, including Masai tribal dress and bronze Benin heads from southern Nigeria. Layered around the image of the slave ship's belly, these references carry a message of endurance and pride, despite, as Tinnie says, "the horror of the Middle Passage."

CARLOS BETANCOURT

Miami Beach Artist's "Splintered Vision" at Core of *Fracturism*

June 21, 1994

There's a blue tattoo on Carlos Betancourt's tanned, freckled shoulder, something curling, arching, even beckoning. A mermaid? A scorpion? The Miami Beach artist laughs.

"It's an angel," he says. "An angel looking over my shoulder."

It's not as if Betancourt, 28, needs a guardian angel. His paintings and award-winning furniture designs have caught the attention of the *New York Times, Elle, House and Garden*, and a slew of other publications. He designed the interiors for area clubs like Boomerang and the Butter Club. Sylvester Stallone recently commissioned Betancourt and artist Miguel Delgado to paint murals for his Miami home, among them a 20-by-5-foot replica of Michelangelo's *Expulsion of Eve from Paradise* scene in the Sistine Chapel.

"It was a fantastic experience because I was able to try to paint like Michelangelo," says Betancourt, reverence in his voice.

It's a curious switch: Warhol and Lichtenstein, not the Renaissance master, have been a strong influence on much of Betancourt's paintings, which include enormous Pop-style, ultracamp portraits of Celia Cruz and Miami Beach diva Tara Solomon.

On a sun-blazing Saturday afternoon, in the 90-degree heat outside his Lincoln Road gallery, Imperfect Utopia, the artist is up, radiant with energy. He's lithe and loose in tank top, shorts, and Birkenstocks. Slipping in and out of a shoulder-shuddering salsa, he describes how he danced with actress Marisa Tomei at Stallone's recent Planet Hollywood bash. Now he shifts lightly from one foot to the other, takes a drag on a cigarette, and smiles broadly. He's excited about his show of new work, which will open that evening.

Sheets of white paper cover the storefront window, veiling the new works until nighttime, but a poem Betancourt scrawled across the glass offers some cryptic hints about what's inside. The language is dense, the meter

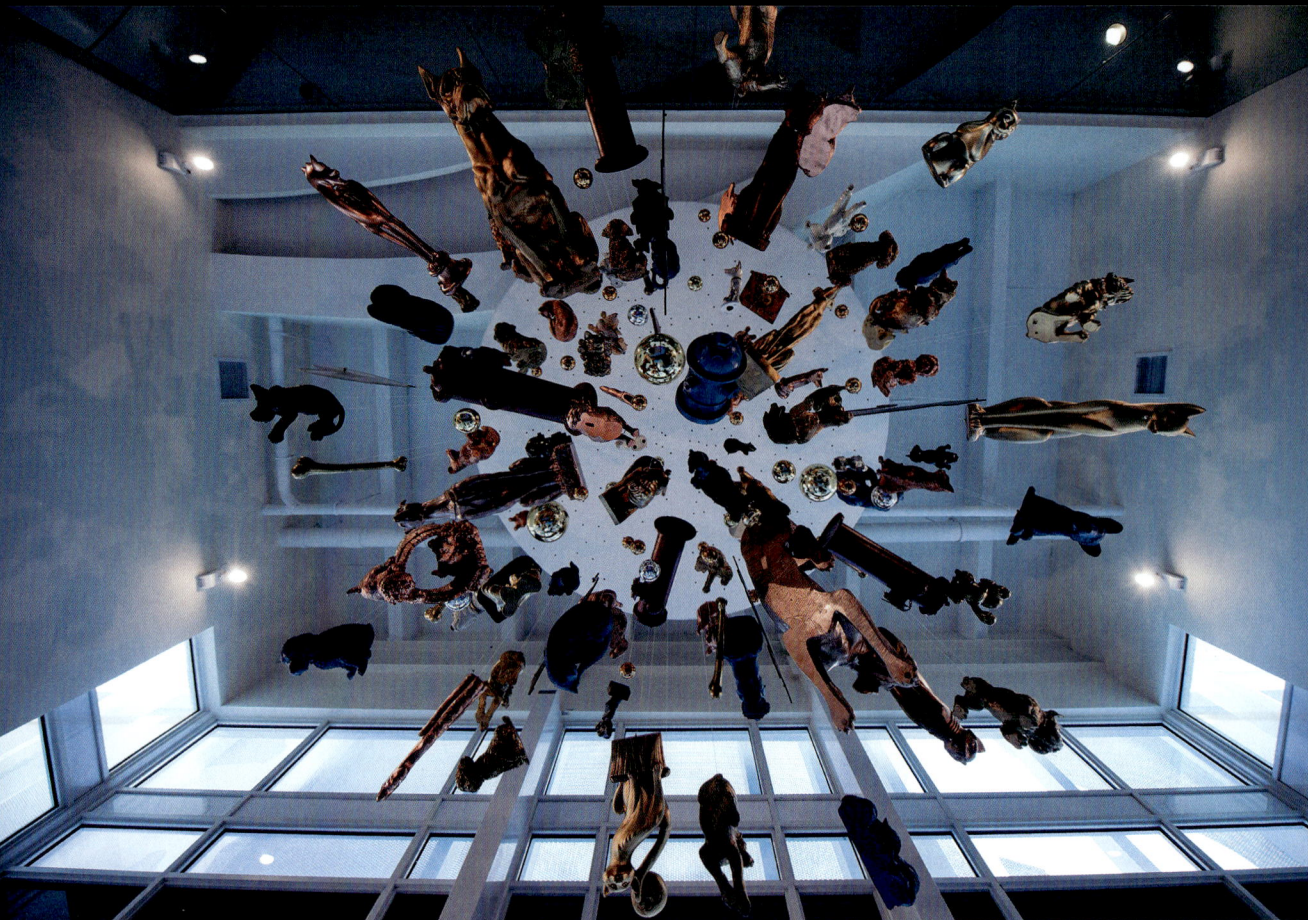

FIGURE 6. Carlos Betancourt and Alberto Latorre, *Splendor in the Shelter: It's Raining Cats and Dogs*, 2014. Mixed media. Miami-Dade Animal Services Pet Adoption & Protection Center, 3599 NW 79th Ave. Courtesy of Miami-Dade County Department of Cultural Affairs, Art in Public Places Trust.

indecipherable, but the last line strikes a chord on this multilingual island of tropical kitsch and thrift-shop glitz. The poem reads, "I long to assemble the splintered vision of all that I know."

"Splintered vision" dovetails neatly with the title of Betancourt's new show, *Fracturism*. The paintings—layered with a noisy web of shattered, broken-up images—were inspired by the multicultural sensory overload the artist sees as a condition of our lives on the edge of the millennium. Of a recent trip to Buenos Aires, for example, he says, "You listen to the music there, and it's a mixture of everything—flamenco-bossa nova, tango-jazz, salsa-flamenco."

His mixed-media paintings feature photo-silk-screened portraits of such varied icons as Audrey Hepburn, male models in Banana Republic shorts, the patron saint of Cuba, and dissident Cuban poet María Elena Cruz Varela. They are interlaced with dreamy blue skies, organic forms—some dripping and bloody, some tender and green—and futuristic drawings recalling the artist's sinuous chairs and lounges. The works are encased in black fragments of mismatched frames, a device that adds to their chaotic energy.

"My works let me express 300 things visually at the same time," Betancourt says.

"They scream at you," says John Casey, who included Betancourt in a show of Miami artists that he curated for a Sarasota gallery in March. "He travels on the edge of this cleft between cultures," Casey says, comparing Betancourt's art to his habit of switching back and forth between Spanish and English. On the one hand, "he's got that very heavy religious element, with a lot of blood and suffering," while other images suggest the inclusive pop sensibility of Robert Rauschenberg.

Betancourt creates just such uncomfortable juxtapositions in *Viaje y destino de Raiza la balsera*, inspired by the wrenching story of a Cuban rafter who survived the perilous crossing with her young son but died shortly after, having given all her drinking water to her child. "It killed me, that story," says Betancourt.

In the painting, a black-and-white silk-screened photo of a child's round face, shaded slightly by a baseball cap, appears several times—floating among blue skies with puffy cumulus clouds, boxed into a radiant orange area near the edge of the canvas (where the artist has written a few lines in his trademark and nearly illegible reverse script). Elsewhere, there is contrasting deep and shallow space, with architectural constructions that seem to begin and end nowhere.

Ready to crush this airy network of sky, faces, and spaces is a torrent of dripping red and blue, like great clusters of tears or drooping hearts cut in half. This emotional outpouring of paint, in contrast to the bland architectural fragments, seems to evoke the mother's great sacrifice, which was her son's tremendous loss and gain.

The work reflects another theme in the show: the artist's fascination with women as icons of beauty and suffering, ravaged beacons of hope and desire. In the same conversation, he waxes rhapsodic about Audrey Hepburn and Cruz Varela. "She had one of the most honest and beautiful smiles you can imagine," he says of Hepburn, whom he met in Miami several years ago. Of Cruz Varela, who has been persecuted and jailed for her poems in Cuba, "What she is is all in her face. Intense. Angelic."

This is just the sort of riveting contrast that Betancourt thrives on: the elegant Hollywood star and the brutally victimized poet, women from vastly different worlds whose soulful likenesses he's brought together in a single work.

There's yet another contrast to experience at Imperfect Utopia—the clash between Betancourt's "screaming" paintings and the sleek furniture he designs. Placed near the center of the gallery is a low-slung wooden chaise, gently recalling the curving facade of Morris Lapidus's Fontainebleau Hotel. Other chairs and sofas, sporting shiny cushions of hot pink or lime green, are crafted from a few airy loops of wrought iron, playful grace notes to his passionate imagination.

Everything at Imperfect Utopia is part of a work in progress for one of Betancourt's biggest fans, Richard Alexander, executive producer of the company that brought *Les Misérables*, *Phantom of the Opera*, and *Miss Saigon* to Broadway and on tour. Alexander—who flew to Miami Beach from New York for the opening of *Fracturism* "even though we were having our opening of *Miss Saigon* that night in Washington with the president"—calls Betancourt "ferociously talented. . . . I think he will be in evolution (throughout) his entire career. He doesn't seem to have any boundaries. He has eyeballs that are on fire."

GROUND LEVEL

Transforming Trash into Objets d'Art

November 19, 1994

Pablo Cano picks up a faded, bottle-green valise. It's the small overnight size, and he opens it quickly, flicking the tarnished contents to reveal hundreds of silver papers, neatly stacked and wrapped with rubber bands like so much paper money. In this town, the gesture reverberates with corny memories of *Miami Vice* episodes in which bad guys loved to snap open smart black attaché cases to show off dazzling stacks of $100 bills.

But the silver in this shabby valise, meticulously saved from cigarette boxes and gum wrappers, is the coin of a very different realm—the realm of artistic imagination where one person's trash is someone else's treasure. Prized for their patina, the silver papers are used to cover Cano's magical marionettes—elegant sculptures of silvery junk. They're also a fine example of what's on view in *Dirty Laundry: The Art behind the Art*, the current show at Ground Level.

The title, say the five artists who've put together this quirky and rambling show, comes from an expression they use to describe the sketches, notes, and accumulated clutter they one day may turn into art. And as visitors will discover, artists Cano, Carlos Alves, Jens Diercks, Linda Faneuf, and Marina Fernandez have a lot of dirty laundry.

You may not find smelly socks here, but you will find Clorox bottles, dragonflies, broken chairs and candlesticks, cracked salt shakers, old letters, vintage beauty guides, and sequined fruit. It's a collection focused less on the result than on the process of art making.

The show is about ideas and where they come from, says Fernandez, whose favorite medium is broken glass collected from the street or from shopkeepers' trash. She melds others' mistakes into fanciful windows, screens, lamps, and fountains.

Alves, a noted ceramist, has built a busy career from broken dishes, fusing them to such things as fountains and to the towering ceramic royal palm that

Art in Public Places commissioned for the Eighth Street Metromover station.

Diercks, who once dismantled obsolete mainframe computers for art parts, currently is making sculpture from discarded chairs. "I see potential in a lot of things," he says. Critical of our throwaway society, he considers it "healthy to embrace things that have been cast out."

Attached to the outside of Cano's old valise is a funky drawing by Faneuf that records the trips she made "trash picking" with Alves and Cano. It shows her two friends riding in the cab of a red pickup truck while she stands watch in the truck bed, shining a flashlight curbside.

In the late 1980s, the three artists made many such late-night forays, greeting dawn on Southwest Eighth Street with breakfast at Versailles. Placemats from that classic Cuban restaurant, covered with Cano's charming doodles of family and friends, are in the show.

"Around Little Havana, there's the best trash," Cano says. "There's a lot of baroque things Cubans love, candelabras, kitschy things." Their trips ended after a *Miami Vice* tale turned into a true story.

"We stopped doing it when Linda and I were robbed," Cano said. "We were held up at machine-gun point . . . two machine guns. Unfortunately for us, these people were looking for a getaway car. They had done a drug deal and had actually shot someone."

That was a few years ago, but the three still have bushels of material from those trips. All agree that their best find was a big pile in front of the house of a widow who apparently had died. "They had just taken her whole life and dumped it on the street," says Alves. There were rocking chairs, dishes, magazines, and a fat cache of letters and records belonging to a woman named Gladys who had been a missionary and beautician.

The letters inspired Faneuf to make her *Gladys* series of collaged paintings about stooped but determined ladies with bulky heels and bulging shopping bags, occasionally attending to the needs of their pets, plants, or husbands. In the many notes and sketches she has included in the show, you can see Faneuf's trenchant, poetic observations of what time does to body and soul.

The installations not only offer clues to each artist's sensibility but also show how specific projects evolved. Alves, for instance, has provided many drawings, some from his teenage years, recording his love of royal palms, a symbol of Cuba and a central image in his Metromover commission. Notes, photos, and ceramics document the history of that project as well as Alves's gift for tropical exuberance.

His accumulations and the others in this show are deliciously eccentric and frank. While this century counts many artists, from Picasso to Rauschenberg, who have turned discards into objects of desire, we rarely get a glimpse of how such alchemy can happen.

CENTER OF CONTEMPORARY ART

Art + Architecture Reflects Miami's Glorious Coming of Age

February 25, 1995

Scooped from sticky swamps, pervaded by the stinging whine of mosquitoes, Miami began life as a place to be made over into newcomers' visions of other, more romantic locales. That legacy persists today, in Mediterranean Revival architecture, in hotel names like the Mandalay and Malibu, the DiLido and Del Rio, the Aztec and Avalon.

But in the last decade, Miami has come into its own images, creating a sense of place out of its recent multifaceted history, both glamorous and gritty. That evolving identity is deftly illuminated in *Art + Architecture = Miami*, the current show at North Miami's Center of Contemporary Art.

In her catalog essay, curator Beth Dunlop charts Miami's maturing sense of place, noting that the plethora of construction here from the late 1960s through the early '80s was "faceless, tasteless." Dunlop, the *Miami Herald's* architecture critic, compares the city to a diffident adolescent: "Emerging cities (and the architects and artists who adorn them) tend to be self-conscious, like teenagers not wanting to stand out, to be different; with cultural sophistication also comes the ability to step away from the crowd, to stand out."

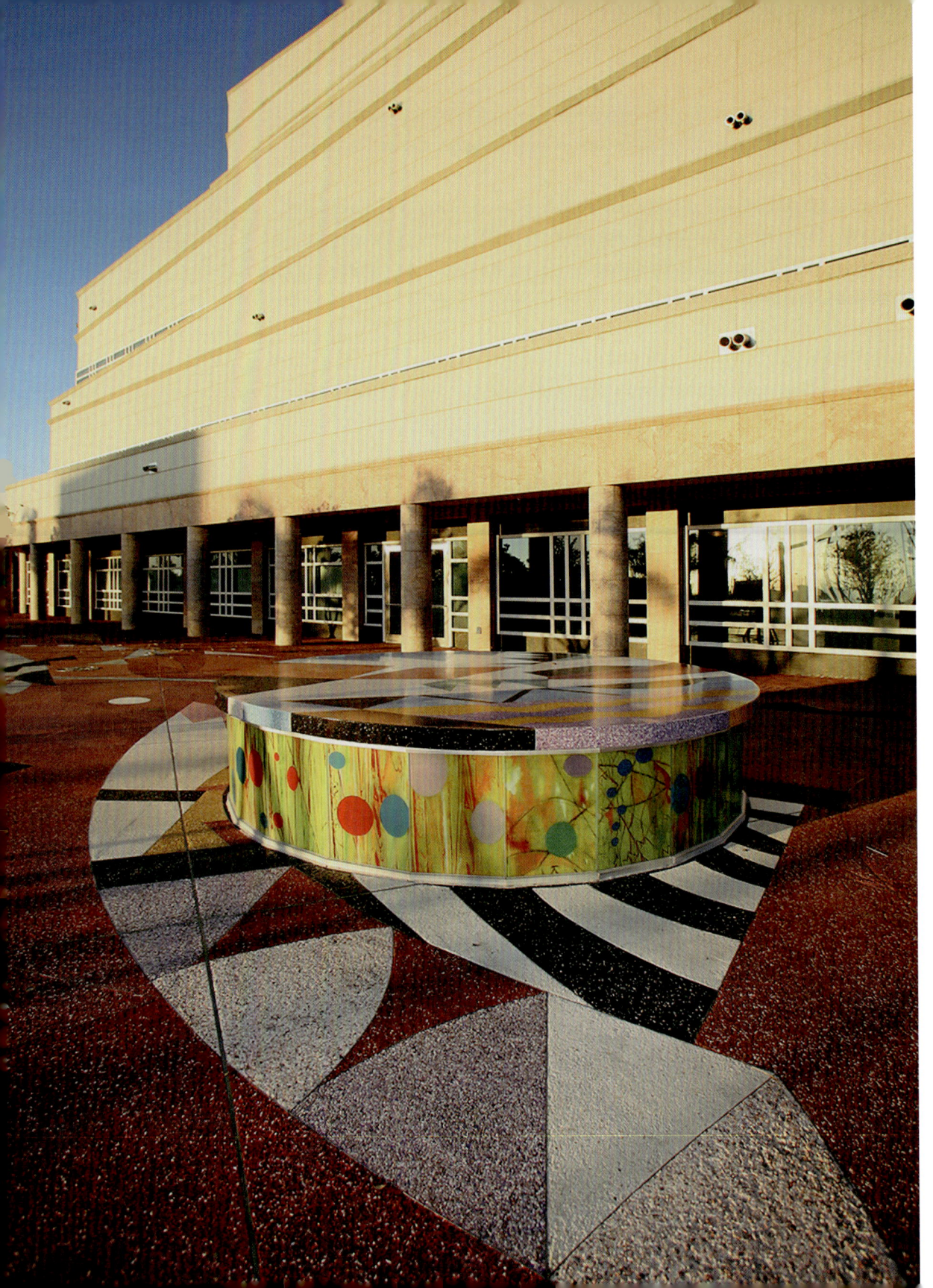

The ability to step away and stand out seems to have crystallized in 1983, when Christo and Jeanne-Claude wrapped islands in Biscayne Bay with 6.5 million square feet of pink polypropylene, summoning world-class attention for *Surrounded Islands*. That year we also were treated to the dashing exuberance of Arquitectonica's Atlantis on Brickell Avenue. With its central cutout housing pool and palm tree, the building was a 24-hour freeze-frame of glamour Miami style, an icon picked up weekly on *Miami Vice*.

While those visual landmarks are familiar to many, this show is not about recycling photographs of completed monuments. Instead, Dunlop holds a mirror up to a community's creative sensibilities by mining a trove of public and private documents. Models, sketch pads, drawings, and paintings—even kitschy artifacts like a burlesque poster—aim to show how such sensibilities spiral outward, often nurturing each other.

The exhibit also includes videotapes that record moments in the making of several works described in the exhibit: Christo and company wrapping the islands, Michele Oka Doner installing her bronze marine forms in an airport walkway, Richard Haas painting his playfully visionary Fontainebleau mural.

Among the show's natural images is a quietly compelling drawing of the mangrove's intricately interwoven root system by Flavio Barney. These looping shapes reflect not only a fragile environment deserving respect but also a formal beauty and energy echoed in the nearby designs of Carlos Alfonzo and Carlos Alves. Visitors can see a photograph and painted study of Alfonzo's *Ceremony of the Tropics* at the Santa Clara Metrorail station. For Alves's *La Palma*, under construction for the Eighth Street Metromover station, there is a dynamic pastel study.

Throughout the show we get to savor the familiar, including the downtown *Dropped Bowl* fountain by Claes Oldenburg and Coosje van Bruggen, and experience more recent projects, public and private. There is an abundance of work from Miami-Dade Art in Public Places, tapping into the city's natural and multiethnic history. These commissions are not so much

FIGURE 7. Gary Moore, *Pharoah's Dance*, 2003. Rustic terrazzo, fused glass, polished steel, lighting. Adrienne Arsht Center, Ziff Ballet Opera House/plaza. Image Robin Hill, courtesy of Miami-Dade County Department of Cultural Affairs, Art in Public Places Trust.

about being politically correct as about finding the past within the present, a crucial step in coming of age.

On display is Christopher Janney's model for *Winds of Sound/Gates of Light*, a walkway greeting international arrivals at the airport that is complete with chirping, rustling Everglades sounds and translucent panels that gently suffuse travelers in light changing from blue-greens to pinks and oranges. The exhibit also documents Overtown's Ninth Street Mall, layered with references to the area's African American heritage, by Gary Moore and landscape architect Gerald Marston.

The fantasy world of Miami's early promoters also finds its way into the present. "Our work—images that bridge the world of reality and the world of dreams" is the notation on a sketch pad relating to the giant red concrete *M* for Miami, an Art in Public Places commission by Roberto M. Behar and Rosario Marquardt with Claudia Bancalari, José Jaén, and Kevin Storm.

Planned to ornament the Riverwalk Metromover station, the *M* has two silvery balls on top, like fanciful earrings, and its massive presence is reminiscent of a child's toy block. Quirky and sophisticated with links to dreams and childhood, it is a wonderful image for a city growing up. And it's just one of many resonant images in this show, calling us to consider reminders big and small of where we've been and where we can go.

LYNNE GOLOB GELFMAN

Reach Out and Touch Artist's Creations, Visitors Don Gloves to Feel Changes in Layers and Texture

March 1, 1996

No matter how tempting the texture or luscious the color, paintings are to be seen and not touched. This rule, meant to protect artworks, keeps museum guards on their toes and most of us at a respectful distance.

In the current show at the Foundlings Club, however, you can don white gloves and touch the paintings, feeling the rippling curves of brushstrokes and the smooth weave of the canvas. *New Paintings: Oil and Sand* features recent work by Miami artist Lynne Golob Gelfman, with 14 selections on canvas and 5 on paper.

Gelfman, whose abstract paintings have often reflected her interest in the interlacing patterns of elaborate iron grille work and handwoven baskets, invites us to touch her paintings in order to feel the traces of her own direct encounter with these handsome surfaces.

Not only have the canvases been painted with a tight gridlike design and swooping baroque flourishes and curlicues, but they've also been heavily sanded with an electric sanding machine so that in some cases the canvas is almost threadbare. We can touch the remnants of that vigorous activity. This sensation adds an extra dimension to what we see, which are the shadows and outlines of exuberantly thick strokes of paint.

The effect is both beautiful and peculiar, confusing our ability to distinguish between what's been wrought by hand and by machine. More importantly, the effect gives Gelfman's enduring interest in overlapping layers of lines and colors an extra punch.

The colors here are somber, mostly deep charcoal or silvery grays with passages of ashy white. Some paintings are darker than others, making the intricate patterns tantalizingly mysterious and obscure. Glimpses of brighter colors sometimes surface, with tiny flamelike curls of yellow in one untitled work, while stains of sky-blue and pale-gold flicker through the graceful and sinuous *Blue Sand*.

These paintings bear traces of a Byzantine complexity, a faded labyrinth of grids and curls that leads the eye through one lattice-like layer into another, through corridors of darkness and light. The journey suggests a metaphor for the creative process of seeing.

"I thought they were stones," commented one visitor to the exhibit, surprised to learn that he was looking at paintings. But they do have the look of worn-away stones, perhaps once encrusted with ornately designed mosaics. This sense of something vanished and something left behind gives Gelfman's newest abstract paintings a presence both tough and poignant.

In memoriam: Lynne Golob Gelfman, 1944–2020

SEBASTIAN SPRENG

Writing and Painting about Chamber Music, Argentine Artist Bound Only by Wheelchair

March 27, 1995

In this porous city, swirling with the accents and customs of many cultures, Sebastian Spreng seems especially at home: a man with a porous imagination who moves freely among the worlds of music, painting, and language, multicultural in a way most of us never dream of becoming. *Chamber Music*, Spreng's show of oil paintings on display through April 5 at the Americas Collection in Coral Gables, is a splendid example of that rich confluence. His work features atmospheric landscapes with fabulous gardens seen from a distance and shimmering expanses of water in which a solitary swimmer often floats. They speak of interior worlds where the imagination roams free.

Spreng, who has been confined to a wheelchair since he was diagnosed with muscular dystrophy at age 14, acknowledges that these swimmers are references to the free movement that eludes him except in the water. But, he is quick to add, the landscapes are meant to be poetic metaphors.

"I paint my interior landscapes. By coincidence, [they are] landscapes I'm living in now," he says, referring to Miami's tropical luxuriance and his attraction to its "strange oneiric" summer nights. "It's like what I have inside."

Even though his work is at times more sweet than compelling, Spreng wields a restrained vocabulary with great sensitivity. And the pieces are, indeed, analogous to the chamber music of the exhibition's title: intimate and subtle with finely etched repetitions and variations.

The parallels highlight Spreng's wide-ranging knowledge of classical music. A native of Buenos Aires who moved to Miami in the late '80s, Spreng, 38, is the Miami correspondent for the glossy magazine *Clasica*, published in Buenos Aires by Radio Clásica. (Florida Philharmonic fans may already be familiar with his paintings, which appear on five of the orchestra's nine playbills this season.)

Even the catalog for the show begins with a poem from James Joyce's youthfully romantic collection *Chamber Music*. The opening lines of the first poem—"Strings in the earth and air / Make music sweet"—inspired American composer Samuel Barber's 1935 song, whose title is taken from that line; it was one of many songs Barber set to lyric poetry during his career.

"They are exquisite pieces of music," Spreng says. Making a reference to the lovely, bittersweet quality of the 1935 song, as he does in this show, was "a way of putting together music, painting, and literature."

It's a synthesis Spreng deals with daily, spending some eight hours listening to classical music while painting. And of

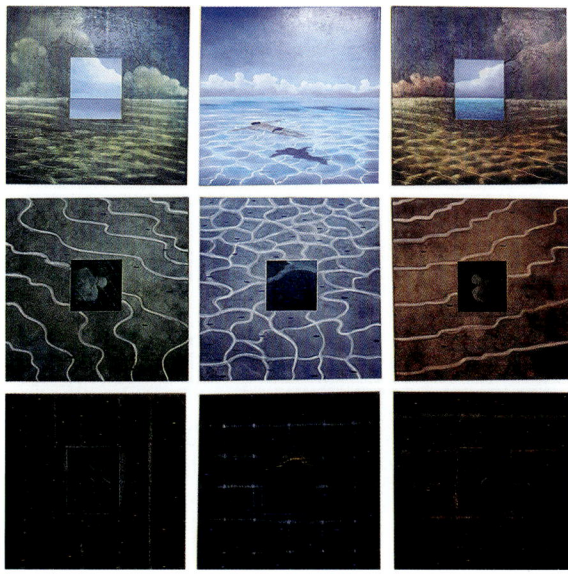

FIGURE 8. Sebastian Spreng, *Nonet for the Long Journey*, 1995. Oil on canvas in nine parts. Stephen P. Clark Government Center. Image Ryan Holloway, courtesy of Miami-Dade County Department of Cultural Affairs, Art in Public Places Trust.

course there is his work for *Clasica*, which includes interviewing visiting musicians such as violinist Pinchas Zukerman and soprano Barbara Hendricks. "It's fascinating," he says of these interviews. "You are in contact with another world. When you by chance mention that you are an artist, that you paint, the whole thing is much more relaxed. I'm not trying to do a critique but to have an interchange of ideas." What's equally fascinating is the way music and water have shaped Spreng's own artistic sensibility. He recalls visiting Teatro Colón, Buenos Aires's turn-of-the-century opera house, as a high schooler.

"We [toured] the bowels of the theater. It was like *Phantom of the Opera*," he says. "The orchestra was 10 meters above us, playing Wagner, and the music was like water, falling over us, as if you could touch it."

"My love of music started there," he says. "It was so important in cultivating a sensibility."

If his feelings for music developed during high school, Spreng's longing for marine vistas began much earlier, during his childhood in the Santa Fe province. "I was always fascinated by the ocean, always," he says. "In Argentina I lived in the middle of an ocean of wheat, the pampas." As a child, he drew and painted obsessively, making maps of imaginary countries. There was much time for these solitary pursuits, since Spreng had had trouble walking from the age of 3. For years it was thought he had cancer or tuberculosis; it wasn't until he was 14 that the MD diagnosis was made.

Only when pressed will he talk about his disability—and then he recounts, in a thin, tense voice, a harrowing tale of a narrow escape from Argentine police during the turbulent 1970s.

Spreng prefers to talk about his newest work, a group of nine 24-by-24-inch paintings commissioned by the Miami-Dade Art in Public Places program. The works, to be unveiled this fall, will hang in the Stephen P. Clark Government Center as a memorial to George Armitage, a local advocate for the disabled who died in 1991 at the age of 66.

"There will be three levels of three paintings to form a puzzle—like a big painting because I cannot paint big," Spreng says of his serial composition. "This disadvantage gives me an advantage. I try to see my whole life like this. . . . The lower levels are like webs, labyrinths, jails. The figure inside is very dark. In the upper level, you have this magnificent ocean." In the ocean Spreng will paint a swimmer, a reference to the one activity in which he himself can move freely.

He's not concerned that his work will hang in this specific context. "Everybody has some kind of handicap," he says, adding that the series is really about "the path from darkness to light." Vivian Rodriguez, executive director of Art in Public Places, agrees. The commissioned works, she says, will make a statement about "dealing with universal disabilities, whether they are physical or from being an imperfect human being."

The Politics of Boats at Dade Library Shows
Highlight Fears and Dreams

August 13, 1995

Boats have a particular resonance here in South Florida, from the pleasure yachts anchored along our coast to the rickety vessels that deliver refugees from Cuba and Haiti. Put artists at the helms of our boats, and you sign on for a voyage that calls on many ports of the imagination but remains always moored in our complex history. It's a voyage freighted with the richly powerful human experience of fears, dreams, and memories.

That's just the combination that has guided two compelling shows at the Miami-Dade County Main Library: *Boat Images from South Florida Collections*, a handful of large paintings and sculpture in the auditorium, and *Becalmed in Miami: Three-Dimensional Boats by South Florida Artists* in the second-floor exhibition area. Both were organized by the library's Barbara Young, supervisor of art services.

In *Boat Images*, the political is visual, with abundant references to the issues of immigration and exile. Consider Aramis O'Reilly's painting *Passage*, for example, with its ghostly, overlapping scenes of islands and ocean travelers; or Paul Sierra's *Gently into the Night*, in which a dreaming, levitating figure floats above a boat drifting along a current of memory. While these paintings are not the strongest in the show, they underscore the themes that pull all the works together.

Sherri Tan's untitled construction, resembling the wooden piling of a dock draped with massive ropes, is especially fine. The ropes, twisted and fraying, are like lines used for docking ships, yet their ability to hold anything secure and steady has unraveled. Rectangles of yellowed text—in English, Spanish, and Creole—are collaged onto this column of wood. They transform a simple shape, one that evokes both an abstract form and a useful nautical structure, into a provocative record of interrupted stories, many voices speaking at once. All are wrapped around a place that should stand for safety but doesn't, evoking the insecurity of a new home.

Other powerful works come from the considerably different visions of Lydia Rubio and Luis Cruz Azaceta. Rubio's *Barco de Tierra* (*Ship of earth*) is a round oil on wood, typical of her exquisite draftsmanship, featuring a ship that cleaves a rippling, golden-grained expanse that could be land or water. With this luminous, strange scene framed by a square drawn inside a circle, the piece is at once realistic and chimerical, as full of contradictions as memory itself.

Next to the streamlined elegance of Rubio's painting, Azaceta's *86½ Days Journey* has the raw, messy energy of graffiti. At the center of this work on paper is a screaming head, a grotesque face bobbing in a tiny boat. Scrawled in wavy, undulating rows across the entire piece are numbers 1 through 86½. It's a crude countdown that works on many levels: jamming the numbers of days and victims into a mind-numbing, anonymous progression while offering a wrenching twist on the cool, serial forms of minimalism.

Upstairs is a fleet of nearly 50 boats, smallish objects created for *Becalmed in Miami*. They demonstrate again how boats may enthrall creative minds, becoming capacious metaphors for the body, for flight, for magical journeys, as well as for sleekly formal designs that cut through all the baggage other pieces have welcomed. The result is an intensely varied show, with more discoveries than disappointments.

Among those discoveries: Dinizulu Gene Tinnie's fanciful, fragile *Celestial Vessel* and Carol Cornelison's *Bird's Nest Boat*, made of fiber and twigs and bringing a playful sense to soaring dreams of flight, of airborne escape from the tedious and earthbound.

Steve Bollman also plays with the notion of flight in a powerful untitled work. The pared-down, boatlike form of wire mesh is filled with feathers and accommodates references not only to flight but also to the body and a coffin. Its presence is vividly tactile, soft and thorny, welcoming and forbidding, and offers a poignant homage to the risky refuge promised by leaky, frail crafts braving the waters leading to Miami.

Risk and sacrifice propel boats in which bodies become sails, as in the computer-generated imagery of Tom Schmitt's *Bit Byte Boat* and the ceramic vessel of James Herring's *Sailor Man*. Another ceramic piece, Connie Lloveras's *Idea Vessel*, is heavily scored with markings that suggest safe havens lost and found.

If brevity is the soul of wit, it is surely the soul of the austere wit embraced by the starkly simple works of Teresita Fernández and Rafael Salazar. Fernández's gleaming, stainless steel gravy boat is a trenchant pun on the lure of domestic comfort, while Salazar's panoramic photographs of sea and sky have been crisply folded into little paper boats that would easily fit in a child's hand. They sum up the large-scale, generous visions of the many small works in this deeply engaging summer show.

In memoriam: Tom Schmitt, 1929–2018

BARBARA NEIJNA

New Work Shaped by Ancient Florida

October 7, 1995

There are eight tiny drawers in Barbara Neijna's massive installation, *Interior Landscapes*, at the Center for the Fine Arts. The drawers are lodged in the center of silvery black, shell-encrusted cement blocks, mounted on the wall like gigantic filing cabinets, and half of the drawers can be opened to reveal minute artifacts—ancient fossils of sea creatures and sepia-toned snippets of the artist's old family photographs.

Gingerly open the mirror-lined drawers, and you'll reveal yourself. You'll see your quizzical reflection become entwined with this personal and primeval assortment.

This is by design.

"We're all an accumulation of the past, [and] we're inextricably part of our environment," says Neijna, a South Florida sculptor who constructed this installation for the CFA's *New Work* series.

Interior Landscapes is imbued with a strong sense of South Florida. It

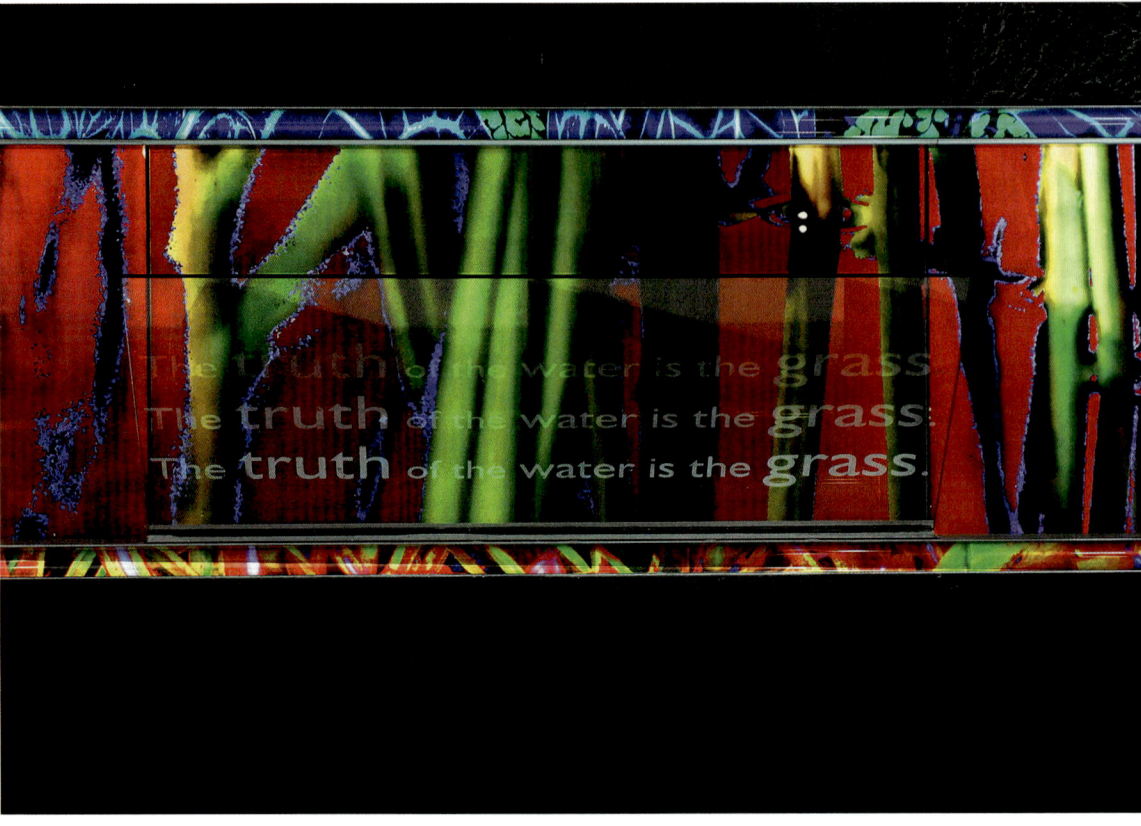

FIGURE 9. Barbara Neijna, *Foreverglades*, 2007. Epoxy terrazzo, acrylic and precast stone mixed-media bas-relief panels, and glass. Miami International Airport Concourse J. Image Marcos Martinez, courtesy of Miami-Dade County Department of Cultural Affairs, Art in Public Places Trust.

meshes the urban with the oceangoing, the poignantly human with the Everglades-earthy. Tinted cement and industrial gray fiberglass scrim accompany pounds of crushed seashells and "magnificent Florida muck," as Neijna calls the moist black earth lining an enormous mesh cone suspended near the entrance to her installation.

Like all of Neijna's many works of public art in Philadelphia, Atlanta, South Florida, and elsewhere, this piece lures the viewer into a textured, contoured space to be experienced from many angles. In her permanent outdoor commissions, plazas and pathways offer a sense of scale that easily shifts from the monumental to the intimate. Here, with the tiny drawers on one wall and a seemingly vast, crumbly slope of 10,000 pounds of seashells on the opposite wall, Neijna has accomplished similar shifts in scale. These shifts create handsome formal tensions, and beyond that, they reflect Neijna's fascination with fusing the small and large histories of our world, the humanly personal with the mysteriously primeval.

Echoes of the long-ago past, and especially of the sweeping, prehistoric-looking expanses found in the Everglades, have become a more dominant presence in Neijna's work in the past 10 years. To her, those expanses are massively sculptural as well as hauntingly fragile, and an awareness of the besieged ecosystem has gradually informed her work. She has moved from using welded aluminum to more natural materials such as Florida's fossilized limestone and cement packed with shells.

Accordant Zone, the piece she created last year with sculptor Ned Smyth on five acres at Fort Lauderdale's new Judicial Complex, includes immense Florida limestone and concrete forms—her signature sphere, cone, and disk—and a section of marshland. One of 29 works cited in *Art in America*'s prestigious 1994 review of public art, *Accordant Zone* embraces the weighty architectural forms and fragile natural elements also present in *Interior Landscapes*.

As visitors enter the CFA, they'll see *Stele*, a cement and limestone disk 84 inches in diameter, glinting with shades of pewter and charcoal. A subtle line of shadows divides the disk into four quarters, suggesting an earthly globe and propelling us toward the huge earthy cone suspended at the doorway to the *New Works* gallery.

Once viewers edge past this cone, they enter a room with the cabinet-like grid of drawers at one end and Neijna's encrusted *Shellscape* opposite, sloping toward the floor from a point near the ceiling. It resembles an ancient tidal avalanche, weighted not only with billions of shells but with the appearance of vast space and time.

In the middle of the room are two fiberglass scrims hanging from the ceiling and a collection of spheres on the floor. A shell-encrusted cement cylinder hangs from one scrim, as if floating miraculously in space, or as if some of the loose shells have already been rolled up, compacted, and distilled into pure, poetic form. Walking among these scrims and objects gives viewers a subtle stream of changing images, massive and intimate, textured and blurred, old and new.

Neijna's installation is wonderfully compelling. It beautifully evokes a sense of artistic form and South Florida place. That *Interior Landscapes* exists despite its tough technical demands is a tribute to the CFA's commitment to contemporary art.

MUSEUM OF CONTEMPORARY ART

Thoroughly Modern MOCA Cutting-Edge Institution Comes of Age with a Splash

February 18, 1996

There's a tiny tin of chocolate that comes with the invitation to Friday's gala celebrating the opening of the Museum of Contemporary Art in North Miami. Say "MOCA"—the name they use for cutting-edge institutions in Los Angeles, San Diego, and Chicago—and you'll get the wordplay.

There's a suggestion of confection, too, in the multihued pieces of MOCA's new $3.5 million, 23,000-square-foot building, designed by noted New York architect Charles Gwathmey.

But there's more than a candy-coated gimmick behind South Florida's dashing new museum space. (If you didn't get your sweets in the mail, don't despair; they'll be for sale at the gift shop.)

Timely items in international magazines such as *Art & Auction* and *Flash Art* are noting the coming of age of an institution long prized by locals for bringing artists and audiences closer together. But beyond the chic and spacious new building, it is the museum's distinctive programming and tightly focused mission that account for the buzz.

By pulling together a splashy cluster of art world connections—collectors, dealers, curators, critics, and artists themselves—those at MOCA's epicenter are securing a spot for South Florida in international art world sensibilities.

"We have a critical mass [of institutions]," says Bonnie Clearwater, chief curator, who with executive director Lou Anne Colodny and board chairman Richard Shack forms the triumvirate most responsible for making things go at MOCA. "That makes this a destination for the international art world. If they come here, it's not just for one thing; there are a number of things to check out."

For starters, consider MOCA's inaugural exhibit, *Defining the Nineties: Consensus-Making in New York, Miami, and Los Angeles,* rounding up 82 works by 25 artists who've seen their reputations flower in one of those three cities.

"There hasn't been a survey of artists who've emerged in the '90s yet," says Clearwater, who curated the show. "We've taken a lead in trying to examine what's happening."

It's a show about who's becoming hot—and hotly collected. Represented among works loaned by a who's who list of internationally recognized collectors is the late Félix González-Torres, who made his name in New York with pieces, among others, about the fragility of life in the age of AIDS. From Los Angeles is an installation and videos by Matthew Barney, a specialist in exotic, tongue-in-cheek performance art. From Miami comes José Bedia, whose installations and paintings mix the old and new with references to contemporary kitsch and to Native American drawings.

"If we had just opened with something that was safer, I don't know if we'd have had the same response from collectors, curators, and critics," says Clearwater, who runs down a list of gala "promises" from pop artist James Rosenquist to Kevin Consey, director of Chicago's MOCA. "They're looking at this as a very fun event."

George Adams, a New York dealer who, along with Fredric Snitzer in Coral Gables, represents Bedia, has been watching MOCA grow: "It's a fabulous facility . . . and it puts a real emphasis on how strong the arts are down there. . . . I'm interested in the fact that Miami has incredible resources, and not just MOCA," he says, citing the Center for the Fine Arts, the Art Museum at Florida International University, and the Centre Gallery at the Wolfson campus of Miami-Dade Community College.

"You can't have just one institution. You have to have a dialogue."

The new site, on Northeast 125th Street, is next door to the tiny municipal office space where MOCA began life in 1978 as a North Miami satellite of the ill-fated Metropolitan Museum and Arts Center. The center withdrew its funding in 1981 and later disappeared altogether.

Colodny, who began as a volunteer, and Shack, a collector and performing arts promoter, managed to keep things together with help from the city of North Miami. In the decade that followed, the North Miami Museum and Art Center—and later, the Center of Contemporary Art, or COCA—developed a name for engaging Florida artists in innovative programming: 1991's *Round 'n Round Again*, for example, was a giant, magical collaborative sculpture of woven saplings by Ron Fondaw and Karen Rifas of Miami and Patrick Dougherty of North Carolina, artists who'd never worked together before.

Colodny, whose gift for linking artists and audiences comes naturally, not from formal training, attributes the success of the museum to its openness and innovation. Artists were invited to curate exhibitions, and there were annual shows of work by winners of the Florida Arts Council of Fellowships and exhibits highlighting area public art. She transformed modest resources into a major regional catalyst for an emerging art scene. She expects the museum to be accredited by the American Association of Museums by 1998.

Remarkably consistent leadership through the years—Colodny and Shack have been the mainstays—kept MOCA on track in spite of minuscule budgets. It was retired US Representative William Lehman's clout in nailing a $2.5 million federal redevelopment grant that secured the museum's new home.

The new building—designed with high-ceilinged galleries that flex well to showcase the wildly diverse shapes and materials of contemporary art—is named for Lehman's wife, Joan, a sculptor.

Now, in defining the '90s, MOCA is also redefining itself, looking beyond its regional emphasis to the broader contemporary scene—linking artists, collectors, dealers, and the public who help forge the consensus on what artists are most noticed right now.

The savvy hand of Clearwater, involved as a consultant before she became curator in 1994, has lent a quickening kind of magic. Long associated with contemporary art collectors and institutions, she brought the connections to advance the strategy.

"I can't wait to introduce my friends in New York, Los Angeles, and

Chicago to my friends in Miami," says Clearwater, copublisher, with her husband, James, of Grassfield Press in Miami Beach. "It creates this whole new network."

The result is a museum that stands a reasonable chance of claiming the national cachet it seeks: its "national honorary hosts," for instance, are New Yorkers Evelyn and Leonard Lauder of the cosmetics fortune and Eileen and Peter Norton of Los Angeles—both on *ARTnews*'s 1995 list of the top 25 art collectors in the United States.

Miami collectors Irma and Norman Braman and Carlos and Rosa de la Cruz—all on *ARTnews*'s list of the top 200 collectors in the world—are MOCA's "honorary chairmen."

The de la Cruzes are making two gifts and nine loans of work by up-and-coming Latin American artists, including Miami residents Bedia and Teresita Fernández—as well as work by Félix González-Torres, to whom the show is dedicated. The de la Cruzes, along with the Peter Norton Family Foundation, were major patrons of the González-Torres retrospective held last spring at New York's Guggenheim Museum. Irma and Norman Braman have made a gift to MOCA's growing permanent collection of an abstract painting by Gary Stephan.

Adding to the éclat of the gala are Mera and Donald Rubell, also on the top 200, who are hosting a party Thursday night for MOCA donors of $500 or more. Their downtown Miami warehouse space—40,000 square feet, open only by appointment—holds significant installations of contemporary art and is a frequent stop for those on Miami's visual arts circuit. MOCA's inaugural exhibit includes two loans from the Rubell Family Collection, work by New York artists Janine Antoni and Gary Simmons.

"I think that MOCA is a miracle," says developer Mera Rubell, who divides her time between New York and Miami. "It's extraordinary at a time when, across the country, there's tremendous cutback of support for museums."

Adds Norman Braman, who owns auto dealerships and has never before donated a work of art to a local museum, "This is the most exciting event in Miami in terms of the arts since [1968] because it's focused on contemporary art, and the community has needed this for a very long time."

How did those collectors get into the MOCA loop?

Clearwater's association with the Lauders (he was president of the board of the Whitney Museum of American Art from 1990 to 1994) dates to 1982, when she advised the couple on purchases as well as loans and gifts to museums. Through them, she tapped into the influential New York network of auction houses, galleries, and museums.

Clearwater was a consultant, too, to Norton in the establishment of the Santa Monica–based Peter Norton Family Foundation, known for grants supporting the work of emerging and underrecognized artists, especially African Americans. For *Defining the Nineties*, the Nortons have lent two photographs by Los Angeles–based artist Catherine Opie.

Fran Seegull, curator of the Nortons' personal collection and foundation, will attend the MOCA opening. "The Nortons spoke with [Bonnie] during the development of the exhibition," says Seegull. "They will watch the museum closely."

Rosa de la Cruz is another collector who believes patrons play a vital role in cultivating a climate that allows artists to thrive. "My definition of collecting is not about keeping art in my house," she says. "I want the work to be seen and recognized for its own aesthetics. I believe it's important to have an institution like MOCA in your hometown."

And now, we do.

Many of the new gifts to MOCA will be exhibited this summer in *Highlights from the Permanent Collection*—including a painting by Alex Katz from New York dealer Robert Miller, work by Quisqueya Henríquez from the de la Cruzes, and 50 works on paper by Scottish artist and poet Ian Hamilton Finlay, this from Miamians Ruth and Marvin Sackner, who've never made such a large donation to a Miami institution but did make a similar gift to the prestigious Houghton Library of Harvard University.

The show has a niche in an eye-catching first-year lineup that ranges from tattoo art organized by New York's Drawing Center to a survey of Robert Rauschenberg's sculpture from the Modern Art Museum of Fort Worth.

Closing the year is a "firework finale," as Clearwater puts it: *Mexican Modernism from the Jacques and Natasha Gelman Collection*, an assembly of masterworks showing how prominent collectors in the 1940s nurtured the careers of then-contemporary, now-famous artists such as Frida Kahlo and Rufino Tamayo. As with just about everything at MOCA, the exhibition schedule gleams with the kind of smart marketing it takes to get people looking and talking about art.

Indeed, observers here and elsewhere see MOCA's opening as a landmark in a region's cultural coming of age.

"It was a helluva ride," muses Shack, looking back on the youth of South Florida's newest art jewel. "This is different."

In memoriam: Richard Shack, 1926–2012
Ruth Sackner, 1936–2015
Marvin Sackner, 1932–2020
Rosa de la Cruz, 1944–2024
Quisqueya Henríquez, 1966–2024

CÉSAR TRASOBARES

A Tryst with Chairs at Ambrosino Gallery

March 15, 1996

The art of César Trasobares has traveled a long way, from the fussy and fancy to the sleek and sharp.

In the late 1970s and '80s, Trasobares explored lacy rituals of the Quince, honoring a girl's 15th birthday, a celebration popular in Miami's Cuban exile community. He gathered up bits of ornate gowns, party souvenirs, and other fanciful artifacts, arranging them in collages and boxes.

The look was playful, but with an ironic edge. His works dissected and documented the nostalgic extravagances of an exile culture, wrapped in a cocoon of gilded memories.

Since then, Trasobares has addressed issues of cultural identity, and how they intersect with the making of art, in other ways. A 1993 installation at the Center for the Fine Arts, for example, was a tipsy tower of director's chairs.

In this piece, *Tumbling Chairs: Museum of American Democratic Art*, the chairs were stamped with acerbic phrases that dissected strands of vociferous debates about multicultural themes in museum exhibitions. "Curator, Mainstream," read one. "Curator, Political Correctness," read another. The tone was strident and blunt.

In his latest work, *Tryst*, on display at Ambrosino Gallery, Trasobares is still doing chairs, but without the obvious barbs. The mood is meditative, stripped of direct commentary, his drawings and chairlike sculptures steering the viewer back to intimate encounters with the art object itself.

The show begins with a row of drawings encased in sleek, light-colored wood boxes. Combining sharply outlined chairs and blurry, nearly abstract suggestions of faces, the drawings evoke a personal reverie on what happens when familiar, homey objects are wrenched from their daily context.

At least in the scenario Trasobares has carefully orchestrated with this exhibit, what happens is that something stultifyingly familiar becomes wonderfully open-ended.

His "chair sculptures" are arranged in pairs, setting up a visual dialogue. They invite us to contrast their proportions and design, noting how one might seem stronger, more heavily weighted than the other. References to the human figure also invite us to compare these pairs to couples. As with any relationship, subtle differences become more obvious the longer we look, even though all the chairs are built of bland, blond wood in sharp-edged, minimal designs.

Some chairs incorporate open rows of shelves, housing blocks of pink, white, and gray marble that playfully resemble books or cushions. Elegantly arranged on other shelves are marble trays and goblets. These sleek marble objects, while recalling the monumental presence of grand-scale marble sculpture and architecture, give the glossy stone a new identity—one intimately scaled, definitely domestic.

Here, a public material like marble gets up close and personal, fitting for a show called *Tryst*. That's especially true in the only work that doesn't include a reference to chairs. *Falling Leaves*, a pile of 38 fleshy-pink marble blocks shaped like tears or leaves, pays tribute to all the bodies implied by—but missing from—Trasobares's "chairs." While this might suggest an homage to lives lost to AIDS, it is also a moving coda to a show that mines the subtle ways we relate to art and to each other.

CENTER FOR THE FINE ARTS

True Vodou Far from the Silly Misconceptions, Haiti's Vibrant Folk Religion Enriches Its Art with Spirituality

September 22, 1996

Dolls stuck with pins. That is the image many Americans may associate with voodoo. Others probably remember George Bush spelling voodoo with "economics" attached, suggesting a scathing new theory on black magic in the marketplace.

A term reeking with silliness and sorcery, "voodoo" sums up American prejudices about Haiti's folk religion.

But in Haiti, the common spelling is Vodou, and dolls are not stuck with pins to cast evil spells, nor is the word normally associated with the economy.

In Haiti, Vodou is a vibrant religion born of slavery, revolt, and multiculturalism long before the m-word reached the shores of our politically correct consciousness. The word means "sacred" in the African language of Fon.

And Vodou is at the heart of Haitian art, a distinctive and spiritual tradition blending dazzling colors and images of old and new worlds.

Over the next few months, South Floridians will get an eyeful of that artistic tradition, beginning with two current exhibits, one at the Center for the Fine Arts and the other at the South Florida Art Center.

In Haitian art, stories of colorful Vodou spirits dance through oil paintings and temple murals. Their triumphs and trials mirror the whole spectrum of human nature, from birth to love and lust to death. Vodou symbols of hearts and roosters, skeletons and serpents are spangled across gorgeously sequined flags used in rituals or sold to tourists who prize their exquisite craftsmanship.

Vodou, with its rich network of symbols and signs, has nurtured Haiti's wealth of art and culture, even prevailing over desperate politics and poverty.

Vodou took hold in the New World with an inclusive roster of roots from Africa, Europe, and native cultures of the island, now called Hispaniola, which Columbus mistook for India half a millennium ago.

In Vodou beliefs and altars, Central and West African deities mingle with Catholic saints, Masonic symbols, and Celtic myths. Between 1804, the year Haiti won its independence from French colonizers, and 1860, when the Catholic Church returned to Haiti, the evolving lore of Vodou spirits, or lwas, flourished unchecked.

It served up daily spiritual sustenance to a passionately independent, impoverished people. Vodou opened the door to a new identity for a new nation.

RESHAPING MISCONCEPTIONS

This year, just as Haiti tries to reshape its government and economy after years of turmoil, a range of art exhibits in South Florida aims to reshape American misconceptions about Haiti.

The largest is *Sacred Arts of Haitian Vodou*, organized by the Fowler Museum of Cultural History at the University of California, Los Angeles. It runs from September 20 to December 1 at the Center for the Fine Arts and features a stunning collection of 500-plus objects, from altars to oil paintings, all inspired by the Haitian religion of Vodou.

A more focused show is *Invoking the Spirits: Haiti's Charged Murals*, which opened last weekend and runs through October 26 at Ground Level, South Florida Art Center. Presented by Miami's Haitian Cultural Arts Alliance, the exhibit features paintings by Haitian muralist Charlemagne Celestin and 30 color photographs by South Florida resident Pablo Butcher. Butcher traveled to Haiti six times over the past 10 years, documenting hundreds of political murals painted all over Port-au-Prince.

The murals, many anonymous, sprang up as a spontaneous sort of public art unleashed by the fall of Jean-Claude Duvalier's regime in 1986, an event many likened to liberation from slavery. Rich with patriotic colors of red and blue, laden with Vodou symbols and portraits of popular former president Jean-Bertrand Aristide, the murals recount events marking the country's tumultuous steps toward democracy.

Finally, two more Haitian art shows come to the Lowe Art Museum at the

University of Miami. They are *Masterworks in Haitian Art* from the Davenport Museum of Art (in Davenport, Iowa) and *Haitian Beaded Flags* from the Sheila Natasha Simrod Friedman Collection, running from February 6 to March 30. *Masterworks* will present some 60 paintings and sculpture, from 1945 to the present, by influential schooled and unschooled Haitian artists, a collection the museum has cultivated since 1967. *Beaded Flags* will unfurl the sparkling sacred art of flags sequined with Vodou symbols and created for ritual ceremonies.

HISTORY OF DEMONIZATION

American defamation of Haiti's religious traditions has many precedents. Books published during the US Marines' occupation of Haiti from 1915 to 1934 offered sensational accounts of a primitive, savage island in desperate need of white civilization and spawned a series of Hollywood horror movies about zombies, fearsome figures prevalent in Haitian folklore who were thought to stalk about in the catatonic trance of the "living dead," under the spell of Vodou priests.

In the 1940s, the Catholic Church kept up this demonization of Vodou, launching an "Anti-Superstition Campaign," supported by the Haitian government and bourgeoisie. Temples were sacked, ritual objects burned, and Vodouists arrested in a vigorous yet failed effort to ban beliefs Westerners found barbaric.

"There's probably no religion in the world that's been as denigrated as Vodou has been. . . . The whole folklore of the word 'voodoo' is about not making sense," says Donald J. Cosentino, UCLA professor of African and Caribbean folklore and cocurator of *Sacred Arts of Haitian Vodou*.

Of Vodou's intricate, intercontinental collage of saints, spirits, and signs, Cosentino says, "It makes a great deal of sense. It makes aesthetic and historical sense. It is not some mishmash of crazy ideas, but it is the hard-wrought and hard-won expression of the culture of African life in the New World. Vodou is the response made by African people to conditions they had to confront. These are people who've always been in a pretty desperate game and have made an extraordinary culture and art out of that experience. I think you have to be open to the idea that Vodou might be worthy of respect and even, God forbid, admiration."

DISTRUST AMONG UPPER CLASSES

Even now, says Mireille Chancy Gonzalez, a local businesswoman, art collector, and president of the Haitian Cultural Arts Alliance, "among upper-class Haitians, there is distrust of Vodou. They do not want to go back to their roots."

Gonzalez recalls her childhood in a wealthy Port-au-Prince family: "We were raised as very strict Catholics. Our parents always described Vodou as a sin." Seeing *Sacred Arts* when it opened in Los Angeles, she says, "was an education. I was able to see that it was beautiful and not something that is bad."

That beauty is reflected in vivid ways: from ornate drawings known as vèvès and sequin-ornamented wine bottles, to Kongo-style charms wrapped in brilliant cloth, beads, and feathers.

Vodou, in fact, thrives on rich layers of images and colors. It has produced an intensely visual culture—as Haitian-born painter and poet Marilene Phipps, a recent Guggenheim fellow now living in Boston, points out. "Every activity, every interpretation of daily life is colored by Vodou lore. The art is very enriched by all of this," she says. Each spirit, for example, is linked to specific places and plants, colors and Catholic saints, dress and demeanor, even animals, food, and days of the week. Such symbols stake out fertile ground for metaphor making.

DIVERSE ARTISTS

Echoes of these powerful symbols also find their way into the paintings of artists as diverse as the legendary Hector Hyppolite (1894–1948) and Haitian-born South Floridian Edouard Duval-Carrié—both represented in both *Sacred Arts* and *Masterworks*.

Hyppolite had lived most of his life as an obscure Vodou priest and house painter, using chicken feathers if brushes were scarce, when in 1945 he was invited to join the Centre d'Art in Port-au-Prince, an art center recently opened to nurture Haitian painters and sculptors. In the last three years of his life, he produced more than 250 paintings. Their so-called naive or primitive style places Christian and Vodou figures amid boldly patterned landscapes and captivated French surrealist André Breton, who arranged for enthusiastically received shows of Hyppolite's paintings in Europe in the 1940s.

As a contemporary artist, Duval-Carrié adapts that mélange to his own postmodernist ends. His provocative paintings draw on Haitian history, from Duvalier's brutal regime to the symbolic legacy of crumbling French colonial–style architecture. They show vignettes with Vodou spirits, including the light-skinned temptress Ezili Freda and the top-hatted, skull-faced trickster spirit Bawon Samdi. The settings are luxuriantly tropical, a wry spin on the now overworked decorative tradition of Haitian landscapes.

NAIVE ART'S POPULARITY

That well-known and wildly popular tradition burst full-blown on the world in 1944 when the Centre d'Art was opened by an American language teacher and would-be artist, DeWitt Peters. In promoting "naive" paintings by Hyppolite and others, it attracted international collectors, including Cuban artist Wifredo Lam, Jacqueline Kennedy Onassis, and New York's Museum of Modern Art.

In recent years, this visionary style has been mired in coconut-sweet clichés crafted for tourist consumption. It's what Cosentino calls a "really shlocky, Harry Belafonte view of the Caribbean." In response to the clichés, Carol Damian, an art professor at Florida International University, curated an exhibit of alternative Haitian art last year at the South Florida Art Center.

"Haitian art has been so muddled by commercialism. Sometimes we tend to overlook the incredible beauty and artistry of the work," she says.

Phipps, whose painting of a Vodou priest at his altar was included in that show, says the marketplace was notorious for determining the look of Haitian paintings. "The true naive artist is more rare," she says. "One gallery in Port-au-Prince made a fortune in keeping standards of stylization of naive art. A lot of it is very lyrical, beautiful, and joyful in the way Western society expects naive art to be. People go to the islands for vacations, and they want to bring back souvenirs that involve coconuts and bright flowers and smiling natives," she adds.

BRIGHTNESS IS MISLEADING

Yet in the same breath, Phipps says the happy, radiantly colored jungles can be misleading: "Haiti is a very troubled island. People have manifested a lot of ingenuity in their survival, and their art reflects that. One should not necessarily attribute the bright colors to joy. In some forms of art, bright colors are associated with brutality and conflict."

Sacred Arts and other exhibits demonstrate there's much more to Haitian art than the sunny appeal of exotic souvenirs. And as Haiti desperately seeks a more stable political future, the country's art is changing along with our perceptions of it.

"This whole thing of the jungle scenes that never existed in Haiti, I think this has stopped," says Duval-Carrié. "The tourists are not there anymore, so the artists are more true to themselves."

CENTER FOR THE FINE ARTS

Celebratory Exhibition of Sacred Arts Takes Voodoo Out of Vodou

September 22, 1996

Sacred Arts of Haitian Vodou is full of fiercely festive charms and unforgettable images:

Sequined flags flashing with the shocking beauty of stained-glass windows and carnival costumes. A sinister altar crowded with a cross, skull, and Darth Vader toy. Wooden drums carved with dazzling skill, wrapped with snakes and palms.

Recycled bottles once holding perfume and wine, now beaded and beribboned, holding aloft peacock feathers. Dolls and spoons, candles and coffins, roosters and mermaids. Catholic saints, Masonic symbols, and African serpent spirits.

You could go on and on with this litany of visually stunning objects. They are all artful devices for summoning the spirits of Haitian Vodou, who are sought for the advice they offer as mediators between God and humans. *Sacred Arts*, which opened Friday at the Center for the Fine Arts, lures you into this world, revealing at least some of the magic, power, and spiritual energy making up Haiti's often misunderstood Vodou religion.

The exhibit seeks to take the "voodoo" out of "Vodou" and shows how it is an abundantly Creole creation. Like the African-derived religions of Santería in Cuba and Candomblé in Brazil, Vodou arose in the New World by remaking many old traditions.

HOLLYWOOD MYTH

Sticking pins in dolls to bring enemies bad luck is not a ritual practiced in this religion but most likely a Hollywood myth. Yes, there are cloth dolls in the show, but they're ritual objects for carrying messages—sometimes written on paper and attached with pins—to spirits combining the qualities of African deities and Catholic saints.

And yes, the way these objects touch both the physical and the spiritual worlds is indeed haunting. A photograph shows one such doll carefully tied to a tree with a scuffed pair of shoes because, according to the label, the doll "has a long way to go."

In paying homage to the rich cultural and spiritual integrity of Vodou, the show also pays little heed to those 1940s horror movies featuring Haitian zombies, frightening figures with death-warmed-over stares, supposedly under the spell of Vodou priests.

"We don't deal with zombies because they aren't part of the religion of Haiti; they are part of the folklore," says Donald J. Cosentino, cocurator of the exhibit and professor of African and Caribbean folklore at the University of California, Los Angeles.

With fellow curator Marilyn Houlberg, professor of art and anthropology at the School of the Art Institute of Chicago, and many other researchers here and in Haiti, Cosentino put eight years into organizing this show for the University of California, Los Angeles Fowler Museum of Cultural History.

PROJECT DELAYS

Sacred Arts was so long in the making because political turmoil in Haiti caused delays. But delays also came when two funding requests, made to the National Endowment for the Humanities during the late 1980s, were denied on the grounds that the proposed show was "too celebratory."

Eventually, supported by the Rockefeller Foundation and the National Endowment for the Humanities of the Clinton administration, the exhibit was funded. It opened at the Fowler in October 1995 to outstanding praise.

The exhibit is most certainly celebratory. At the CFA, a spectacular installation, overseen by associate curator Kate Rawlinson, leads us through the fascinating network of Vodou sources and symbols, with videos showing actual ceremonies.

Everything in the show is embedded with the story of how enslaved West Africans, cut off from their families and others who spoke their language, were exiled to the Caribbean island of Hispaniola, first colonized in 1492 by the Spanish.

And so began the bloody history of cultural genocide, begetting Vodou. Spain soon killed the native Taíno population; two centuries later the country ceded a third of the island, now called Haiti, to France. The French forced enslaved peoples to convert to Catholicism, yet they simply adopted Christian symbols as a way to hide their practice of African beliefs.

THE WEAVING OF VODOU

These beliefs, also weaving together remnants of Taíno lore with Catholic and Masonic practices, evolved into the revolutionary rites of Vodou.

In the first section, a group of 20th-century paintings remind us of crucial events in Haiti's history. Dieudonné Cédor's 1948 *Ceremony at the Bois Caiman* shows the sacrifice of a black pig in 1791, a ritual that sparked Haiti's 13-year-long rebellion by enslaved people with African roots.

Next, visitors will find that *Sacred Arts* does an admirable job of sorting out the complex families of Vodou spirits, or lwas. Two sets of glass cases display ritual objects of the Rada families, the gentle water spirits, and of the fierce, fiery spirits called Petwo.

You'll also find that the Rada temptress spirit Ezili Freda not only loves jewels, lace, and the color pink but also Anaïs Anaïs perfume and Virginia Slims cigarettes.

High points of the show are fascinating examples of images of African talismans, Masonic garb, and Catholic statuary, all presented to show how their imagery has been transformed into Vodou flags, drums, paintings, sculpture, and utterly astonishing altars. The show has an extra flourish not available to other venues: an altar painting of the dark-skinned, earthy spirit Ezili Dantor by Haitian-born South Florida artist Rara Kuyu.

There's also an installation by Edouard Duval-Carrié not traveling to other venues. It's *Les Capteurs des Esprits*, airy bronze statues of Rada spirits created several years ago for a Vodou festival in the African Republic of Benin.

Here the statues rise from a bed of sand. But in Benin they were placed on the beach, as if catching Haitian spirits flowing back across the watery Middle Passage to find their ancestral roots.

Like these sculptures, *Sacred Arts* catches us to find the true roots of Vodou.

RUBÉN TORRES LLORCA

The Start of a Beautiful Friendship

October 14, 1996

In the 1960s, there was a movie that Cuban television played again and again. Each time, it captivated the adventurous soul of a young boy. He was a painter's son, growing up poor in a tough Havana neighborhood, raised by a widowed mother who sewed for a living.

The movie was *Casablanca*, and the boy was Rubén Torres Llorca, an artist who moved to Miami with his family from Mexico in 1993. He still savors that schmaltzy cinematic experience—particularly memorable in Havana, where "for many years you never saw an American movie [in theaters]. You saw a lot of boring Soviet and Hungarian movies about communism."

"When I was a child, *Casablanca* taught me that nothing can be only for show. In a good story, everything is essential. *Casablanca* is the perfect thriller. It has all the clichés—adventure, love triangles, emigration problems—and it has the best song." In spite of, or perhaps because of, those common devices and problems, "it's a magical movie," he says.

A MOVIE FAN

"I am a movie fan," admits Torres Llorca, breaking into a sudden smile as he puts the final touches on his new installation at the Center for the Fine Arts and absently tugs on his thick black beard, flecked with a few silver strands that seem premature for his 39 years. "Movies have this fascinating quality. You enter that room, and you belong to that story."

Something of the cinema pervades his artwork, particularly in *Eight Visits to the Artist's Studio*, which opened Friday at the CFA. It's a commissioned, site-specific piece that's part of the museum's *New Work* series.

Here, visitors meet up with a movie-like mélange of vignettes. To experience Torres Llorca's work, you must wend your way through eight small rooms and along a hallway filled with assorted objects, photographs, and text. Recurring scenes of splashing surf, rustic carvings of beds and boats, and heartfelt tales of desire and loss greet you.

YOU'RE THE ARTIST

Pay attention. Torres Llorca is urging you to direct your own story or movie, your own artwork. Enter into the episodes—from childhood, dreams, love—that he describes in each room. If you rise to the test, you may find that the experience of art can transform your daily life, even perhaps your daily bread—just as it has for Torres Llorca and for the seven other artists whose stories are woven throughout *Eight Visits*.

"I really want you to become the artist," he says to those who will see his work. "I try to give you the clues and all the instruments for you to become the hero in the piece. You need to build your own story."

But why expect so much effort from us? Whose studio is this?

Granted, art isn't a cure-all for our stress-ridden, secular times. But for Torres Llorca, it possesses a curative and spiritual presence, much like the charms and altars in the Latin American folk and religious art he admires. Art, Torres Llorca believes, offers "the space for having an adventure of the spirit."

OTHER INFLUENCES

Handcrafted altars and charms influenced Torres Llorca as much as American movies and kitschy popular culture when he was a young artist in Cuba. In Havana, he made an enormous multipaneled relief that included images of his family, a Hollywood starlet, Humphrey Bogart, and Cuba's patron saint, Caridad del Cobre, for the city's Second Biennial in 1986. He shares his interest in popular culture with others in the much talked about "'80s generation" of innovative contemporary artists in Cuba, some of whom have also moved to South Florida, including José Bedia, Consuelo Castañeda, Juan-Sí, and Glexis Novoa.

But there's a lot more to Torres Llorca's work than pop imagery. "He seems to have some anthropological interest in thinking about how images are therapeutic," says Charles Merewether, Special Collections curator at the Getty Research Institute in Los Angeles, who participated in a public discussion of Torres Llorca's work Saturday at the CFA. Merewether came to know Torres Llorca while in Cuba selecting work for *Made in Havana*, a show Merewether curated in 1986 for the Contemporary Art Museum in Brisbane, Australia.

Though circumstances kept Torres Llorca's work from being in that show, which included Bedia and Castañeda, he exhibited in the São Paulo Biennial in 1989. So far his work has been shown more widely in Latin America and Europe—he's represented in a survey of 20th-century Cuban art that opened this month at the Centre d'Art Santa Monica in Barcelona—than in the United States. In February he was included in *Defining the Nineties*, the inaugural exhibit of North Miami's Museum of Contemporary Art, and a show is planned for a New York gallery next year. But he has yet to draw the considerable critical and commercial support that's come the way of his close friend and former Havana classmate Bedia.

"HANDICRAFT"

Bedia, who wrote an essay for this CFA exhibit, says that both his work and Torres Llorca's can be thought of as "handicraft," because a fascination with the spiritual power of folk talismans surfaces in their work. Torres Llorca speaks with as much enthusiasm about Mexican handicrafts as he does about movies. In his home is a collection of toys, masks, and Day of the Dead figurines purchased from street merchants in Mexico.

Their magical presence—like the mestizo paintings of Catholic saints with the eyes of Mexican spirits, which he once saw in a monastery near Mexico City—moves him to make his own talismans for today's crowded global village.

Solace for the spirit, Torres Llorca believes, is in short supply.

EDUARDO DEL VALLE
AND MIRTA GÓMEZ

Maya Hut Exhibit Preserves 2,000-Year Tradition

February 19, 1997

South Florida artists Eduardo del Valle and Mirta Gómez are on a mission. Since 1994 they've made frequent trips to Mexico, rambling rutted roads in a four-wheel-drive jeep to photograph thousands of mud, pole, and thatch huts in Mexico's Yucatán Peninsula.

The huts have been built the same way in this corner of the world for more than 2,000 years. But that tradition, currently carried out by descendants of Mexico's powerful Maya civilization, is rapidly changing as industrialization forces builders to use new materials and methods.

Mindful that time is running out, del Valle and Gómez are compiling house-high stacks of images. Thirty color photographs from this series make up *The Mayan Dwelling*, an exhibit of their work at the O. K. Harris Gallery in New York's SoHo neighborhood. The exhibit runs through March 1.

ENDANGERED BY PROGRESS

The photographs record changes courtesy of rapacious industrialization in the name of progress and fancy Cancun resorts.

Hay for crafting thatched roofs, for example, has become so scarce it must be imported from Guatemala, an expense many of the Yucatán villagers can't afford. The villagers, whose ancestors constructed thatch huts among the stone towers of Chichén Itzá, are turning to more readily available materials: cement blocks, tar paper, bottle caps. Odd hybrids happen: in one hut, slender wooden poles support a paper roof spangled with metal disks sporting soft-drink logos.

To capture such surprising and unsettling details, finely etched by tropical morning light, del Valle and Gómez rise at 4 a.m. when they're in Mexico. They're out taking pictures by 6 a.m.

The two—a married couple and an artistic team since 1970 whose work is owned by New York's Museum of Modern Art and the Bibliothèque Nationale de France in Paris—are profoundly moved by what they see: modest homes built to ancient specifications, tenaciously evolving or rotting into extinction; centuries-old contours colliding with television antennas that pipe in spicy novellas and *Miami Vice* reruns.

Frequent visitors to Mexico since the late 1980s, they've watched how a domestic icon has been displaced, destroyed, and forgotten or transformed into something rough and new.

They can identify with the domestically displaced. Both were born in Cuba, moving to Miami in 1961 when Eduardo was 10 and Mirta was 8. "We are first-generation immigrants," says del Valle, a slim, graying man who's been teaching with his wife at the art department of Florida International University since 1984. "We feel that all the time, the sense of cross-culturation. That's what these homes are going through now."

He laughs, delicately sifting through photographs. "So maybe that's why we feel at home there. We are going through the same thing in our own heads."

MIRRORS OF HUMANITY

In fact, the two really see their work as portraits. Their photographs turn these homes into poignant mirrors of human endeavor. Without the slightest bit of sentimentality, they talk about the "bone structure" and "face" of their subject matter. A future series will pair photographs as "couples," showing how a hut has aged over the passage of time.

In one especially compelling photograph, a home is a mere skeleton of sticks, a breezy wraith vanishing into an ethereal landscape of clouds and grass. In another, a miniature hut balances on a tomb amid white stone statuary in a cemetery. Spanish inscriptions, Catholic Virgins, and colonial grillwork are everywhere. This Maya dwelling remains a sturdy, muscular thing, vigorously real compared to a surrounding parade of bluish shadows shaped like angel wings.

The images are powerful.

"You surrender yourself to your subject," says Gómez. "You hope the subject will surrender itself back. That's all you can really hope for."

MIRA LEHR'S WATER WORLD REFLECTS BEAUTY, DESPAIR

June 20, 1997

Miami Beach artist Mira Lehr, whose work is in a solo show, *Icarus Series*, at the Continuum on Miami Beach's Lincoln Road, is accomplished at conveying the fluid charms of the "water planet."

Her art recalls *Welcome to the Water Planet*, an extraordinarily beautiful print by pop artist James Rosenquist. Considered a superb example of printmaking (it was completed in 1989 at Graphicstudio, the noted fine art printshop affiliated with the University of South Florida in Tampa), *Water Planet* is an aquatint in velvety shades of black, pewter, and white, the color of moonlight, showing one of the artist's luscious lilies nestled in a gleaming pool of water as stars glimmer overhead.

But while Rosenquist's singular work is all shades of gray, the "color" washing across our field of vision like a magical liquid balm, Lehr's palette contains blues, oranges, and greens. Nevertheless, a watery, wavering feeling likewise pervades her landscapes and still lifes.

Lehr's mixed-media paintings—a gestural mix of acrylic, pastel, charcoal, and collaged Japanese rice paper—have always flirted with the pretty and decorative, though the best maintain a slippery edge. Not all paintings in this show are equally strong, and a few smaller ones are blatantly precious, but several are far more substantial than their subject matter.

DANGEROUS CURRENTS

Unlike Rosenquist's water imagery, which promises to heal, Lehr's scenes swirl with more dangerous currents. You often have the sense, when looking at her paintings, that you're seeing a limpid, moist place of sun-kissed colors floating—or is it sinking?—under water. Translucent petals overlap, skies stream into trees, and nothing looks solid. Lehr's water world is undeniably seductive but so lacking in terra firma that it's frightening as well. Movement appears slow and heavy, weighted down by a rippling, rolling tide.

Icarus Series features 11 works produced in the past year. As you'd expect, birds are present in the paintings. Black, beaky, and ominous, they are apparently trying to wing—or claw, hampered in flight by the many currents of form and color—their way to the bright, dry air high above the water planet. We already know such effort produces a devastating fate, according to the Greek myth of Icarus, who melted his superhuman waxen wings by getting too close to the sun.

DROWNING WORLD

In *Meltdown*, for example, a dripping, drowning world is evoked by the presence of three blue horizontal lines. Like multiple horizons—suggesting an optical illusion created by the experience of swerving downward—the lines divide her landscape of spotted lilies, an acrid orange sun, and blue-green swampy vegetation into an alluring but perilous and dissolving place.

Lehr, a Miami Beach native who received a degree in art history from Vassar College in 1956 and has studied painting at Boston's Museum of Fine Arts school and sculpture at the University of Miami, has lived in Miami Beach with her family since 1960. Her work has been included in only a handful of group shows—at the Museum of Contemporary Art in North Miami, Fort Lauderdale's Museum of Art, and in a space run by the National Association of Women Artists in New York City—but her persistence attests to a delicately realized vision of how art mirrors both beauty and despair.

In memoriam: Mira Lehr, 1934–2023

SHEILA ELIAS'S SECRET GARDENS EXPLODE WITH COLORS AND TEXTURES AT THE LOWE

August 10, 1997

There's no secret to the riotous abundance coursing through paintings in *Sheila Elias: Secret Gardens*, the second exhibit in the Lowe Art Museum's annual *Florida Artist* series. *Secret Gardens*, which opened Wednesday and runs through September 7, fairly vibrates with a hothouse assortment of color, shape, and texture.

Exploding sunflowers, spiraling rose petals, and sprawling green vines bloom thickly among the collaged, elaborate surfaces of these works on paper and canvas and on the handful of boxy wood sculpture.

This selection of 23 works by Elias, who has lived in South Florida since the late 1980s and maintains a studio in North Miami, was curated by Denise Gerson, the museum's associate director of curatorial affairs, and ranges from 1992 to the present. It doesn't always show off Elias at her best, as her imagery suffers from an indulgent penchant for busy decoration.

Her work does invite comparison with French master Henri Matisse, another artist sometimes accused of being overly decorative. Reminders of Matisse's luxuriant floral patterns streak through Elias's art, rendered by her collaged elements made from photocopied bits of ornate lace and tulle and of handsomely printed papers.

The large painting *Red Garden*, for example, with its twitchy and textured composition of flower arrangements lurching across a red ground, seems to pay homage to Matisse's 1911 masterpiece *The Red Studio*, in which vines curve sinuously from a long-necked vase in a vast red room.

Other sources, with roots in far more distant art history, also plant themselves in her work. Elias loves to paint and cut out images bursting with the classic curves of ancient Greek vessels. A favorite is the two-handled amphora, which she ornaments with lacy designs or with a running warrior boasting splendid musculature.

Her quotations from the past are steeped in her own past.

Elias was born in Chicago, and she recalls her first visit, at age eight, to the treasures of that city's Art Institute.

"I just loved it. I told my mother I wanted to quit school and go to that building with the lions [out front] every day. There was something about the Matisses that made me want to live in front of them," she says, describing the awe she felt when seeing, up close, the spritely acrobatic forms dancing through the French artist's famous series of paper cutouts.

Much later, visits to the antiquities collection at New York's Metropolitan Museum of Art and to the Brooklyn Museum of Art's trove of Egyptian art stirred her fondness for the stately simplicity of centuries-old vessels.

Still, you'd never call *Secret Gardens* simple and stately. Many pieces in the show, such as *Water Garden*, are a hectic and quirky mix of landscape, still life, and patchwork quilt. Her exaggerated, repetitive style makes such work swerve close to caricatures of paintings.

More interesting is the 1997 *Tondos Rondo*, a collection of 24 round canvases, ranging in diameter from 8 to 24 inches, installed on the wall to create a floating web of juicy color and jazzy bursts of voluptuous, flowery forms. Released from the insistent framing device of the conventional rectangular painting, these secret gardens blossom in space with the fresh vigor of dandelion seeds flying in the wind.

This solo show follows a fairly steady stream of Elias shows in commercial galleries in New York, Miami, Chicago, and Los Angeles since 1985, with occasional group exhibits in regional museums. It will travel to the Art and Culture Center/Hollywood and to the New England Center for Contemporary Art in Brooklyn, Connecticut.

A smartly produced 48-page exhibit catalog—funded by Chase Manhattan Private Bank, the exhibit's corporate sponsor and a collector of the artist's work—smacks of overkill for this redundant survey. (It does include a gracefully researched essay by New York art critic Alexandra Anderson-Spivy covering the garden in art history.)

A year ago, the Lowe mounted the first show in its annual *Florida Artist* series, featuring the photography of Clyde Butcher. Next year's artist to be featured is ceramics sculptor Christine Federighi. Such exhibits—though occurring in the art season's cruelest month, August—are a welcome dividend of the Lowe's recent expansion. The series joins the efforts of other area institutions to spotlight the individual achievements of South Florida artists.

CARLOS ALFONZO

Exhibit a Moving Tribute to Talent Cut Short

December 21, 1997

The last time I spoke to South Florida artist Carlos Alfonzo, bombs were exploding. It was the evening of January 16, 1991, the start of the Gulf War, and my television screen was consumed with scenes of horrific conflagration.

Alfonzo telephoned to tell me that his paintings would be included in the 1991 Biennial exhibition at the Whitney Museum of American Art in New York, which would open in April. It was a great coup, especially for an artist who had been working seriously in this country only since 1982. I remember trying to balance that moment of intensely conflicting emotions—joy for an artist whose talent I believed deserved such recognition and shock at the destruction I'd been witnessing.

That explosive experience of death and joy seems like an epiphany now, prophetic of the arc Alfonzo's career was already taking. Although I traveled to see his accomplished, brooding paintings in the biennial, Alfonzo did not. He died that February 19 at South Miami Hospital. At age 41, he suffered a cerebral hemorrhage, brought on by AIDS.

With a far greater impact than I ever imagined, the Miami Art Museum presents Alfonzo's work in a superbly installed exhibit. *Triumph of the Spirit: Carlos Alfonzo, a Survey, 1975–1991* opened Thursday and runs through March 8. It is guest curated by Olga Viso, assistant curator at the Hirshhorn Museum and Sculpture Garden in Washington, DC, where the show will travel in June.

This show has been long awaited by many in South Florida who knew Alfonzo, watched his art flourish, and grieved at his early death. As a tribute

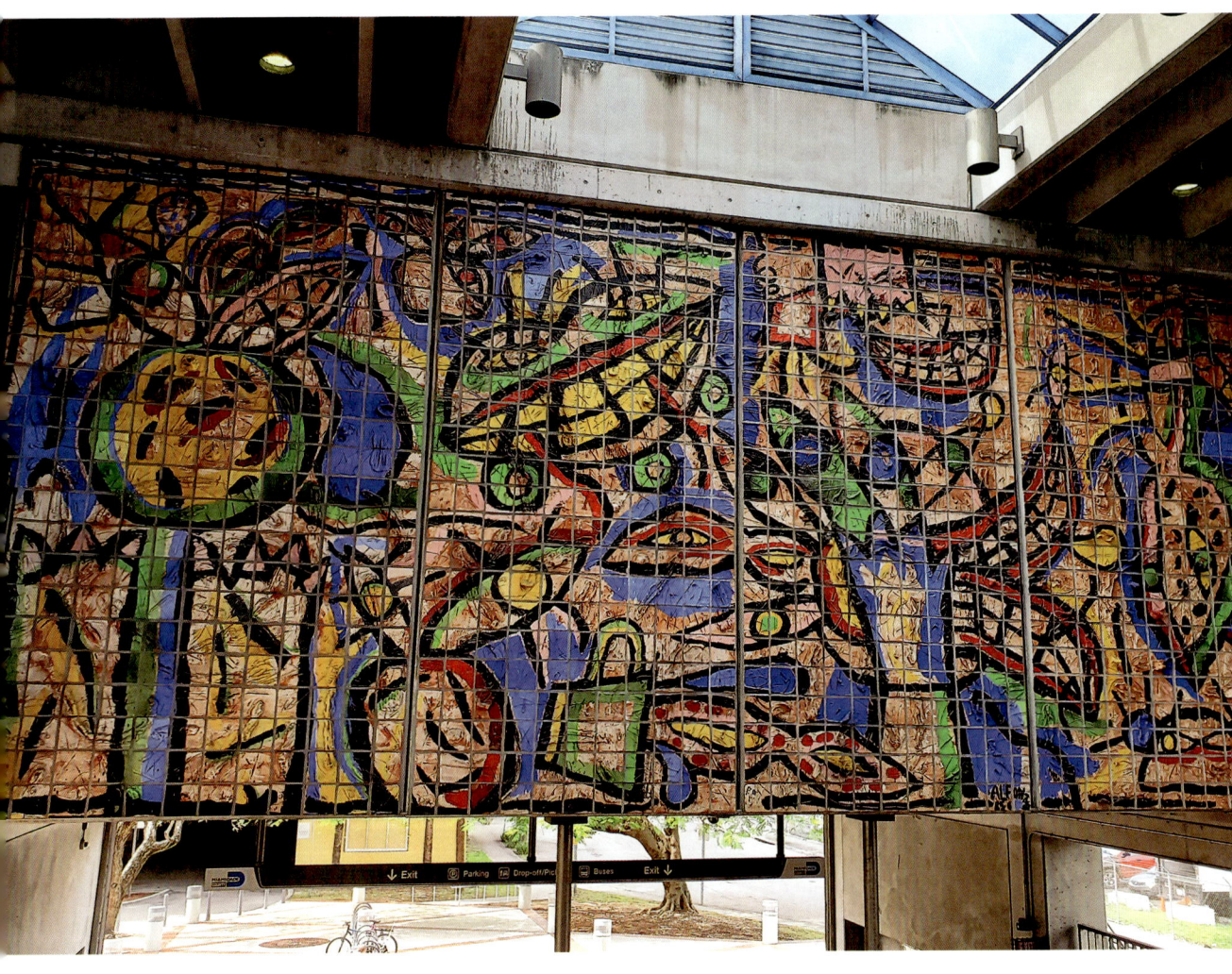

FIGURE 10. Carlos Alfonzo, *Ceremony of the Tropics*, 1986. Glazed ceramic tile mural. Entrance of Santa Clara Metrorail Station. Courtesy of Miami-Dade County Department of Cultural Affairs, Art in Public Places Trust.

to Alfonzo's remarkable art and his swift rise to national notice, it's the culmination of more than two years of exhaustive research conducted by Viso and the MAM staff, including curatorial assistant Amy Rosenblum. *Triumph of the Spirit* brings together 71 works, chiefly paintings, with a handful of drawings and sculpture.

POWER OF PAINTINGS

The exhibit is also an immensely moving witness to the power of the painted image. It shows how Alfonzo, who was born in Cuba in 1950 and arrived in Miami in 1980 as a Mariel refugee, shaped a unique vocabulary. His best paintings gleam and clash with emblems of desire, sacrifice, death, and spiritual change.

The tumult of his imagery is fabulously hectic, in which symbols continually overlap and fuse. There are tongues and telephones oppressively pierced with daggers and flashing eyes that become transformed into swollen tears and phalluses. There are jittery coffee cups in which cartoonish signs for a delectable aroma blossom, with amused irony, into more fat, juicy teardrops.

Alfonzo once wrote that in his art, "tears are a symbol of exile," but his work surely leaps beyond personal experience into a universal arena of deeply felt passion and loss.

"I think he was incredibly brave in his devotion to painting," Viso says. "He could deal with emotional and passionate themes and the work never became over-sentimentalized."

And like the artist whom she never met, she bristles against stamping his art too hard with the label "Latin American." "He matured as an artist in the US looking at work by artists from all over the world," she says. "Jackson Pollock is equally important as any of the Cuban masters in his development."

Michael Auping, chief curator of the Modern Art Museum of Fort Worth, Texas, who met Alfonzo in Miami and included his work in a 1988 group show of emerging artists in New York, also recalls the painter's impressive gift for international style and synthesis.

"What sets Carlos apart is the incredible mental energy that he put into his paintings," he says. "They were physically layered with images, and they were layered in terms of content. Now cultural diversity has become a clichéd term, but in the 1980s Carlos was making a fusion of Cuban and American culture that was not clichéd. It made his work sometimes beautiful, sometimes potent, sometimes very angry. It all melted together into a kind of erotic violence."

That dynamism seeped into his studio visits with the artist, he says. A visit with Alfonzo was like drinking "six cups of coffee. . . . I've always thought of him as a shooting star. He started to shine really bright, and he just burned up."

In the paintings at MAM, geometric cubes burst with radiant lines of light. They evoke searing moments of intense pleasure and insight as well as the artist's formal skills for weaving an intricate composition together with dashing lines.

Crosses are also a constant, sometimes flowing into knives, melding into imagery associated with Roman Catholicism and with the Afro-Cuban cult of Santería. Both contain rituals, symbols, and beliefs that fascinated Alfonzo during his years growing up in Cuba.

Especially as his talent matured in the United States, he proceeded to mine the dramatic, seductive potential of these loaded images by thrusting them into ever more flashing and whirling compositions.

In the mid to late 1980s, his taste for rich, alluring metaphor led him to study the Tarot cards of Rosicrucianism, a mystic philosophy dating to 17th-century Europe. It's a belief system, as Viso explains in her catalog essay, that's designed to lead devotees to a transcendent state of consciousness, spurred by contemplating ancient Tarot symbols and imagining them animated in space. In one of his last works, the 1990 *Told*, a scythe-like shape, similar to the Tarot card of Death, appears sucked into the spiraling, overlapped shapes of a skull and kneeling figure.

TWO FIRSTS

This exhibit is the first traveling museum show that MAM has organized under director Suzanne Delehanty, who had joined the Center for the Fine Arts as director in 1995 and became MAM's founding director in 1996. This is also the first career survey of Alfonzo. Certainly this is the most ambitious effort MAM has initiated. Delehanty finds real significance in Alfonzo's art and the community he worked in. "I think [Carlos's] presence here parallels Miami's development as a creative community and acted as a catalyst in that development," Delehanty says. "Alfonzo really gives Miami a mirror of itself: energy, a respect for solid training, and a sense of adventure."

Says César Trasobares, a close friend of Alfonzo and a fellow artist, "I think the show is a testament to the strength of the work and is a major coup for MAM."

The show charts the development of his imagery, beginning with examples of his tightly compressed, calligraphic ink drawings from the 1970s, made in Cuba. It shows the aggressive, colorful pace of his evolving style in Miami, in which Viso and critic Dan Cameron, in his catalog essay, find links with the flamboyant, energetic approach of 1980s Neo-expressionism. Yet this was a style that became so packed with "fireworks," as Alfonzo himself once called his bravura way with paint, that it risked falling into self-parody. Instead, his art evolved in a new direction in his last year of life.

The show concludes with Alfonzo's moving "black paintings" of the late 1990s. They are marked by the presence of a figure that seems both supplicant and fetus, radiant and mournful, one transformed by the premonition of death and the promise of yet more changes.

Coursing through all the changes are Alfonzo's fluid, fluctuating brushstrokes. They switch back and forth from our fondest dreams to our most fearsome nightmares. This is art you can't forget.

In memoriam: Carlos Alfonzo, 1950–1991

VISUALLY ON THE VERGE, 1998–2000

From 1998 to 2000, the art community in Miami and South Florida moved forward to leverage its proximity to the Caribbean and Latin America with promising accomplishments. Exhibits at Miami-Dade County Public Library System proved a catalyst for change and reflection. Still, there were times when this forward movement stumbled and not all worthy initiatives reached fruition, often because of a lack of funding or sufficiently broad-minded imagination or both.

Given Miami's location as a favored destination for risky ocean crossings, artists created vivid, poignant imagery inspired by the experience of Cubans and Haitians attempting to reach Miami. Part 2 begins with reviews of art by Lydia Rubio and *Touched by* AIDS exhibits. Times of crisis form the backdrop of each, addressing urgent national topics of immigration and the AIDS epidemic. Those overlapping crises demonstrate how South Florida's recent art history provides a nuanced portrait of the region as it evolved in the late 20th century.

A haunting portrayal of journeys at sea, merging dreams with reality, characterized Lydia Rubio's paintings and sculpture in her 1998 exhibit at Fort Lauderdale's Museum of Art (now NSU Art Museum Fort Lauderdale).

Her paintings depicted dangerous journeys over water, recalling the horrific "rafter season" during the summer of 1994—when hundreds of Cubans attempted to cross the Florida Straits in makeshift boats. That was one of many moments when chaotic disruptions in Castro's Cuba led to chaotic disruptions in South Florida. These rafters were known by the Spanish word *balseros*, derived from the Spanish word *balsa*, meaning "raft."

During the "rafter season," barely seaworthy rafts were found adrift in the Florida Straits. Did they silently tell of lives lost or lives brought to shore? Hard to say. "Cuban women rafters plead for rescue, during massive flotillas in fall of 1994," reads a caption for a wrenching photograph by *Miami Herald* staff photographer Charles Trainor Jr. His photo shows two women and a child screaming in what looks to be a small, crowded boat and accompanies the story "How Events in Cuba Shaped and Reshaped Miami" by *Miami Herald* staff, updated November 26, 2016.

"*Touched by* AIDS Honors Pivotal Figures of Miami's Art Scene" in 1998 was presented at two galleries of Miami Dade College, Wolfson Campus. It announces broad historical threads in part 2 by presenting work by Miami artists whose thriving careers were cut short.

Among those were Sheldon Lurie, who ran the gallery program of the Wolfson Campus from around the 1980s to 1990. He was an especially pivotal figure, encouraging fellow artists. *Touched by* AIDS placed their art in a national context through its connections with the Los Angeles–based Estate Project for Artists with AIDS, which organized the exhibit. "I think some artists who have AIDS really focus on their condition," said Patricia Jones, South Florida coordinator of the Estate Project, "but the majority of these artists were busy simply producing the work they loved and cared about. This show is really about the triumph of the spirit and continuing to work as long as possible."

Photography becomes a significant genre during these years. In the 1998 review "Florida Center for Photography: Three Exile Voices Remember Details from the Voyage," I wrote that Silvia Lizama's photographs gave us a sense of how the exile journey was manifested in places like Miami. Photographs by the late Roberto Machado depicted classic scenes of Cuba before Fidel Castro seized power in 1959; in this context, they portrayed exiles' longing for what no longer existed. To highlight the photographs' impact as reflections on the nature of Cuban exile, they were curated in visual conversation with poetry by Richard Blanco at the short-lived Florida Center for Photography in Coral Gables.

Reviews and profiles address work by additional photographers Mario Algaze, Michael Carlebach, William Maguire, and J. Tomás López. Some photographers were featured at the Miami-Dade County Public Library System downtown, which also presented important exhibits inviting this community to contemplate its past and future.

In 2000, Miami-Dade County Public Library System curator and educator Barbara Young mused on the late Fernando García's green-and-pink road maps of Miami, part of *Cultivated under the Sun*, the library's look at 30 years of South Florida art. These maps told a story about a city where people came to reinvent themselves—yet still found themselves attached to their previous homes.

Young reflected on *Cultivated* with veteran artists Carol Brown and César

Trasobares. They remember when, in the absence of serious museum attention, artists were nurtured by inventive, low-budget programs at the library and at the old Center of Contemporary Art, the precursor to the Museum of Contemporary Art North Miami.

After putting together *Cultivated under the Sun* with fellow curator Margarita Cano, Young and former *Miami Herald* art critic Helen Kohen planned an ongoing visual arts archive to document Miami-Dade County's arts scene from the postwar years to the present.

The decision to create these archives was a milestone, encapsulating the art community's growing self-awareness. "It's time to recognize the years of contributions that artists, collectors, and their supporters have made to build Miami into an international cultural center," said Kohen, the *Herald*'s art critic from 1978 to 1995. "We're not a very prideful community," she acknowledged, "and I think this kind of thing says that it [the art scene] is real and that it's been here for a very long time." This initiative became the Vasari Project, named after 16th-century Italian artist Giorgio Vasari, who penned pioneering artist biographies.

New levels of sophistication developed. Ramón Cernuda opened Cernuda Arte gallery in 2000, intending to compensate for what he and others perceived as a lack of consistent attention to Cuban art history in local museums. Juan A. Martínez, an art professor at Florida International University and author of *Cuban Art & National Identity*, believed that more wide-ranging attention was necessary. "With the exception of Mexican art, I think the rest of the art of the Caribbean and Latin America has been underestimated because this country has always looked to the North and to Europe," he said.

A heady amalgam of international foods and festivals transformed Miami Art Museum with a visceral sensation of abundance, the signature of boundary-breaking artist Antoni Miralda. For *New Work: Miralda*, recipes were tacked to walls and painted on plates. MAM collected some 40,000 paper placemats passed around schools and libraries, recording local tastes, from Mauritius lamb curry to Nicaragua rice pudding.

It was admirable that MAM gave this validating, vigorously communal attention to Miralda. Afterall, Miami seemed a perfect place to highlight his highly experimental, multicultural aesthetic linking art and food—often overlooked in standard art history books. But as a Spanish artist inspired by years of international travel, he has maintained close ties to Barcelona and Miami and is a treasured part of Miami's cultural community. In April 2025, there was an outpouring of grief and support in Miami for the artist when his longtime wife and partner, entrepreneurial chef Montse Guillén, died in Barcelona.

During the years 1998 to 2000, this art community witnessed false starts, missteps, promises failing to deliver on their potential. One art institution that had faltered in its mission was the Bakehouse Art Complex. It looked scruffy and sad when I wrote about its 10th anniversary in 1998. The Bakehouse has since blossomed into one of Miami's most robust art organizations. Guided by the leadership of executive director Cathy Leff since 2018, it has cultivated the international connections making 21st-century Miami a desirable destination for cultural tourism and business. Bold murals on the exterior extend the art inside into the surrounding community.

Languishing for years on the Bakehouse east wall was a mural by Miami's well-known self-taught artist Purvis Young (1943–2010). Produced circa 1998–2003, it is near the entrance but was easy to overlook, quietly fading into obscurity underneath the harsh glare of intense sunlight.

Rosie Gordon-Wallace, now president and lead curator of Diaspora Vibe Cultural Arts Incubator, was a board member of the Bakehouse Art Complex in 1998. She made it possible for Young to paint his mural at the Bakehouse. For the book *Making Miami: The Story of an Art Community*, published by Jayaram and EXILE Books in 2023, Gordon-Wallace recalled that process. After Young had run afoul of the law, Diaspora Vibe Gallery became his probation officer. She oversaw his required 100 hours of community service by commissioning him to paint a mural at the art complex. "We bought him paint and left him paint by the wall at night," she wrote. He painted every night until the mural was finished and his probation requirements were fulfilled.

Gordon-Wallace was honored in April 2024 for her innovative leadership of Diaspora Vibe Cultural Arts Incubator. She was the first to receive the Miami-Dade County Mayor's Legacy in Arts Award at that year's Serving the Arts Award Ceremony. Said Mayor Daniella Levine Cava, "Our community is recognized across the globe as an arts and cultural capital with artists that showcase their creativity with a unique Miami flair. For over two decades, her work has nurtured and developed diverse voices in the arts and has been instrumental in making our community the international artistic center it is today."

In 1999, Young's growing career received an extraordinary boost when internationally known contemporary art collectors Donald and Mera Rubell of Miami purchased the contents of his studio—around 4,000 paintings, drawings, and books. Thirteen years after Young's death, his legacy brought another major coup for Miami. His Bakehouse mural joins over 200 projects and cultural treasures around the world conserved with funds from the Bank of America Art Conservation Project since 2010.

Thanks to the Bank of America grant, RLA Conservation repaired and conserved Young's deteriorating Bakehouse mural in 2023. "The fact that we were able to bring what we thought was a lost work back to life is incredibly gratifying," Leff told the *Miami Herald* then. "It's a relief. It's a gift to the community. It's a gift to us."

Deep connections to African customs and religious lore formed a strong presence in work by prominent Caribbean artists in Miami during this time—José Bedia, Charo Oquet, and Edouard Duval-Carrié. These artists remain an active force in the community. Their personal stories intersected with closely observed insights into the cultural heritage of their native countries.

The 2000 profile of Green Family Foundation president Kimberly Green provides a detailed introduction to her philanthropic family history, which surely paved the way for the many inclusive opportunities for Miami artists she established in 2020 with Green Space Miami.

Though it may seem like a small event, Miami art history is indelibly marked by Jamaica-raised Michael Richards's drawings shown in 2000 at Ambrosino Gallery. One drawing suggested a thematic echo of Richards's iconic 1999 sculpture *Tar Baby vs. St. Sebastian*, which was inspired by the underrecognized, racially segregated World War II Tuskegee Airmen. In 2021, the sculpture was part of his first museum retrospective at the Museum of Contemporary Art North Miami. It was a tragic, long-overdue recognition. Richards was killed in the 9/11 attack.

Three years before the inaugural Art Basel Miami Beach, "Visually on the Verge: With Tropical Clichés Safely in the Past: Could South Florida's Art Future Be Something Great?" asked the headline to my early January 1999 story. These were days and nights when art lovers' agendas were packed—with visits not only to the fair Art Miami but to spinoff events.

"Obviously, Miami is a hot scene," said New York Metropolitan Museum of Art curator Lowery Sims, who accepted an Art Miami invitation for the first time that year in 1999. "It's very strong in Latin American art and the visual arts in general. I'm coming down to see how it all goes together."

Miami's major challenge was to push the momentum of this "most happening week" into the months ahead, sustaining excitement after crowds departed. Much more needed to happen for art to become a year-round source of interest. "I think the problem remains that we are lacking an enthusiastic audience that recognizes what the outside recognizes, that Miami is a great cultural mix," said Miami art dealer Fredric Snitzer.

A year later, momentum continued to build. The January 2000 chronicle of that art-filled week, one year before Art Basel Miami Beach was supposed to arrive, showed the art community taking an activist role by making its own adventurous opportunities for displaying homegrown talent. A gathering of new, site-specific work by 44 Miami artists in an empty Brickell Avenue bank building drew large crowds for the time and high praise from Miami collector Dennis Scholl. It was, he said, "a defining moment for Miami, showing the community how many excellent working artists there are here. I got a chill walking up and down those floors."

Working nonstop during less than a week's time, established artists and ambitious high school and college art students filled eight floors of the soon-to-be-demolished building with an impressive range of work. Despite some uneven and grandstanding moments, the multistoried megashow was well worth the attention of the 1,200 visitors who showed up for the opening-night gala, a fundraiser that raised $7,000 for the New World School of the Arts, where Snitzer has taught sculpture for years.

As curator of the event, he estimated that another 1,200 people passed through the bank's transformed cubicles and corridors during the project's three-day public showing. While these figures don't sound impressive in current times, they were in the year 2000.

Roberto Behar and Rosario Marquardt watched visitors step inside their collaborative work. "It's like a small apartment with a big dream," as Marquardt described the piece, articulating a perfect metaphor for Miami at that time.

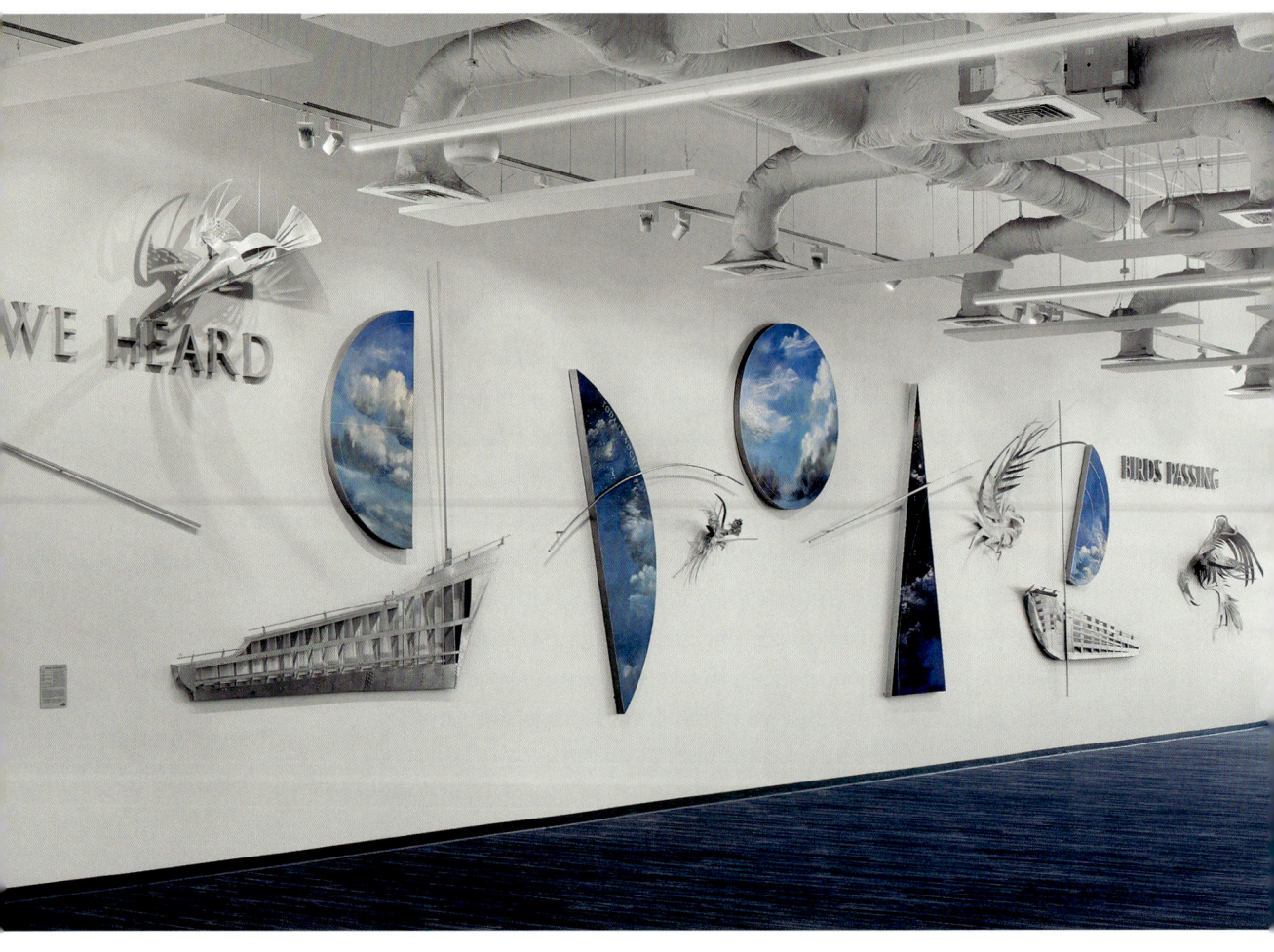

FIGURE 11. Lydia Rubio, *All Night Long, We Heard Birds Passing*, 2002/2023. Aluminum, oil paint. PortMiami–Terminal F, 1015 N American Way; 2, Ticketing, Carnival Cruise Line. Image Zachary Balber, courtesy of Miami-Dade County Department of Cultural Affairs, Art in Public Places Trust.

LYDIA RUBIO

Exhibit's Voices Speak of Perils of Exile Journey

March 7, 1998

Ships at sea ply the crosscurrents of dream and reality, fiction and fact in *Fragments of the Sea: Works by Lydia Rubio*, at the Museum of Art in Fort Lauderdale (now NSU Art Museum Fort Lauderdale). Paintings by this South Florida, Cuban-born artist are gracefully wrought but gleam with wry spins on the sun-kissed clichés of Caribbean seascapes.

Her paintings are spliced with written references to maritime metaphors from such writers as Pablo Neruda, Joseph Conrad, and Cuban novelist Reinaldo Arenas. They offer glinting images of dangerous journeys over water, with vignettes showing, for example, a freighter on fire, an abandoned raft, and an ocean liner aglitter with *Titanic* glamour. The work also recalls the horrific "rafter season" during the summer of 1994—when hundreds of Cubans attempted to cross the Florida Straits in flimsy makeshift boats.

This solo show of paintings and a few works of sculpture brings together 24 works from 1994 to 1996 and is curated by Jorge Santis, the Museum of Art's curator of collections. Most of the artwork in *Fragments of the Sea* was exhibited in shows at Gutierrez Fine Arts in Miami Beach in 1995 and at the Joyce Goldstein Gallery in New York City in 1996.

It's too bad that this exhibit is so narrowly focused. Visitors might have a better understanding of the evolution of Rubio's work if *Fragments* had included a few of her earlier, nearly nostalgic landscapes—constructed with surrealist sleights of hand in which, for example, silken tablecloths drift magically into velvety sand dunes shaded by palm trees. There could also have been an effort to connect this work to her current series of painted and collaged boxes, *Alphabet of Invisible Islands*, now on exhibit at Bridgewater/Lustberg Gallery in New York City through March 14.

Such connections would be useful because the fluid melding of fiction and fact is a constant in Rubio's career, even as her art has veered into regions less easily fathomed than the disarming landscapes, which gently summoned up an exile's memories of an island homeland. (Rubio, who grew up in Cuba in the 1950s and immigrated to Puerto Rico with her family in 1960, lived and worked in the Northeast before moving to Miami in the mid-1980s. Her work was included in the recent *Breaking Barriers: Selections from the Museum of Art's Permanent Contemporary Cuban Collection* at the Museum of Art in Fort Lauderdale.)

Her artwork has become less stand-alone images and more akin to stanzas in a poem or chapters in a novel, all exploring the resonant theme of ongoing journeys. Those journeys point specifically to an exile's perilous passage. Rubio also makes her marine metaphors expand into spiritual tales about the travels we all take through time and memory, shifting from places of peril to those of haunting beauty.

With those stanzas and chapters comes Rubio's love of labyrinthine word games, forging tenuous connections among these "fragments of the sea." For example, in her *Map of Pathways*, a gracefully drawn map of the Caribbean that functions as a kind of map for this show, with references to her paintings sketched among the islands, there's this poetic puzzle: a triangle stacked with the letters ARMAR AL MAR. They're arranged to spell out Spanish words for sea and soul and the expression "to give power to the sea."

A section of this show is devoted to her *Ships of the Elements* series, with four round oil paintings on wood and four corresponding ship-like sculptures constructed of metal and wood.

There's the painting *Barco de Fuego* (*Ship of fire*), in which roiling tongues of fire and plumes of smoke envelop a ship, melting it into a smashed composition of geometric shapes so that it becomes a shattered puzzle of its former self. There's the ghostly *Barco de Aire* (*Ship of air*), in which a vessel pared down to its metal ribs floats above a gently curling sea, like the barest outlines of an unrealized dream.

Many of these paintings, like those in the *Ships of the Elements* series, have the sepia tones of old photographs, giving the works a deceptive gloss of fact. The facts are that Rubio is an inveterate poet, weaving intricate episodes from life's churning voyage.

TOUCHED BY AIDS HONORS PIVOTAL FIGURES OF MIAMI'S ART SCENE

March 14, 1998

Touched by AIDS touches the determined heart of art making. It also revives what was once the creative heart of Miami's nascent art scene, which grew with poignant zest even as the national art scene felt tremors of the coming deadly calamity.

Focusing on artists who helped nurture local culture in the 1980s, *Touched by* AIDS opened Wednesday at the Centre Gallery and the Frances Wolfson Gallery of Miami-Dade Community College, Wolfson Campus.

In the Centre Gallery, you'll see paintings, sculptures, and works on paper by Carlos Alfonzo, Cesar Augusto, Jose Bernardo, Wil and Jon Fernando Brito, Craig Coleman, Humberto Dionisio, Fernando García, Juan González, Sheldon Lurie, Carlos Maciá, Adolfo Sanchez, and Tomas Touron. Lurie, who ran the gallery program of the Wolfson Campus from around the 1980s to 1990, was an especially pivotal figure, encouraging many of his fellow artists.

Anyone who remembers those days will be touched by the entrance to this show. Right away you encounter one of Lurie's piercing self-portraits, in which he wears a T-shirt bristling with Alfonzo's energetic symbols. Look to your right and you'll see those larger-than-life symbols in an Alfonzo sculpture.

In the Frances Wolfson Gallery are more works by these artists as well as costumes, books, paintings, ceramics, and even drag-queen dolls created by the current lively but HIV-aware, mostly South Beach, community of companions and colleagues of those represented in the Centre Gallery. There's Rafael Salazar's astonishing photo-collage portrait of García and Ali's campy shots of divas.

The core of the show is in the Centre Gallery, where some artists' legacies stand out more than others. Connections among the works do not dominate the show, but there is a strong sense of invention, of exacting commitment to form, and a sensuous delight in the manipulation of symbols, whether plucked from touristy kitsch or Roman Catholic shrines.

All the artists in this gallery have been lost to AIDS. The presence of that loss is an insidious undercurrent in a show marked by richly diverse talent—from Brito's iridescent collages and painted plates to García's arch conceptual games mingling math with Miami maps, from Lurie's exquisitely deft drawings and stenciled poems to Touron's painted canvases layered with images of spiked flesh and upward-swimming fish. Bernardo's baroque-styled celebration of pop decorative arts, in his quirky ceramic sculpture, is another highlight, as are the surreal drawings of González and Maciá.

"Not one of them was anywhere near the end of his career," says former *Herald* art critic Helen Kohen, who curated *Touched by* AIDS with Margarita Cano and Barbara Young—all veteran art supporters who knew these artists as they approached their primes.

AIDS NOT SOLE FOCUS

While this is a show tragically shadowed by our postwar plague, AIDS is not the overt subject, says Patricia Jones, South Florida coordinator of the Los Angeles–based Estate Project for Artists with AIDS, which organized the exhibit.

"I think some artists who have AIDS really focus on their condition," she says, "but the majority of these artists were busy simply producing the work they loved and cared about. This show is really about the triumph of the spirit and continuing to work as long as possible."

Alfonzo, who was one of the only two to achieve national recognition during their lifetimes—the other was González—is also the focus of a major retrospective revealing that urgent kind of creative dedication: *Triumph of the Spirit: Carlos Alfonzo, a Survey, 1975–1991*, organized by the Miami Art Museum, where it closed earlier this month. It will travel in June to the Hirshhorn Museum and Sculpture Garden in Washington, DC.

While *Touched by* AIDS was timed to follow the Alfonzo retrospective as a way to draw attention to those working around the same time as Alfonzo but whose careers did not rise to similar heights, the show also coincides with the current Keith Haring retrospective at the Museum of Contemporary Art. Haring died of AIDS in 1990 at age 31. A sense of apocalyptic urgency—as well as his signature freewheeling love of line—informs his later paintings.

What does it mean that we're seeing so many examples of creativity cut short? "It means to me that within the curatorial community, there's a growing confirmation that this work is of interest for lots of reasons, aesthetic and social," says Patrick Moore, director of the Estate Project. "You can look at it as a work of art but also as a record of the horrible past 10 or 15 years we've lived through."

KEEPING WORKS ALIVE

Founded in 1991, the Estate Project advises artists—visual as well as performing—about how to ensure that their work will survive their death. (Copies of the project's pamphlet *Future Safe: Estate Planning for Artists in a Time of* AIDS are available at the Centre Gallery. *Future Safe* and its Spanish translation, as well as related documents, are also available online at www.artistswithaids.org.)

The project's activist agenda includes arranging for storage of work by artists touched by AIDS at the New York Public Library and the Academy Film Archive in Los Angeles. Thanks to the project's collaboration with the Getty Information Institute in Malibu, California, art by the Centre Gallery artists will be part of a huge digital archive documenting more than 3,000 examples of work by artists with AIDS or HIV, says Moore.

Exhibitions also make up the agenda. New York's Solomon R. Guggenheim Museum is preparing a show of film and video preserved by the project. Moore hopes that Miami's *Touched by* AIDS, with its focus on a specific community of artists, many of them Cuban American, will be a national model for other community-focused exhibits.

To some extent, this is a show touched by two conflicting aims—to memorialize the toll exacted by untimely deaths and to recognize the art left behind. But a funereal memorial service can sentimentalize our view of the art's vitality.

Touched by AIDS, insists Moore, "is not a funeral. True preservation involves preservation of the artists' careers. The work was at the core of their existence, and its continued life means that a central part of each person continues to live on."

In memoriam: Helen Kohen, 1931–2015
Margarita Cano, 1932–2024

FLORIDA CENTER FOR PHOTOGRAPHY

Three Exile Voices Remember Details from the Voyage

March 21, 1998

Memory comes in many colors for three generations of Cuban exiles, whose poetry and photography form a triangle of longing in the current show at the Florida Center for Photography in Coral Gables.

There are poetic musings on exotic, hard-to-translate shades like chartreuse that crammed the crayon box of a new Spanish-speaking kid on the block; the frilly pink sleeves of a leggy mambo-dancer-cum-kitschy-lamp that adorned a television in a modest apartment in Rochester, New York; and the crisp white sail of a boat reflected in the silvery Almendares River of pre-1959 Havana.

Generations: Silvia Lizama, Roberto Machado, and Richard Blanco is a charming, sweet show, even if the overall nostalgic tone may be excessively familiar. It includes the hand-colored photography of Lizama, a widely exhibited South Florida artist whose family arrived in Miami in 1960 when Lizama was a toddler. Her subjects range from televisions plopped in small shops throughout Latin America to scenes of vast urban upheaval, as captured on I-95 construction sites in the early 1990s.

Paired with her photographs are excerpts from *City of a Hundred Fires*, a book of poems by Blanco to be published later this year by the University

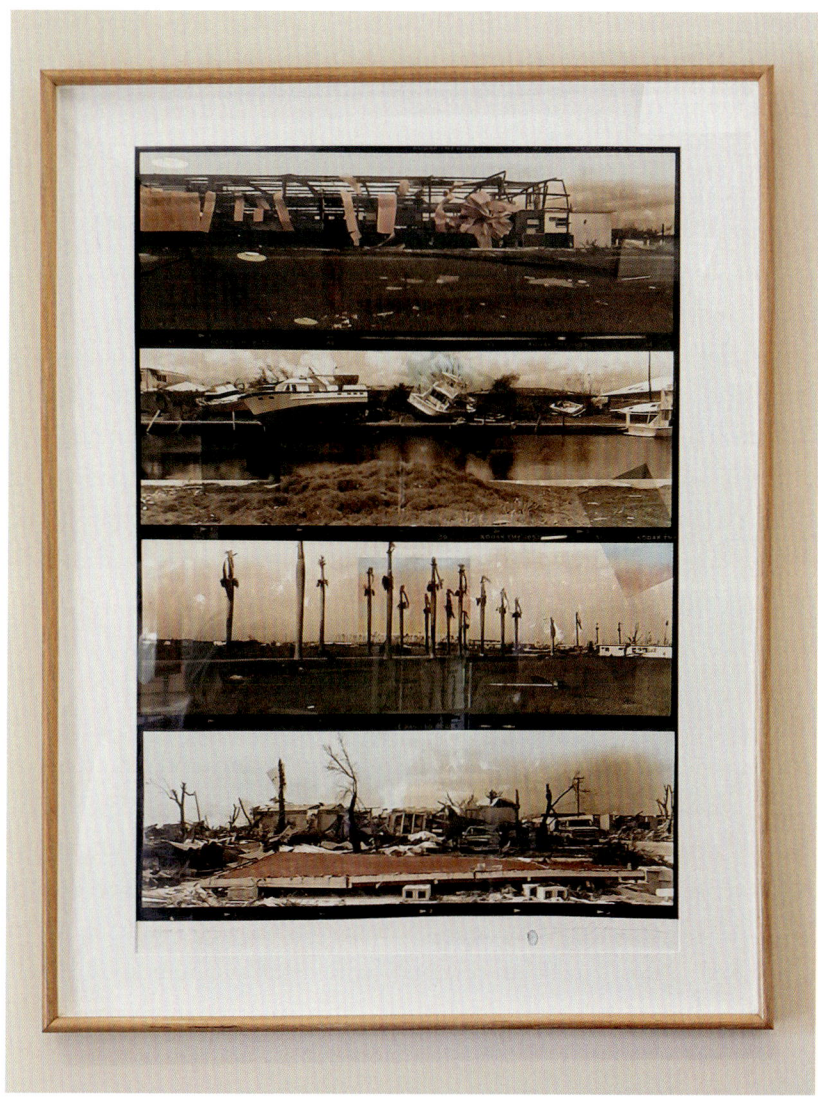

FIGURE 12. Silvia Lizama, *Welcome to the Sunshine State, FL 4/93*, 1993. Hand-colored gelatin silver print. Image Yusimy Lara, courtesy of Miami-Dade County Department of Cultural Affairs, Art in Public Places Trust.

of Pittsburgh Press. Born in Madrid in 1968 to exiled Cuban parents, Blanco grew up in New York and Miami, receiving an MFA in creative writing from Florida International University in 1997.

The senior member of this trio is Dr. Roberto Machado (1905–79), a physician in Havana for many years who emigrated in 1960, eventually settling in Maryland. He was also a fine amateur photographer, as revealed by these crystalline shots of strollers along Havana's waterfront Malecón, canecutters in the countryside, and a broom seller on a Havana street corner.

Lizama learned of Machado's photography when she met one of his sons in Mexico four years ago. In January, the Machado family gave her permission to print his negatives—an experience she recalls as a "treasure hunt for beautiful images of a land I had only heard about but was now experiencing through the eyes of a fellow photographer." Machado's posthumous prints form an eloquent backdrop to the current hunt, carried by younger artists, for telling emblems of an exile's journey.

DAVID ROHN AT GALERIE DOUYON

Sweet colors also suffuse an intriguing group of paintings and sculptures by South Florida artist David Rohn in the exhibition *David Rohn: Recent Sculptures and Paintings*. Nostalgia is nowhere to be seen in this edgy gathering of pink-fleshed musclemen and eerily human-eyed barnyard animals on display in his solo show at Galerie Douyon. The tone of these works shifts between affection and assault, particularly in the three lumpish and humorous papier-mâché sculptures of yellow-suited wrestlers. They're locked in a progressively more intimate—and more confrontational—embrace.

Rohn celebrates the fleshy vulnerability of life, whether he finds it in ambiguous relationships among men or in humanity's self-serving connection to domesticated animals. There's an endearing but provocative clumsiness to his *Four Chicken Faces*, portraits of hens and roosters. They're gifted with a knowing gaze that makes them not quite cute enough to find their way onto Williams Sonoma tea towels—but human enough to resist being marketed as macho trophies.

BAKEHOUSE

10 Years Old and at a Turning Point

May 3, 1998

At the Bakehouse Art Complex, the gallery is locked up tight, condemned by the City of Miami. Salty bits of beach sand, residue from a 1920s recipe for concrete, are causing the gallery's concrete beams and columns to crumble. Termites have threatened the original maple floors in the rambling, coral-pink building, a former bakery in Wynwood converted into nonprofit artists' studios and an exhibition space, which was fully open in 1987.

Artists cleared out from its studios for two days last month when an exterminator's circus-sized tents covered the building. They've since moved back in; the director's office, however, remains empty, a casualty of sporadic funding.

"We need to breathe some life in the structure, because we could definitely go belly-up," says furniture designer Matt Zbornik, president of the Bakehouse's long-dormant but newly active artists' association.

And when record crowds of some 1,000 visitors trekked to the Bakehouse for the Easter Sunday opening of two exhibits, the *Tenth Anniversary Show* and the *Caribbean Art Show*, it was clear that a spirit of revival was in the air. Artists and board members of the no-frills facility, dedicated to giving artists at all stages an affordable place to work and gather, are joining forces to make things work.

The Bakehouse artists, who currently number 53, rallied together to promote the opening, painting walls and mounting lights from the closed gallery in a warren of hallways lined with their studios. The halls function as an impromptu gallery space for the current exhibits.

"The artists in the last few months have done more than they have in quite some time," says Zbornik, who believes that the resignation of director Pola Reydburd in October and the departure of interim director Peggy Johnson in February helped spur the current level of initiative.

Not having the gallery "galvanized the artists," says Bakehouse artist Necee

Regis. "We started having meetings to discuss how to get more people interested in coming to the Bakehouse and how to make it a more vital place." Preparing for the 10th-anniversary show was a priority, she said. "We felt that if we didn't do it, nobody else would."

GAINING STABILITY

On Thursday, after two-and-a-half years of uncertain finances, the Bakehouse closed on a five-year, $225,000 mortgage with City National Bank of Miami, says board president Robert Apfel, a Miami Beach dentist and glass artist who once had a studio at the Bakehouse himself.

"The next five years should be a lot easier for us. This is the first time we've had some predictability, financially. Now the fundraising can go more toward a secure directorship," he says. Support for a director has been spotty in the last two years, he says, because the board has been busy raising $70,000 to pay for desperately needed renovations, required by the bank before it would extend the mortgage. Renovation of the gallery, for example, is scheduled to start this month.

Apfel expects an interim director will be hired for two or three months after the 13-member board meeting on Wednesday and then hopes to find a director "obviously as soon as possible."

Gaps in leadership and funding have plagued this ambitious cultural institution, which offers artists low-cost workspace and provides educational outreach programs for surrounding inner-city neighborhoods. Though its artists over the years have been promising (photographer María Martínez-Cañas was a Bakehouse tenant early in her career; Jean-Claude Rigaud, whose abstract steel sculpture was included in the 1995 traveling *Caribbean Visions* exhibit, is a current tenant), its exhibits have been wildly uneven.

"It's very difficult to maintain a low-rent facility and have the resources to pay for administrative infrastructure," says former director Reydburd, now a consultant. Reydburd says she wrote 21 grants during her tenure while also taking the Bakehouse's guard dogs to the vet and buying toilet paper for its bathrooms: "I was using most of my time to perform menial or clerical duties that wasted my professional background and did not contribute to advancing the goals of the Bakehouse."

"[Reydburd] wanted a full-time assistant and we could not afford one," says Apfel.

Partially funded by public money, the Bakehouse, according to Apfel, has an annual budget of approximately $140,000. Its 32,000 square feet features an underutilized exhibition space of handsome proportions and 72 studios with monthly rents ranging from $150 to $400. (Apfel says the 75 percent studio occupancy rate has held steady for the past several years.)

ARTISTS' HAVEN

The size of the Bakehouse makes it a unique resource among the many local arts groups that work with the Miami-Dade County Cultural Affairs Council, says Rem Cabrera, chief of cultural development at the council. The Bakehouse is also different from the ArtCenter/South Florida on Lincoln Road, which also houses an exhibition space and artists' studios, in that it has work areas for dealing with industrial materials as well as zoning for glassmaking and welding.

Supporters are anxious for the Bakehouse to put aside the crises of the past 10 years and move ahead.

"We've had intensive meetings with their board and our staff over the last few years," says Michael Spring, executive director of the Miami-Dade County Cultural Affairs Council, which distributes grants and offers advisory services to local arts organizations. "We lock ourselves in a conference room and go through budgets, vision, and come up with pathways for the Bakehouse."

The board, Spring says, "is showing the resourcefulness and creativity to prevail, like restructuring the mortgage, coming up with board members who dedicate 300 percent of their time, and continuing to attract artists. The Bakehouse is a critical link in the support network for individual artists. It has to survive and thrive."

The reinvented bakery is ripe for a stronger identity, says Zbornik, by "transforming itself into a truly professional organization where people get paid, [with] a consistent salary for a director and facilities manager."

"The Bakehouse is on the cusp of change," insists board member Rosie Gordon-Wallace, a Searle pharmaceutical representative who has also served on the Miami Light Project board. Two years ago in a rented space at the Bakehouse, she founded Diaspora Vibe Gallery to present work by artists of Caribbean descent. "We've had mishaps. I think we're going to come out of that cloud and attract new members and corporations to partner with us."

Gordon-Wallace also feels the complex should collaborate with other arts organizations. Apfel, hoping to capitalize on the increasing sophistication of Miami's cultural scene, would like to see local collectors sponsor Bakehouse residencies for out-of-town artists whose work is in their collections. Zbornik, too, would like to see the facility bring in exhibits from alternative spaces around the country, such as PS 1 Contemporary Art Center in Long Island City and the Mattress Factory in Pittsburgh.

"I really want to see young graduates from Miami's art schools look toward the Bakehouse as their artistic home," says Gordon-Wallace. "On Saturday mornings I'd like to see Wynwood families let their kids come in and paint. Who is to say who is going to be the next major artist?"

JULIO LARRAZ

Diary of a Soul Travels through Tradition

May 10, 1998

So much talk about Latin American art has been laced with mapmaking and magical realism. Maps imply a sense of travel, of displacement and change, and these are ideas that smolder on the surface of paintings by such different, internationally known contemporary figures as José Bedia, a Cuban-born artist living in Miami, and Guillermo Kuitca of Argentina.

Earlier this century, European surrealists were enchanted by the intimations of magic in the flowery vistas of Haitian painter Hector Hyppolite and in Wifredo Lam's piercing visions of sugarcane fields seething with Afro-Cuban spirits and spears.

Julio Larraz: Diary of the Soul, on exhibit at the Boca Raton Museum of

Art, seems to glide sweetly into this tradition of travel and transformation. In Larraz's 1995 painting *Conclave at Boca*, a crate of pomegranates, packed for shipping, are rosy and robust, fleshy and lush. Their snipped stems resemble tiny crowns, and the more one looks at this oversized close-up of queenly, voluptuous fruit, the more bizarre it becomes.

Diary of the Soul was organized by the Boca Raton Museum of Art and brings together some 40 still lifes and figurative works, primarily oil paintings, with an occasional pastel drawing and bronze sculpture. Most of the art is from the 1990s.

Larraz, born in Cuba in 1944, immigrated to Miami with his family in 1961, resettling two years later in New York City. A gifted draftsman, Larraz began publishing political caricatures in the *New York Times*, the *Washington Post*, and *Vogue* magazine.

By 1967, Larraz dedicated himself to painting full time and has been recognized with a series of shows in galleries in New York; Dallas; Santa Fe, New Mexico; and Colombia, as well as a 1977 exhibit at New York's American Academy of Arts and Letters. His work was included in the traveling 1987 *Outside Cuba*, organized by the Jane Voorhees Zimmerli Art Museum of Rutgers University, and in a 1993 survey of 20th-century Cuban art at the Museum of Art in Fort Lauderdale. Since 1986 he's lived in Miami.

IN TOUCH WITH HISTORY

A prolific and painstaking artist whose realist style can veer toward the conservative and commercial, Larraz never studied painting formally in the United States or Cuba. It's clear, however, that he's steeped himself in a range of art historical precedents.

His spare, radiant still lifes recall the luminous orbs of fruit and glowing folds of cloth in paintings by Francisco de Zurbaran and Luis Meléndez, 17th- and 18th-century Spanish masters. A taste for out-of-kilter compositions, such as a white rose politely floating amid clouds, may remind viewers of Belgian surrealist René Magritte, while other imagery also evokes comparisons to Americans Georgia O'Keeffe and Andrew Wyeth.

What's most striking about the current exhibit is the ironic way Larraz deals with these so-called Latin American themes of travel and magical realism. Certain paintings surely make sly references to the fact that many scholars have challenged the popular view that Latin American art is "art of the fantastic," arguing that such a label is another Eurocentric misinterpretation of a region's diverse New World culture.

"You want journeys? You want fantasy?" this exhibit seems to ask. Viewers get plenty of both in *Diary of the Soul*, but with a particularly surreal, space-age twist that dovetails with recent tabloid chatter about extraterrestrial sightings. This show projects an unexpected sense of humor at once subtle and slapstick.

Larraz's 1997 *Sombrero*, for example, shows a bowler hat gleaming with an aluminum sheen, its wide brim a near ringer for a flying saucer. This fantastic "sombrero" floats, and even appears to vibrate, against a serene backdrop of blue sky and green trees. *Continental Breakfast*, also from 1997, serves up another otherworldly scene with a jumble of breakfast objects—white china cups and saucer, loaf of bread, oranges, and coffeepot—floating against the deathly blackness of outer space, hovering just beyond a bulging blue glimpse of Earth. It's a most unstill still life.

Lest you think such works are simply recent spatial aberrations, consider the 1994 bronze sculpture *Space Station*, a tipsy-looking tower of white coffee cups balancing a coffeepot on top.

A NEW SPIN

As a result of these images, a silly brio invades this show, with mixed results. *Into the 6th Dimension* of 1997 offers an overstated, unsuccessful attempt to upend the traditional Spanish-style still life that Larraz paints with such rich dexterity. Here, a bowl of squash and fruit is represented both in loving detail and as fractured, jittery lines of hot colors.

Black Hole, from 1998, moves Larraz's appetite for ironic fantasy in a slightly more compelling direction. A delectable red apple sinks into the black dimple of a deep shadow, nearly engulfed by a wavering field of charcoal gray.

Lost in space? Fruit in search of a still life? Or an artist in search of a new, mysterious spin on old, familiar territory? The answer is most likely yes to the first two questions and certainly yes to the last.

MUSEUM OF ART
IN FORT LAUDERDALE

Trio of Exhibits Taps South Florida's Cultural Mosaic

May 10, 1998

Visitors this spring and summer will find a stimulating trio of shows at the Museum of Art in Fort Lauderdale, with a sharp focus on South Florida talent.

Exquisitely crafted works probe the rough, raw edges of growing up in *María Brito: Rites of Passage (Sculpture and Painting 1988–1998)*. Our picture-postcard scenery gets a wide-angle look in the 24 paintings by six artists featured in *Tropical Terrain: South Florida Landscapes*. A love of telling stories—whether visionary vignettes or acutely personal anecdotes—is woven through *Two Narratives: Paintings by Peter Olsen and Rebecca "Betty" Pinkney*.

Together, the shows survey the surprising range of expression making up the cultural and geographic mosaic that's South Florida.

The solo show dedicated to a decade of artwork by María Brito is the strongest and most moving of the three. Brito, who was born in Havana in 1947 and has lived in Miami since arriving here in 1961, is widely admired for her sculpture made from elaborate reworkings of domestic carpentry and furnishings.

Her art has been included in group exhibits at the Museum of Art in Fort Lauderdale, the Norton Museum of Art, the High Museum of Art in Atlanta, and the Santa Monica Art Center in Barcelona, among others.

An accomplished painter with a startling ability to evoke what could be called a kind of "everywoman" within her own acute likeness, Brito has also produced many canvases. The paintings rarely stand alone and are often incorporated into her sculptural assemblages—as with the aluminum bucket attached to her 1993 *The Traveler (Homage to B.G.)*, poised to catch rivulets of clouds "weeping" from the painting.

Her sculptures and canvases meld bravura quotations from Renaissance paintings, showing virginal figures suffused with sacrifice and saintliness, with dreamy but ominous scenes of children and mothers, often posed too close for comfort.

EMOTIONAL INTENSITY

Brito makes assemblages in the manner of overgrown boxes by American surrealist Joseph Cornell. Her art is layered with the emotional intensity coursing through self-portraits by Frida Kahlo and earthy, body-inspired installations by Brito's late compatriot, Ana Mendieta.

Chairs, beds, cribs, doorways, cabinets, even light bulbs and mirrors: throughout her career, Brito has nailed these mundane housebound fixtures into a body of work that could be dubbed the Home Depot of the Soul.

Like much of the art by Cuban Americans of her generation, Brito's work has been discussed as emblematic of the anguish of exile, of the pain of cultural upheaval. That personal history of displacement speaks clearly through this retrospective, but images of enclosure and escape are equally dominant.

"Overprotection," she says, is the word that best sums up her memories of a 1950s Cuban childhood—later mixed with the frustration of "finding myself as a young teenager having to deal with customs carried over from one country to another" and discovering that many of those customs were "very passé. I was chaperoned until the day I was married," she admits, referring to her first marriage at age 19.

Her art offers claustrophobic, labyrinthine journeys for the eye and mind. Elaborate installations such as 1993's *Merely a Player* and the 1995 *Trappings* lead us into restricted areas. These boxy spaces are where Brito's eccentric cluster of objects, from a tiny virginal altarpiece encased in a bird cage to a vintage sketch of fishermen snagging a big catch, play out dramas of women molded for a narrow housebound role and released, sometimes, into a broader arena.

Though *Merely a Player* was shown at the Norton just four years ago, it's such a rich, theatrical piece that this current exhibit would not be complete without it.

One person at a time, you can actually walk through its maze of small rooms and passageways, confronting its little mirrors, masks, and cleansing basins, as well as the tiny black-and-white video of a girl endlessly knocking on a door that never opens. At last you find a narrow door, open it, and depart.

Leaving behind those child-sized rooms is the defining moment of Brito's *Rites of Passage*.

SHADES OF THE TROPICS

Tropical Terrain: South Florida Landscapes is an unexpectedly inviting show, given that tropical vistas inspire so many clichéd renderings in all imaginable shades of fruity bubble gum and sherbet. Artists represented here are James Couper of Miami, Joseph Davoli of Fort Lauderdale, John David Hawver of Islamorada, Roslyn Kirsch of Boca Raton, Fenol Marcelin of Miami Beach, and Mary Louise O'Sullivan of Palm City.

Hawver's faux impressionist style is grating, especially in the tedious parade of blue dots in *Tribute to the Banality of Just Another Day in Paradise, Ho Hum*. But Couper proves himself once again to be a master at limning the swiftly changing shades of blue, green, and amber rippling across a stretch of sawgrass and mangroves.

While there's a strong preference for the idyllic—as well as the fanciful in Marcelin's jungles sparkling with dewy leaves and preening birds—Davoli is the only one to acknowledge that South Florida is a densely populated place, where green Edenic locales are fraught with canals and bridges. Such frankness gives his shimmering brushstrokes an urgent and beyond-prettiness punch.

Two Narratives spins tales of biblical revenge with Peter Olsen's apocalyptic, pop-culture visions of cartoon characters roasting in hell or rising among angels. But his style is marred by an abundance of flashy 3D effects, giving his paintings the busy look of a video arcade. Rebecca "Betty" Pinkney's lively memory paintings are much more engaging, drawing us into richly detailed and sometimes harrowing episodes from her life growing up as a Black person in rural Florida in the 1960s.

In memoriam: James (Jim) Couper, 1937–2023

FLORENCIO GELABERT

Exhibits Transmogrify Natural Images

May 16, 1998

The hand-honed integrity of tools has always sliced to the core of sculpture by South Florida artist Florencio Gelabert, represented in a solo show a year ago at the Museum of Art in Fort Lauderdale. That exhibit resonated with tools as political and cultural emblems of protection and violence.

His current show, *Florencio Gelabert: Sound of the Forest* at Miami's Ambrosino Gallery, moves forward his signature reworking of axes, scythes, and knives. *Sound of the Forest*, with eight recent sculptures and installations, gives his arsenal a trendy ecological twist.

Knives, axes, and spades become not only spare sculptural instruments imbued with a respect for manual labor and skill but also devices capable of wreaking havoc on their maker's natural world. One untitled work shows a triangle-shaped mosaic of wood blocks, matching the proportions of a human torso. Some of the golden-brown blocks have been polished to reveal a web of concentric circles, a quietly beautiful but aborted record of a forest's growth.

A handsomely crafted wooden picture frame, its border lined with shimmering Astroturf but lacking any picture inside, seems to evoke the emptiness of ravaged terrain—which has been sacrificed for fashionable objects like this one. But this heavy-handed piece is downright dull, like a worn-away blade.

Other pieces are more complex, delicately dovetailing imagery of vulnerable bodies and forests with the legacy of the well-turned tool. Most show how Gelabert, born in Cuba in 1961 and working in Miami since the early 1990s, is expanding his vocabulary in inventive ways.

With a catalog essay by Miami-based art critic Tami Katz-Freiman, this show will travel to contemporary art museums in Panama, Guatemala, and Costa Rica.

ANTONI MIRALDA

Tongue in Chic in His Food, Tradition

November 8, 1998

It's a fair question to ask the artist who's making art from a smorgasbord of Miamians' favorite recipes. What's your favorite?

Antoni Miralda, salt-and-pepper hair pulled back in his customary ponytail, is shy to share it at first and then begins an animated description. His hands slice and caress the air. His words conjure a pungent aroma and juicy taste. It's easy to see why the sensuous, life-celebrating aura of food has seduced his sensibility throughout his career. This is the aura that pervades portions of his most recent work, *New Work Miralda: Grandma's Recipes—Miami Bureau*, at the Miami Art Museum through January 10.

His answer: "A slice of bread, tomato very well sautéed in good, good olive oil, and salt," he says. "It's very Mediterranean. This is our fast food. This is," he says, giving the next word a deliciously sonorous roll so that it may sum up centuries of good taste, "ancestral."

The cultural ancestry of food lies at the core of his art making. Serving up a postmodern spin on age-old customs, his art links his love of festivals to a love of a well-crafted meal. With pop art irreverence and the ephemeral drama of performance art, his work is about how and why people gather for special times, special food.

At MAM, there are recipes tacked to the walls, painted on plates, and posted on his website at https://www.foodcultura.org/ More are on the way, as MAM collects the some 40,000 paper placemats the staff has passed around to schools and libraries. Written and illustrated by hand, they record an overwhelming range of local tastes, from Mauritius lamb curry to Vietnamese pizza to Virginia spoon bread to Nicaragua rice pudding.

With tongue-in-cheek puns, the show looks at the most basic, physical origins of taste, regardless of the language or "tongue" that claims a particular dish. Taste buds are everywhere—on fat plastic tongues mounted on the wall with meat hooks, shiny photographs of real tongues, and symbolic "tongue tapestries" made of cans for Latin American soft drinks, all purchased in Miami, like Inca Kola and Milca.

SIMPLE SANDWICH

Miralda's favorite, the simple sandwich, isn't the elaborate paella one might expect from the Spanish-born artist, an internationally known figure who divides his time between Barcelona and Miami—when he isn't traveling to spice markets in Istanbul and date markets in Morocco, or building a temporary tombstone with eggplants to mark the demise of the legendary market in Paris called Les Halles, or orchestrating vast festivals to celebrate the "marriage" of Christopher Columbus to the Statue of Liberty, part of his *Honeymoon Project* that took place in Europe and the United States, including Miami, between 1986 and 1992.

To the art world, his work has been something of a tough sell. Despite participating in international events including biennials in São Paulo in 1983, Venice in 1990, and Istanbul in 1997, Miralda draws little attention in recent art history books covering postwar art—far less than Christo, for example, to whom he's sometimes compared.

ATTACK OF "OUTSIDERNESS"

He suffers from "outsiderness," says Paula Harper, a University of Miami art professor. "It's hard to include him in any movement. He operates in the real crack between art and life, in between things that haven't been explored before."

Folk art is another renegade ingredient. Miralda admires the fleeting kind, such as street murals made of petals for the spring rite of Corpus Christi in Spain or frosted sugar skulls created for Mexico's Day of the Dead on November 2, a festival honoring deceased family members and evolved from Aztec rituals.

"You have to think of these things as votive objects, to give thanks," says Marion Oettinger, senior curator and folk art scholar at the San Antonio Museum of Art, of the edible skulls and petal paintings. The essence of their appeal, he says, is that they're crafted from materials "ephemeral, sweet, and available." The festive celebration, not the object, is what comes down through generations.

A NOVEL BLEND

Ephemeral, available, sometimes more savory than sweet—those are the qualities that season Miralda's unique confections of food, festival, and art.

The Honeymoon Project, a madcap monument to the 500th anniversary of Columbus's arrival in the Americas, is his most vivid synthesis of that trinity. Based on cultural exchanges between Europe and the Americas, it was laced with droll wit, leavening the caustic tone of much politically correct Columbus-inspired artwork. It included Miss Liberty's 900-pound fuchsia petticoat, billowing in the atrium of Miami-Dade Community College's Wolfson Campus, 10 years ago this fall.

Honeymoon ended with 20 white limousines parked at Red Rock Canyon, near the world's wedding chapel capital of Las Vegas. Each limo's trunk was packed with Old and New World foods, from almonds to avocados. The cars surrounded two huge sculptures shaped like pelvic bones—a rice-covered papier-mâché one for Miss Liberty and a bronze one for Columbus—and then the party began, with Catalan music and huge photographs of the couple projected, Mount Rushmore style, on the Nevada mountains.

PHOTO PROJECTIONS

His work at MAM, curated by Sue Graze, assistant director for programs / senior curator, also features photo projections, but the scale is more intimate. They flicker with startling portraits of many Miamians' tongues. One sparkles with a silver stud, another pops out of its owner's mouth like a ripe strawberry, still another strikes a lip-caressing pose. Along one wall is a large range, with a computer offering access to Miralda's website blinking away where you'd expect to find a bubbling casserole. Silvery rows of 12,000 canned foods are lined up along the walls and stacked like a Mexican step pyramid, courtesy of Publix Supermarket Charities and destined for Camillus House when the show ends.

New Work: Miralda lacks the sensuous spectacle of his older work. What's most revealing is that his departure point is not the usual grand public procession but instead, two of the most private locales of all: inside our mouth and our family kitchen. Those spaces have produced recipes for foods in sharp contrast to what's in the generic cans. With subdued flair, he brings those individual recipes to one public banquet.

Standing next to plates painted at the opening and now laid out on the floor as if waiting for a picnic, Miralda sums up why he loves festivals, especially the Day of the Dead and its bright, sweet skulls, which he exchanges with friends. "People have this tendency to be so closed and finally, so boring. It's a way out of that. To play with the dead with all respect and make a little corner of the cemetery into a feast—it's fantastic to me. There's this real heavy ritual, but also the best colors and sharing, sharing every moment."

In memoriam: Paula Harper, 1930–2012

VISUALLY ON THE VERGE

With Tropical Clichés Safely in the Past, Could South Florida's Art Future Be Something Great?

January 10, 1999

We're deep into the high-energy, head-spinning odyssey of "the most happening art week in Miami," as South Florida artist George Sánchez-Calderón puts it. These are the days and nights when art lovers' agendas are packed—not only with visits to Art Miami, the five-day international fair that wraps Tuesday at the Miami Beach Convention Center but to a host of spinoff events that have helped lure a globe-trotting crowd of collectors, curators, dealers, and artists to town.

It's the heady time when, navigating Art Miami booths of close to 100 galleries, you can see a wide range of works by European, American, and

Latin American artists—from Henri Matisse, Robert Rauschenberg, Judy Pfaff, and Kiki Smith to Wifredo Lam, Rufino Tamayo, Marta María Pérez Bravo, and Ernesto Pujol—and enjoy substantial fare as well at local museums and galleries.

Though Art Miami is still behind the first-rank American and European art fairs—those held in Basel, Switzerland; Chicago; and elsewhere—it's steadily improving. And a similar progress report could be made for the South Florida scene as a whole. Museums are in an unprecedented expansionist mode, artists' organizations like ArtCenter/South Florida and the Bakehouse are refurbishing facilities and missions, and an international aura pervades outstanding private collections located here and the work many artists are making here.

"Obviously, Miami is a hot scene," says New York Metropolitan Museum of Art curator Lowery Sims, who accepted an Art Miami invitation for the first time this year. "It's very strong in Latin American art and the visual arts in general. I'm coming down to see how it all goes together."

This week, it all goes together like a resounding orchestral overture, with international visual arts cognoscenti clogging area hotels, taking in the scene. But the real challenge is to push the momentum of this "most happening week" into the months ahead, to sustain excitement about the visual arts after all the crowds are gone.

One year before the millennium turns, South Florida stands between a provincial past steeped in tropically colored clichés and an ongoing push for a visual arts agenda that's increasingly sophisticated—and even trendsetting—in some genres.

"We are in a crossover time, and Miami is a crossover place," says Samuel Keller, a spokesman for Art Basel, which plans to stage a local event, possibly to coincide with a future Art Miami.

The momentum is there for the region to take the next leap forward, capitalizing on rich crossover credentials that have attracted not only the astute, moneyed interests of art fair organizers but also the questing talents of visual artists from Cuba, Jamaica, Peru, Argentina, Spain, and other points across the map.

CULTURAL BLEND

We're an artistic entry point at which Caribbean and Latin American influences mingle with mainstream art world trends, swirling together to produce a distinctive blend. Consider the series of bronze heads sculpted by South Florida artist Edouard Duval-Carrié. While he's not the first contemporary artist to tweak the heroic conventions of classic European sculpture, he's probably the first to layer that visual language with the bristling, sensual symbols of Haitian Vodou spirits.

Eduardo del Valle and Mirta Gómez, an artistic team and married couple who teach at Florida International University, won Guggenheim fellowships in 1997 to continue shooting their photographs of one-room dwellings constructed by Mayan descendants in Mexico's Yucatán Peninsula. Their handsomely detailed images recall the frontal "portraits" of industrial architecture by influential German couple Bernd and Hilla Becher—included in local contemporary art collections of the Rubell Family and Martin Z. Margulies.

But they do something else too. Del Valle and Gómez capture fragments of regional history in the Americas, showing how Indigenous materials like mud and sticks have gradually given way to cement blocks and corrugated tin, modern cast-offs of an ever-more-urbanized era.

IMAGINATIVE EXHIBITS

Then there's the case of a young artist like George Sánchez-Calderón, whose interest in sprawling installations and performance-based political critiques dovetails with his fascination with Cuban culture and history. It's a mix that's drawn him to memorialize the 1961 Bay of Pigs invasion with a project originally scheduled to open this weekend but pushed back to an April 17 opening at vintage Pan Am hangars on South Bayshore Drive in Coconut Grove.

It's an ironically temporary monument, constructed with more than 75 model airplanes, that lovingly, obsessively documents not only the details of the tragic event but the marginal way it's remembered in the minds of most Americans.

Museums are reflecting the imaginative zest that pervades the best art coming out of South Florida these days. Their programs have never looked better. Some of the significant exhibits in the last 12 months have been generated by local institutions, such as the Miami Art Museum's commissioned installation by Ann Hamilton, who was tapped to represent the United States in this year's Venice Biennale, and the survey of late Cuban American painter Carlos Alfonzo—as well as the current *David Smith: Stop/Action* at the Museum of Contemporary Art and a selection of photography from the Martin Z. Margulies Collection at the Art Museum at Florida International University.

Add to the mix wide-ranging permanent collections at the Lowe Art Museum.

Area artists, collectors, dealers, and art aficionados credit the efforts of MOCA, MAM, the Rubell Family Collection, and FIU in particular with ratcheting up the visual arts bar. Not only are exhibits getting stronger, but after-hours programming is becoming more imaginative and enticing.

"I think the museums are doing a much better job of getting out to the public," says local art dealer Fred Snitzer.

Witness the standing-room-only crowd in December at MOCA for a lecture on sculptor Smith by eminent art historian Irving Sandler, a friend of this American master during the most productive years of his career, or for a performance of Pablo Cano's magical marionette play, *Cavaletti's Dream*.

This past summer, recalls MAM director Suzanne Delehanty, close to 100 people came to a Thursday-night drawing class organized with FIU and the New World School of the Arts—including firemen dressed in yellow flame-proof garb. "I thought, my God, do we have an emergency? But they had just come here after work."

To kick off the museum's new series of "Third Thursdays" evening events in September, local musician Nil Lara was invited to perform, drawing a crowd of 700 when, Delehanty says, she had anticipated 400. "We were just stunned by the turnout and the ages, from 25 to 45. I think a broad base audience for the arts is growing here. All the museums are working hard to serve as many people as we can."

WORK'S NOT DONE

But much more needs to be done. Finances are always an issue: "The community is still striving to get on its feet, with the NEA down and corporate giving down, and with the losses of major corporations," says FIU Art Museum director Dahlia Morgan, referring to the recent departures of Knight Ridder and others.

The gallery scene is lagging. "People continue to feel that they need to have their opinion vetted in New York," says collector Maggie Hernandez, a Museum of Contemporary Art honorary trustee and board member of Friends of the Lowe Art Museum. She's referring to local collectors who shop up north, even purchasing art there by South Florida artists affiliated with galleries here.

"That's really hard on the whole art scene," Hernandez says. "For artists to exist here, you need to have local people acquiring [their] art."

Says Snitzer, "I think the problem remains that we are lacking an enthusiastic audience that recognizes what the outside recognizes, that Miami is a great cultural mix."

Clearly, New York offers seasoned collectors a comforting critical mass of museums and galleries, with an unparalleled range of choices. But there are qualitative differences as well. While Latin American painters are represented in abundance in galleries lining Ponce de Leon Boulevard in Coral Gables, there's less attention paid to more experimental art that could inject greater visual challenges into the local scene.

Nor is there much crossover between museum and gallery offerings—as is common in New York, enriching private collections. The current show of paintings and works on paper by Russian artist Maxim Kantor, at both the Bass Museum of Art and Virginia Miller Galleries, is one exception.

STILL "TRAINING AN AUDIENCE"

The root of the gallery issue seems to go back to a deeply conservative strain that has traditionally pervaded dealers and audiences alike. "We're really in the business of training an audience right now," says MAM assistant curator Amy Rosenblum, who would have liked to see a more ethnically diverse audience at, for example, the MAM opening for Ann Hamilton or at a gallery opening this summer for Cuban-born artist Carlos Cardenas. "It's understandable, but I think we could work on mixing it up more."

Yet, says Miami dealer Genaro Ambrosino, "the crowd in my gallery has changed drastically since I moved from the Gables. I get fewer people with money but more people interested in contemporary art. I see a lot of young people who are usually not drawn to art exhibitions but who feel something is happening and they want to be a part of it."

The artists themselves are taking a more active role in mixing things up these days, generating events that feed upon the Art Miami week's global and local synergy. Compared to museums putting on big-budget shows or private collectors amassing internationally known works, their efforts seem modest. But they are critical to the community's creative future.

KEEPING MOMENTUM

The projects of artists like Tom Downs, Robert Chambers, and Sánchez-Calderón help keep the momentum going with innovative ways to cultivate audiences and generally support the production of art.

Tucked among a row of auto-body shops in Miami's warehouse district, Sánchez-Calderón's studio is lined with the art magazines and books you'd expect to find in the digs of a former student at the Rhode Island School of Design, from where he graduated four years ago. It's also home to maps of Cuba, photocopied State Department documents about the island, schematic designs of the Douglas A26 "Invader" flown in the April 1961 Bay of Pigs invasion, and a miniature brigade of sage-green model airplanes also flown in the ill-fated attack.

The planes—along with a tethered 30-foot helium balloon of a "really p—ed-off" pig aimlessly floating about—make up his monument. He says they'll resemble "a parade going nowhere" and are the fruits of a year's worth of research and conversations with Bay of Pigs veterans. Sure to be controversial, the project dives into a defining moment of South Florida history. Sánchez-Calderón says it will pay certain homage to an event that's considered in more heroic dimensions here than anywhere else.

It's just the beginning of his plans. An ebullient figure whose conversation jumps between jokes about James Bond's military exploits to an earnest discussion of the social activism of German artist Joseph Beuys, he says he wants to form a nonprofit corporation that would support an alternative space and dispense grants to artists. "I really want to make Miami stand out because I like it here. As an artist, if you go to New York, you're a sponge, but if you stay in Miami, you make roots here. Art isn't just something that goes on the wall that you sell—it's about making the community you live in a better place. I want to make some noise. I will not go quietly into the night."

LEADERSHIP ROLES

Other artists are taking leadership roles as well. Downs, a video artist whose work was shown last summer at MAM in *New Work: Words & Images* along with the multimedia installations of Janet Cardiff and Vernon Fisher, put together a video and film screening last weekend at the Wolfsonian-FIU of work by an international group of young artists—Tacita Dean, Mona Hatoum, Liisa Roberts, and Sophie Tottie—along with a new work of his own, *Coil*.

Compared to the sparkling and flashing video sculptures by the long-established Nam June Paik, whose works are showcased at several galleries at Art Miami and whose 1963 show of altered TV sets in Germany was most likely the first video art displayed anywhere, these provocative pieces are less about high-speed technology and more about the nature of narrative, immersing viewers in the painstaking process of examining conflicting bits of visual and written information.

Speaking from his sleek office in Avalon, a Coral Gables film production company where he works his day job (he's a 1988 graduate of the University of Miami's School of Motion Pictures), Downs admits that "it's a difficult thing to make art and put together shows as well." His motivation was to offer an edgier alternative to the video offerings at Art Miami, which have traditionally been slim, and to show visitors examples of cultural activity generated here.

"I think the art fair is a great place to go to get out of New York when it's cold," he says, speaking in laconic tones that mirror the minimal, understated look of his quietly confrontational video. "But I also think it's a time to look at work in Miami, as opposed to it being a kind of convention where people enjoy South Beach nightlife."

MATCHING ARTISTS

The peripatetic Chambers, who shuttles between Miami and New York, is another innovator on the South Florida scene. This inventive installation artist, who always seems something of a conceptual Peter Pan even as shades of gray tint his curly black hair, has traveled in the past year to London and Mexico City, hobnobbing with artists and networking with curators to explore organizing shows that would match Miami artists with artists from those major international art centers.

He has discussed a Mexico City–Miami exchange with Monica de la Torre, director of visual arts and literature at the Mexican Cultural Institute in New York; she says a Miami show could happen in the fall. The two met while working on the *Cambio* shows, which exhibited more than 40 emerging artists from New York and Mexico City in venues in both places during 1997 and 1998. The venture was supported in part by Mexico's National Fund for Culture and the Arts and the Rockefeller Foundation.

"We're trying to create links between artists," says de la Torre, "so that they can grow and create opportunities for themselves."

"If you go out and approach people, things start to happen," says Chambers—not to mention becoming exposed to new ideas from new places. That information, he says, "is fed back into your own cookpot, and you end up with a more interesting dish. It pushes everything to a higher speed."

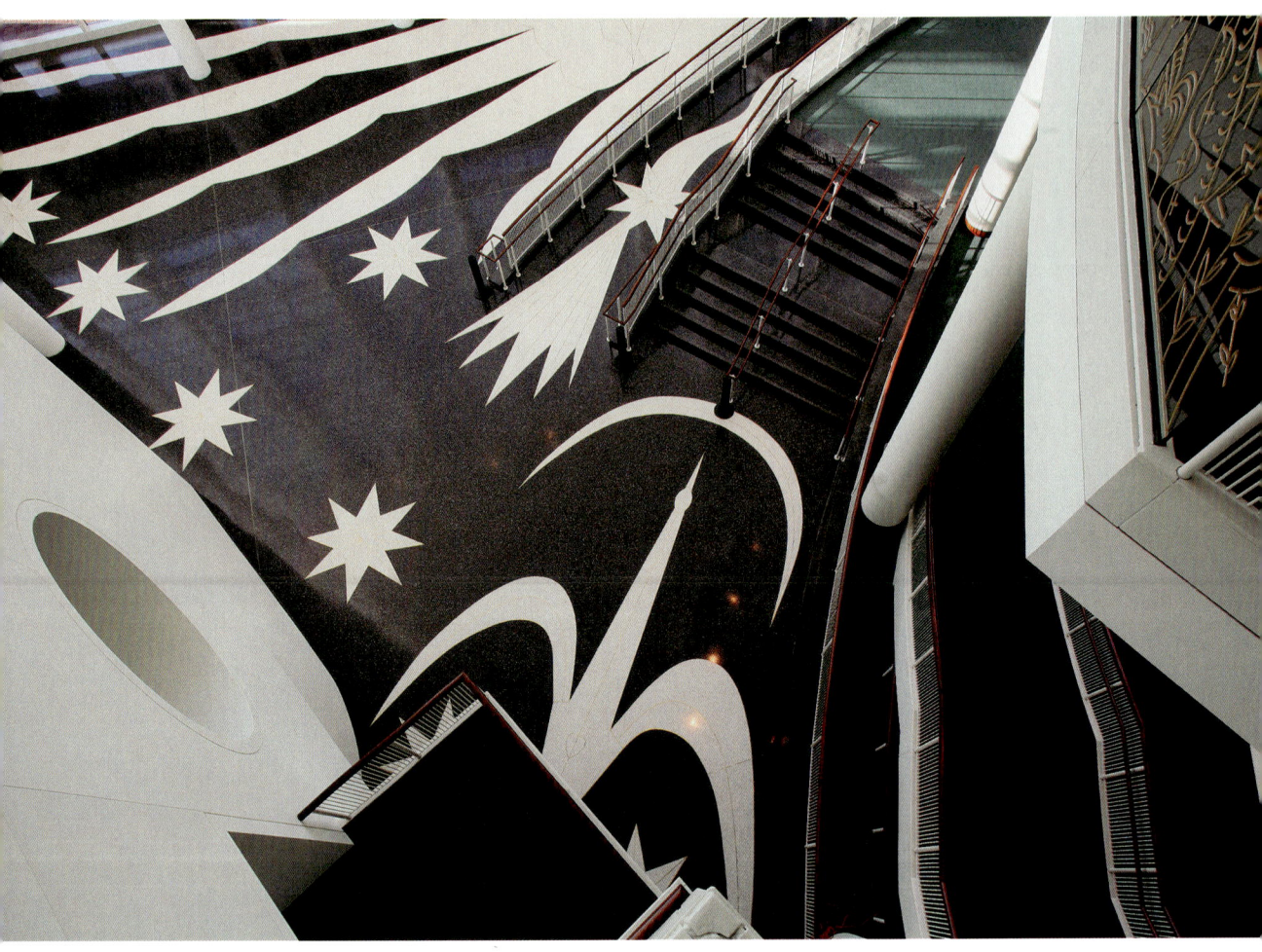

FIGURE 13. José Bedia, *Untitled (Ziff Ballet Opera House Terrazzo Floor)*, 2006. Epoxy terrazzo floor. Image Robin Hill, courtesy of Miami-Dade County Department of Cultural Affairs, Art in Public Places Trust.

JOSÉ BEDIA EXPLORES LINKS
BETWEEN CUBAN AND AFRICAN ART

February 28, 1999

Leaning on a ladder splattered with the black paint that's a constant in his vivid visual narratives, the Cuban-born South Florida artist tilts his head back reflectively. His thick, brown, wavy hair seems to curl even closer to his waist. He is getting ready to tell the tale of San Lazarus, the subject of a still-wet silhouette he's painted on the gallery walls of the Art Museum at Florida International University, site of *José Bedia*, the fierce and fascinating solo show of his never-exhibited personal collection of paintings, drawings, and sketchbooks.

His eyes widen. The story begins.

"San Lazarus was a prince—a rich, wealthy, handsome man. He had a lot of lovers, a lot of women. So he was asking a favor from Olofi [the Yoruba god], if he can have all the women he wants."

Bedia goes on. The favor was granted, so long as San Lazarus reserved Thursday as a day of rest from lovemaking and prayed to God instead. But San Lazarus forgot his promise and soon became sick with leprosy. Forgiveness was granted again, but his rich grandeur did not return. "He loses his crown," Bedia says. "He was homeless, a lone traveler, lying down in the street."

In Cuba, Bedia says, "they have two San Lazaruses," referring also to the Saint Lazarus in traditional holy robes. "But the San Lazarus of the people is the guy with crutches, Babaluaye. He looks so weak, but he is so powerful. If you promise something to him, you have to pay for it. Otherwise, you'll be in trouble."

The Lazarus legend comes to new life in *Mi Coballende (Protector of Patron Saint)*, an installation Bedia created at FIU, dominated by an engulfing, electrifying silhouette. A man's black torso rises from the floor, tattooed with curvy chalk lines pointing to earth and sky, emblazoned with Afro-Cuban symbols standing for the crossroads between life and death. Vast arms extend around corners, one morphing into a giant dog's head, another draped with a tattered roll of burlap, emblems of the humbled but now beneficent Lazarus. Outlines of thorny trees sprout from his body; a tiny leggy man seems to race desperately along one gangly arm. As the work tells its story, boundaries between myth and man and forest blur.

It's a vivid example of the sort of work that's brought Bedia international acclaim—particularly since he left Cuba for Mexico in 1991, eventually settling in Miami with his wife and son. His art stands out for its elegant and assertive draftsmanship and the way it's often laced with deft homages to Native American drawings on animal hide and to action-figure comic books.

Even more striking, though, is the way Bedia transforms eloquent scenarios expressing Afro-Cuban imagery and spiritual values into his own brand of contemporary art. This comes through in his direct graphic style, which he compares to "a primitive comic." It also surfaces in his love of symbolically loaded materials—whether it's the beaded Afro-Cuban ritual staff or even the weighted diving shoes, metaphors for mining primal myths, that are part of his installation here.

"For me, the object is very important," Bedia says. "It's a fetish—to have this thing that connects you with people even though they lived hundreds or thousands of years ago."

NON-WESTERN VIEW

His is an alchemical process that is gaining more notice amid the art world's current interest in work removed from the dominant American culture.

"I think Bedia's art is actually about providing an alternative, even a warning against Western culture," says South Florida art historian Roni Feinstein, who wrote the catalog essay for the FIU show.

In Bedia's primal universe, no one is truly disconnected from the natural world. In the rhythmic and bilingual *Nkunia Brava (Fierce Forest)*, a wilderness of angular branches is rendered as an elaborate network of limbs and heads so that plant, animal, and person become one vital hybrid.

"In a world where everyone is sending each other email and going shopping on the internet, his work is a reminder that there's another world out there with real, physical experience, with spiritual values," Feinstein says.

Yale art historian Robert Farris Thompson, author of essential books on African and African American culture and the opening-night lecturer for the Bedia show, praises Bedia's fluid adaptation of image and idea from non-Western sources—and especially from the extraordinarily rich Kongo culture of West Africa, carried across the Atlantic to emerge in the Afro-Cuban religion of Palo Monte. (Palo Monte, meaning "trees of the sacred forest," venerates spirits living outside crowded cities.)

This is not a matter of amateur anthropology—even though the artist himself jokes that if he hadn't been so seduced by filling up sketchbook after sketchbook with restless drawings, he might well have entered that field.

A friend even once called him a frustrated anthropologist, Bedia says. And certainly, he's fed his muse with what some might call field studies. These include an apprenticeship in 1985 to a Lakota shaman on the Rosebud Reservation in South Dakota and, more recently, a visit to the Southwestern Yaqui tribe during Easter week, when the Yaqui mount their own "Days of the Deer" festival.

"I learn things from my eyes and ears. This is different from when you learn only from books," he says of his travels. Archaeology, another way to recover the past, has also fascinated him ever since he began finding carved shards of Cuba's native Taíno and Siboney history buried in the island's soil and sand.

An endlessly inventive artist, Bedia has dedicated his career to alternative ways of digging, and his creative excavations have struck not only past but present truths. Deeply influenced by his direct involvement with Native American and Palo Monte rituals, his art is in sync with the changing urban landscape.

"Bedia's right at the forefront of contemporary art and culture. America has become the first universal nation on this planet," says Thompson, noting the evermore visible presence of people with Asian, Native American Indian, African, and Hispanic roots. "Particularly in Miami. Miami is teaching the world what it will be like in the 21st century, and José is teaching us how to move into this multiethnic situation. He is at the very least trilingual."

Bedia's paintings and drawings are nearly always inscribed with sayings in Spanish or the Kongo language so that their observations and admonitions mingle with scenes of people and animals negotiating crossings of earth, sea, and sky. Their migrations tell the story not only of exiles and immigrants but of moral choices that define life's journeys through a universe fraught with intricate connections.

"Who knows more, Isabel or Isabelita, who knows more?" is a typical translated inscription. "It's a sermon about paying attention to our elders," says Thompson, "instead of just shoving them into a condo for old people."

THE OTHER "MAMBO"

This query is called a mambo, a Kongo expression meaning "most important matters." These mambos are not the foot-tapping dances of 1940s Cuba but moral guides for living. Often, they remind us that time is running out for everyone. Even for the rich and handsome.

The cautionary tale of the once-handsome Lazarus, steeped as it is in Afro-Cuban lore carried so long ago to the Caribbean, is really not so different—as Bedia will tell you with a burst of bemused laughter—from the catastrophe that beset a famous fallen charmer of Irish extraction, the terribly two-faced Dorian Gray.

The "Cuban Dorian Gray," which Bedia's syncretic mind has suddenly dubbed Babaluaye, is just one example of his love of layered narratives. Another is the story about a 10-year-old Cuban kid who recklessly clambered up a fence, only to fall and chip his two front teeth so that, forever after, they formed an odd little space, shaped like a triangle. "He was spoiled," Bedia confesses.

When the kid grew up and found himself doing a six-month compulsory military stint in Angola for Cuba in 1985, imagine his surprise to see tribesmen in southern Angola pointing at him. "They made a joke with me about my teeth," he said. "Mostly the men speak Portuguese, but my Portuguese was so bad, we were just talking with each other by gestures and laughing."

It turned out that the soldier's smile bore an uncanny likeness to those of various tribesmen in Angola. In the southern part of the country, men customarily cut their teeth to form a similar triangular pattern as a way of paying homage to the cattle that are the focus of their nomadic life. In the north, men of another tribe cut their teeth so that they form a triangular opening, making it easier to chew a sugarcane-like fruit during ritual ceremonies.

The 10-year-old kid was Bedia, of course. His tale of the chipped teeth resonates as an especially striking coincidence, for Bedia's work is marked by his passionate fascination with the art and culture of West Africa and by his profound awareness of how that intricate system of imagery and values has wound its way into the Afro-Cuban religions of Santería and Palo Monte.

Frustrated with the academic approach offered by his art training in Havana, Bedia was grateful when one teacher introduced him to the links between Cuban and African art. His later initiation into Palo Monte, he recalls, "was a conscious idea to recover my culture. When you are connected with [this tradition], many things develop for you. You can read reality in nontraditional ways. They teach you many things about the forces of nature in the river, the mountain, the sea, the ocean, the wind."

Not only does Bedia collect cross-cultural stories; he collects objects too. His Miami home is filled with dozens of African as well as Native American artifacts, from painted drums used by the Tarahumara tribe in Mexico to carved shell objects of Taíno and Siboney origin, which the artist found as a teenager along beaches and hills in Cuba.

"When you live inside this environment, you must learn something," Bedia has said. "For at some moment, the symbol must open up to you. That is my technique. I try to find knowledge from many different places."

Perhaps the place that's given him the most knowledge is the sacred shrines of Palo Monte, which he began visiting in Havana at age 16 with his mother. Less than 10 years later, in 1983, Bedia was initiated into the priesthood of Palo Monte. A night of song and dance unfolded in a room painted brilliant blue with blazing stars, evoking the world's wheeling cycles between night and day, life and death.

Thompson, who was initiated with Bedia at his side a few years later, recalls the circular and cross-shaped Kongo designs, drawn in white chalk on the floor. Called "cosmograms," they represent the intersecting forces of life and death, God and man. "That's where you stand and swear to be a better person," Thompson says.

The cosmograms, also sliced with a knife into an initiate's skin as signs of spiritual strength, appear on figures in countless paintings and drawings by Bedia. At FIU, they score the shoulders of a lone, lean, silhouetted figure in the painting *De Vuelta al Barrio* (*Return to the neighborhood*). Carrying a suitcase in each hand, he seems nearly trapped in a chasm of bleak apartment buildings, their windows resembling ominous eyes—yet this figure's restless, taut posture suggests a defiant and mobile vitality very much at odds with the barren cityscape.

More Kongo circles, spun into a concentric maze, appear in another painting at FIU, *Isla Sola* (*Lone island*). The circles revolve inside the silhouette of a large, disembodied head, which appears to be watching a swimmer fleeing a moonlit shipwreck. It's a dreamlike scene, with the man's head seemingly laced together by a network of tree branches so that he also resembles a forested island.

Both paintings pull us into a vortex of unsettling migration and cyclical motion, themes that South Florida poet Adrian Castro—a Bedia admirer—considers both consummately Caribbean and truly universal. Born and raised in Miami by parents from Cuba and the Dominican Republic, Castro shares Bedia's deep sensitivity to the rich themes of Afro-Caribbean culture. Not only has Castro translated into English the Spanish works, laced with African expressions, by 1930s Puerto Rican poet Luis Palés Matos, but the Miami poet is a Babalawo Ifá priest of Santería.

Asked to read from his new book of poems at this exhibit on March 17, Castro also wrote the poem "Para la installation de José Bedia" for a 1996 Miami Light Project performance at the Rubell Family Collection soon after Bedia created a room-sized installation, *Naufragios* (*Shipwrecks*), for the collection.

Born in Havana in 1959, Bedia studied art at Escuela de Arte de San Alejandro and at the Instituto Superior de Arte. He is the best known among the group of "'80s generation" Cuban artists, whose work represented a significant break with tradition.

In the late 1980s, Bedia began to chart a place on the art world map when his work appeared in biennials in Havana and São Paulo and in the 1989 *Magiciens de la Terre*, a prominent show at the Centre Georges Pompidou in Paris. In 1993, he was the youngest of five Cuban-born artists tapped for the landmark *Latin American Artists of the Twentieth Century* at New York's Museum of Modern Art.

For the past two years, Bedia has been developing designs for the Opera and Symphony Hall lobbies of Miami's new Performing Arts Center (now the Adrienne Arsht Center for the Performing Arts of Miami-Dade County). These projects were commissioned by Miami-Dade County Art in Public Places.

"José Bedia will measure up as very important," says Amy Cappellazzo, director of the Rubell Family Collection, though she admits that, despite Bedia's growing reputation, visitors to the collection aren't always familiar with his distinctive style and materials. "A lot of Europeans see the work by Jeff Koons here and they nod approvingly, but when they see José, they fall off the map. It has a whole different set of African and Caribbean references that don't even register on their scale."

Bedia's accomplishments register for Roberto Matta, the legendary Latin American master and 1940s surrealist. After a meeting was arranged between the two artists at Matta's request, the elder Latin American attended a brunch at Bedia's home in January 1998. The dozen guests included Bedia's dealer, Fred Snitzer. "Matta was very charming, holding court," says Snitzer, "and he loved José's collection [of African and Native American art]. He kept saying, 'Ooh, can you get me one of those?' But it was clear that he recognized something in Bedia as very special."

In memoriam: Robert Farris Thompson, 1932–2021

TAMI KATZ-FREIMAN

Curator Defines Cuban-Israeli Link

June 20, 1999

Tami Katz-Freiman sips cappuccino at a café just across from the ArtCenter/ South Florida gallery on Lincoln Road, where crowds gather for an opening on a recent Saturday night. The moist, sultry blue thunderclouds overhead remind her of dawn breaking over St. Mark's Square in Venice, a spectacular sight she saw while making her way to the airport for a flight back home from the Venice Biennale.

Combating jet lag with Italian caffeine, Katz-Freiman talks about the ArtCenter exhibit, *Currently: Art Focus 1, Summer 1999*, which she curated with Goran Tomcic, director of the Centre Gallery, Wolfson Campus, Miami-Dade Community College. "This was a challenge for us to make our mark," she says. "It's an interesting job, being a curator. In a way, it's like gambling. You gamble on some people that you really believe in. They're very young, but they're very promising," she says of the artists, ages 24 to 28, in the show.

These are the types of risks that Katz-Freiman, 44, a writer and former curator at the Tel Aviv Museum of Art, loves to take. With her quick sense of humor, corkscrew blond curls, and owlish, tortoise-shell glasses, the Israeli-born and -educated independent curator has been an active player in Miami's museum and gallery scene since arriving in 1994 with daughter Noa and husband Mooli Freiman, whose business in Latin American agriculture brought them to South Florida.

She's made her mark here with adventurous shows, thoughtful essays, and passionate enthusiasm for the artists she champions, from both South Florida and Israel. Her most ambitious project to date was the well-received *Desert Cliché: Israel Now—Local Images*, a survey of contemporary Israeli art that she curated with Amy Cappellazzo, which opened at the Bass Museum of Art in 1997 and traveled to New York, Atlanta, and San Francisco.

RETURNING TO ISRAEL

In August, Katz-Freiman and her husband will return to Tel Aviv because their daughter, now a teenager, wants to attend high school in Israel. But this isn't merely another symptom of South Florida's elasticity, with talent often moving in and out, but also an example of how traveling curators can spread the word about visual artists from one region to another. Sometimes that word can embody startling insights, such as the connections Katz-Freiman is defining between Cuban and Israeli artists.

"I'm not the same person I was five years ago," she said during a recent interview at her art-filled North Miami Beach home. "I opened myself to an unknown world for me, which was the Latin scene, about which in Israel there is no knowledge at all. Israel is totally oriented toward European and US art. It was a revelation just to look at all these Latin motifs and to witness all the changes that have happened here," she says, referring, among other changes, to the opening of the Museum of Contemporary Art and the Rubell Family Collection.

On her desk is a sheaf of proposals for shows that are currently "cooking," as she puts it. They are, so to speak, spiced with her exposure to South Florida and Cuban artists, though it's too early to say which ones.

BEDIA TO JERUSALEM

One project is certain. "I'm bringing José Bedia to Jerusalem," she says of the internationally admired Cuban exile artist who settled in Miami in the early 1990s. Katz-Freiman is one of 13 curators chosen to select artists to exhibit in October in Art Focus 1999, the third edition of Jerusalem's biennial. She's tapped Bedia and Israeli painter Tsibi Geva, whose abstract imagery recalls the kaffiyeh, the traditional Arab head covering that has become a loaded, pervasive image in Israeli culture. Each will create a site-specific installation for the event, which includes some 70 artists from Israel, Cuba, China, Europe, Japan, and the United States.

Her pairing of Bedia and Geva is, she admits, an early chapter "in a big story, in an exhibition with Cuban artists from Cuba, Cubans from Miami, together with Israeli artists, in as many venues as possible, including Miami and Havana."

"I know this is utopia right now. I know how many mines I would find in the way," she says, taking a deep breath, but "in five years from now . . . maybe things politically will change."

She's traveled to Cuba three times since February 1998, once to give a lecture about Israeli artists at the Wifredo Lam Center of Contemporary Art in Havana, and is amazed by the parallels she finds among Israeli and Cuban artists.

"Of course there are a lot of differences, but there are aspects that make the linkage very interesting," she says. Artists from both countries speak of the conceptual influence of Marcel Duchamp, Hans Haacke, and Joseph Beuys and are interested in manipulating nationally charged visual icons, from the kaffiyeh to the balsero.

BOTH ISLANDS IN OWN WAY

Both countries share a fierce sense of isolation. Cuba "is a small island, and we consider Israel an island among all the Arab countries," she says. "In Israel we have the Arabs, and the Cubans have the Western world and the Clinton administration. There is a political tension and passion in Cuba that makes me as an outsider feel at home."

Katz-Freiman, a supporter of Israeli Prime Minister-Elect Ehud Barak and his peace-minded mandate, is quick to emphasize that Israel is a democratic country with freedom of speech, unlike Cuba. Still, she says, politics are intensely personal in both places: "If the government of Israel decides something about the Palestinians and Lebanon, it has to do with your own life, with your children. It's the same in Cuba. It has to do with what [you] will have to eat."

Looking forward to developing this groundbreaking tale of two islands, she pauses to look back at her time in South Florida. "This was a peaceful place for me to develop my career and my understanding of the world. It was a break from the hysterical situation I'm used to."

Many people, of course, would say South Florida is fraught with its own brand of hysteria.

"OK," she smiles, "they should come to Tel Aviv and see what is hysterical."

WILLIAM MAGUIRE

Night Vision Inspires Photographer's Work, Array of Snapshots on Display

June 23, 1999

It was an accident that drew William Maguire into the nightlife, into the after-hours world of lonely Southern streets, neon-lit strip malls, and rain-slick parking lots.

It happened in 1972 in Chicago, where he was a graduate student at the Institute of Design. Trapped in a traffic jam in rapidly fading light, he stuck his camera out the window of his van and snapped a picture.

"I had no notion about photographing at night," said Maguire, whose work is presented in the current Visual Arts Faculty Exhibition at the Art Museum at Florida International University. "I just wanted to shoot with a new lens."

Then, he says, breaking into a metaphor made for a photographer, "a light went on. . . . I think lots of wonderful things come from unexpected sources."

Night shots spoke to him then, and still do now, for their "theatricality, their quality of stillness."

Out of that vision, Maguire has built a solid body of work that shines gently into drowsy, banal edges of Americana—from a gas station in Bull Gap, Tennessee, to a Twistee Treat ice cream stand in Sebring, Florida.

It's a vision that manages to be unblinking and kind at the same time, recording run-of-the-mill places with a ghostly and sad dignity. It bears the imprint of two of Maguire's favorite American artists, painter Edward Hopper and photographer Walker Evans.

In the current exhibit of photographs from 1993 to 1998, Maguire illustrates his knack for using that theatrical aura to spotlight, for example, scenes that almost look like accidents: the ugly white boxes in a lot in Lake City, Florida, that are prefab homes for sale; the twin signs announcing "Auto Repair" in two side-by-side buildings separated by a strange fountain of light; the shabby downtown storefront painted with the message "Holiness Is Beautiful," as if daring the eye to find loveliness on this nondescript and forlorn street.

LACKING SENTIMENT, CHARM

Robbed of sentiment and charm, these places resonate with the simple strength of formally balanced compositions, documenting the rhythms of urban growth and decay as they unfold under the silvery glare of streetlights.

Only rarely does Maguire veer too far into a region he calls "sweet," flirting with sentimentality, as in his shot of a ramshackle Key West cottage shrouded with vines.

His vision shines best in a work like the one that shows a florist's shop in Maysville, Tennessee. It's a squat building dwarfed by a big, asphalt-colored sky heavily crisscrossed with power lines. Wreaths hang in the window, fussy with the tiny, hard-to-see details that celebrate a town's births and deaths.

"Here's this humble little store that seems lost in the godforsaken darkness of Maysville," says Maguire. He's interested in places like this, as well as in the equally squat Tastee Treat stand shaped like an ice cream cone, "not in a kitschy way," he says, "but in a way [that will] cast them in our memory."

A VISIT TO BOLIVIA

A good portion of this show is devoted to photographs Maguire took last summer during a visit to La Paz, Bolivia, and during a field trip with students to San Pedro de Atacama, Chile, a small town in the Atacama Desert.

These were shot mainly in the late afternoon, when intense sunlight softens and shadows become a bit sharper, and they lack the theatrical flair of Maguire's nighttime scenes. These images might have been better served by a break from the artist's persistent use of the 11-by-14-inch print. A larger scale might give viewers a closer encounter with the still-quiet but more monumental presence marking many of these landscapes.

Maguire says that for this work, he was inspired by Timothy O'Sullivan's landmark images of the similarly barren and dry American Southwest, shot shortly after the end of the Civil War. Admittedly, a well-known work like O'Sullivan's *Sand Dunes, Carson Desert* is only 7¾ by 10⅝ inches, but this show of so many modestly scaled images cries out for a few bold variations.

IMAGES OF DRYNESS

Maguire, nevertheless, is skilled at rendering telling details in the scorching desert light—surely a sensibility suited to one who can ferret them out in dusk and darkness. Instead of focusing on his signature darkness, these images are about dryness. They show the searing lack of moisture shaping a curving rock and adobe fence or the circular remains of a pre-Columbian dwelling rising from a sandy moonscape.

Other images document a place rather than a mood, including chess players on a narrow street and what's known as the witch's market in La Paz, where medicinal herbs and other organic materials are sold. Here, Maguire has trained his lens on the unsettling spectacle of fetal llamas with gawky necks and big birdlike eyes.

Despite all these accomplished vistas of distant and dry regions, the best is a rare night vision: a hilltop view of the lights of La Paz. Lights twinkle in tiny, fuzzy white orbs, scattered over a rambling mass of tile roofs, apartments, and shops. The few buildings that stand out are gracelessly functional; as always, Maguire has an honest eye for humble, even desolate architecture.

But with that honesty comes a mind for magic, too, for the transforming luster unique to night.

Silly/Sad Photos Disarming—but Shoes Have Sass

August 1, 1999

Michael Carlebach has a keen eye for accidental humor. Barbara Young has an artful flair for topics both amusing and thoughtful. Put their sensibilities together and you get a disarming pair of summer shows at the Miami-Dade County Main Library.

In the auditorium is *This Way to the Crypt: American Studies by Michael Carlebach*, some 100 black-and-white photographs Carlebach shot in travels through Florida and other Southern states, the Northeast, Midwest, and West from the late 1960s to 1998. In the second-floor exhibition space is *All God's Children Got Shoes: Artists' Shoes*, curated by Young, the library's art services supervisor, showing how shoes can leap from plodding apparel to sculptural object.

In this era of celebrity photographs and digital wizardry, Carlebach affectionately stakes out the unfamous with deceptively simple, straight shots in the tradition of Walker Evans, Robert Frank, and Mary Ellen Mark. He looks for the collision of consumerist and corny Americana—Elvis impersonators, an alligator-themed tourist trap, Burger King billboards, satellite dishes—with unassuming settings and then quietly snaps a serendipitous picture that's both familiar and startling.

His 1992 photo in Kelly, Wyoming, shows a satellite dish plopped on the forested hills of a ranch, hardly a radical sight till you realize it's silhouetted against a Native American tepee.

Or there's the heavily made-up bleached blond in a wrinkled Marilyn Monroe T-shirt, looking like an aging Marilyn herself, wielding a camera at the 1995 Luciano Pavarotti concert in Miami Beach. There's the mother with her preschool- and middle-school-aged sons dressed in white Elvis suits and pomaded hair, waiting for the 1993 Elvis Parade in Kansas City to begin.

"A couple of people were celebrating the fat Elvis, but mostly it was this exuberant Midwestern celebration of an iconic pop figure," remembers

Carlebach, a University of Miami professor of communications and American studies who has written two books on photojournalism. "There was an Asian Elvis who sang 'Rub Me Tender.' There was a Fishing Elvis who had a jelly doughnut attached to his fishing rod. They weren't taking themselves or Elvis seriously," he says. Carlebach, too, is not afraid to be silly, documenting a sign for a "Jelly Sale" next to Piggy's Nude Review in Goulds, Florida.

His gift for humor is a leavening complement to the harsher, angrier locales in what he calls our country's "peoplescapes." This comes through in his image of a goofy, touristy Keys billboard scrawled with "Hang Angela Davis Now" or of a comatose-looking hospital patient, hooked up to all sorts of tubes, in a room framed by a computer-printed banner proclaiming, "Merry Christmas."

But that's as you'd expect for a funny-sad series called *This Way to the Crypt*. "It's a sign I saw many years ago in St. Paul's Cathedral in London," Carlebach explains. "We are all headed to the crypt, but there are going to be some good moments along the way, and I want to photograph them."

THE ART OF BEING WELL-HEELED

"Do shoes," said Barbara Young, and they did.

They did brake shoes, shoe trees, shoofly pie. They did spike heels and espadrilles, clunky shoes that grow moss, and tiny ceramic pumps that sport wings. They dissected a loafer and lavished a satin slipper with feathers and dolls.

Artists have obliged Young with inventive responses to the offbeat themes of her summer shows at the Main Library for several years (past themes included books, boats, and even bookmarks). The witty current show pairs the charming with socially charged images. It finds room to reinvent the Cinderella story, with shoes by Monica Eichmann, Karen Rifas, and Susan Banks, and to revisit the African American legacy of a shoe shiner's toolbox in an assemblage by Mildred Howard.

All God's Children Got Shoes: Artists' Shoes is on view on the second floor of the Main Library, presenting more than 50 works by artists chiefly from South Florida. A smaller companion show is *Shoes of the 20th Century*, with footwear from 1900 to the present from the collection of the International Fine Arts College Historical Costume Museum, curated by Charlene Parsons and ranging from sparkly antiques to a new punkish number shining with safety pins.

WHY SHOES?

It's a personal summertime thing, says Young. "I grew up with Buster Brown shoes. . . . It was a big deal in the summer to get new shoes. I always got red sandals," she acknowledges with a laugh and then steps into a more aesthetic mode. "I like the form of shoes. Everyone has them. They are a personal object."

The show's title comes from a verse in the African American spiritual "All God's Children Got Wings," echoing what you might call the universal characteristics of shoes. Young underscores that notion by noting that the United States produces 250 million pairs of shoes each year and imports another 850 million.

The artfulness of footwear might be less obvious, though no less an artist than Andy Warhol began his career with his now-famous drawings of shoes and other fashion accessories for *Vanity Fair*, *Glamour*, and *Mademoiselle*. Like some of the artists in this current show, including Dina Knapp and Sherri Tan, Warhol could slip into puns. He did that in his 1960 drawing *Who's Pussyfooting Around?*, in which women's footwear is adorned with the face of a smirking feline—an image that goes on view this month in a show of Warhol's drawings at the Walker Art Center in Minneapolis.

Shoes, as it turns out, fit into a sizable number of artful media and styles, though the immense variety of women's shoes seems to prime the imagination more than men's workaday models. There's photography by Alexis Rodríguez-Duarte (he zooms in on Celia Cruz's unique pumps) and collages by Bud Lee, as well as sculpture, books, and conceptual objects.

Shoes can point the way to flights of fancy or the carnivalesque excess ornamenting Charo Oquet's *Mojo Shoe*. They are versatile emblems of journeys variously dangerous or humorous, such as in the ominous pun present in Robert Huff's steel *Gunshoe* or in Elmer Craig's found object piece, a pair of Honda brake shoes called *Stop That Running*. They can be stand-ins for the body, even vehicles for ironic social comment—witness Rafael Salazar's coolly designed shoe box with photographs of a foot and linen espadrille, titled *Shoe Box* and *Vegetarian Shoe*.

These pedestrian accessories even spring into poetry. University of Miami art historian Paula Harper accompanied a tangle of tired party shoes with her droll poem describing a feminist journey via shoes fit first for baby, then babe, then a bemused celebrant of orthopedically correct comfort. Who knew shoes could support such creative activity?

In memoriam: Paula Harper, 1930–2012
Robert Huff, 1945–2014
Dina Knapp, 1947–2016
Michael Carlebach, 1945–2023

WALTER DARBY BANNARD AND CARLOS ALVES

Mixed Media, Cracked Crocks, and Puddles of Color

August 8, 1999

Fractured light; fractured pots and plates. Kitschy colors of flamingo pink and Venetian Pool blue. Yellow starfish and orange sunsets. They're ingredients for an only-in-South-Florida mosaic of tantalizing textures, one pieced together with wildly different methods, marked by the delicate shadings of hand-rubbed drawings and the fat, muscular lines that industrial-strength brooms leave when they're loaded with paint and shoved across a canvas.

This mosaic makes up two summer shows, *Florida Artists Series: Carlos Alves, Recent Works* and *University of Miami Faculty Exhibition: Darby Bannard, Paintings, 1987–1999* at the Lowe Art Museum, University of Miami.

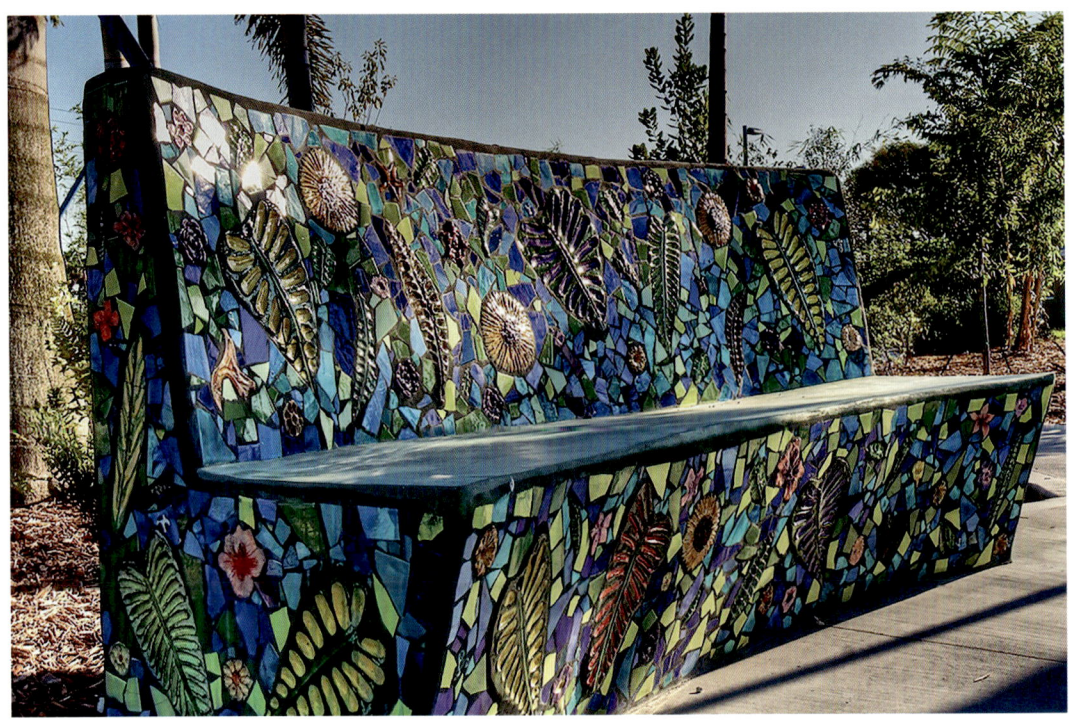

FIGURE 14. Carlos Alves and JC Carroll, *Verde Garden at Verde Gardens*, 2011. Ceramic mosaic tile installation spanning five gardens. Verde Gardens Affordable Housing, 12550 SW 282nd St. Image Yusimy Lara, courtesy of Miami-Dade County Department of Cultural Affairs, Art in Public Places Trust.

Alves is a prolific ceramic artist known for his distinctive urban makeovers, which include the delightful cracked-crockery fountain on Lincoln Road Mall and an exuberant Art in Public Places mural of recycled demitasse cups and dominoes, among other examples of tropical Cuban American nostalgia, at the Metromover station for Eighth Street. For this exhibit, he's created a new ceramic installation as well as graphite rubbings of mosaic floors that he's made for various commissions throughout the United States.

Bannard is a long-standing, dyed-in-the-canvas abstract painter whose debts to Jackson Pollock and Helen Frankenthaler are evident but who stubbornly makes their abstract expressionist and "color field" tradition his own at the end of a century in which painting is repeatedly reported (a) to have died or (b) to be in the throes of a struggling comeback. Since living in South

Florida for most of the decade, he's found that the moist, iridescent lushness of our skies and flora has seeped into his paintings.

"The damned stuff won't go away," writes Robert Sindelir in his catalog essay about Bannard's dedication to the purely painted surface. "There are unredeemable practitioners of this Jurassic pastime right under our noses—people who cannot be dissuaded by an amount of evidence or argument."

People like Bannard. In this series of 44 paintings and works on paper from 1987 to 1999, we see Bannard obsessed with the slash, smear, and pull of paint stretched in thick and thin lines across the flat canvas. There's the sense of yellow-tinted, salmon-colored planes of color floating farther back into space or gently pushing toward us as Bannard plays around with the illusion of depth. Then there's the messy, gyrating, heavy gobs of paint that stick resolutely to the painting's true flatness, seducing our eyes with their rich, luscious puddles of colors.

WET PAINT?

More recent works have grown even more lush, glinting with iridescent gels of paint in colors like aqua, rose, lapis lazuli, orange, and lime green. They still seem wet, as if sticky to the touch. Occasionally, they descend into a swampy murkiness that finally obscures the delicate tensions between surface and depth that have animated Bannard's fascination with form. Named for Florida places—like *Tomoka*, recalling the Tomoka River—these glowing abstractions suggest a humid, fecund world but don't always possess the engaging, muscular rhythms of the large 1987 painting *Aurora*.

While this selection of paintings does get repetitive in that several works seem indistinguishable from each other, Bannard's smaller works on paper are the quiet highlights of the exhibit. Created with oil stick, Krylon spray, and powdery pigments, they demonstrate an impressive range of textures—from the fuzzy, atmospheric orange glow that evokes a hazy sunrise in *Early Riser* to the foamy slashes of white and deep blue that swipe a fluid diagonal stream across the lovely but intense *Clay River*. Bannard lets his love of the natural landscape mingle more obviously with his passion for abstraction in these smaller works, and that's the source of their strength.

MUTED WORKS ON PAPER

For those familiar with Carlos Alves's carnival-colored ceramic pieces, ingeniously layered with unlikely treasures from his collection of smashed plates, pots, and garish knickknacks, this exhibit will be a surprise. It's mostly muted works on paper, graphite rubbings of large-scale installations that can't be moved. There is a large sand-and-broken-ceramic fish sculpture that rests on the floor and three murals of recycled ceramics and fused glass tiles. The murals are charming enough, though they contain too little of Alves's often gritty and irreverent exuberance. The fish piece, *Pescado Grande*, doesn't seem to be finished, suggesting a concept that awaits a stronger execution.

The rubbings themselves are more intriguing, as memories of something we know to be harder and brighter and as subtle shadows and trace marks in their own right. Lobsters, snakes, seashells, and even a shark are enmeshed within a crazy-quilt pattern of broken triangles and circles. They look surprisingly fragile. Given that some of the titles sound an environmental SOS, as in *Save Water*, that fragility may be a concern Alves can express more poignantly in these rubbings than in his lively mosaics.

In memoriam: Walter Darby Bannard, 1934–2016
Robert Sindelir, 1932–2021

MICHAEL CARLEBACH

A Labor of Love Recalls the Way We Were

September 6, 1999

A country milkmaid and a fleet of FedEx carriers are stomping about in Michael Carlebach's office, joined by tinsmiths and carpenters, women rolling cigars, and a man wielding a block of ice.

They make up an impromptu—and, of course, wholly imaginary—Labor

Day parade, for all these workers are in fact memories of real laborers past and present. They live on in photographs that Carlebach, a professor in the Communication and American Studies departments at the University of Miami, has assembled into a remarkable record of the way we once worked.

Most of these images—except for the energetic workers of various ages, genders, and colors whose photos decorate a white FedEx box—are from the late 19th century. They are the size of a compact mirror, printed on thin sheets of blackened iron coated with collodion.

Called tintypes, they were once hugely popular, a cheap alternative to the more expensive and fragile daguerreotype. More durable than a pair of overalls, tintypes reflected the Kodak moment of choice for thousands of American workers who paid a few pennies for the pleasure of acquiring a small self-portrait with the tools of their particular trade. You could keep it in your pocket, stamp and mail it to distant relatives, tack it to the wall with a nail.

After the rise of factories in the 20th century, this process died out; it now seems quaint. Historians have largely overlooked these modest but resilient mementos of a very different workplace, Carlebach says. But to him, the turn of our own century is the right time to rediscover the story tintypes can tell.

"The place of work in American culture is not the same place it was 100 years ago," he says. "Work is a way to get rich, to go to the Gap and the Shoppes at Sunset Place. It's not so much an ideal in and of itself. Back when these pictures were made, there was a nobility to work, whether you were a fence maker or a milkmaid. These people were proud enough of what they did to present themselves as workers. We don't do that anymore."

ITINERANT PHOTOGRAPHERS

A gifted photojournalist, Carlebach speaks almost affectionately about the direct, artless technique of tintype photographers. They were itinerant workers likely to set up shop at county fairs and have remained as anonymous as their subjects. Often, they'd add a rough dollop of pink to a woman's cheeks, a bit of gold to buttons. Their cloth backdrops, featuring leafy glens and shadowy castles, sometimes sagged, spotlighting their clumsy trompe l'oeil settings.

Carlebach holds up one of his favorite tintypes, a man dressed in overalls and tie holding a hammer at his side with the resolute posture of a soldier with a bayonet. Then there's the dashing young man in a sporty cap and bow tie standing next to a bicycle with gleaming spokes. "I love this guy. He's probably a messenger, perhaps even with Western Union. You can see this man is proud of what he does. He has a good job with a modern bike. Maybe he sent it to his mom."

Think about it. When was the last time you went out of the way to have your picture taken with your computer? And in family photos, workaday tools can't compete with the charm of pets, kids on new Rollerblades, and trips to the beach or the mountains.

"Labor Day," muses Carlebach, "used to honor the working man. Now it's a vacation. It's also a day to go out and spend money on the things we are proud to be photographed with."

This change in attitudes toward work had caught the attention of Mark Hirsch, senior editor at the Smithsonian Institution Press, which has published two books by Carlebach on the history of American photojournalism. Hirsch says he's in the "talking stage" with the UM professor about his proposed book on the often touchingly earnest and intent workers in a collection of some 80 tintypes owned by New York photographer Ken Heyman, Carlebach's cousin and coauthor for this project.

"I think what Mike is trying to get at is the transition from a society that celebrates making things to a society that celebrates owning things," says Hirsch. "To me, it really points up a respect for physical labor that is clearly evident in America before and after the Civil War and is less evident today."

WORKING WITH PRIDE

That attention to the hands-on tools of labor—rather than its fruits—is part and parcel of the post–Civil War era, when the economy was battered by a severe depression and when having a good job was a particular source of pride.

Still, it's the pride in craftsmanship that seems most striking—and fleeting—in these shiny pocket-size portraits. Hold one in your hand, tilt it in the light, and watch it flicker in a second from a window into the past to a blurry mirror of present surroundings.

"All of our crafts are sold through Pottery Barn," grumps Carlebach, managing a smile at his overstatement. "This is looking into a piece of American culture—one which if it isn't altogether gone, it's fast disappearing."

Alison Devine Nordstrom, director of the Southeast Museum of Photography in Daytona Beach, shares Carlebach's affection for these no-nonsense workaday images.

INNOCENT REFLECTIONS

She points out that the genre hasn't completely vanished but that its decline holds up a compelling mirror to a past that can look almost innocent to us now, especially as collectors and scholars begin to focus more on the social history embedded in antique, anonymous photographs. "I've seen a couple of pictures of people peering into microscopes. I've seen pictures of people at the typewriter, mostly women, and I've certainly seen a lot of pictures of women at the stove. . . . But the craft industries, like carpentry, are on the decline, and service industries are on the ascent. It's much harder to represent a service industry. There's something wonderful about making things, and that kind of labor we miss."

Today's images of labor can be packaged as artfully as the tintypes were artless. Consider the calculated sense of pep permeating the Madison Avenue–styled FedEx workers on the box in Carlebach's office. These folks hold their rapid-delivery packages with the stylish fervor usually reserved for models in J. Crew catalogs. Smartly turned out in navy shorts and shirts, they could be performing a corporate line dance. These FedEx workers promise an indispensable alternative to that bike-riding, bow-tied messenger of decades ago, and they're surely helping us sprint into a century during which few would notice if tinsmiths and milkmaids disappeared from the dictionary.

Just as important, despite their slick and cool efficiency, the FedExers represent a racially diverse population, one that's conspicuously absent from these tintypes.

"African Americans would have run into considerable resistance from white photographers. We were thoroughly racist back then," says Carlebach. In the late 19th century, however, "there were Black photographers, and there's probably a cache somewhere of tintypes of Black people. There's so much that hasn't been discovered. People overlooked this because they thought it wasn't worth anything."

In memoriam: Michael Carlebach, 1945–2023

CHARO OQUET

Soulful Journey Leads to Gallery

September 26, 1999

It took a long time to get to the party that night in early September. The sky was stained an angry indigo, lashed with the rain of hurricane season in Miami. On the way, artist Charo Oquet had to pass through waterlogged crossroads, and she had quite a few bundles to carry.

But when she finally arrived, dressed in pink and draped in beads, Oquet was ready to celebrate. There were cakes to eat, music to make. It had, after all, taken her more than 10 years to get here, perhaps most of her lifetime.

Hers was a far-reaching pilgrimage, spanning the Pacific and Atlantic, stretching all the way from lush New Zealand forests moist with geothermal steam to sun-bright sugarcane fields in the Dominican Republic. It took Oquet on a roundabout trek from little girls' fancy dress shops to Goodwill stores before the trip ended at the altars of Ambrosino Gallery in Miami.

It was a sojourn, she later reflected, that seemed destined to reach Miami. And that night it did, the night of Oquet's opening at Ambrosino, a cavernous space in an alley of auto-body shops, where the altars glistened. The gallery's spotlights, which have shone on a variety of contemporary works from austere curls of intravenous tubing by Donald Lipski to sleek, oversized tools by

Florencio Gelabert now illuminated a dazzling crush of crepe-paper streamers and torrents of silk and satin heavy with fringe, sequins, and dolls—her syncretic art stitching together the bright allure of birthday piñatas, Roman Catholic icons, and Dominican Vodou parades through sugarcane.

"I've been charged to know more about my own culture, so this has really been a journey," Oquet, 47, said a few days after the opening night of her show, *The Kingdom of Our World*. Wearing a simple linen shirt and khaki skirt, her tousled auburn-tinged hair signifying a busy woman, she settled down on a sofa in a gallery corner to talk not only about her newest work but about her evolution as an artist.

It's a career set within the typically fluid landscape of modern Caribbean life. When she was 10, she and her upper-class family fled the Dominican Republic in the wake of dictator Rafael Trujillo's assassination in 1961. Everyone, including her father, a military officer who took part in the coup, confronted a more humble existence in Bayonne, New Jersey. "My mother didn't even know how to cook anything," Oquet remembers, "and she had to clean other people's houses."

KEPT IN TOUCH

Summer trips and a stint at art school back home kept Oquet close enough to her roots, but it was travel halfway around the world that pushed her face-to-face with her Afro-Caribbean heritage—usually glossed over in Oquet's Roman Catholic upbringing. During the 1980s, before settling briefly in a Dominican neighborhood of Manhattan's Upper West Side, she spent five years in New Zealand with her husband at the time, a filmmaker with whom she later had two children—Jack, now 8, and Gabrielle, 12. It was a productive period, good for painting, but something was missing.

"When I was in New Zealand, I was the only Dominican there that I knew of. . . . It's very Anglo, kidney pie," she says. "There was a total absence of Black culture. Somehow, that part of me came out really needy. I would go to Santo Domingo, and I would bring back images, like the Mami Watta," a water spirit worshipped throughout Central and West Africa.

It was an auspicious and telling choice. The Mami Watta turns out to have a passport even more heavily stamped than Oquet's. Some images show a mermaid that recalls the figureheads on early European ships sailing to Africa. In others, she's a powerful tamer of water snakes—an image traced to a 19th-century German circus poster, which also made its way to Africa via sailors, according to Henry Drewal, an African art history professor at the University of Wisconsin. And as traders traveled between Bombay and the West African country of Togo, the Mami Watta picked up multiple arms and a resemblance to Hindu spirits. In the New World, her way with snakes became saintly. Dominicans call her Santa Marta la Dominadora (the dominating one) or Santa Marta Africana.

She brings wealth to her worshippers, but the price for such success is childlessness.

Though Oquet knew little about the Mami Watta then, she was enthralled by her strength. "She had this wild hair and is just dominating that snake."

THE SNAKE TAMER

She painted the snake tamer many times, and her career blossomed. Later a friend pointed out that Oquet's paintings recalled African carvings of the mermaid spirit, and to this day Oquet marvels at how during those years doctors repeatedly told her she was sterile. Her children arrived and put her art on hold, Oquet says, only after she put away those paintings and the little Mami Watta chromolithograph from a Dominican market.

Mami Watta resurfaces in *The Kingdom of Our World*, in an altar that displays not only her chromolithograph, framed in sequins like a Vodou flag, but a chubby doll with a tiny mermaid stuck to her chest. The doll is swathed in plastic and silken green snakes, radiating multiple, mismatched plastic arms.

Such imaginative adaptations of this globe-trotting water spirit have caught Drewal's admiration. He notes that Mami Watta has inspired countless altars in Africa—beautiful and orderly profusions of flowers, perfume, and color, which are also, he says, "artistic creations." Oquet's work will be part of a show he's curating on the arts of Mami Watta.

A SPIRITUAL WORLD

In town when *Beads, Body, and Soul: Art and Light in the Yoruba Universe*, which he cocurated, opened this summer at the Miami Art Museum, Drewal visited Oquet's studio, filled with the nearly completed altars. He was struck by their extravagant presence. "I felt like I was moving into a spiritual land, a kind of sacred forest of cloth, with streamers, dolls, and photographs. The richness of the materials created a very intense, spiritual feeling. She is drawing on many kinds of sources, as she connects with Haitian Vodou and African beliefs and practices in the Dominican Republic and with her own background," he says. "I think that's the richness. . . . She's kind of a diviner in her own way."

In Oquet's show, there are dolls everywhere—Barbie and Ken, Black and white Cabbage Patch dolls, even Spider-Man. One doll is attached to the black hose of scuba gear, in quirky homage to water spirits. While the artist brings a distinctive take to her materials, Drewal points out that dolls are ubiquitous sacred icons in the African diaspora, where they became veiled versions of African carvings, thus seen as nonthreatening by colonial masters.

Several altars rise upward in swirling layers of bright fabrics and ornaments—reminiscent of the Haitian Vodou "poto mitan," a sacred pole said to link the worlds of spirits and mortals. Drewal compares another altar with long flaps of brilliantly beaded cloth to a Yoruba Egungun costume, with its lengths of cloth in rich patterns that whirl when worn in a ceremonial dance, evoking a powerful spiritual presence.

There are many lavish streams of fabric here, beginning with the dusky blue drapes that surround the clustered altars, requiring visitors to find a way inside. Once in, one finds a scene part carnival parade and part sacred space, with a piñata's explosion of toys thrown in for good measure. You'll see divinely dressed altars sparkling with riotous detail, one circled with offerings of food and drink. There are jingle bells, froufrou pink tutus, a fiery-red Santería robe, a recycled blue ball gown the color of medieval stained glass from House of Lanvin in Paris.

Many of the altars are dressed in clothing and toys scoured from Miami flea markets and Goodwill stores—"places where everybody else finds stuff they send to Haiti and the Dominican Republic," Oquet says. They are often old gifts and rite-of-passage party dresses bound for new uses and places, giving her work a sense of gaudy celebration and magical transformation.

The whole place is spangled with a constellation of star-shaped paper bows, like the bows adorning musicians and marchers in Gagá processions, the Eastertime celebrations in the Dominican Republic that sprang from Haitian Vodou and African Kongo religious rites.

Oquet first learned about Gagá groups when she met Robert Farris Thompson, Yale scholar and influential historian of African and African American art, who has written a short essay about her new work. They met 10 years ago in a museum in the Dominican Republic, where he was with students watching a documentary about Gagá groups' vivid rituals and music performed deep within sugarcane fields. She was fascinated and wanted to see them for herself.

"I had to find my way there," she says. "Since I'm a Dominican bourgeoise, going to the sugarcane fields by myself was not something I could do. I was frozen by that fear of how to get there. Maybe if I was a foreigner I would have just taken a taxi."

Almost seven years later, she found her way. Since then, she's taken many photographs of the groups performing their whirling dances, wearing glittering hats and costumes streaming with bright scarves. She's shown her photographs at Española Way Art Center in Miami Beach, sometimes accompanied by Dominican Vodou-styled flags she has helped students make at Allapattah Middle and Elementary schools during the Dominican Youth Arts Festival.

Not everyone liked the photographs. "I got a phone message that said, 'You'd better not be saying this about Dominicans. We don't do Vodou. I'm going to break your windows.'"

It was a sentiment that did not surprise Oquet, but it is one she finds sadly out of sync with what has made Miami such a special destination for her. "When I lived in the Dominican Republic, I never knew about Haitian culture, Cuban culture. I never went to either country. But living in Miami makes you want to discover all those Caribbean and South American countries and get the bigger picture of your own culture. It's all right here."

HISTORICAL MUSEUM OF SOUTHERN FLORIDA

Cultural Legacies of South Florida and Caribbean History Are Served Well in Ambitious Exhibit

December 5, 1999

The food here is for thought alone, but it's telling that the first thing you see when you enter the newest exhibit at the Historical Museum of Southern Florida is a recipe—a spicy mix of Chinese spinach, salt pork, coconut milk, and hot pepper sauce. Cook them together with other assorted ingredients and you'll have a Trinidad-style treat called callaloo, a Caribbean stew that serves up a surprising variety of tastes and textures. (Historical Museum of Southern Florida is now renamed HistoryMiami Museum.)

As a New World stew that's at once sharp and sweet, callaloo becomes a tangy metaphor for the various objects—from capacious, earthy-colored pre-Columbian vessels to glinting green Coke bottles—that, when joined, tell the story of South Florida.

Myths and Dreams: Exploring the Cultural Legacies of Florida and the Caribbean begins with the shapely tools of Taíno tribes living a millennium ago in what is now the Dominican Republic and leads us through centuries of tragedy and mosquito-braving derring-do, sacred rituals, and shopping trips.

All these fables and foibles come through in this lively exhibit, curated by Florida International University art historian Carol Damian and organized by Miami's Jay I. Kislak Foundation in conjunction with the Historical Museum of Southern Florida. Still, with so much fascinating territory to cover, it's a shame that the show has such a squeezed look about it.

Myths and Dreams is an ambitious undertaking that could use a more expansive treatment—and could benefit from a more inclusive approach showing how this legacy plays out in fine art as well as in cultural artifacts by incorporating painting and photography by such varied artists as Lydia Rubio, Eduardo del Valle, and Mirta Gómez.

That said, *Myths and Dreams* is an often clever weaving of image and historical narrative, especially with its gracefully honed pre-Columbian works, many on loan from the Kislak Foundation. These vessels and tools are paired with 18th-century engravings showing French depictions of Florida Indigenous peoples, including women whose hair falls in Botticelli-like curls, a curious omen of the way the New World would be further fashioned by European egos and desire.

An even earlier engraving by Theodore de Bry gives us a rare chance to study the lengths of that desire, showing a geographically incorrect, sawtoothed map of coastal Florida. Despite the misshapen perspective and forbidding scale, we can see a toy-like galleon sailing determinedly for the craggy coast, just missing a scowling sea monster.

Other mythic representations of Florida from this period include a scene of ostrich-sized spoonbills, alligators with sunbursts carved on their backs, and trees with huge leaves shaped like arrows. The fantasy world they evoke and the wealth such dreams inspired are underscored by the presence of glittering silver bars and coins, unearthed in the Florida Keys by Mel Fisher from the 1622 wreck of the Spanish galleon *Atocha*.

As the show rushes forward to a 20th-century Florida replete with Caribbean influences, there are examples of Florida cracker cabins, cruise liners, art deco hotels, touristy kitsch, and inventive Miami botanica icons blending New and Old World beliefs. There's also a speedy look at the legacy of the cruel trade in enslaved West Africans, with a selection of Yoruba carvings, ritual objects of Haitian Vodou, and iron shackles from the 18th-century slave ship *Henrietta Marie*.

A nearby section crams together Seminole and Miccosukee objects, including a beautiful cotton skirt striped in red. Its brilliant hue connects with the heart appliquéd 1920s quilt from northern Florida, which in turn leads the eye to an over-the-top sculptural concoction of red satin and lace, Charo Oquet's altar to Dominican Vodou deity Ogun.

That's just one example of the rich visual narrative spicing of this show, coursing through layered chunks of history that should have been ladled out in more generous portions.

PRE-BASEL GROUP SHOW, DENNIS SCHOLL CALLS THIS A DEFINING MOMENT FOR MIAMI

Artists Bond in Doomed Building

January 30, 2000

Last weekend was a time of excellent art adventures in Miami.

There was a national-class art fair in Miami Beach and talk of a world-class art fair heading there in the near future. There were lively shows of art sprinkled about Greater Miami, in private and public settings. Artists even took over a condemned building, transforming it into an exciting experiment in public exhibitions.

The weekend was, in short, a milestone in the area's coming-of-age saga in that it demonstrated a clear desire for innovation in the visual arts and a real hunger for challenging exhibition spaces.

As art lovers attended a host of events last weekend, including parties at two internationally admired private collections in warehouse spaces near downtown Miami—the Rubell Family Collection on Northwest 29th Street and Martin Z. Margulies's newly installed contemporary photography collection on Northwest 27th Street—there was abundant buzz about an impromptu art exhibit taking over yet another commercial building: the unprecedented gathering of new, site-specific work by 44 Miami artists in *Departing Perspectives* at the former Espirito Santo Bank Building at 1395 Brickell Avenue.

The exhibition was, according to collector Dennis Scholl, "a defining moment for Miami, showing the community how many excellent working artists there are here. I got a chill walking up and down those floors."

Working for five days at a feverish pace, established artists and ambitious high school and college art students filled eight floors of the soon-to-be-demolished building with an audacious variety of work. Despite a few uneven and grandstanding moments, the multistoried megashow was well worth the attention of the 1,200 visitors who showed up for the opening-night gala, a fundraiser that raised $7,000 for the New World School of the Arts.

Miami art dealer Fredric Snitzer, who curated the event, estimates that another 1,200 people passed through the bank's transformed cubicles and corridors during the project's three-day public showing. It was a diverse crowd that included artists and their friends, parents and kids, collectors and curators, as well as *Art in America* editor Elizabeth C. Baker and author Brian Antoni.

From Karen Rifas's oak leaves, which dangled in delicate strands next to elevator doors, to Purvis Young's frenetic horses painted next to bland travertine floors, the mood was ephemeral in a generous and daring way, igniting a spirit of community among artists and audiences.

Marveling over the colorful portraits painted by New World High School art students in an eighth-floor office space, Rifas looked almost stunned by the bustle of activity animating the doomed bank tower.

"It feels to me like the high after Christo," she said, recalling the brief but immensely memorable *Surrounded Islands* transforming 11 Biscayne Bay islands in 1983.

"This was so energizing. We should have done something like this a long time ago," added María Martínez-Cañas, who papered a window office with a new, meandering view of her deep-blue photographs of shadowy botanical shapes. "Normally you're working all alone—here we were all asking, 'Do you have a broom? Do you have a drill?'"

New Jersey artist Willie Cole, in town for his solo show at the Miami Art

Museum, said the project inspired him to think about similar opportunities in Newark buildings slated for demolition. Luring artists to recycle and re-invent discarded workaday sites, he said, is a chance to reveal "the presence of thinkers in the community."

"The concept is thrilling, and the quality and variety are just dizzying," added Nancy Wolcott, a member of the Miami Beach Cultural Arts Council.

It was a fascinating and fleeting chance to savor South Florida creativity in all its various strands. Hernan Bas, who works with the artist collective known as Team Waif, turned in a deliberately facile, conceptual piece tucked in the corner of a blue-carpeted cubicle. An amusing riff on Félix González-Torres's sparkling piles of cellophane-wrapped candies—as well as a puckish nod to the South Beach cult of glamorously hard bodies—Bas's work was a cascading pile of strawberry-flavored SlimFast titled *Fat Free Corner*.

Eugenia Vargas also played with local allusions to airy esprit de vivre with her glass-enclosed room billowing with constant, mechanically produced bubbles—a spectacle that charmed viewers as they stepped out of a stairwell.

"Bubbles are happy, and they also describe Miami," Vargas said. "I had a lot of fun with this. It's not about the frenzy of 'We have to make a great piece and see if we sell it.' It's all about the pure pleasure of making."

Other routine offices were transformed with rich layers of detail—sometimes suggesting stories and inviting visitors to interject their own narratives, at others offering engaging imagery that refashioned industrial structures. Among the many intriguing works on view were installations by Annie Wharton, Robert Huff, Robert Chambers, Rubén Torres Llorca, Marisa Tellería Díez, Lydia Rubio, and Carol Brown, as well as a striking collaboration by Julian Picaza, Jay Hines, and Bhakti Baxter.

Roberto Behar and Rosario Marquardt clearly enjoyed watching visitors step inside their collaborative work—two connecting rooms reconfigured into a child's simple bedroom and a sandy, candlelit dreamscape dominated by a large paper boat made of maps. It was an enchanting, welcoming refuge.

"It's like a small apartment with a big dream," Marquardt described the piece.

With that remark, she touched on a mighty metaphor for Miami's once-provincial art scene—except that on this weekend, the big dreams turned into reality.

MIAMI-DADE MAIN LIBRARY

Past, Present, and Future, as Seen by *Cultivated* Curator and Artists

August 6, 2000

Barbara Young is musing on the late Fernando García's green-and-pink road maps of Miami, which are part of *Cultivated under the Sun*, the Miami-Dade Public Library System's look at 30 years of South Florida art.

The maps are arranged like a quirky patchwork quilt, part of an adventurous project from the 1980s. In this activity, one that might have sent less-stable souls on an obsessive handwashing spree, participants dug up dirt and transplanted the grimy residues from one neighborhood to another, which were identified on the maps.

García's work is just one of many in the show that prompted Young and artists Carol Brown and César Trasobares to gather at the library and reflect on how Miami's art scene has evolved—for good and ill.

They remember when, in the absence of serious museum attention, artists were nurtured by inventive, low-budget programs at the library and at the old Center of Contemporary Art (now the Museum of Contemporary Art). Things have altered mightily since 1987, when Brown was allowed to show her sculpture for two weeks outside the Center for the Fine Arts (now Miami Art Museum) but, as she recalled, received an icy stare when she asked to show her drawings inside.

On this day, they chat about how the current sophisticated level of activity was fertilized by the creative work represented in *Cultivated under the Sun*.

PUTTING ART ON THE MAP

When Young talks about García, it's easy to see how the artist's project, dirt and all, migrated into a witty metaphor of Miami. It tells a story about a city where people come to reinvent themselves—yet still find themselves attached to reminders of a previous address.

"This was part of a show that had three different locations," says Young, who has been a curator and educator at the Miami-Dade County Public Library System since 1976. "During October, he had a show at the south campus of Miami-Dade Community College, at a bank in Coral Gables, and at the Coral Reef Library. As part of the exhibit, he has these activities that were going on. Fernando would get tons of people involved. There were people that helped him dig, that would photograph him digging. He was funny and intense and always full of ideas."

She moves from talking about earth art to cow art—those wildly painted, highly hyped cows in Chicago that recently became a peculiarly Midwestern brand of public art. Way before Chicago had cows in the street, though, Young says Miami had set up artist-designed dominoes on Biscayne Boulevard. The 1981 project was conceived as a way to publicize the library's move from its old downtown site to its present one on West Flagler Street.

"The original thought would be to have all these dominoes lined up from Biscayne Boulevard down to [Flagler], and then we thought maybe that wasn't practical," she says with a laugh. "That just grew into the idea that we could have huge boxes decorated by artists."

These big, beautiful pieces were set in motion one windy Sunday afternoon, tumbling in a crowd-pleasing cascade of color down streets blissfully free of traffic.

TEACH THE CHILDREN WELL

Brown admits that, as an artist, she looks at *Cultivated under the Sun* with a very different kind of nostalgia.

"When most of this work was done, there were really so few little avenues for us to ever do anything in this town," she says. "It was really frustrating. The difference between then and what we have available to us now is like night and day."

As a sculptor who also speaks passionately about teaching college art students, Brown admits that what she has to say next may sound like sour grapes, but her voice reveals genuine worry.

"What scares me a little bit are the younger artists that are so successful, that are having so many people looking over their shoulders," she says. "When are they going to have the opportunity to let the work really incubate and grow? Some ideas are lousy and you need a chance to throw them away."

When Trasobares, a Cuban-born artist and arts administrator, surveys the drawings, bookmarks, tiny boats, and photographs in *Cultivated under the Sun*, he says he's struck by "the idea of the more senior artists participating in all these activities."

"I studied with [sculptor] Bob Thiele at Miami-Dade Community College in 1969," he says. "I remember that we as kids really admired the fact that artists like Thiele were not only teaching, but there was this mentoring, this transfer of energy over the years that's visible in this room."

"I'm looking at Bob Huff's magnificent early silkscreen," Trasobares continues, pointing to a rainbow-hued work on paper by Huff, a painter, sculptor, and teacher. "At the time it was, like, 'Oh God, Bob has done a silk screen with 30 colors, and it is perfectly registered.' And over the years I've seen him grow into larger pieces. There is this kind of seed quality to the work here, a seed that has blossomed."

LOOKING AHEAD

Talk among the three eventually turned to ideas and admonitions for building on the surrounding heritage of Miami art.

"I hope that Art Basel week is not so crammed with activities that people can forget about Miami the rest of the time," Brown says in reference to the acclaimed Swiss art fair, which is coming to Miami Beach in December 2001. "There's going to be so much to do, and none of us are going to get any sleep, and there won't be time to seriously look. You need a little time to look at art. I hope all of our resources won't be given to just that week."

Reflecting on a failed proposal during his tenure at the helm of Art in Public Places to give a free museum pass to high school students and community college humanities students, Trasobares says he hopes local cultural institutions will move toward more collaborative activities that cast a wide, welcoming net.

"In the arts community, we have our own set of issues," he says. "But for the larger community, we want to see art everywhere. There are a lot of people interested in doing art that could be published in the newspaper, in the media, in things that all benefit from this very broad kind of thinking."

In memoriam: Fernando García, 1945–1989
Robert Huff, 1945–2014

MIA GALLERY, J. TOMÁS LÓPEZ

Fly over to Airport for Sea of Imagery in Digital Collages

August 18, 2000

You could swim your way into this sort of art, as long as you keep an eye out for the frequent tidal waves of images. It is an art of digital collage and deep-sea diving, of computer screens and scuba gear flung into a whirlpool of sex, money, and politics.

The whirlpool is new; the water is not.

For two decades Miami artist J. Tomás López has built a reputation by going underwater. He has photographed men and women floating in pools, their bodies twisting in sensuous motion, by turns grotesque or full of grace.

Sometimes they break the surface; sometimes they sink toward the bottom.

Such black-and-white photographs linger in your memory. They summon a stop-in-your-tracks contrast to López's new digital collages, frenetic and colorful inkjet prints on display for the first time. The computer-generated prints are part of a provocative if uneven group exhibit called *The Persistent Image* at MIA Gallery in Miami International Airport, a show that also includes work by South Florida photographers Elizabeth Cerejido, Fernando E. García, Mark A. Koven, and Ramón Williams.

López, 50, easily the most seasoned in this group, has work in the permanent collections of the Smithsonian American Art Museum, Bibliothèque Nationale in Paris, International Museum of Photography, and the Lowe Art Museum, among other institutions.

And the submerged life hasn't been an excuse for dreaming of mermaids or carting about a fancy camera. Instead, says López, an artist who loves to scuba dive at night, it has been a "metaphor for being out of my element . . . another world where one doesn't quite belong, but a place where one must adapt."

That dislocated mood spilled over into portraits López created in the early 1990s—close-ups of people with AIDS, such as the one of a toddler named Glenda wearing a lace collar, her sweet face glazed in a vacant, milky stare.

"His work has never been embarrassed to be beautiful. It's not merely decorative; it's intellectually interesting," says Alison Devine Nordstrom, director of the Southeast Museum of Photography in Daytona Beach, who invited López to take part in a February group show about contemporary Cuba.

Four of the five artists on display in the airport gallery, including López, were born in Cuba. And though all five work in wildly varied styles, gallery director Yolanda Sanchez, in the show's catalog, says their photography is charged by a desire to connect with the past, to construct persistent images that may keep those memories fade resistant.

López's images persist in the mind in a hyperactive way. They're radiant with drama, seduction, and illusion—surely a channel-surfing metaphor for the Miami he says "feels like a soap opera."

"I never lived in a place that's this dramatic. There's something wonderfully garish about South Beach and the costumes people wear," says López, who, in 1956, emigrated with his family from Camagüey to Long Island and taught at the Rochester Institute of Technology in New York before moving to South Florida in 1994, where he teaches photography at the University of Miami.

In this new body of work, which overlays dreamy slices of cathedrals, coral reefs, and 1950s snapshots of Camagüey, there are lots of SoBe colors and sexy shape-shifting—weaving together, for example, erotic shots lifted from Madonna's *Sex* book, then stretched and distorted into quick glimpses.

For an artist similarly accomplished with camera, keyboard, and oxygen tank, the new works also simmer with a subtropical tension akin to "the wonderful sense of anxiety on a night dive," he says.

The aquatic overtones converge in their own soap opera. In one print showing a baroque flurry of turquoise, there are two octopuses, "and you don't know whether they are fighting or making love," he says.

Two other prints are awash with even more conflict, evoking the flag-waving Miami of recent months and the division sparked by the plight of Elián González and the Immigration and Naturalization Service (INS) decision to seize him from his family's Little Havana home.

If you look closely at this pair of prints, which hang side by side in the gallery, this is what you'll discover: horizontal bands of blue, green, yellow, and magenta, in which silvery palm trees and Cuban passports, bookshelves and body parts swim into view and then dissolve as your eye travels over their seductive contours.

You can barely distinguish news shots of tires burning in Little Havana, shadows of police garbed in riot gear.

Stand back and you'll see that in one, called *Resignation*, the kaleidoscopic patterns click to resemble the Cuban flag, and in the other, *Parasite Marries Climber*, a digitized version of the Stars and Stripes emerges. Dead center in the second piece is a tiny shot of the INS agent clutching Elián to her chest during the raid.

"I'm just trying to make sense of the myriad of conflicting information," López says. "I understand the exile view, but I also see the American side. That kid was so politicized by everyone."

The title of *Parasite Marries Climber*—a piece bordered with rows of ladder-climbing figures culled from Eadweard Muybridge's famous motion studies— refers to the kind of polarized point of view that's the exact opposite of López's cascading, layered composition. The title comes from a headline about Prince Andrew's marriage to Sarah Ferguson, López says with a dry chuckle.

Printed in a Mexican socialist newspaper, it shouted a sharp contrast to

"Prince Marries Princess," the headline that ran the same day in a conservative paper. Neither paper could see the other's point, López says.

When two sides are so rigid, so lacking in humor and empathy, the artist asks, "How do you come to a problem with a fresh eye?"

FORT LAUDERDALE MUSEUM OF ART, DAVID NOVROS, AND ROBERT HUFF

Two Wrongs and One Right among Local Arts Changes

September 3, 2000

In one of Richard Serra's *House of Cards* sculptures from the early 1970s, three five-foot-tall metal plates balance delicately against each other, creating a scene of tension and grace.

But you could also read into these cards a lesson on the importance of knowing when to hold and when to fold.

Playing a cunning hand of poker seems an unlikely metaphor when talking about art, but the comparison isn't so far off if we're talking about a growing arts community that also needs to know when to hold and when to fold—or what to keep and what to discard.

Recently, we've been dealt a hand that includes two at-risk public artworks and the apparent demise of the Fort Lauderdale Museum of Art's Hortt Annual Memorial Competition and Exhibition, a 41-year-old artists' competition. And while there is reason to mourn the artworks' plight—each is a valuable, taxpayer-purchased part of South Florida's youthful but growing visual arts culture—we should welcome the passing of the competition. (Fort Lauderdale Museum of Art is now renamed NSU Art Museum Fort Lauderdale.)

The threatened public works are David Novros's 1984 abstract frescoes in the courtyard of the downtown David W. Dyer Federal Building and US Court-house and *Transpontine*, a boldly colored tile mural that Miami artist Robert Huff created in 1996 for Concourse D at the Miami International Airport.

Novros's work, which is in need of repair, is set to be painted over instead of being restored. Its demise is being blamed on the fact that it was not reviewed under the National Historic Preservation Act when it was com-missioned—at a cost of $52,500—by the General Services Administration, which places art in federal buildings.

Huff's work, a $155,000 work commissioned by Miami-Dade Art in Public Places, is slated for demolition because it's an obstacle to the airport's plans to expand that concourse to accommodate larger gates and airplanes, says Vivian Donnell Rodriguez, executive director of Miami-Dade Art in Public Places.

IMMINENT LOSS?

As for the Novros murals, those who've protested the decision to remove or cover them up include the Florida Art Museum Directors Association, South Florida collector Martin Z. Margulies, and Michael Spring, director of Miami-Dade County Department of Cultural Affairs.

The loss of the murals seemed imminent earlier this year, but perhaps owing to the protests, the government is now in a holding pattern.

"We are working on the best way to cover the murals and how to incor-porate that work into the entire courtyard renovation schedule," says GSA spokeswoman Viki Reath. "We hope to have that schedule in six months—not later than a year from now."

Novros, who turned down the GSA's offer to pay him to create another work for the Dyer Building, is adamant that his murals stay.

"We're trying to find a more creative way of dealing with this situation rather than destroying the art," he said.

One proposed solution has the Art Museum at Florida International University acquiring the work for its collection.

"Although the work remains on site, we would be responsible for it," says Dahlia Morgan, the museum's director. "It's under discussion. It's not just because David Novros is such a good artist, but I really feel an artist's work needs to be protected."

Protection is not in the cards for the lustrous 19,000 tiles that make up Huff's airport mural. No date has been set for its removal, although destruction could begin in a month.

Rodriguez says that when she learned of the plans to expand Concourse D, she had hoped to relocate the mural, but it turned out that the tiles can't be moved without being shattered.

Huff has agreed to create a work for another site at the airport for the same fee, meaning that not only will a valuable piece of art be lost due to poor planning but replacing it will require a redundant use of tax money.

"I was concerned at first," Huff says of his mural's fate. "I probably will be [again] when I see it being torn down. But we live in an age of totally disposable architecture, and anything that is site specific in a building is in jeopardy."

Huff's relationship with Art in Public Places is far more cordial than Novros's relationship with the GSA. While it's distressing to see two public artworks imperiled, Novros's case seems more egregious because there's no physical expansion taking place at the courthouse.

Nevertheless, all public art—just as with bridges, roads, airport concourses—is susceptible to urban growing pains, Rodriguez says.

"I think the benefits of working in this public arena far outweigh the potential impact of growth," she says. "We've installed 25 to 30 projects at the airport, and only one is being impacted."

HORTT HIATUS

The loss of either of these works would be lamentable. But the time has come to say goodbye to the Hortt exhibit in hopes that this dusty South Florida rite can be reconfigured into something more meaningful.

Last month the museum announced that the Hortt would not be included in this season's schedule of exhibitions. Instead, the museum will represent the work of 37 South Florida artists with three solo shows and two group shows that will be part of the museum's *Contemporary Artist* series.

Museum of Art director Kathleen Harleman says putting the Hortt on hiatus could lead to a more innovative way of helping area artists establish their links to the larger world of contemporary art.

In memoriam: Robert Huff, 1945–2014

MICHAEL RICHARDS

Grounded Dreams at Ambrosino Gallery

October 2, 2000

The buoyant drawings of Michael Richards stand out for their clarity of fleshy detail, their forays into surrealist fantasy, and their poetic lines of text penned in a calligraphic style.

But wrapped within this formal elegance are stories of dreams that never quite get off the ground.

Richards's drawings are featured in *Escape Plan 2000* at North Miami's Ambrosino Gallery, complementing his sculptural works from *Passages: Contemporary Art in Tradition*, a show organized by the Studio Museum in Harlem on view at the Miami Art Museum through November 26.

That this solo show is at Ambrosino signals a small but important change in the local art scene. For a number of reasons, local galleries in South Florida rarely feature artists showcased in current museum shows. This is especially unfortunate given the caliber of contemporary work we've seen in recent seasons at MAM, the Museum of Contemporary Art, the Art Museum at Florida International University, and Fort Lauderdale's Museum of Art.

This has kept many commercial galleries lagging behind the accelerating quality of museum programs, even as artists based here are stepping up their presence in museum schedules.

Richards, who lives in New York, has ties here. This spring he completed a visual arts residency with Miami's National Foundation for Advancement in the Arts (now YoungArts), a program that culminated with a summer show at the Corcoran Museum of Art in Washington, DC.

At Ambrosino, one of his drawings hints at the failure of Icarus's wings in the Greek myth. It shows the curled tendrils of a feather grazing a foot, and the text below reads, "The feathers he saved in secret, hiding them until he had enough to form a ladder. But his feet were sensitive and his laughter gave him away."

Concise and compelling, Richards's drawings occasionally bring to mind the spiritual integration of image and word present in the visionary poems of 18th-century English artist William Blake.

They are also visual narratives—like the artist's sculptural homage at MAM to the underrecognized, racially segregated Tuskegee Airmen of World War II—that unfold episodes of loss throughout American culture.

In memoriam: Michael Richards, 1963–2001

PURVIS YOUNG

Forever Young

October 11, 2000

Purvis Young picks up a wooden crate, turns it around, and sits down. This quick gesture of recycling, turning a crate into a stool, is typical for an artist who turns crates into paintings museums covet.

Behind him, on a bleak street corner in Overtown, is a warehouse stuffed with more crates, piles of wood, strips of carpet, a dozen-plus bicycles, and cans of paint. An iridescent figurine of a rearing unicorn glistens on one of several dusty TV sets while a book about Vincent van Gogh is tucked in the basket of an old bicycle.

When visitors show up, Young turns his back on this impressive clutter

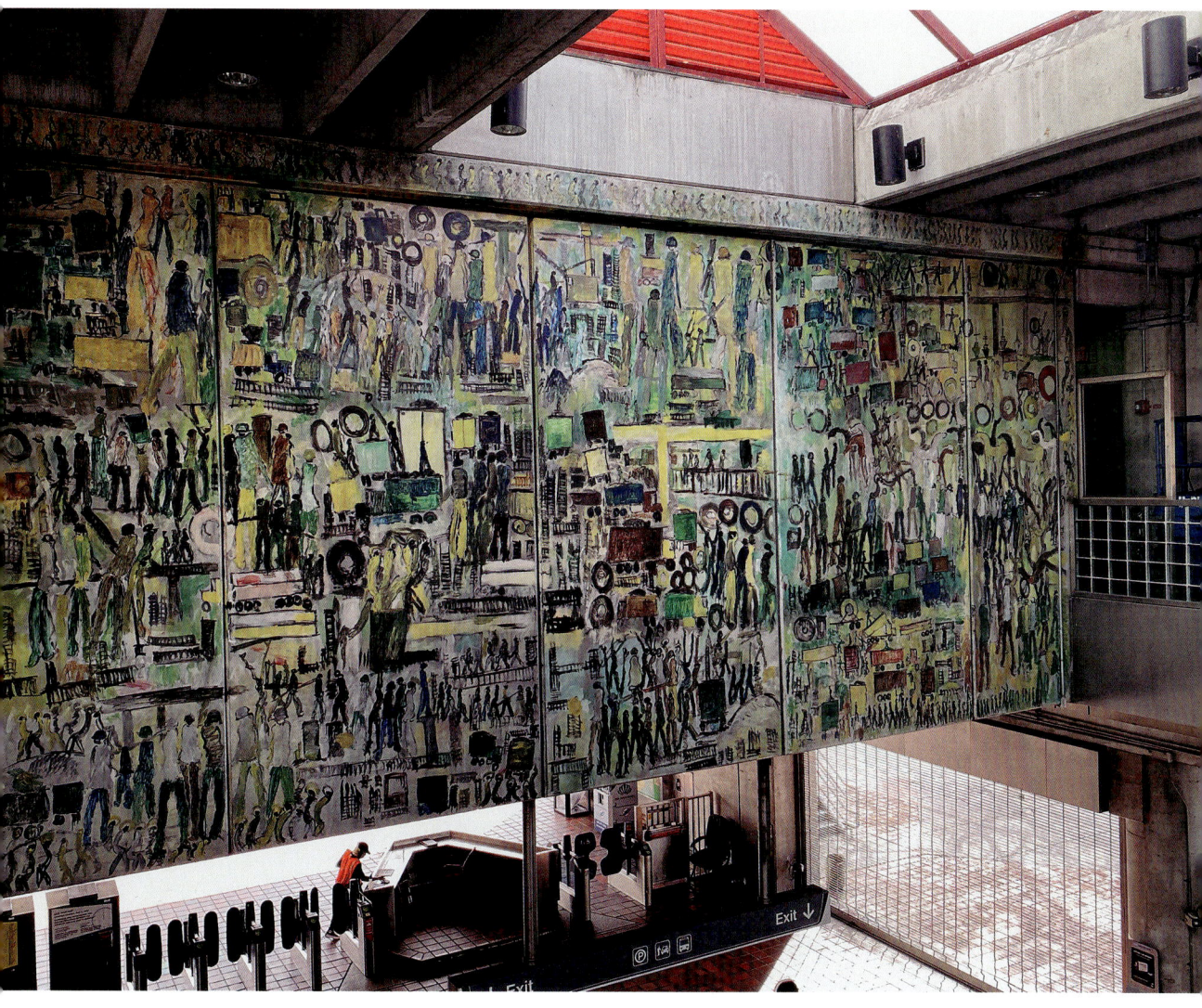

FIGURE 15. Purvis Young, *Untitled*, 1986. Enamel paint on treated surface. Northside Metrorail Station, 3150 NW 79th St., escalator. Courtesy of Miami-Dade County Department of Cultural Affairs, Art in Public Places Trust.

that is both his studio and his home and hunkers down on his makeshift stool, facing the street corner.

He lets his art speak for itself. Fantastic stories tumble out in his paintings on wood and other grimy materials. In luminous shades of house paint no one else has ever mixed, Young tells of the despair and dreams of job seekers, basketball players, pregnant women, and Haitian boat people. There are also angels the color of flames and spectral herds of rearing horses—graceful as unicorns but far more impassioned.

Rendered in Young's undulating brushstrokes and rhythmic compositions, the scenes eloquently chronicle life in Miami's once bustling Black neighborhood of Overtown.

"You got my paintings," he has said, "you got my soul."

Now that soul is poised on the cusp of a substantial breakthrough. Young's art hasn't changed dramatically in his 30-year career, but the fickle world of contemporary art has. So-called outsider artists like Young—who have taught themselves, developing far from the world of academe—are increasingly being accepted into the ever-more-diverse mainstream.

And Young's not the only outsider breaking through. Paintings by Thornton Dial, who worked for years in an Alabama boxcar factory, were part of this year's Biennial at the Whitney Museum of American Art. James Castle, a self-taught deaf artist who lived with his family in Idaho, had more than 100 minute drawings on matchbooks and cigarette packs shown at New York's Drawing Center in March.

"I do think that the tides are turning and that we are going to see a lot of artists we support become more integrated into the larger art world," says Brooke Anderson, curator of the Contemporary Center at New York's Museum of American Folk Arts. "The reason is that the work is really strong. It's all art of our time. That kind of integration can allow new scholarship, new ways of seeing."

Things began changing for Young last year, when internationally known contemporary art collectors Donald and Mera Rubell of Miami purchased the contents of his studio—around 4,000 paintings, drawings, and books. A fraction of that is on view in their two-story warehouse on Northwest 29th Street.

"For me, Purvis is a kind of prophet artist without being pedantic," says Mera Rubell, who, like Young, won't discuss terms of the sale. "He makes us focus on neighborhoods, on people that are not part of the glamorous vision of America. He glamorizes the uniqueness that exists in every person regardless of their economic or social position."

MUSEUM IN THE WORKS

Young may soon have his own museum show, culled from the Rubells' holdings.

"Our objective is to have a traveling museum exhibition and to donate work to all institutions that have a show of his work," Mera Rubell says. "I wouldn't be surprised if we are talking about half a dozen institutions in the US and Europe. . . . The world knows Purvis Young."

In preparation, the Rubells' staff has embarked on a Herculean task, fumigating, photographing, and documenting Young's work. Binders will be created, says the collection's director Bill Begert, with photographs of pieces in the collection, allowing curators to choose works to show or acquire.

Young's talent has been recognized by curators and collectors for years. In the early 1970s, he found champions in Miami-Dade County Public Library System librarians Margarita Cano and Barbara Young (who is no relation to the artist), who shared art books with him. In the past decade, Young's work has been shown at museums in Alabama, Florida, Ohio, New York, New Jersey, and Virginia and at galleries in Miami, New York, Philadelphia, New Orleans, Chicago, and Cologne, Germany.

But most of this recent attention has come at a price: not only has Young been promoted as an outsider artist—a problematic term many find patronizing—but he has had troubling relations with dealers who, friends say, did not compensate him fairly.

He also extricated himself from an exclusive contract with former South Florida dealer Joy Moos. (Young says now he never signs a contract without consulting his lawyer, and his current Miami dealer, Fredric Snitzer, says Young receives the same commission that the gallery's other artists receive.)

On a recent weekday, Young stared out at the street and talked about what was on his mind. A bearded, barrel-chested man in shorts, sandals, and a shirt with cutoff sleeves, he launched into a purely Purvis conversation—one both rambling and right on target.

"That's all I do is fantasize," he announced. "As I get older, I feel like I was a Zulu: I was no chief, I was just part of the Zulus. I look at Rembrandts, I look at all old masters. I listen to opera because opera's telling a story."

A fan of public television, he says, "One night I woke up and they were telling a story about Col. Rhodes, you know, of Rhodesia, and how he went to the British authority and got orders to conquer that part of Africa. . . . Zulu was a tribe the British always had problems with. The Americans had problems with the Sioux and the Blackfoot. . . . You know, they was takin' land. The same thing went on in Africa."

Moving on from colonial Africa and 19th-century America to the present day, Young continues to rail about oppressor and oppressed, a theme that runs through his art. He mentions "those two dudes on death row that didn't do nothing. Innocent they find them."

Eventually, an apocalyptic vision surfaces.

"I look at mankind and the problems," he says. "I see a lot in America, but I don't speak out, I just paint. As I get older, I see eyes of fire, fire burning up the world."

In talks like this, Young slips seamlessly between real-world knowledge and the visionary quality that makes his art so remarkable. That quality is "astrologic, like something he sees in the sky. He lays down and dreams, and then he can paint," says close friend Silo Crespo, a Santería priest and retired merchant seaman who shared his Overtown home with Young for years.

Other knowledge, says Barbara Young, comes from his favorite populist sources: public libraries, public television, and national public radio. But as willing as he is to expound on what he has learned about Mozart, John Brown, and John Coltrane, he's guarded about his personal life.

"Some folks don't take me serious. They come to my place and want to talk about the bikes I got," he complains. "If you don't talk about my paintings, I don't want to talk. God put me here to be an artist."

God sent Purvis Young to Miami's Black neighborhood of Liberty City in 1943, where he was one of three boys and two girls born into a family of Bahamian descent. As a boy, he frequently suffered the wrath of his grandmother, according to Crespo, who says Young "grew up in fear."

LOOKING BACK

Young remembers doodling submarines and horses as a kid, but his schooling did nothing to nurture that talent. Even worse, he saw an uncle who carved wooden figures lose control, only to be carried off by the police.

"I don't know what caused his mind to get messed up. He always stayed by himself. It's the same with me," said Crespo.

Young admits, "Someone said, you know, your uncle might have seen the same things you see. The world ain't changed too much."

A fearful childhood spiraled into an adolescence of crime, and Young dropped out of Booker T. Washington High School. By the time he turned 18, he was doing time in Florida's Raiford Prison for armed robbery.

Jail proved to be a vast improvement over high school. A jailer gave him pencil and paper, and Young discovered he could draw. A few years later, that discovery became his destiny when he happened upon a book illustrating the *Wall of Respect*, a legendary Chicago mural filled with portraits of African American leaders.

MYTHIC PAINTINGS

Finding out more about the late 1960s movement to create murals in Black, Latino, and other ethnic neighborhoods, Young "saw that ordinary people could paint the stories of their own communities and give them mythic importance," wrote University of Miami art historian Paula Harper in a 1992 essay.

So he began painting his own stories of urban struggles, of figures behind bars reaching upward. Some of the first stories appeared in Goodbread Alley as a makeshift mural Young began attaching to tumbledown buildings on Northwest 14th Street around the early 1970s.

"I think it was a kind of nervous energy he had to channel. At that time people in his community were very angry," artist César Trasobares, who is writing a book on Young, says of the mural, which was torn down in the mid-1970s to make room for a park next to the Culmer/Overtown Branch Library. "Not only was it a way to channel that energy, but it was a vehicle for ideas. Much later I learned about the African tradition of the griot, and in a way Purvis had become that," he adds, comparing Young to the African public speaker who recites a village's oral history.

Young did another mural, also since destroyed, inside the old downtown Miami-Dade County Public Library in 1983, recounting Miami's race riots. Two other murals from the mid-1980s are still in place: one on the outside of the Culmer Library and one at the Northside Metrorail Station. They tell of basketball players and construction workers—common people caught up in a griot's vivid narrative.

"LET ME WANDER. . . ."

Fast-forward to the present, and Young is still the griot, compulsively drawing what he sees on the streets and in his dreams, even during doctor visits to treat the diabetes he developed about six years ago. The man, who once gave a boy a quarter for a poem and has worried about children coming into the world without families to care for them, now frets that kids eat too much greasy food.

Once so shy that a 15-minute conversation was a challenge, Young recently spoke for an hour and a half to New World School of the Arts students who visited his current show at Fredric Snitzer Gallery.

While a larger audience and more recognition are surely on the way, Young remains fiercely independent and rooted to his surroundings. When asked if he'd like an air-conditioned condo, he says he has a fan and lets it go at that.

"If you're happy, don't try to tell me how to live my life," he says. "Let me wander and do what I want to do."

In memoriam: Silo Crespo, 1929–2003
Purvis Young, 1943–2010
Paula Harper, 1930–2012

GROWTH SPURTS, GROWING PAINS, AND FLOCKS OF KITSCH— WHAT'S NEXT?

October 29, 2000

If you were to look back at snapshots of South Florida's arts scene this fall, you'd see pictures that reveal both growth spurts and growing pains.

For starters, there was *Cultivated under the Sun*, the Miami-Dade Public Library's absorbing survey of art collected during the past 30 years. So captivating was the exhibition, two of its curators were inspired to embark on a more far-reaching project.

After putting together the library show with fellow curator Margarita Cano, Helen L. Kohen and Barbara Young plan to develop an ongoing visual arts archive to document the Greater Miami area's arts scene from the postwar years to the present.

It's time to recognize the years of contributions that artists, collectors, and their supporters have made to build Miami into an international cultural center, says Kohen, the *Herald*'s art critic from 1978 to 1995.

"We're not a very prideful community," she acknowledges, "and I think this kind of thing says that it [the art scene] is real and that it's been here for a very long time. These days depend on those days."

Kohen plans to interview artists, collectors, arts patrons, and anyone else concerned with the visual arts.

"I want everybody's story," Kohen says. "I want gossip as long as it's printable, because the truth is in there somewhere—the failures as well as the victories. We want to make sure that no artist gets overlooked."

The effort—tentatively called the *Vasari Project* after 16th-century Italian artist and writer Giorgio Vasari, who was admired for his pioneering biographies of major artists—promises to be a fascinating community resource. A bonus is that it would be supplemented with an illustrated book listing artists, museums, art centers, and galleries.

Kohen hopes to get the project under way by the first of the year, though funding is not yet in place. The archive will be sponsored by the Miami-Dade County Public Library System, which is providing office space, and the Miami-Dade County Department of Cultural Affairs, which is helping identify sources of funding.

FRUITFUL EXCHANGE

A second notable growth spurt came from the most recent meeting of the Miami Art Exchange—a loose coalition of artists, dealers, collectors, and others. The Exchange has become a forum for announcing grant and exhibition opportunities and for updating the visual arts community on plans for January's Art Miami and for the arrival of Art Basel Miami Beach in December 2001.

This trading of information, says Rem Cabrera, cultural development chief at Miami-Dade's Department of Cultural Affairs, is a long-overdue sign of a maturing arts community. But the meetings have produced more than just talk.

At this month's get-together, dealer Bernice Steinbaum announced she is providing space for area artists not represented by a local gallery to store their résumés and slides. A team of 15 curators, Steinbaum promises, will review this material when they choose art for shows mounted in and near the Design District during Art Basel Miami Beach.

If handled with an imaginative eye, this project could provide an opportunity to discover adventurous voices. But given that the Exchange's website (www.miamiartexchange.com) has been funded by $1,000 from its sponsor, Bernice Steinbaum Gallery, Cabrera would like to see this loose organization evolve into a nonprofit arts group.

"It just doesn't seem right for any one individual to address the needs of the artist community," he says. "If they go for a nonprofit, they can go for funding of the website and raise money from dues. It's also an issue of determining a focus. I think formulating a nonprofit with a clearly stated mission would provide them with that."

BIRDS OF PARADISE

We may live in a subtropical paradise, but a countywide show, *Flamingos in Paradise*, sounds more like a growing pain than a spurt. It resonates with tired, copycat thinking.

The project was announced at the Exchange meeting by Sandy-Jo Gordon, secretary-treasurer of Miami-Dade Art in Public Places Trust. The facts: Between 300 and 500 larger-than-life-sized flamingos will be embellished by local artists and placed around the county from November 2001 through April 2002. In May 2002, the faux birds will be auctioned at the Miami Seaquarium to benefit charity. Organizers include the Miami-Dade County Tourist Development Council, Greater Miami Convention and Visitors Bureau, and Bank of America Coconut Grove Arts Festival, as well as the public art programs of Miami-Dade and Miami Beach.

"We'll put together a panel of local art professionals and curators to select the artists," says Miami-Dade Art in Public Places director Vivian Donnell Rodriguez. "It isn't serious."

Flamingos is modeled after the widely publicized *Cows on Parade*, a herd of artist-decorated sculptures that populated Chicago in the summer of 1999. The idea came from Zurich and has since spread to more than 30 North American cities.

Chicago's parade turned into a cash cow according to the *Chicago Tribune*, which reported that the herd drew a million visitors to Chicago and generated $200 million in economic activity—estimates the paper termed "generous."

It is "lowest-common-denominator art," Michael Lash, director of Chicago's Public Art Program, told the paper. But he found it entertaining and publicly engaging, as did Stanley Murashige, chair of the art history department at the School of the Art Institute of Chicago.

Some South Florida artists aren't so sure flocks of kitschy sculptures will put Miami's growing arts community in the best light when visitors arrive for Art Basel Miami Beach, which will take place while the flamingos are on display. Nor are they convinced it will engage local interest in the more thoughtful work on view.

"This is fluff," says sculptor Carol Brown, who teaches at the New World School of the Arts. "I would hate for someone to say, 'Well, we did the flamingos so why bother to go to the Miami Art Museum?'"

"Anything for money," adds artist David Rohn. "It would have been cool if they'd used manatees. Manatees get right to some serious environmental issues, but they're obviously going to reject anything that doesn't promote tourism."

In memoriam: Helen Kohen, 1931–2015
Margarita Cano, 1932–2024

RAMÓN CERNUDA

Art Critic

November 3, 2000

It's not unusual for art collectors to become art dealers. And vice versa.

But Miami collector and educational publisher Ramón Cernuda says he has entered the gallery world not for commercial reasons but to fill a major gap in the area's offerings in Latin American art.

Despite the wealth of contemporary Latin American art for sale in galleries and the offerings on view in museums, there's still a conspicuous lack of attention paid to the historical range of art from the region, particularly Cuba, he says.

And when it comes to artists who are exhibited here, the major museums have proven "too New York–centric," Cernuda complains.

"We get people coming here from out of town who are looking for the vibrancy of Latin American art, to see precisely what our museums are trying to ignore," he says.

To counter some of those omissions, Cernuda's new gallery, Cernuda Arte, tonight unveils *Calentando Motores* (*Warming up the engines*), a gathering of

46 paintings by 22 Cuban artists, from early 20th-century figures like Amelia Peláez and Wifredo Lam to later masters like René Portocarrero and Cundo Bermúdez. The show will also feature Cuban American artist Demi and Flora Fong, who paints lush, semiabstract landscapes in Havana.

But in addition to presenting prerevolution artists, Cernuda says he'll also show artists still living in Cuba.

"We're not going to exclude artists on the basis of geographical location," he says. "It's not right to censor the arts."

Cernuda, whose gallery opened last month, is an early warrior in Miami's censorship battles. In 1988, he presided over a controversial auction that included work by artists living in Cuba, prompting one irate protester to burn a painting by Manuel Mendive.

The following year, federal agents confiscated some 200 of his paintings, alleging that their purchase violated the US trade embargo against Cuba. But US District Judge Kenneth L. Ryskamp ruled that the collector's freedom of speech rights were violated by the seizure.

South Florida has hardly ignored Latin American art. In the last five years, the region has welcomed a major show of modern Mexican masters and solo exhibits of Pablo Cano and Teresita Fernández at the Museum of Contemporary Art, surveys of Latin American drawing and art by Latin American women at the Miami Art Museum, and solo shows featuring Guido Llinás and José Bedia at the Art Museum at Florida International University.

NOT ENOUGH

In addition, contemporary artists like photographer Marta María Pérez Bravo of Cuba and conceptual artists Ernesto Neto of Brazil and José Clemente Orozco of Mexico have also been included in group shows; the Bass Museum of Art presented a historical survey of art from the Dominican Republic; and the Museum of Art in Fort Lauderdale hosted *Breaking Barriers: Selections from the Museum of Art's Permanent Contemporary Cuban Collection* and a traveling solo show of cutting-edge installations by Chilean artist Alfredo Jaar.

But Cernuda and others argue that hasn't been enough.

Juan A. Martínez, an art professor at Florida International University, author of *Cuban Art & National Identity* and curator of this month's exhibit at the Lowe Art Museum culled from its Cuban collection, believes that more wide-ranging, historical attention is needed.

"With the exception of Mexican art, I think the rest of the art of the Caribbean and Latin America has been underestimated because this country has always looked to the North and to Europe," he says. "There just hasn't been an exhibit here that looks at Cuban art historically and thematically. The shows have been mostly contemporary."

A veteran collector of 19th- and 20th-century Cuban art and a former board member of the Cuban Museum—an institution whose art collection has been absorbed into the Lowe's—Cernuda, 53, has spent 2½ years developing his gallery's inventory of paintings by 19th- and 20th-century Cuban artists.

SHINING THROUGH

One artist whose legacy could benefit from the brighter spotlight is Carlos Enríquez, whose breathtaking 1954 painting *Caballo Rojo* (*Red horse*) is included in Cernuda's show. Enríquez, who died in 1957, was eclipsed by the growing interest in abstract art and is now a footnote in American art through his marriage to celebrated portrait painter Alice Neel.

In memoriam: Juan A. Martínez, 1951–2020

EDOUARD DUVAL-CARRIÉ

Wall of Vodou

November 5, 2000

With his quick wit and deep, infectious laugh, Edouard Duval-Carrié would be a perfect fit as a social director on a Caribbean cruise.

You can imagine him introducing guests to one another, cajoling people

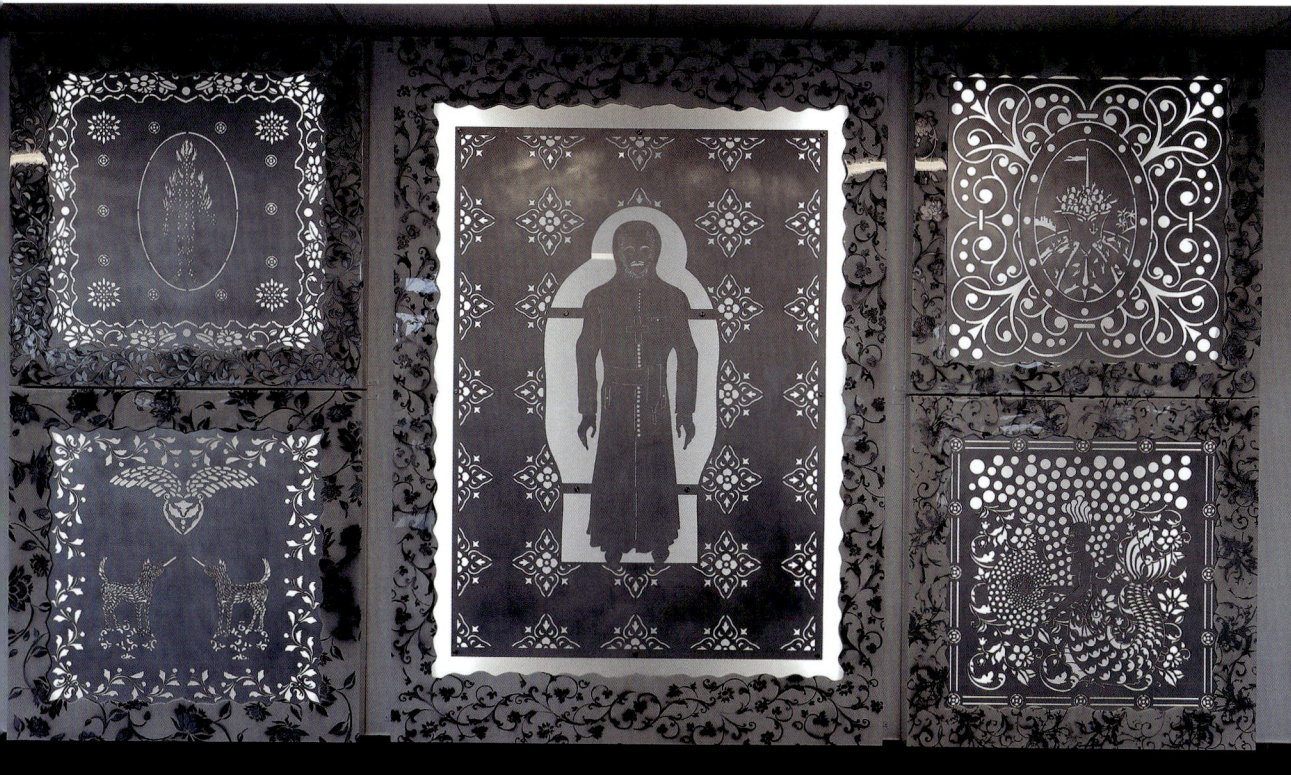

FIGURE 16. Edouard Duval-Carrié, *Oak Grove Rhapsody*, 2019. Painted resin panels, water-jet cut metal, etched acrylic, LED fixtures. Father Gerard Jean-Juste Community Center at Oak Grove Park, lobby, 690 NE 159st St., Miami 33162. Image Carl Juste, courtesy of Miami-Dade County Department of Cultural Affairs, Art in Public Places Trust.

to share a drink or tell a story, and chatting up an audience in English or French—or even in the Spanish he learned as a teenager living in Puerto Rico.

He became an artist instead, although he aims to make plenty of introductions these days. He indicated as much to a standing-room-only crowd at the opening of his latest exhibition, *New Work: Edouard Duval-Carrié, Migrations*, an exploration of Haitian culture, Vodou spirits, and the current desperation on the island now on view at the Miami Art Museum.

But these introductions concern desperate travelers in rickety flotillas and vivid migratory Haitian Vodou spirits of love and death, not tanned passengers sipping rum on multimillion-dollar ships.

"Here is this whole culture that you might not be aware of," said Duval-Carrié, a worldly and jocular figure dressed in a natty black suit. "But it may be heading your way, so let's get accustomed to each other."

Presented in a tour de force combination of painting and sculpture, *Migrations* is a spirited encounter made for South Florida, a community of immigrants suffused with much of the Caribbean. (Another collection of Duval-Carrié's work, *Edouard Duval-Carrié: Landscapes, Real & Imagined*, is showing at the Bernice Steinbaum Gallery in the Miami Design District through December 7.)

And fittingly, the MAM show is scheduled for its own significant encounter. In the spring of 2002, *Migrations* will meet up with three of the artist's previous installations that probe complex African, American, and European strands interlacing Haitian culture and its history, originating from the brutal Middle Passage. The quartet is uniting for a show organized by the Davenport Museum of Art in Iowa, a venue known for its large collection of Haitian art, and the Bass Museum of Art in Miami Beach, which owns the artist's caustic portrait of deposed Haitian dictator Jean-Claude "Baby Doc" Duvalier and his family, a seminal riff on European court painters.

MILESTONE EXHIBITION

Duval-Carrié's first traveling museum exhibit will mark a milestone in a prolific career, and both *Migrations* and the traveling show should solidify Duval-Carrié's reputation as a major voice sifting the New World–Old World mélange of the Caribbean with the inventive materials and international outlook of contemporary art.

The just-published *Oxford History of Western Art*, in fact, is already linking Duval-Carrié's art to the blend of European modernism and Afro-Cuban rites forged by Cuban master Wifredo Lam.

"It's very second millennium," MAM senior curator Peter Boswell says of the artist's work. "He's a great synthesizer. He's bringing in those influences from other countries. This is really a dominant trend in art right now, with artists who are global but also regional at the same time."

And the polyglot, Caribbean-colored landscape of Miami, Boswell adds, "is very good at fostering that type of sensibility."

"It's so refreshing to have a voice like Edouard's, that openly talks about Vodou and treats it with the respect it deserves," says Leonie Hermantin, executive director of the Haitian American Foundation, which today is cosponsoring a round-table discussion on issues raised by Duval-Carrié's exhibition. "His art shows that when we move to another land, we use our memories of religion to help us adapt."

As Duval-Carrié spoke at MAM, subdued laughter rippled through the crowd. The artist may be a clever charmer, but the urgent reasons behind his get-accustomed offer are close to the surface.

"In time, God knows, the island will get its act straight," but for now, he continued, "the crisis in Haiti seems unending."

The artist puts it more emphatically in an interview in his Little Haiti studio, a workspace lined with art books, antique maps of Port-au-Prince, and an orange iMac computer.

"The Vodou spirits are splitting! I am having the whole pantheon pick up and leave," he says of the premise driving *Migrations*, in which the Vodou spirits flee the island. "It's funny, but at the same time it's very tragic. I decided to address the problem of Haiti losing itself, of dying. People are in total dire straits."

BITTERSWEET STORIES

During Duval-Carrié's visit to Port-au-Prince five months ago, a gunman fatally shot his cousin, a prominent radio newscaster critical of the Duvalier regime. That violent scene—and many others—are rendered in the MAM show in painted panels that include a faux marble wall relief reminiscent of a Roman Catholic altarpiece.

In one panel, a lush tropical forest smolders, while in others a tattooed goddess dances in a South Beach strip joint and a warrior spirit in gold epaulets mans a tank in the Gulf War.

They deliver bittersweet stories of a besieged country, represented by rural spirits migrating into new urban contexts. The spirits are a testament to the fluid energies of Vodou that Duval-Carrié has always admired. He calls Vodou—with its syncretic assortment of Yoruba, Kongo, and Roman Catholic deities—"a guerrilla religion."

"It refuses to have strict canons," he says. "You have new gods coming in, other gods forgotten. It recovers anything that might be of use to survival of the people."

Loosely reminiscent of a Vodou temple, *Migrations* is perfumed with lilies strewn on the floor like offerings and fraught with the rococo curves of crumbling colonial French architecture, replicated in ornate urns laden with more offerings of glazed fruit.

Throughout is the festive sparkle of Vodou altars to "Mistress" Ezili Freda, the vampish light-skinned goddess of love and luxury. A devotee of pink cake, lace hankies, and Anaïs Anaïs perfume, she is a poor country's fantasy of ravishing wealth—and emblematic of colonial Haiti's vanished natural resources.

At MAM, she's the dominant voyager in a peculiar flotilla of boats suspended from the ceiling, their hulls glistening in melting pink shades of mock marble and inscribed with lacy ritual drawings that invoke Vodou spirits. And like the glowering, scar-faced Bawon Samdi, a Vodou spirit at home in cemeteries but tucked here in a listing skiff, Ezili is heading for the exit and away from Haiti.

Their uprootedness is familiar to Duval-Carrié, 45. He is, writes Latin American art historian Edward J. Sullivan, "acutely aware of the disorientations caused by migration [which is] the defining issue in the history of the islands."

STUDIED ABROAD

After spending his boyhood in Haiti and his adolescence in Puerto Rico, the artist shipped out to college in Montreal to study urban planning, though he was more engaged by painting than planning. In the 1980s he returned to Haiti to help manage his father's construction business, where he witnessed the 1986 downfall of "Baby Doc" Duvalier and the chaos that followed.

Two years later the French government invited him to a formative residency at the Museum of African and Oceanic Arts in Paris. In 1992, he traveled to Benin, home to Haiti's African ancestors, for an international reunion of Vodou cultures, and a year after that, he settled in Miami with his second wife, Nina, an English film producer, and their sons, now 8 and 10.

Along the way he has exhibited at the contemporary art museum in Monterrey, Mexico; biennials in São Paulo and Havana; and the 1996 Cultural Olympiad in Atlanta.

Raised Roman Catholic in an upper-middle-class family that typically finds his interest in Vodou "off the wall," Duval-Carrié recalls constant drumming coming from the mountains surrounding Port-au-Prince.

"You got to know it, if you liked it or not. There's no way you can be shielded," he says. "When I was a kid the maids took me to something that was supposedly church-related, but it was really a pilgrimage to Ezili. It was just like a party, and they would serve you a Coke. You could even visit the temples and go into the back rooms where the sacred objects are. There would be tables full of cakes for Ezili, and you'd have rows of perfume bottles, some appropriated from my mother. Visually, it's very stunning."

SCARRED BY BRUTALITY

Affected by the flashy panoply of altars and fantastic colors of traditional Haitian painting, the artist was also scarred by the brutalities of the Duvaliers, who jailed his brother Robert for more than a year. And while he is not unique among Haitian artists of his generation in reinventing his country's intensely visual heritage, Duval-Carrié is a leader in this trend, says Veerle Poupeye in the 1998 book *Caribbean Art*.

"His work evokes," she writes, "the magic and mystery of the Vodou universe and comments on Haiti's history and sociopolitical realities with sharp, surreal wit."

In his first show in 1980 at the Centre d'Art in Port-au-Prince, his evocations went too far. Centre director Francine Murat advised him against adding his portrait of Baby Doc in lacy drag with a pistol pointed to his head, a nod to rumors that the iron-fisted dictator was gay and to Ezili's patronage of homosexuals.

"Do you want to have us all disappeared?" Duval-Carrié remembers Murat asking. "That would be signing our death warrant."

Six years later, the portrait finally surfaced publicly as a poster celebrating Duvalier's flight from power. Vodou scholar Donald J. Cosentino says it indicated how Duvalier's lavish kleptocracy kept itself afloat by playing into Ezili-inspired fantasies of Haiti's poor.

Given his view of Haiti's current fortunes, Duval-Carrié says migration is a more pressing issue than ever. But by devising a scenario in which even the country's spiritual essence is departing, the artist has delayed his own dream of painting murals in a Vodou temple in Haiti.

The stay is only temporary, he promises. As icons of Haitian culture, the spirits are, he insists, international and can return to the island just as easily as they left.

"They can travel back and forth," he says. "That's the state of things these days. Nobody's stuck in one place."

A+ RESOURCES, DIASPORA VIBE

Local Galleries Showcase Diverse Caribbean Artists

November 12, 2000

Art flavored with the Creole cultures of the Caribbean islands is particularly visible in South Florida now, with Edouard Duval-Carrié's *Migrations*, a tragicomic homage to mercurial Haitian Vodou spirits, taking center stage at the Miami Art Museum.

But the intricate visual traditions that thread the work of contemporary Caribbean artists are also on display in *Caribbean Unexplored: Belkis Ramírez* at the A+ Resources and *Caribbean Crossroads Group Show* at Diaspora Vibe Gallery at the Bakehouse Art Complex.

The A+ Resources exhibit of woodcut prints and wooden sculptural reliefs by Dominican artist Belkis Ramírez is a well-considered addition to this mix. A commercial gallery opened two months ago, Denise Andrews's A+ Resources promises to give a heightened profile to work by artists of the African diaspora, a mission that is similar to Diaspora Vibe's.

Ramírez's wood reliefs were last seen here in 1996 at the Bass Museum

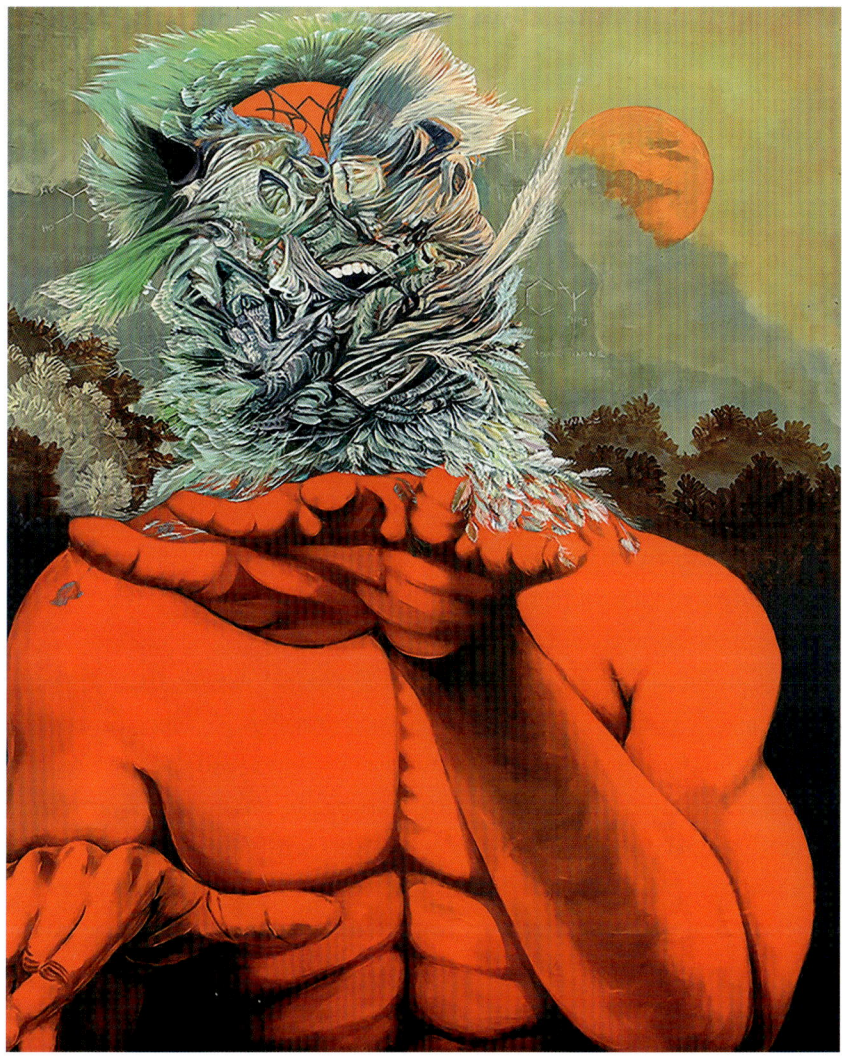

FIGURE 17. Asser Saint-Val, MSLITHP NGODA, *I have allowed you to perform your task (Magical Entities Series)*, 2019. Mixed media on board. Courtesy of the artist, courtesy of Miami-Dade County Department of Cultural Affairs, Art in Public Places Trust.

of Art in the traveling *Modern and Contemporary Art of the Dominican Republic*. And while her large-scale installation was uncomfortably wedged into a narrow gallery there, the smaller works at A+ Resources benefit from more generous breathing room.

In this selection of around 20 works from 1991 to the present, Ramírez shows herself as an emphatically figurative artist, limning faces from wooden surfaces that emerge as multiple shades of brown and embedding the human form in a pliant material that reminds us of the Dominican Republic's imperiled forests. Two of the larger works here make pointed comments about corrupt judicial practices and prostitution.

But while her works don't shy from political statements, formally they possess a vigorous, swooping sense of line that, in works such as *Heart without Feeling*, seems to equate the leafy tendrils of forests with the lined textures of human flesh and hair. Thus, Ramírez can create a rice-paper print with a foreshortened view of feet, endowing these anonymous, awkward bits of humble anatomy with energy.

The *Caribbean Crossroads Group Show* at Diaspora Vibe rounds up the work of eight artists. Featuring mostly paintings and drawings, it's a show that could benefit from sharper curating and a more ambitious use of varied materials.

Nicole Salpétrier, who was born in Martinique and works in Paris, contributed a series of delicate, flowery landscapes with many debts to French impressionist painting. Individually, they possess a gracious sweetness—especially one that incorporates a brightly colored wooden cottage into a lush garden.

But overall there is a bland sameness.

Corinne Wakeland, a Miami artist who was formally trained in Jamaica, has produced murals at Tropical Park and other sites in conjunction with Miami-Dade County programs for at-risk youth. Her paintings, with their bold, black outlines of women's faces rendered in the searing shades of tropical flora, seem better suited for a large-scale presentation than the easel paintings here, which suffer from a simplistic composition.

Also in the show is Haitian-born Asser Saint-Val, who is showing a promising evolution in his approach to painting the human figure, especially female nudes suffused with coppery shades. He has fractured a larger painting into a series of small squares, evoking various perspectives and blending fragments of the sensual backs of odalisque-like figures into nearly abstract patterns or hard-to-define landscapes.

KIMBERLY GREEN

Family Wealth Brought Social Obligations

November 15, 2000

Hers was a charmed childhood. Pouring bottled water into a crystal glass and sitting down for a talk among the orchids and photographs of Bill Clinton and Mother Teresa that line her office, Kimberly Green owns up to starting out with lots of good luck.

In her family, there was always money to pay for horseback riding, for dance and piano lessons, and later for boarding school in England and trips to Europe.

Her glamorous mother, a one-time model and Miss New York, signed her up for acting classes. Her father, a self-made millionaire and current US ambassador to Singapore, shepherded his daughter around art museums.

SOUP KITCHENS

But growing up, first in Miami and later in Boston, Green also remembers visits to soup kitchens with Mom. They began when she was in sixth grade. On weekends, she helped serve hot meals to homeless men and women.

Those visits marked her first foray into philanthropy, a family custom. As an adult she's continuing that custom with compassion and charm, as well as with a spiritual sense of mission evolved from her religious studies at the College of Santa Fe in New Mexico and with Buddhist monks in Tibet.

Green is a graceful 29-year-old with long auburn hair, curious hazel eyes, and a cartoonish ankle tattoo just visible beneath her gray pants suit.

Since 1997 she has led the Green Family Foundation in Miami Beach, which was established in 1991 by her parents, Steven and Dorothea Green.

Her father, a graduate of Miami Beach Senior High and the University of Miami, is a former chairman and CEO of Samsonite Corporation.

The largesse of the family foundation has touched a vast swath of South Florida, from Habitat for Humanity and the United Foundation for AIDS to the Lowe Art Museum at the University of Miami and the Ambassador Steven and Dorothea Green Library at Florida International University. Funds also support grassroots arts programs run by Miami City Ballet for lower-income children and early childhood development by UM's Department of Pediatrics.

Major gifts have included $250,000 to Camillus House apartments for formerly homeless families, $1 million to the United Way, $1 million to the Red Cross for disaster relief and swim programs, and $2.5 million to FIU. The state of Florida matched the FIU gift, creating the $5 million Steven and Dorothea Green Endowment Fund to support programs for the Art Museum at FIU.

For this youngest Green—friends call her Kim—such giving back goes way back to values instilled by parents who insisted that their two daughters heed the social obligations that come with wealth.

"We had been given a lot, and they made us volunteer," she says simply of herself and big sister Andrea, a lawyer in San Diego.

In elementary school, doing good works was a bit like forced labor, Green admits, but by the time she hit high school, her attraction to altruism blossomed.

"I loved it so much," she says. "It was just something that was innate with me."

Throughout high school and college, Green spent part of her summer vacations volunteering as a Head Start counselor on the Pine Ridge Indian Reservation in South Dakota and as an arts teacher in a Catholic home for abused children.

HANDS ON

All those community service hours set the precedent for the hands-on approach Green brings to the foundation. Her vision has also been shaped by coordinating special events at the United Way in Miami and, about 10 years ago, by working for the fundraising arm of the New York–based Children's Health Fund, a nonprofit cofounded by singer Paul Simon.

"It was really eye-opening," she says of the New York experience, during which she spent one week out of every month working in medical buses making the rounds of homeless shelters. "We knew exactly what we were working for. I think a lot of agencies become so financially goal-oriented that you forget who you are raising the money for."

As a result, she and the foundation's executive director, Angela McBride, often take part in the efforts they support. These include children's programs at the Miami Rescue Mission initiated by Bessie Garrett, a nurse at the Miami Veterans Affairs Hospital.

"We decided we would much rather be down with Bessie doing something with the kids than going to a cocktail reception at the Delano," says Green.

She got to know Garrett two years ago when the nurse was one of 10 winners of the annual Green Family Foundation United Way American Values Award, which honors the volunteer activities of public servants with dinner at the Biltmore and checks for $5,000.

Touched to hear that Garrett planned to use her $5,000 to fund a trip to Disney World for children and their welfare-to-work mothers, Green was "the first to come forward and say let us help you do that," says Tamara Klingler, senior vice president of the Miami-Dade United Way. "She very much follows in her family tradition of doing good and giving back and understanding how important that is."

The Disney trip has since become an annual excursion for some 50 kids, who each receive $20 to spend on toys; it's funded by the Green Family Foundation and an anonymous donor.

GUT-WRENCHING

"On the first trip, some of the kids were coming up and asking us if they could use it [their $20] to buy bread on the way home," recalls Green, who says she is continually moved by the generosity of people with modest resources. "Here are these kids who have the opportunity to get a new toy and they want to take food home to their families. It was gut-wrenching."

She also sees unselfishness in friends who are teachers, bartenders, and waitresses who donated supplies to a public school and picked up hammer and nail for a Habitat for Humanity project in Little Haiti.

"Getting my friends to volunteer was easier than getting a check out of someone who lives on Fisher Island," she says. Volunteering "is not about money. People love doing it because it makes them feel good."

Green's own generosity is deeply affected by her interest in the spiritual dimensions of various cultures. Dennis Kendrick witnessed that when he invited Green, soon after she'd moved back to Miami from Santa Fe in 1996, to teach a course in world religion with him at Bay Point School, a nonprofit boarding school in South Dade for juvenile delinquents.

Kendrick, an adjunct religion professor at FIU, says that "despite all her advantages, she shows great empathy and sensitivity. She can communicate the cultural values of different religions. She really did relate to the students."

The experience at Bay Point also tested Green's dedication.

"It was very hard. They all towered over me; they didn't take me seriously at first," she recalls. "You had Guatemalan gang members fighting with Ecuadoreans, Haitian gang members fighting with African Americans."

She began talking about Buddhism. "They would say, 'How the hell could Buddha walk and flowers come out of his feet,' and I would say, 'Well, how did Jesus die and come back to life three days later?' It was showing them how other cultures don't necessarily have the same mindset."

CHILDHOOD STORY

The Green family's magnanimous mindset elicits Kendrick's admiration, especially for a young woman who could easily find far less demanding things to do. He recalls a story Green's mother shared with him about her daughter as a child: Green looked at the colorful, hovering figures in a Picasso painting her parents had just bought and pronounced them guardian angels. The comment was telling.

"She really is a guardian angel herself, along with her parents," says Kendrick. "They look out for the poor and disadvantaged."

MARIO ALGAZE

Cuba Proved the Missing Link in My Career, Photographer Says

November 30, 2000

Mario Algaze left Cuba as a teenager in 1960. He returned last year for the first time, camera in hand.

During that visit, the South Florida artist crisscrossed the island, snapping nearly 500 images in three weeks. Traveling in a 1982 Soviet-made Lada prone to frequent breakdowns, he captured the crumbling elegance of Old Havana and sea spray crashing over the city's famed Malecón.

He also photographed a schoolchild holding a Cuban flag in Trinidad, a vast field of malanga in the countryside, and a lone bicyclist in Matanzas.

A dozen or so of those vivid black-and-white images go on view Friday in *Mario Algaze: Cuba, 1999–2000* at Books & Books in Coral Gables.

Algaze has taken his camera all over Latin America, and his work has been collected by museums in the United States and Mexico. But there was, he says, "a missing link, and the missing link was my homeland."

Invited to Cuba by the Casa de las Américas in Havana, Algaze said he agreed to come only on his terms.

The visit would have to be "an apolitical trip . . . without any involvement whatsoever from any government agency," he said.

Plus, he wanted to photograph "during the early winter, when the light is magical at that time in the tropics."

Not only was the light right for his trip, but so was the timing for this one-month show.

"There are some people in Miami that won't welcome any contact with the island, but I think the majority has outgrown that," says the artist, who has won fellowships from the National Endowment for the Humanities, the South Florida Cultural Consortium, and the CINTAS Foundation. "I'm just being neutral and trying to follow my own visual vocabulary and not somebody else's agenda. I've always dreamed of the day I could go back and photograph Cuba."

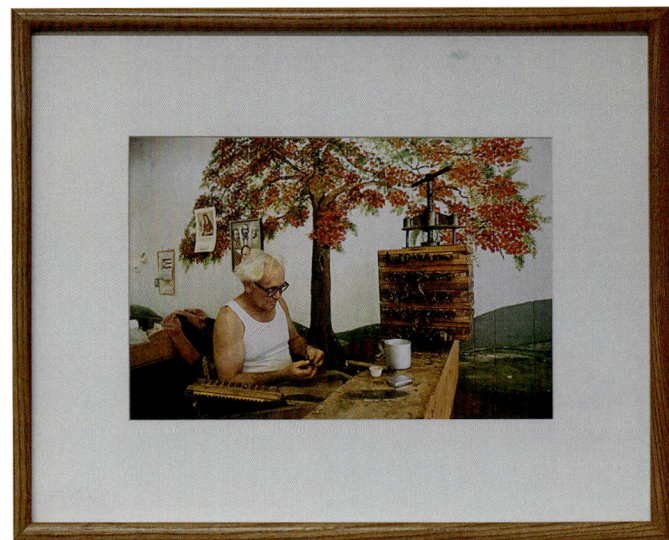

FIGURE 18. Mario Algaze, *Little Havana Series (Rolling Cigars)*, 1984. Color photograph. Image Ryan Holloway, courtesy of Miami-Dade County Department of Cultural Affairs, Art in Public Places Trust.

FIGURE 19. Mario Algaze, *Lummus Park*, Circa 1989. Selenium-toned silver gelatin print. Image Ryan Holloway, courtesy of Miami-Dade County Department of Cultural Affairs, Art in Public Places Trust.

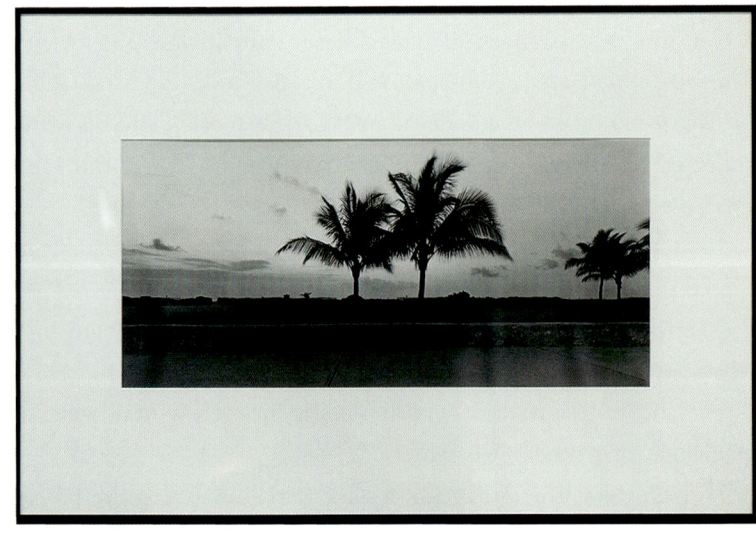

While he was disappointed to see how people on the island struggle to make ends meet, Havana charmed him utterly.

The city may be like "a beauty queen devoid of a good manicure and facial," he insists, but "she's still the grande dame. There's nothing like that in all of the Americas."

Mario Algaze is the first show at Books & Books's new quarters on Aragon Avenue and is accompanied by a catalog.

A larger version of the exhibit goes on view in April at Throckmorton Fine Art in New York City.

In memoriam: Mario Algaze, 1947–2022

ALL SEEMS PROMISING
FOR SOUTH FLORIDA EDITION
OF WORLD'S TOP ART FAIR

December 16, 2000

Samuel Keller looked thrilled with Wednesday's moonlit evening after the downpours that recently drenched South Florida.

As director of Switzerland's Art Basel, the world's largest and most prestigious art fair, Keller was here to host an invitation-only reception at the Miami Beach Convention Center. That's where the Basel fair will stage its first North American event next December. And the good weather seemed like a good omen.

The most recent Art Basel, the 31st, drew 55,000 visitors and 270 galleries from Europe, the Americas, Australia, and Asia. Hailed as a tremendous coup, the South Florida version will be called Art Basel Miami Beach and is expected to generate as many as 1,500 hotel bookings on peak nights and attract 150 major galleries.

But when the idea of Art Basel in Miami Beach moved closer to reality last year, on the eve of Art Miami's 10th anniversary fair, it fueled heated debate over both events. The clamor has since quieted, with Art Basel agreeing on a December date and Art Miami retaining its January schedule. So it was no surprise that Keller's reception was not only rain-free but shining with South Beach charm. As guests walked down a runway into a white gossamer tent lit with a mirror ball, 10 leggy models in white gowns greeted them in 10 languages.

"I'm delighted that Art Basel will soon have a sister in this glamorous city one year from tonight," Keller told a crowd of 350 and a who's who of players from South Florida's visual art scene.

Among the collectors on hand: Norman and Irma Braman, Martin Z. Margulies, Donald and Mera Rubell, and Richard and Ruth Shack.

"Our vision is to make Miami Beach a gathering place for the finest artists, collectors, art dealers, critics, and museums," said Keller. "South Florida art museums will play a central role," he promised.

A stylish dresser with a shaved head and a warm smile, Keller has been traveling regularly to South Florida since Art Basel signed a contract with the Miami Beach Convention Center last June. In October, he slipped into a seat next to the Rubells at a lecture at the Art Museum at Florida International University and later attended a dinner party for patrons of the Museum of Contemporary Art.

His visits also have included meetings with local art consultant Stefanie Block Reed, who says she's targeted more than 30 US museum groups to attend Art Basel Miami Beach, and independent curator Amy Cappellazzo, who's organizing parallel exhibits outside the convention center.

"This is a way for people who live in the city to discover art and for guests to discover the city," Keller said.

Born and bred in Basel, Keller is married and has an 8-year-old son. Early on, a rained-out field trip to the countryside led to his first encounter with art when a teacher took the 11-year-old Keller and his classmates instead to see the witty, clanking sculpture of fellow Swiss Jean Tinguely.

"I was very surprised to learn that art didn't just hang on the wall," he recalls, "but could make noise."

He went on to study art history at the University of Basel and became fluent in English, French, German, and Italian. And he's still not satisfied.

"I hope my Spanish will improve," he says. And because Art Basel Miami Beach will feature more Latin American galleries than the fair in Switzerland, Keller has the rest of his organizing team taking Spanish lessons as well.

Before taking the helm of Art Basel last January, Keller, 34, worked for five years as the fair's communication manager.

That experience has served him well in dealing with the press. When asked to be more specific about crossover programs, Keller politely but firmly sidesteps. "It makes no sense to tell one year in advance. Then when the events come, people could say, 'Oh, we've heard it before,'" he says. "We are working on a major film night, fashion show, something with architecture."

Especially architecture. Keller is smitten with the art deco ambience of Miami Beach: "You see some pictures from Ocean Drive and you think maybe the art deco is just some houses that people show the tourists, but it's a whole part of town where people live and where there are cultural institutions. This area has such a vibrant cultural life."

And it will grow more vibrant next December.

In memoriam: Richard Shack, 1926–2012

PART III

MIAMI /
"A LOT OF
FREEDOM TO
EXPERIMENT,"
2001–2004

For the most part, the years 2001 to 2004 were rewarding to witness. An emboldened art community flexed its creative muscle. Artists and collectors as well as museums and galleries became more proactive by nurturing Miami-based talent. When in 2001 the inaugural Art Basel Miami Beach was postponed one year following the 9/11 terrorist attacks, the art community did not shelve plans to highlight local talent in December of that year but rallied to continue them. Artists did double duty as curators, exploring new opportunities for other artists and for themselves. This moment saw the art community grow in national and international cachet when the inaugural Art Basel Miami Beach and satellite fairs at last arrived in 2002. Out-of-the-way neighborhoods were tapped for innovative art projects by those who saw their potential when others did not. And once again, some promising initiatives did not bear fruit.

Part 3 begins with "Miami Arts Project: River Dance," recounting ideas from the ambitious but short-lived nonprofit Miami Arts Project (MAP) to rethink the Miami River area, an unlovely and unlikely location for art. MAP commissioned artists outside Miami to create images for billboards near the workaday river. They were Dan Graham, Jack Pierson, Andrea Robbins and Max Becher, and Mark Robbins and Carrie Mae Weems. Images were to be in conversation with the mélange of neighborhoods the river traverses, a typically South Florida mosaic of Black, Hispanic, and white neighborhoods along the river in Allapattah and East Little Havana, Overtown and Spring Garden.

MAP's efforts dovetailed somewhat with Miami River Commission goals to make the river more pedestrian friendly by establishing a Miami River Greenway. To that end, MAP also commissioned Stalker, a group of Italian artists and architects, to create *Domino Miami*, an installation at Miami's new alternative art space, Locust Projects. It featured video and a sculpture shaped like giant domino blocks, displaying aerial photographs of Miami River neighborhoods and labeled with names of cultural groups—from Yoruba to Mayan to Pennsylvania Dutch—that occupy Miami.

Yet in my February 17, 2001, *Miami Herald* column "Miami Arts Project Misses the Boat," I wrote that MAP did not live up to its potential. It needed a more organic relationship with the city for which it was named. There was poor communication with the public regarding where the billboards were located. Additionally, the project lacked substantial programming to underscore the intent of spotlighting Miami's diverse neighborhoods through contemporary art. MAP might have made more impact if there had been a series of public talks at various locations to engage audiences or even a sequence of thematically connected exhibits.

Briefly recalling *Surrounded Islands* on a much smaller scale, this project also involved out-of-town artists choosing unlikely locations in Miami for creating contemporary, experimental art. But MAP offered little or no interaction with the local community and with Miami's own creative energies. There was nothing even approaching the fiercely committed, on-the-ground engagement with Miami that Christo and Jeanne-Claude famously brought to Miami and to their projects in other locations.

In 2001, the year it was involved with MAP, the nonprofit alternative art space Locust Projects was an upstart in a little-known upstart arts neighborhood called Wynwood. A few years later the art space moved a few blocks away to the Miami Design District. In 2023, its address changed again, further north to Little River / Little Haiti to a much larger, over 8,000-square-foot industrial warehouse.

For years, Locust Projects has sought to energize Miami's art community by enabling artists outside Miami and from Miami to go beyond market constraints. Founding artists were Westen Charles, Cooper, and Elizabeth Withstandley; only Westen Charles still lives in Miami. A conversation with Charles, Withstandley, and artist Jonathan Pylypchuk speaking about the early days of Locust Projects is documented in the 2023 book *Making Miami: The Story of an Art Community*. Said Withstandley, "It's 25 years after we started Locust, which sounds crazy, and it's nice that it still exists and is providing opportunities for artists. I'm involved with the open-call process, and I try to make sure that there are elements of some of our origins. Wes is still on the board there and he's very involved. I just don't run across many new organizations like Locust." Currently, Locust Projects is led by Lorie Mertes.

Artists themselves took on more visible roles as curators, bringing inside perspective to the accelerating activity. Artist-curators Martin Oppel, Bhakti

Mar Baxter, and Tao Rey of The House, then one of Miami's newest art venues, had another home temporarily in 2001. They became curators of an exhibit at the Museum of Contemporary Art in North Miami.

Later that year, Robert Chambers curated *globe>Miami>island* at Bass Museum of Art in Miami Beach, featuring work by 30 artists. Reviewed in "Global Perspective," December 23, 2001, it was distinguished by a pervasive generosity of spirit. And that spirit was both a weakness and a stubborn strength. At the show's entrance, there was a muddled variety of art pointing to a chaotic mix of directions.

Despite such flaws, the show was a memorable highlight for Miami's maturing art community. Bringing these artists together with others with ties to Miami, such as sculptor Ursula Von Rydingsvard and Janine Antoni, amounted to something of a homecoming, a panoramic take on the Miami art scene.

Chambers's experience brought to this show an effervescent sensibility, matching the sensibility erupting from his own eccentric installations. Amy Cappellazzo wrote an essay for the catalog documenting this show, as she did again for the one Chambers curated in 2022, *The BluPrnt Show*. Commemorating the 20th anniversary of *globe>Miami>island*, it was a must-see event for Miami Art Week 2022. Chambers credited an "all-volunteer team of participating artists, assistant curators, art historians, and producers," as he explained on its website. The location was the venerable Bridge Red Studios, a North Miami warehouse with artist studios and an admirable commitment to presenting work by mid-career artists.

On December 26, 2001, as described in "Basel Leaving Imprint on Mix of New Events," there were numerous events that happened that year in December, despite the one-year postponement of Art Basel Miami Beach. This lively, if uneven, flurry of events testified to the self-starting drive of the art community.

Earlier in 2001, solo museum shows for Pablo Cano and the duo Roberto Behar and Rosario Marquardt of R&R Studios reflected Miami's capacity to engender storytelling spiked with fantasy, perhaps as a result of the city's ever-evolving exile culture, in which abruptly displaced exiles often reconstruct dreams in newly discovered surroundings, generally working with materials common to Miami. Such reconstructed dreams have happened in a place perennially reinventing itself in the wake of the region's boom-and-bust-and-boom-again cycle of real estate development and its heavily marketed glamour in boom times.

The March 25, 2001, column "Puppet Master" reviewed Cano's show and performance at the Museum of Contemporary Art. Puppetry, poetry, and trash have beguiled Cano for years. To this trinity of sources he brought a magical spirituality nurtured by art of the past and thrift-shop decor of the present. This new work, lorded over by a prideful peacock with red fingernails rearing from an aluminum trash can, was called *To Sin or Not to Sin*.

It's possible to trace Cano's appropriation of such odds and ends to the works of Robert Rauschenberg and Marcel Duchamp and to early 20th-century collages created by the rebellious founders of the Dada movement, which foreshadowed surrealism and its peculiar dreamscapes.

The short 2010 documentary *Pablo Cano: The Blue Ribbon* from Miami-based Wet Heat Project takes us on a late-night visit to Cano's Little Havana studio to see his unusual marionettes come to life. It explores his meticulous craftsmanship and loving rescue of peculiar thrift-shop finds entwined with disarming appropriations of art history icons, from Andy Warhol's soup cans to early Renaissance portraits by Piero della Francesca. *The Blue Ribbon* was Cano's 2008 multimedia performance at North Miami's Museum of Contemporary Art in homage to 10 art historical masterpieces.

Constructing another arena for figures playing out fantasies in a dream-like setting, there was *Roberto Behar and Rosario Marquardt: Card Sharks*, a review from April 27, 2003. It was as if Miami had become these visionary artists' playroom, a big city deserving big toys and dreams to match. Their latest living-large toy was a festive house of cards—perhaps about to collapse but perhaps not—built for the Miami Art Museum (MAM) and presented in the museum's *New Work* series.

At MAM, the house of cards was a 12-foot-high mansion of make-believe, built with cards that were 2.5 feet tall. Surrounding them was a wooden scaffold, suggesting a place that had not yet taken its final shape.

So much of Behar and Marquardt's work has been fashioned for a young city with arrivals from all over the map. Like the house of cards, their art is often scaled too big or too small for staid grown-ups. It is, however, sized just right for minds open to multiple possibilities in new, evolving places.

As artists did their part to expand the art scene, several collectors took their role as patrons to another level. They commissioned new works by Miami artists for their homes and places of business as reported in "Miami Collectors Commission Art," November 3, 2002.

To avoid major misunderstandings, collectors worked with artists whose work they already knew and admired. Some talked with the artist about their hopes for the space and may have approved a maquette or drawings, but the key to a successful commission, they said, is to let the artist work unimpeded. The collectors were Jeff Gelblum, Milton Ferrell Jr., and Ruth and Richard Shack. Gelblum commissioned new work by Glexis Novoa, and Ferrell commissioned new work by José Bedia, Carlos Betancourt, and Rubén Torres Llorca for his law firm in downtown Miami.

The Shacks chose artist Karen Rifas. They had puzzled over a narrow horizontal section of wall space just above windows overlooking Biscayne Bay and the bridge to Key Biscayne. They asked many artists for suggestions, but it was Rifas's proposal for the space that won them over. After showing them a maquette, she spent hours installing multiple strings of oak leaves that float above the window and, in a magical bit of rhyming, re-created the contours of the bridge and islands below.

"I like to do things that are site specific, that bounce off an environment," said Rifas, who stitched leaves together on a 30-year-old Singer sewing machine.

When I visited their home in 2002, Richard Shack (1926–2012) and Ruth Shack were prominent civic leaders and collectors in Miami. From Richard's *Miami Herald* obituary posted on the blog of fellow collector George Lindemann: "The Shacks' Brickell Avenue penthouse became 'a well-known stop on the Art Basel VIP circuit,' said fellow collector Dennis Scholl, vice president/arts for the Knight Foundation and, like Dick Shack, a founding board member of North Miami's Museum of Contemporary Art."

After her election to the Dade County (now Miami-Dade County) Commission in 1976, Ruth Shack made her mark as a passionate advocate for civil rights and for art and architecture. In 2016, the Miami-Dade Cultural Affairs Council honored her with the Culture Champion award. "Ruth Shack's leadership contributions are far reaching, to national and international levels," said Adolfo Henriques, chairman of the council, at the 2016 ceremony honoring her. "Cultural pioneers like Ruth Shack paved the way. Presenting Miami's Cultural Champion Award to Ruth means so much to so many, including national arts leaders, international philanthropists, artists, performers, and cultural visionaries. Her accomplishments are legendary."

In 2019, Rifas won the $75,000 Oolite Arts Michael Richards Award. For this award, she was selected by a jury of national and local artists and curators. Rifas was recognized for her art aiming to reconfigure and reimagine space, as demonstrated by the spare precision of her sculptural cord and leaf installations as well as her disciplined line drawings. Her richly colored solo show devoted to overlapping geometric shapes in 2018 at the Bass Museum was preceded by solo shows at the Museum of Art and Design at Miami Dade College, the de la Cruz Collection, and the Savannah College of Art and Design.

Those proactive collectors who commissioned new work by Miami artists in 2002 may have anticipated the visionary program Commissioner, begun in 2018. It has established innovative ways to encourage collectors to support Miami artists. Founded by Deja Carrington and Rebekah Monson, Commissioner is an art membership program pairing artists with collectors in order to commission new work by local contemporary artists. Innovative events enhance community connections with art by offering members visits to studios and galleries, snorkeling expeditions, and art tourism travels to Mexico City and New Orleans. It was launched with the support of the Knight Foundation's Arts Challenge. Fiscal sponsors are the Miami Foundation and Diaspora Vibe Cultural Arts Incubator. For Miami Art Week 2024, it organized a program of select fairs and events, including performances and talks at The Carter Project, Wynwood Norte, and a visit to the live movement and sound performance of *GeoVanna Gonzalez: Flowing Pathways* at the Museum of Art and Design at MDC College, Downtown.

Stimulating if rarely market-friendly experimental electronic media became more apparent around the years 2002 and 2003 as organizers and artists sought a wider audience. *"Cutting-Edge Art Will Leave You Flarbbergasted"* in 2002 looked at a series of video and film screenings produced by The Experimental Show, a forum to showcase new electronic art forms. The invented word *flarbbergasted* was an editorial wordplay on the name FLARB2, the experimental video and film program founded on a shoestring budget by artist Elizabeth Hall. She joked that Flarb could also stand for Florida Art Bureau. "If we want to raise the level of discourse, and if art is to have an enduring dialogue with science and technology, then we need to talk to more people," Hall said. "We have to open it up. The reason we're seeing new media is that artists are yearning to say more and speak to different levels." A year later, the 2003 review of *Plugged In: New and Electronic Art* at the Art and Culture Center/Hollywood assessed this gathering of mostly underrecognized South Florida artists. When commercial galleries don't show high-resolution videos, Hall remarked, it's easier to avoid predictable paths. "The good thing about Miami is that there is a lot of freedom to experiment," she asserted, "and not conform to what a gallery would want."

During this time, three pairs of artists who often share space and ideas spoke to me about their artistic practice: Beatriz Monteavaro and Gavin Perry, Hernan Bas and Naomi Fisher, and Dara Friedman and Mark Handforth. These free-flowing, spirited conversations took place across Greater Miami. They were a revealing chance to gain unscripted insights into how and why each became artists as all their careers progressed.

For April 2002's "Gavin Perry and Beatriz Monteavaro: Profiles in Collecting," I visited their studios at the Miami Beach ArtCenter/South Florida, now dramatically changed as Oolite Arts. I was curious about their lively collection of toys—chiefly action figures and miniature low-rider cars—and how that had shaped their adventurous art. As artists now living and working in Miami, their recognition continues to grow. In recent years, the art membership program Commissioner has commissioned new work from both.

For January 2004's "Amazing Journey: Naomi Fisher, Hernan Bas Connect in Life and Art," I visited their shared studio in the Miami Design District, currently a retail space. Together they contributed to Miami's artistic community by cofounding the nonprofit Bas Fisher Invitational (BFI), a nomadic space inviting artists to experiment and thrive as a community. BFI marked its 20th anniversary in 2024, with support from the Knight Foundation, Andy Warhol Foundation, Miami-Dade Department of Cultural Affairs, and others.

For April 2004's "Mark Handforth and Dara Friedman," our interview took place in their apartment in an art deco building in Miami Beach. Since 2004, they have exhibited widely internationally but maintain close connections to Miami. Friedman has spoken compellingly about her research in Calusa Indigenous culture and its influence on her filming a radiant sunrise and sunset over the Everglades during an AIRIE (Artists in Residence in Everglades) residency.

In the May 2004 story "Creating Public Treasures," I recounted a hard-hat tour of what was then known as Miami's Performing Arts Center (PAC) when it was still under construction. This was to preview PAC's commissioned art by Miami-Dade Art in Public Places. Only the vibrant glass mosaic mural *Ways of Performing* by Cundo Bermúdez was completed, but it was not yet installed. That day, workers carefully laid out sections of the mural on a concrete floor. The elderly artist, 89, was present. It was a touching, historic moment when he saw the mural in its entirety for the first time. The mural's rich, glowing hues created a stark contrast with its raw concrete surroundings. The actual drama of any performance seemed very far away when the harsh cacophony of hammers and drills pierced the air. Two years later, the PAC opened under a new name as the Carnival Center for the Performing Arts, thanks to a pledged gift of $20 million from Carnival Corporation. Also in 2006, the Knight Foundation donated $10 million to the PAC. As a result of this donation, the center's Carnival Concert Hall was renamed the John S. and James L. Knight Concert Hall.

Plagued for years by rising costs and delays, the long-awaited venue in downtown Miami was sharply criticized for being built "too big and too soon." It had been touted as a world-class center to revitalize the city's moribund downtown, but many might not have been comfortable attending at night. After one year, it was operating in the red, with disappointing ticket sales and changing leadership.

In 2008, there was another multimillion-dollar gift and another renaming. Philanthropist and former Total Bank chair Adrienne Arsht gave $30 million to the center. In her honor the center was renamed the Adrienne Arsht Center for the Performing Arts of Miami-Dade County. Over the years since 2008, downtown Miami has become much more vibrant. There's a glamorous skyline with many places downtown to live, work, and play.

And during that same time, the Arsht has offered a range of programs. Some might be called more mainstream, such as the musical comedy *Mamma Mia*, but others draw on Miami's diverse cultures in sophisticated ways. Classics have been reinvented. In particular, the Miami City Ballet has drawn rave reviews for performances at the Arsht and at Lincoln Center in New York City. Coinciding with Miami Art Week in 2022 and 2024, the center has presented multimedia productions by the celebrated South African visual artist William Kentridge.

In 2019, Johann Zeitsman became president and CEO of the Arsht. Soon after arriving, he developed "Arshtconnect," a comprehensive strategic plan based on gathering extensive community feedback. As of 2022, during his tenure he has overseen more than 400 performances, supported increased arts education at the Arsht, and took part in greeting the five millionth guest to enter the Arsht for a performance.

In April 2024, another impactful gift to the Arsht was announced. This was a $2.5 million gift to support arts education, including free performances for Miami-Dade County Public School students, from the Miami-based Green Family Foundation.

The August 2003 review of Kerry Stuart Coppin's photographs at the Lowe Art Museum mirrored how Miami led to a new stage in this prolific Black photographer's career. He photographed the African diaspora in the Caribbean and North America, from Little Haiti to Havana, and traveled to Senegal to document links between the not-so-new world on this side of the Atlantic and urban, Westernized cities in West Africa. Several of his photographs in Senegal belong to the Miami-Dade Art in Public Places Collection. There seems to be a calculated, subversive irony at work in Coppin's photographs. They show how traditions borne of colonizers' brutal slave trade have been reinvented in modern times for the Caribbean tourist trade. These include his photograph of Afro-Caribbean Santería ceremonies performed before an eerie mural, painted with multiple eyes, in Havana and the "Crop Over" parade in Barbados. "Crop Over" festivities date back to celebrations for enslaved laborers permitted by plantation owners in Barbados and other Caribbean islands when the notoriously backbreaking work of harvesting sugarcane was finished. Barbados, where sugarcane plantations date back to the 17th century, was one of England's most commercially successful colonies. Deputy director of the Barbados Museum and Historical Society Kevin Farmer told the *New York Times* that generational wealth acquired from sugar and other crops through the late 19th century in the New World was only possible due to the "blood, tears and death" of millions of Africans whose labor had been stolen. The Kerry Stuart Coppin photographs of Barbados, Cuba, Senegal, and the United States were donated to the Smithsonian Anacostia Community Museum in 2006 by the artist.

In the world of 1950s pinup beauties, Bunny Yeager was both the gorgeous girl in front of the camera and the photographer snapping the picture. Working from her studio in Miami Shores in the 1950s and 1960s, Yeager sold beauty and the beach with catchy style. Though Yeager's market dwindled in the 1970s, her vintage photos had come back in demand when shown at Javogue & Ingalls Fine Art in North Miami and reviewed February 2003. That demand continues. The 2023 documentary *Naked Ambition: Bunny Yeager*, directed by Dennis Scholl and Kareem Tabsch, won a Made in MIA feature award when screened at the 2024 Miami Film Festival.

Timed to open for Art Basel Miami Beach 2003, the fair's second iteration, Miami Art Central (MAC), was a new venue conceived to showcase programs of art, music, and film, as the November 2003 "New Space—and Its Artists—Has a Lot of Potential" column reported. MAC's 33,000 square feet of galleries announced bold potential. Despite several years of engaging and challenging programs, among them solo shows for Carmen Herrera and William Kentridge, ultimately MAC did not succeed.

On January 1, 2007, *The Art Newspaper* reported that Miami Art Central and Miami Art Museum could merge to create a collaborative MAC@MAM initiative. In my March 18, 2007, *Miami Herald* column, I reported that MAC would close April 15. "MAC will evolve inside MAM's premises," a spokesperson told me. But that did not happen, as plans for MAM's new identity took shape without MAC. In 2013, MAM was renamed the Jorge M. Pérez Art Museum (PAMM) of Miami-Dade County when it moved to a 200,000-square-foot facility overlooking Biscayne Bay in Museum Park.

Nervy exhibits at a loose network of artist-run spaces remained active through February and March 2004, recounted in "Way Outside the Galleries,"

February 2004. Clustered in the Design District, Wynwood, and Edgewater neighborhoods, these spaces included The House, Placemaker Gallery, World Arts Building, and FoodCultureMuseum. Setting the tone for them was The Free Spirits Artists' Lounge, installed temporarily with locally produced art at a Miami Beach bar during the 2003 Art Basel Miami Beach fair. "It was spontaneous, and the variety of projects and how they used the space had a great energy. It seemed very homegrown and genuine," said Miami Art Museum curator Cheryl Hartup.

During these years, important attention came to Latina artists with ties to Miami: María Martínez-Cañas, Teresita Fernández, and Eugenia Vargas. (Only Martínez-Cañas still lives and works in Miami.)

The May 2002 review of *María Martínez-Cañas: A Retrospective* at the Museum of Art in Fort Lauderdale, now NSU Art Museum Fort Lauderdale, described a prescient video self-portrait of Martínez-Cañas in 1984, when she was 24 and a graduate student at the School of the Art Institute of Chicago. The video foretells her tightly composed photomontages, with glimpses of vulnerable bodies set amid fluid designs evocative of islands and geometric enclosures inspired by maps of colonial Cuba, maps she studied in Spain in 1986 on a Fulbright-Hays grant. The 2002 retrospective surveyed her career as a nationally prominent photographic artist, including her representation in *Arte Latino: Treasures from the Smithsonian American Art Museum*. Today her professional website documents many national and international institutions that collect her art. In 2020, she received the Oolite Arts Michael Richards Award and in 2016 a Pollock-Krasner Foundation Photography Fellowship.

For the December 2002 profile of Teresita Fernández, we spoke about her ongoing interest in rainbows, clouds, and intricately landscaped gardens on the occasion of her solo show then at the Miami Art Museum. I wrote that she mingles natural forms with carefully constructed ones to create spare interiors that visitors can walk through, spurring eventful trips in their imaginations. In 2019, she returned to Miami for a solo show at the Pérez Art Museum Miami. Her career has flourished with prestigious awards and international recognition. Fernández became a MacArthur Fellow in 2005.

In 2003, Miami-based Eugenia Vargas was chosen to represent her native

Chile for the 50th Venice Biennale. Not only was it a coup for the artist, but it could be seen as a stunning recognition of Miami's growing art scene. For the first time in recent memory, an artist working in Miami was tapped for the Venice Biennale. In part 3 are two stories about Vargas's representation in *An Archipelago of Images*, a series of solo shows by artists from nine Latin American countries organized by the Italian–Latin American Institute in Rome for the 50th Venice Biennale. They are "Eugenia Vargas: A Dream Made Real," written in Miami after a studio visit with the artist and published May 2003, and "Eugenia Vargas: Slice of Latin American Spirit Spices Up Jaded Venice Crowd," written on assignment in Venice and published June 2003.

It was especially exciting for me to follow her career during the years 2001 to 2003. Vargas is a photographer and performance artist who lived and worked in Miami in the late 1990s before moving back to Chile in 2003. While she was in Miami, she drew admiration for the generous, activist spirit animating the *Home Shows*, which she staged intermittently at her home in North Miami. For these *Home Shows*, she gave artists free rein to convert nearly every room into an impromptu gallery for showing such varied work as sculpture, photography, installation art, video, and painting. Artist william cordova curated one of these shows, she recalled to me then, and Robert Chambers curated the last one in September 2002, which remained in place until January 2003. Today she's known as Eugenia Vargas-Pereira. Vargas-Pereira currently lives and works in Tucson, Arizona, and Santiago, Chile.

MIAMI ARTS PROJECT

River Dance

February 17, 2001

The Miami River runs through it.

"It" is a mélange of neighborhoods and a collage of history; a typically South Florida mosaic of Black, Hispanic, and white families living along the water in Allapattah and East Little Havana, Overtown and Spring Garden.

The river flows past the pre-Columbian mysteries of the Miami Circle, an 1840s plantation cabin built by enslaved Africans in Lummus Park, and a lot where float builders craft their magic for the Orange Bowl Parade.

Cargo—legal and illegal—has long traveled here: rum runners from Bimini slid through during Prohibition, while today the river is a conduit for smugglers of drugs and refugees. Amid pelicans and manatees, Caribbean and Central American freighters crammed with everything from refrigerators to bicycles jockey for position with luxury yachts heading upriver for repairs.

Now urban planners working with the Miami River Commission and a handful of international artists and architects are pushing their vision for a kinder, gentler river—one welcoming to pedestrians but still true to its hardworking self.

To suggest ways to rethink the river's identity and recognize its fascinating history, six artists have designed 44 billboards posted near the river. The billboards—including 6 more in Hialeah, Opa-locka, and Medley—were installed in mid-January and will remain up through March 31.

The work was commissioned by the nonprofit Miami Arts Project, as was *Domino Miami*, a related exhibit of sculpture and video by Stalker, a group of Italian artists and architects. Stalker's work is on view through March 3 at Locust Projects, an alternative arts venue in Miami.

Carrie Mae Weems, a New York–based photographer whose evocative images and text make up some of the MAP billboards, calls the river an "amazing" place where cultures collide.

"Not only do you have mega money," she says, "but you have Haitians trying to fend for themselves, you have Cubans and Dominicans coming to this first port of call from the south. And when you start thinking about the ideas of exploration, and that 400 years ago it was relatively easy to sail to Florida, you start to understand how water is so important to colonial expansion, and that it's still taking place."

The river, she says "really becomes a great cultural and social exchange on every level."

But many Miamians see it as little more than a roadblock.

"The river is a border that divides communities," says Lorenzo Romito, a Stalker member who visited South Florida last March with Weems and others to study the river for MAP.

"People see it as a place where you get stuck [by drawbridges] and have to wait five minutes as boats pass by. The only people we saw walking along it didn't have money for a car."

A NICE PAUSE

A video at Locust Projects shows Stalker members passing out coffee to drivers waiting while the Flagler Street Bridge is raised one March morning. Drivers were wary but also welcomed this chance to "get out of their cars and face the river," explains Romito, "and catch a positive little parenthesis in their life."

Stalker has crisscrossed Italy, France, and Germany, attracting public appreciation of underused urban spaces through a number of offbeat projects such as dyeing streets blue or hanging hammocks in a decrepit Roman alley—a move that lured musicians and others to picnic in the usually shunned spot.

At Locust Projects, the group is showing a sculpture shaped like giant domino blocks, coated with aerial photographs of Miami River neighborhoods and labeled with names of the 63 cultural groups—from Yoruba to Mayan to Pennsylvania Dutch—that occupy Miami.

Their project was partly inspired by Stalker's encounter with domino players at Lummus Park, but at Locust, visitors can move the blocks around, bringing diverse groups together.

The MAP billboards also contain specific references to local history and landmarks. One, by Dan Graham, shows a crocodile tussling with an alligator, an allusion both to the predatory instincts of some real estate developers and to the long-gone Miami River tourist attraction where Miccosukee tribe members wrestled alligators.

To let more residents near the river know about agencies making plans that could affect their neighborhoods, MAP billboards by the artist team of Andrea Robbins and Max Becher are printed with a phone number (305-ONRIVER) and website where people can get information or express opinions about the river's future in English, Spanish, and Creole.

Jack Pierson's billboards are composed of photographs of people he has known who have died, some from AIDS, while Mark Robbins and Weems most successfully focus on the river's cargo and the sociological ebb and flow it implies.

Robbins's photographs, stamped "Import/Export," are based on his interviews with Haitian, Dominican, and Salvadoran ship workers. Their up-close portraits stand before distant backdrops of wealth, such as office towers and cruise liners.

IMMIGRANTS' IMPACT

Weems's billboards bring ravishing energy to banal street corners, paying homage to immigrants from Jamaica, Barbados, Haiti, and Cuba and to their all-seeing Afro-Caribbean spirits. One billboard shows a woman draped in beads, another a watery expanse with a tiny ship or island on the horizon.

This vista is a reminder, says Weems, that water and the river can connect all of us to our primal past.

"You arrived from across the oceans of time," reads her beautiful billboard, "I watched as you labored long and hard to clear this land."

But the artwork by itself isn't enough to effect permanent change along the river. Toward that end, representatives of the Miami River Commission and the Trust for Public Land, a national nonprofit agency, will meet in April with City of Miami and Miami-Dade County commissioners to present their plan for the Miami River Greenway.

"Our goal is to make the river a place where people want to be, to exercise or go for a walk or shop," says Lavinia Freeman, Trust for Public Land's program manager. "It's a tremendous resource."

NO SOUTH BEACH

And while noting that the river is a huge economic engine that helps generate more than $5 billion annually, primarily from the shipping industry, Freeman says her group is "not trying to make the river South Beach. It has its own character, which will be maintained."

The Greenway would line about 85 percent of the river with 20-foot-wide walkways and bicycle paths, skirting existing businesses but still linking neighborhoods by winding along nearby streets. A priority is to develop the downtown section, from the mouth to the Fifth Street Bridge, says David Miller, Miami River Commission director.

Miller envisions a cluster of shops and restaurants that will make the river and the nearby historic Lummus Park more inviting to tourists and residents in the manner of Fort Lauderdale's River Walk and other riverside parks in cities such as Cleveland and Atlanta.

PABLO CANO

Puppet Master

March 25, 2001

Puppetry, poetry, and trash have beguiled Pablo Cano for years.

To this trinity of sources he brings a magical spirituality nurtured by the art of the past and the thrift-shop decor of the present.

Try to picture plastic peacocks preening with the regal audacity of black velvet paintings of Elvis or the *Last Supper*. Then imagine this brazen flock commandeering a rusty grocery cart and clattering through the aisles of

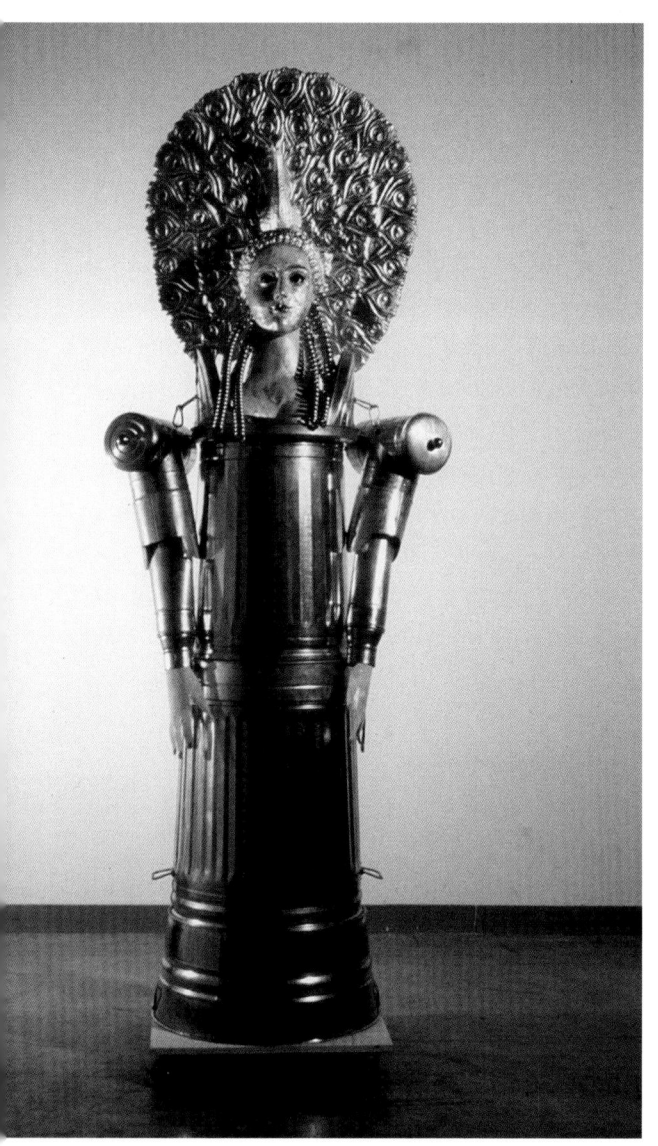

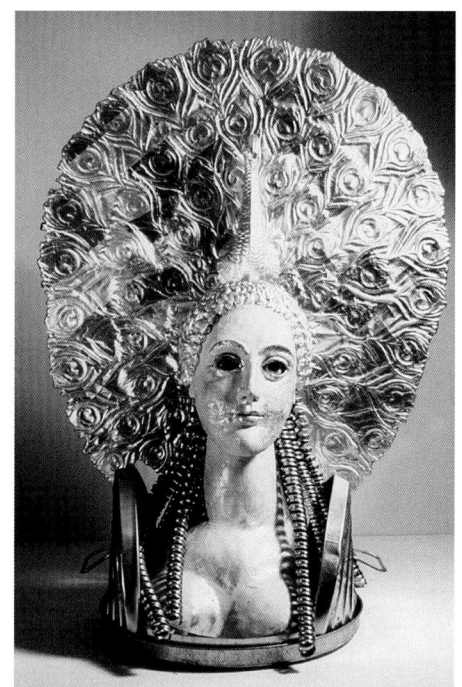

FIGURE 20. Pablo Cano, *Pride*.
Courtesy of the artist.

a medieval cathedral, and you may have some sense of how Cano's elastic imagination wraps around things sacred and silly.

Then again, you might not. Especially if you haven't seen this South Florida artist's fusions of sculpture, found objects, and theater—the most recent of which is now on view at the Museum of Contemporary Art. This new work, lorded over by a prideful peacock with red fingernails rearing from an aluminum trash can, is called *To Sin or Not to Sin*.

The puppet show is accompanied by a lively array of recorded music and voices, including an original score composed by Jason Kunz and performed by William Bilowit.

The voices belong to a sniping but soul-searching cast of characters who represent the wise Archangel Gabriel and the seven virtues and sins—and were partly inspired by the bizarre figures of flesh and fantasy in *The Garden of Earthly Delights*, the 16th-century masterpiece painting by Hieronymus Bosch.

Often, the sins and virtues sound like self-important cousins arguing over their rich uncle's will—until the play closes with a touching poem written by an 11-year-old boy.

Cano's first play, 1987's *Animated Altarpieces*, offered a wry, ecstatic vision of St. Teresa of Avila astride a picnic hamper as she is stabbed with a dart shaped like a model airplane.

Cano's sculptures continue to function as remarkable puppets, telling stories of romance and sacrifice laced with morality tales of good and evil. And along the way, items such as metal gas cans, broken umbrellas, fans, antique chair legs, light bulbs, balloons, crystal chandeliers, and rusty grocery carts are pressed into the service of art and narrative.

It's possible to trace Cano's appropriation of such odds and ends to the works of Robert Rauschenberg and Marcel Duchamp and to early 20th-century collages created by the rebellious founders of the Dada movement, which foreshadowed surrealism and its peculiar dreamscapes.

But despite these modernist influences, it's clear Cano has never strayed far from the whimsical spiritual air of his early *Animated Altarpieces*.

It's this blend of the sacred and silly that drives him, and each time you wonder how long he can keep his work from becoming a parody of itself. How many more sculptures can he make of feminine creatures bearing forward with angelic but rakish elegance, their curvaceous arms clad in chandeliers, their gowns of garbage cans and silvery lampshades eliciting admiring chuckles?

He has gotten away with his mastery of trash and treasure one more time in *To Sin or Not to Sin*, and this time there's less emphasis on creaky romantic plots and more attention to morals, foibles, and fun.

For example, the resplendent peacock lady Cano calls Pride rolls her baby-doll eyes when the glassy figure of Charity wheels on stage and urges her to make a date with Lust.

Gluttony, his belly a balloon, lurches about in a pinstriped shirt looking for cheese cubes while Greed is cloaked in a black umbrella labeled with Paloma Picasso's signature, the sign of a lucrative licensing agreement.

After all the sins and virtues have squabbled about how to get on with life, another little puppet trundles forward and we hear the boyish voice of Wells Weymouth, an 11-year-old family friend of Cano's, reciting his poem:

Talents we are born with, honesty and courage we work for;
Life is a boat across water with storms every day;
You have to live life to the fullest, yet give yourself away.

Then the curtains close and Cano's stage transforms into an old-fashioned magic lantern. His puppets have been attached to two whirling beach umbrellas, creating a wild dance of shadows on the curtains.

And when they swing open for the final time, the merry-go-round of puppets continues, giving away a marvelous balancing act of virtue and vice.

MUSEUM OF CONTEMPORARY ART

Young Artists Find a Temporary Home
at *The House at* MOCA

September 9, 2001

The artists of The House, one of Miami's newest art venues, have a new home for the moment—as curators of the current show at the Museum of Contemporary Art.

It was a risk for director Bonnie Clearwater to collaborate on the curating of a show with such young artists still in the midst of their own education. Yet despite their youth, the artists—Martin Oppel, 24, a New World School of the Arts alum who's pursuing his master of fine arts degree at the University of Miami; and Bhakti Mar Baxter, 21, and Tao Rey, 23, who are both enrolled in the bachelor of fine arts program at New World—have shown a zest for eliciting experimental work from their peers in the few group shows they've orchestrated since December in their downtown Miami home.

Within the context of their down-at-the-heels, two-story white house at 2330 Northeast Fourth Avenue in the city's Edgewater neighborhood, the photography, video, and installation art they've presented can move wildly from the provocative to the tedious. But there's an earnest openness here that's admirable, something you won't find in more structured art venues.

Claustrophobic hallways, closets, a tiny kitchen, a stairwell—even a chimney and rooftop—have become sites for seeing art through intimate, sometimes unconventional encounters.

This is hardly a new concept. Think back nearly three decades to the advent of *Womanhouse*, a collaborative project in which artists in the Feminist Art Program at California Institute of the Arts transformed nearly every square inch of an abandoned Los Angeles home with dramatic installations.

In more recent years, contemporary artists such as Gregor Schneider and Jorge Pardo have adapted the architectural space of a home to probe dark psychological themes and reconfigure formal design.

But in Miami, The House is becoming an open-ended lab for artists to push their talents. It's the refreshing sign of a more independent-minded community of artists defining their own space for risk-taking.

And the Edgewater locale is perhaps the most recent manifestation of such initiative, following in the line of artist Eugenia Vargas's shows in her home and the artist-led Locust Projects, an exhibition space in a remodeled warehouse a few blocks away on Northwest 23rd Street.

TAKING INITIATIVE

"The experience of The House is one of personal empowerment," explains Oppel. "We've taken an initiative to say things the way we think they should be said and to whom they should be said. It is a step away from elitist, market-driven art attitudes and a step closer to honest, nurturing attitudes—without compromising sophistication. We are not playing games."

But translating the intimate approach they've cultivated at The House to a museum was, Oppel admits, a challenge.

Most of the 15 artists included here made work specifically for MOCA, adjusting their vision and proportions to the museum's soaring gallery spaces. As a result, the intimate, casual spirit of a house show has been diminished, but there's still plenty of ambitious work to see and ponder.

Though there's no overt theme, several threads emerge, inviting viewers to follow a loose network of ideas that investigate the legacy of minimalism and the evocative, if at times humorous, qualities of such unassuming materials as dirt, Band-Aids, dolls, strings, and balloons. Design and how functional objects become subverted into new purposes and pleasures is another theme, with some works offering a cool offhand simplicity that becomes both meditative and spiritual.

HANGING BY A THREAD

Threads are literally in evidence in some of the most memorable work here, by Baxter and Frances Trombly.

Baxter's *Light Made Visible* is an ethereal web of strings pulled taut on nails and fashioned to outline a series of triangles that expand outward, like the opening of a camera's aperture. It's lit so that the strings cast shadows of varying thicknesses, resembling temporary line drawings that carve out space with the graceful geometric energy of a wall drawing by Sol LeWitt.

Trombly's *Give and Take* recalls the shivery whirs of Rebecca Horn's mechanized sculptures of machines without an obvious function as well as the push and pull in personal relationships. In Trombly's piece, a pair of machine-operated spools of hand-dyed silk thread is connected by a long strand, which first winds around one spool and then, with a rumble, switches to the other in a comic and cyclical motion.

One of the most complex installations is *People Watching* TV by Jay Hines, another piece invested with subtle humor. It shows three video monitors with repeating loops of two men and one woman watching television, with gray-painted chairs and other domestic props arranged in front of each monitor.

The faces look dreamy, the chairs inviting. And the piece itself invites viewers to stare back, to enter into the dreamlike state of the TV watchers, though their disembodied state and empty chairs are finally unnerving. In this Oz-like tableau, the real objects are gray, and only the fantasy world is in color.

LOGIC DEFIED

Natalia Benedetti has also manipulated the conventions of watching TV with *An Immaculate Murder*, a DVD installation in which we stare at a sweet, fuzzily focused scene of a tabby cat grooming itself while listening to men extol their perfectly planned murder in dialogue from Alfred Hitchcock's *Rope*.

Image and sound defy a logical match, but watch her piece long enough, and they look ominously suited.

In another diverse work, Nick Delaveleye's inkjet print reduces the landscape seen from the Metrorail to a thin band of color traversing a pale-pink ground. It's a ribbon of shifting patterns that recalls Ed Ruscha's deadpan street photographs but interjects a delicate sense of beauty.

A TOUCH OF BEAUTY

In step with a growing emphasis on this once-maligned concept in contemporary art, beauty touches other work here, including Oppel's sparkling, dirt-coated canvases that recall both constellations and James Turrell's spatial illusions; Rey's formal riffs on graffiti; and Tim Curtis's imposing sculpture of charred, wooden boats caught in a cross-shaped gridlock.

Though *The House at* MOCA closes September 21, the doors will remain open to activities nurtured by The House. At 7 p.m. September 23, The House will host a closing reception for its current exhibit, *The Sears Building*, with work by Miami artists curated by artist Robert Chambers.

Some artists in that show—including Cooper, Mette Tommerup, Maria José Arjona, and Maritza Molina—have also been tapped for *Spunky*, a national survey of new artists at Exit Art in New York City, which runs through October 27.

GLEXIS NOVOA, NAOMI FISHER

Flowers, Pay Phones Make for a Compelling Art Pairing

November 18, 2001

Fearsome flowers the color of fire and blood. A flood surging through urban towers and floating with a lifeline, courtesy of Bell South.

Take time to smell the hibiscus only if you dare, but be sure to grab the receiver for your free call.

The combination of a garden gone haywire in Naomi Fisher's photographs and Glexis Novoa's mural of mighty floodwaters afloat with a working pay phone makes for one of the most compelling pairings of work we've seen in the Miami Art Museum's yearlong series of *New Work Miami* shows, which comes to a close with this work by Fisher and Novoa.

Announced more than a year ago as a way to highlight the burgeoning talents of Miami-based artists, the series has produced solo shows for eight artists. And though it has been justly criticized for skipping over or skimping on the considerable range of emerging and establishing artists working here, this final edition is a strong conclusion that should open the door for future attempts to tap the talent developing locally.

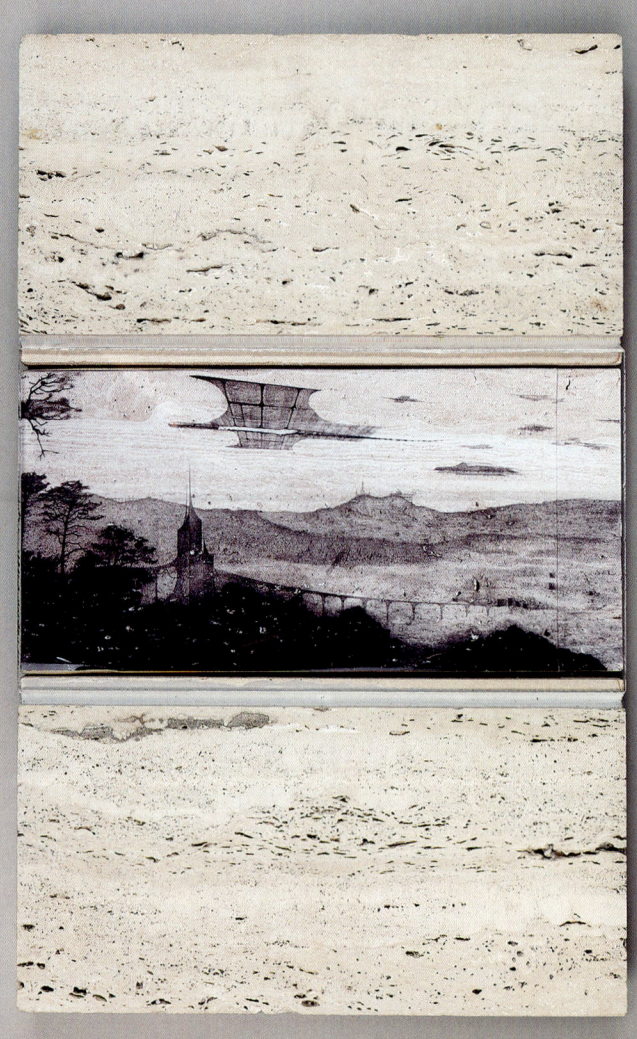

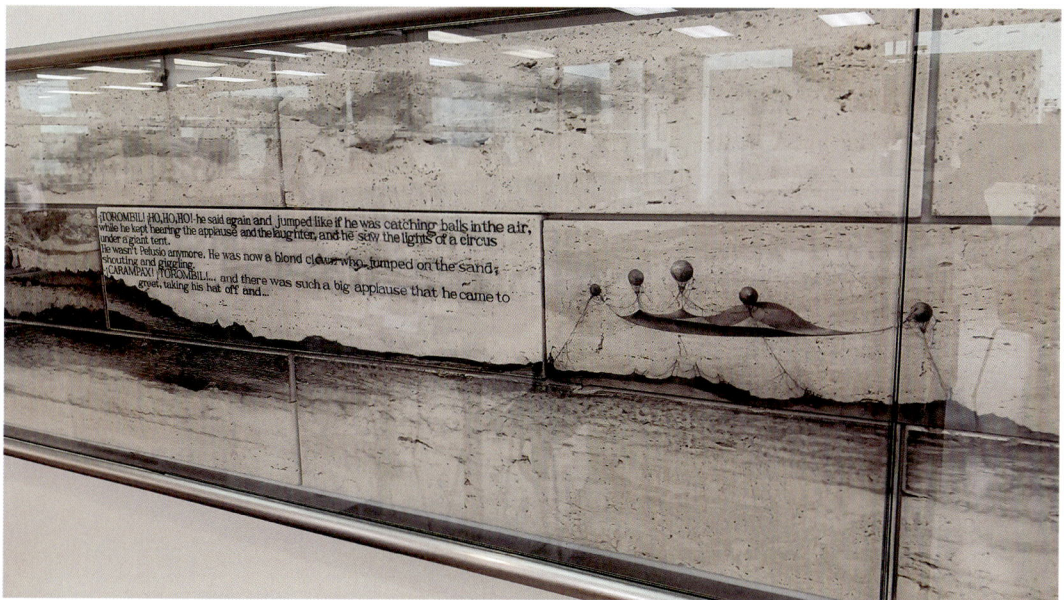

GLEXIS NOVOA

To enter the gallery displaying Novoa's work, you must step through a glass door darkly marked "Exit." It's a move meant to disorient, and it does.

What you see next is a pay phone surrounded by a cloud of random scribbles in the "for a good time call" vein. Visitors are invited to add their two cents' worth and, in the process, place a free five-minute call to any place they like, embarking on another exit of sorts.

The callers' scribbles make up the kind of informal murals that spring up around pay phones in unkempt places, deluging pay phone users with fragmented memories of other lives, other conversations, now recounted in a jumble of throwaway doodles.

On the wall opposite the pay phone is the "real" artwork: one of Novoa's signature graphite drawings

FIGURE 21. Glexis Novoa, *Mock up, Pelusio y el tío Eterio (after an Ivette Vian original story)*, ca. 2009. Image Miami-Dade County Public Library Systems. Digital Collections, courtesy of Miami-Dade County Department of Cultural Affairs, Art in Public Places Trust.

FIGURE 22. Glexis Novoa, *Pelusio y el tío Eterio (after an Ivette Vian original story)*, 2009. Graphite on marble. Kendall Lakes Library. Image Yusimy Lara, courtesy of Miami-Dade County Department of Cultural Affairs, Art in Public Places Trust.

of delicately shaded architecture, typically balancing the exquisite with the ephemeral. It's a more organized collection of memories, recalling places where the Cuban-born artist has lived and traveled but offering moments of recognition for the viewer as well.

Up close, this island of monuments seems like a distant mirage, including a Miami Seaquarium–like dome, church spires, Mexican pyramids, and twin towers. At the edge is El Morro, Havana's landmark fort. Barely moored to the shore are lines to ragtag rafts, some breaking away to tumble into watery depths.

This architectural fantasy island rising up from an oceanic expanse is part of a 110-foot-long mural drawn on the wall. It inscribes the space with a nearly eye-level horizon, dotted with a few other, much tinier islands that soon give you the feeling you're surrounded by water and should probably start paddling.

Novoa has produced a quietly stunning piece, inviting us to become immersed in waves of memory and reflection while also evoking the perils of displacement. His draftsmanship is so agile and inventive, however, that survival, rather than mucked-up nostalgia, remains the guiding current.

NAOMI FISHER

A gifted twentysomething product of Miami's New World School of the Arts, Fisher has seen her career blossom early, with several museum and gallery shows already on her résumé. And Fisher's photographs of female buttocks ornamented with glitter and protruding from floral panties pulled askew have caused a sensation among collectors, dealers, and curators.

Among viewers, they've inspired both intense revulsion and admiration.

Like many young artists, Fisher has been influenced by the props-and-persona mix in Cindy Sherman's classic self-portraits that resemble film stills and dispense feminist critiques of popular stereotypes. Fisher's imagery of bodies enmeshed in exotic floral landscapes is also indebted to Ana Mendieta's self-portraits shrouded in dank earth and bridal-white flowers.

As disturbingly staged tableaux, Fisher's photographs resemble film noir fashion shoots or crime scenes both funny and gruesome. A botanist's daughter, Fisher seeds her art with sardonic takes on flowery feminine styles and a not-so-motherly nature, giving the term "fashion victim" nasty new resonance.

But last year, there were signs that Fisher's photographs were fading on the vine, becoming predictable parodies of her funky-shock school of flesh 'n' flower arranging.

In five new Cibachrome photographs mounted on aluminum, Fisher forsakes those raw, raunchy poses for slightly less predictable—though still bizarre—tableaux of females among flowers.

With heliconia, hibiscus, and birds of paradise shot in jewel-like colors, these compositions bring to mind the brilliantly colored, airless paintings of the 19th-century Pre-Raphaelites, a coterie of English artists who favored romantic, botanically inclined beauties.

In Fisher's photographs, the flowers do more than blossom; they nearly suffocate, closing off mouths and nostrils and veiling eyes with beautiful menace. Throngs of birds of paradise seem ready to slice like power saws, and palm fronds lunge forward like spears. Literary types may see another 19th-century reminder—the garden of deadly delights in one of Nathaniel Hawthorne's allegorical romances, *Rappaccini's Daughter*.

Fisher's mostly female figures can't quite compete with the rapacious energy of these tropical plants. As their bodies become woven ever more densely into this strange landscape, it's not clear whether their destiny is emboldened or buried.

BASS MUSEUM OF ART

Global Perspective

December 23, 2001

There's a great generosity of spirit weaving through the *globe>Miami>island* show featuring work by 30 artists that Miami-based artist Robert Chambers curated for the Bass Museum of Art. And that spirit is both its bewildering weakness and its stubborn strength.

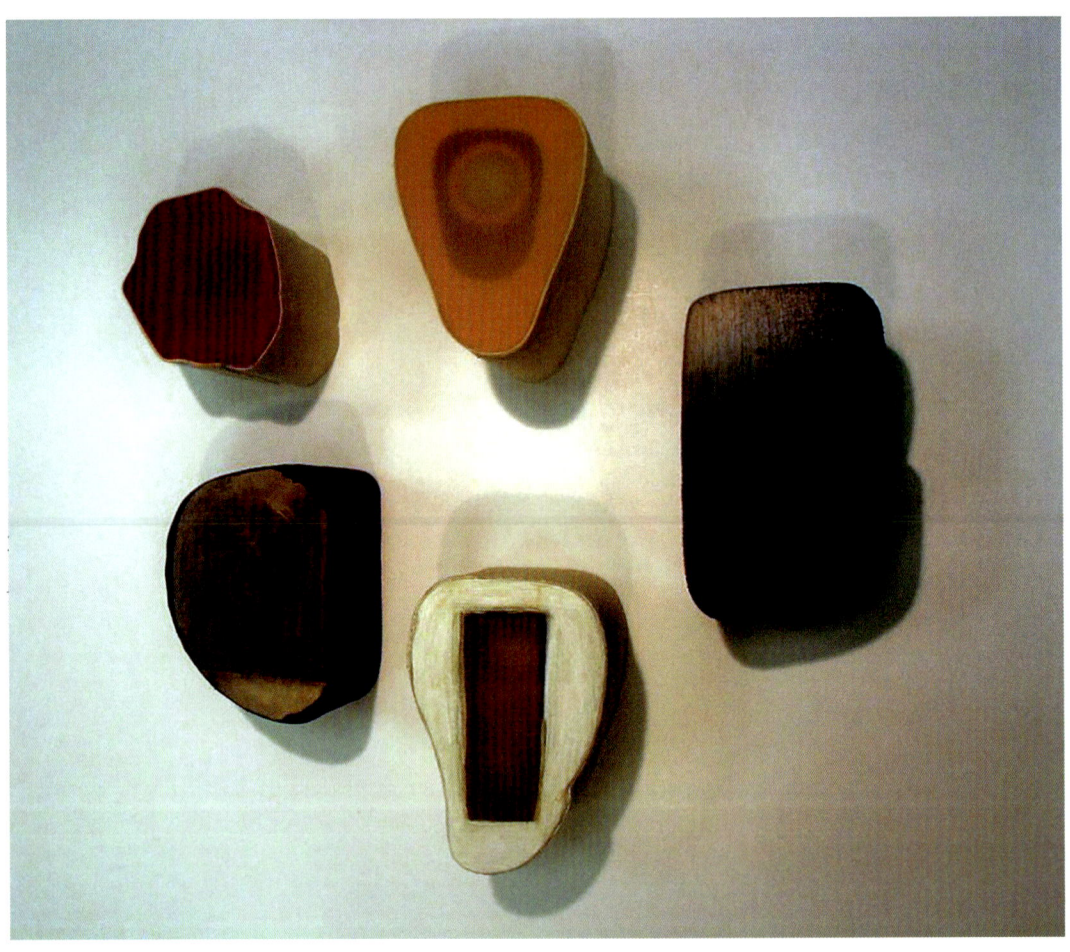

FIGURE 23. Robert Thiele, *A-6 #76 (White and Black)*, 2000; *A-6 #73 (Black)*, 2000; *M 324 (Yellow)*, 2004; *A-6 #121 (White with rectangle)*, 1999; *M 326 (Red)*, 2004. Mixed media. Courtesy of Miami-Dade County Department of Cultural Affairs, Art in Public Places Trust.

It's unlikely a professional curator would have turned out such an undulating, eclectic survey of the Miami art scene. Or that anyone but an artist who has witnessed the area's growth pains, spurts, and stagnating plateaus in art would have had the eye to put this together.

But Chambers's experience brings a unique, effervescent energy and sensibility, matching the varied sensibility erupting from his own eccentric installations that click with kinetic parts and materials both sensuous and scientific.

But within this noisy mix, which spews in a host of directions, there are telling themes. There's a buoyant sense of spectacle, particularly in Bhakti Baxter's airy stream of Royal Poinciana twigs, which seem to float in circles along a partition next to the ramp connecting the museum's first and second floors.

The same goes for the ethereal presence of Karen Rifas's rows of tiny oak leaves dangling from a horizontal net of strings. Both pieces celebrate natural, even uplifting, grace.

More than a few works evoke imaginative places of rising dreams and desires, and injected here are also notions about nurturing, regeneration, and birth. All of this seems wonderfully apt for an event that holds up a mirror—occasionally a wacky funhouse mirror—to an arts scene characterized by growing confidence and diversity as it steps out of a once insular-as-an-island place onto a more visible, if not global, stage.

"SANDWICH" GROUP

As Amy Cappellazzo notes in her essay for the catalog documenting this show, *globe>Miami>island* encircles several generations of Miami artists, ranging from Purvis Young, Robert Huff, Robert Thiele, and Rifas, who worked or taught here at a time when Miami was considered nothing more than a brain-fried backwater by tastemakers in New York, to the current crop of twenty-something artists such as Naomi Fisher, Gean Moreno, and Cooper, whose work has attracted critical attention both here and outside South Florida.

In between these generations are those born in Cuba but raised in Miami, such as César Trasobares and Pablo Cano, whose work can reflect the enervating political nostalgia of exile. Others in these "sandwich generations" are artists such as Glexis Novoa and José Bedia of Cuba and Roberto Behar and Rosario Marquardt of Argentina, who came to Miami from troubled homelands in the 1980s and '90s, then decided to stay.

And finally there are those such as Tom Downs, Teresita Fernández, Quisqueya Henríquez, and Ward Shelley, who made an impression here but have since headed off to New York or other locales.

Bringing these artists together with others with ties to Miami, such as sculptor Ursula Von Rydingsvard and Janine Antoni, amounts to something of a homecoming, a spectacular panoramic take on the Miami art scene like none in recent memory. And there will be more to follow, says Bass director Diane Camber, who's now planning similar surveys every two years.

Still, no one said it was easy to be panoramic and spectacular.

As a result, there are some serious flaws in the show, especially the muddled beginning with its chaotic variety of art presented on walls viewed from the ramp leading to the museum's second floor. There's too much effort expended putting too many artists' work together in this area with its soaring ceilings; it's a place that seems architecturally awkward for looking at art anyway, at least in the manner that it's currently being used.

No one gets any breathing room, and as a result, Luis Gispert's photograph of a hip-hop cheerleader levitating like a baroque angel doesn't make sense jammed in with exuberant, layered abstract paintings by Moreno and Annie Wharton. And Julie Kahn's photograph of Kendall kids at rifle practice and Joanne Rosen's lightbox images of simple domestic light fixtures resembling glowing spaceships make uneasy companions.

MISSING WORKS

Another problem is that some artists, including Elizabeth Withstandley and Adler Guerrier, aren't represented by their most compelling works, while other pieces don't rise to the occasion.

For example, Dara Friedman's photographs of a stylish woman caught in motion like a model at a fashion shoot, her body arching in a balletic arabesque even as she's cramped into a corner, are intriguing. But not as much as Friedman's work in film and video, such as her *Total*, with its startling sequence of a woman tearing apart a room and then, shown in reverse, re-constructing the room with absurd ease.

And Jason Hedges's work, related to his performances and interactive pieces that examine the rituals of meals, remains inexplicable. His *Tartuflo Bianco*, with costly white truffle oil floating inside an electric humidifier, was apparently meant to emit a fragrant scent but, at least during my visit, did not and simply looked out of place.

So those are the weaknesses, the growing pains perhaps inevitable for a show that springs from a youthful scene with such ambitious goals. One artist in the show described the collection of work here as "Robert's diary," a record of one person's journey through changing times.

Chambers himself calls the show a "springboard" for ways to think about contemporary art with a Miami return address.

Diary, springboard, or spectacle, it offers more than enough moments for invigorating reflection. One of the stand-out pieces here is *3:37 p.m.* by Fernández, an artist who has always been fascinated with formal issues of transparency and volume, though this piece shimmers with colored light in a buoyant manner that makes it seem especially suited to this context.

Dozens of tiny acrylic cubes have been glued to the wall, arranged so that they project a rainbow-like spectrum of changing hues. Its gentle, dreamlike aura contrasts with the more earthbound, visceral presence of three works by Antoni, shown earlier this year at the Aldrich Museum of Contemporary Art in Ridgefield, Connecticut. Of particular interest is *Saddle*, made with amber-colored bull rawhide and initially draped over a cast of the artist crawling on her knees.

Part of a series of works that touch on birth and mortality, this piece becomes a translucent shroud of the artist's body and suggests a thoughtful link to *Fontanel*, a DVD by Tom Downs that looks more closely at the harsh pain and sweet promise of human birth.

Those who've followed many of the artists here will find strong examples of their work in the aggressive, altar-like spectacles of Edouard Duval-Carrié and Bedia as well as Charo Oquet's new direction, in which she strips away the glistening fabric of her towering altars to reveal something more bony and vulnerable.

The fine, subtle textures in paintings by Lynne Golob Gelfman and Thiele can be overlooked in all the hoopla here, while Huff's rough pine and plywood sculptures, shaped like forbidding country chapels and clustered outside the museum by its reflecting pool, offer a distinct alternative to the Bass's strict geometric design.

It's the new generation of Miami artists, however, that leaves you with some of the most surprising memories. There's Kevin Arrow's video, projected on a translucent hemispheric form and glimmering with a changing mirage of body and earth, and Norberto (Bert) Rodriguez's *The End*, a sound piece that fills the Bass's elevator with the hilariously triumphant chords from the end of famous movie soundtracks.

In these endings are tantalizing beginnings.

In memoriam: Robert Huff, 1945–2014
Lynne Golob Gelfman, 1944–2020
Quisqueya Henríquez, 1966–2024

BASEL LEAVING IMPRINT ON MIX OF NEW EVENTS

December 26, 2001

One might have expected *Unofficial/Official: The Miami Art Exchange Juried Exhibition* to be dutiful but dull.

After all, it's focused on artists who, when selected by Miami Art Exchange jurors this summer, weren't represented by a South Florida gallery. And it features mostly artists left out of recent shows at the Museum of Contemporary Art and the Miami Art Museum. (The exceptions include Tim Curtis and Tom Scicluna.)

Instead, *Unofficial/Official* is another lively link in South Florida's growing chain of exhibits initiated by artists, including this month's ambitious *Subterfuge* in the Design District and a group of eight solo shows at artist Carlos Betancourt's downtown studio. These recent entries are part of the bustling mix of events generated by an art fair that hasn't happened yet.

Art Basel Miami Beach may have been postponed until December 2002, but it's already showing its muscle as a cultural catalyst. And in this climate, *Unofficial/Official* puts strong work in a chiefly worthwhile context, though it is marred by unevenness, with cluttered installations and so-so paintings.

At the entrance is a striking contrast in scale between two sculptures that suggest transcendent journeys, either promised or lost. Emilio Adán Martinez's slight triangles of treated paper are stitched, like faded but sturdy sails, to Australian pine branches suspended from the ceiling, barely sketching the outlines of a vessel or dreamt-about trips. Curtis's charred wooden hulk of a ship is heavily moored to the floor, spilling over with sand the color of volcanic ash, a becalmed ruin.

And while other shows around town have more overlaps than this one, giving a broader look at artists' work, there are a few connecting threads in *Unofficial/Official*.

Winds, a series of paintings and sculptures by Lydia Rubio, is a poetic extension of a similar series in her current exhibit at Bernice Steinbaum Gallery. In both, the artist disrupts the lush illusions of landscape painting by pairing fragmented scenes with airy sculptures of birds and ships.

Together, they make narratives of displacement, weaving references to cartography with scenes of earth and sky and playful word games. Such imagery circles back on itself to generate rich associations of flight and transformation.

In another link to other shows, Shahreyar Ataie's lethargic video isn't as visually compelling as his piece in *globe>Miami>island* at the Bass, with its strange doll revolving amid a contemplative blur of colors. But in the Miami Art Exchange show, a selective smattering of video includes Scicluna's amusing piece about what appears to be an innocuous patch of oil-stained asphalt.

Microscopic, slow-motion changes cause the shapes to swell and diminish, emerge and vanish. It cleverly makes something out of nothing, taking a cue from Bill Viola's imperceptibly changing video portraits.

Photography includes examples from Eduardo del Valle and Mirta Gómez's fine series documenting Maya dwellings in Mexico; Elizabeth Cerejido's increasingly varied takes on dancers in transition; and Sherri Tan's close-ups of her small tactile sculptures, manual tools collaged with yellowed Latin texts that are unique emblems of hand-eye coordination.

One surprise was Carol Prusa's drawings. Her trio of regenerating blossoms is a fierce and exquisite portrait of organic change that makes us wonder when we'll see more of her work.

SHEKHINAH SCROLLS AND TABERNACLE

South Florida artist Tina Spiro has produced a circular, freestanding mural based on her study of the Dead Sea Scrolls and the Kabbalah, ancient texts of Jewish mysticism recounting stories of spiritual change and creation. Hers is an intricate project aspiring to the texture of long-ago scrolls, ornately inscribed with inspirational texts in English, Hebrew, Aramaic, Chinese, and other languages.

With an original jazz recording by pianist Ben Waltzer playing in the background, *The Shekhinah Scrolls and Tabernacle*, showing at the Buena Vista Building in the Design District, encompasses a vast spectrum of references, from the Kabbalah to Patrick Henry to Bob Marley. Embedded in the text are large Hebrew letters, illuminated with scenes of the artist's family, biblical stories, and idyllic vistas of Jamaica, where Spiro lived and taught painting for more than a decade.

Her scrolls also encircle a group of wooden harps sculpted by Ervin Nichol of Jamaica. The piece is meant to be a place of quiet, healing contemplation. And it does offer an unusual respite from a cluttered world. But its occasional overwrought elements are more opaque than engaging.

GAVIN PERRY AND
BEATRIZ MONTEAVARO

Profiles in Collecting

April 21, 2002

Collecting art and other things is among the most consuming of passions. Even making art doesn't make you immune from such obsessions—from Rembrandt to Matta to Warhol, artists themselves have frequently been struck with the curse of the collector.

Possession Obsession: Objects from Andy Warhol's Personal Collection, a new exhibit at the Andy Warhol Museum in Pittsburgh, showcases the artist's wide-ranging taste, from folk art to costume jewelry to cookie jars. It's a particularly daunting example of how an artist's prized possessions can guide us to insights about sources and ideas within his or her work.

In South Florida, artists who have gathered distinctive collections include Cuban-born José Bedia, whose home resembles a museum gallery showcasing a rich assortment of African and Native American masks, carvings, and dozens of other artifacts. On one wall is an African mask once owned by Latin American master Wifredo Lam; the mask's stark profile often appears in Bedia's figurative drawings, which spring from Afro-Cuban religious rituals.

Other area collections are more quirky, blurring the line between artful artifacts and emblems of popular culture. Bruce Helander's surreal collages, for example, owe much to his stash of vintage sheet music and Bakelite radios. And a barely thirtysomething artist couple, Beatriz Monteavaro and Gavin Perry, are amassing a vivid collection of toys—chiefly action figures and miniature low-rider cars—that has shaped their adventurous art.

Collecting "builds your repertoire, the visual language that you are using to build your work. You pull a part from there, you pull a part here," says Perry, standing in his ArtCenter/South Florida studio next to a table of some 70 gem-bright toy cars, awash in lurid pinks, purples, and shades of green the color of Astroturf.

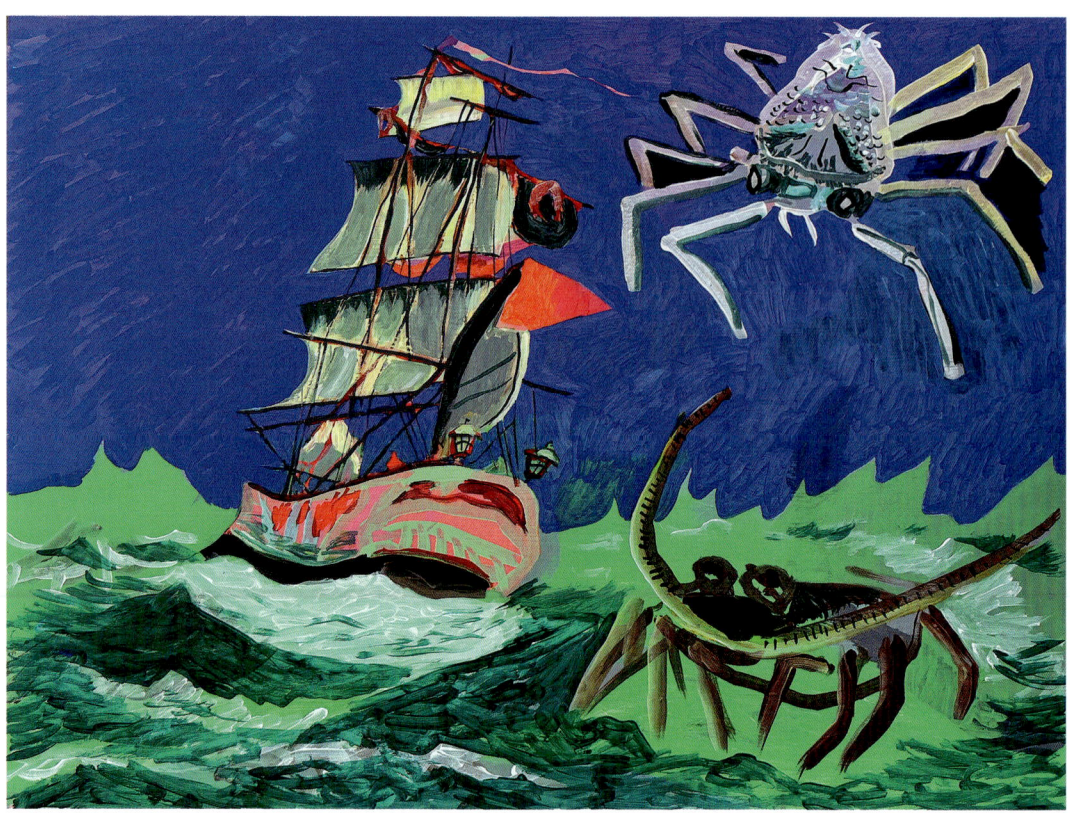

FIGURE 24. Beatriz Monteavaro, *Earth vs. the Flying Spider Crabs*, 2022. Acrylic on wood panel. Courtesy of the artist and Miami-Dade County Department of Cultural Affairs, Art in Public Places Trust.

"I'm really trying to find cars that fit that California mode rather than a Detroit mentality," Perry says. "It's not about how a car goes, but how it looks."

Picking up a bronze and gold model of a 1969 Impala, he says he's intrigued by the aesthetics of what's "predominately a ghetto culture, or more an urban subversive culture now being marketed to suburban kids."

Many of Perry's models sport the down-to-earth profiles of Chicano low-rider cars and feature "chop tops"—roofs lowered for a more streamlined effect. A gaudy model Chevelle boasts a hot-pink interior and a black body that dazzles with pink, silver, and aqua glitter.

"This is insane. You'd think this is only found on a Matchbox car, but no, they actually make paint like that," Perry says, producing one of several books on customized auto bodies he culls for techniques on how to produce the "fetish finish" gleam of his abstract paintings, which are layered with the sheen of auto-body paint and the meticulously lean trails of color pinstriping.

In a stroke of unexpected poetry, the book identifies the paint as a "rainbow metallic flake base."

Perry's canvases have become shinier this year, thanks to an industrial-strength paint gun. And those paintings' garish glow has caught the eye of Montreal dealer Fabrice Marcolini, who saw them at Art Miami in January.

"What hit us most about his work is that it walks this dangerous path," says the Artcore Gallery's Marcolini, who will show Perry's art next fall or spring. "It translates something that is kitsch into something that is fresh. That takes talent."

HERO WORSHIP

Monteavaro's burgeoning collection of plastic superhero and -heroine action figures has also influenced her art. Her interest in the figures began during her childhood in Hialeah, where she was the youngest of four children. She devised solitary games about battling good and bad guys, preferring even the scant ranks of female superheroes such as Wonder Woman to "eternally boring" pink tea sets and Barbies.

"The only fun thing I remember girls ever played was *Charlie's Angels*," she says. "Even today in toy stores the boys' section is full of color, with intricate robots. The girls' section is all pink and purple, and the most exciting thing you'll find is a Barbie that tans. There's no action."

Teased for playing with boys' toys in the second grade, she admits, "I stopped playing with them too early, which is why I think I collect them now—it's like taking back part of my childhood."

Even early on, there was an urge to manipulate these pop-culture artifacts, though the 7-year-old Betty, as friends call her, wouldn't have put it that way. These days she freely modifies her collection by customizing figures for her deliberately cheesy videos about bested muscle-bound villains and her surprisingly elegant drawings, examples of which are on view at North Miami's Ambrosino Gallery through Tuesday.

While the video has a funny, grainy crudeness that makes us look twice at cheap designs that are less familiar than we'd expect, her drawings are the real stars of the show. Her adapted characters bristle with crisply composed details.

Collecting is "a way to make your work your work, and not a generic overview of everybody else's," says Monteavaro, wearing a Wonder Woman T-shirt and standing in her ArtCenter/South Florida studio, where squads of action figures cluster in neat rows on industrial shelving like crowds of stars and extras come to life from old comic books and corny cartoons.

There's a clutch of lizards shaped like bloated, mutant pickles that she identifies as "Godzilla and his family of villains and friends." There's a pack of Disney witches gleaned from fast-food lunches, a tiny doll of Gene Hackman in Lex Luther's purple tights, and Flash Gordon with sidekicks.

TIARA AND BOOTS

Nearby, a vintage Wonder Woman picked up from eBay is clad in a golden tiara and red boots. Sandals would have been the historically correct gear, Monteavaro explains, though she approves of the error, as it jibes with the kind of license she takes with plots and protagonists.

"I don't really think sandals are for superheroes," she says. "It seems to me like her feet would hurt."

Museum of Contemporary Art director Bonnie Clearwater, who included Monteavaro's work in *Making Art in Miami: Travels in Hyperreality* in late 2000, says the artist's alterations give her work a maturing edge.

"She alters the figures so that they take on new characters, not just what some toy company has determined, and she animates them the way a child would so that she can act out stories of good and evil," Clearwater says. "But she makes us question our own beliefs."

In her solo show at Ambrosino, Clearwater says, "the storylines have interesting parables for today, and I think her draftsmanship is quite astonishing. There's a considerable strength and maturity."

With recent shows at galleries in Geneva, Chicago, and Madrid,

Monteavaro's career is moving forward. Still, she and Perry must find work here doing installation jobs for museums, and she also teaches classes at the ArtCenter to make ends meet.

In a way, Monteavaro's collection has become more than simply a source of ideas for art but also a source of the artists' personal experience. As a result, this assortment of action figures offers both artistic and personal sustenance.

"I think a lot of things are parallel to superhero and *Star Wars* stories," Monteavaro says. "There's the hero that goes through the struggle, and 9 times out of 10 they come out winning. This isn't just myth; it's life—we are our own heroes, we go through struggles, and we either wither away or keep going."

MARÍA MARTÍNEZ-CAÑAS

Identity Crisis

May 22, 2002

An eerie specter of a woman dominates one corner of *María Martínez-Cañas: A Retrospective*, now at the Museum of Art in Fort Lauderdale (renamed NSU Art Museum Fort Lauderdale). Glimpsed in the murk of a black-and-white video, she sloshes in a tub, wearing only what appear to be dozens of plastic masks, piled one atop the other.

In a bizarre sequence, the woman pulls off one mask after another. Yet what should be a process of revelation becomes more concealing. We see her body floundering in water and hear her voice in Spanish, but the camera never focuses on her face.

The video is a remarkably prescient self-portrait of Martínez-Cañas in 1984, when the Miami-based artist was 24 and a graduate student at the School of the Art Institute of Chicago. Titled *Un problema de identidad* (*A problem of identity*), it exposes a tense process of watery flux, a peculiar conundrum in which naked flesh on view within a claustrophobic, womb-like space remains a damp mystery.

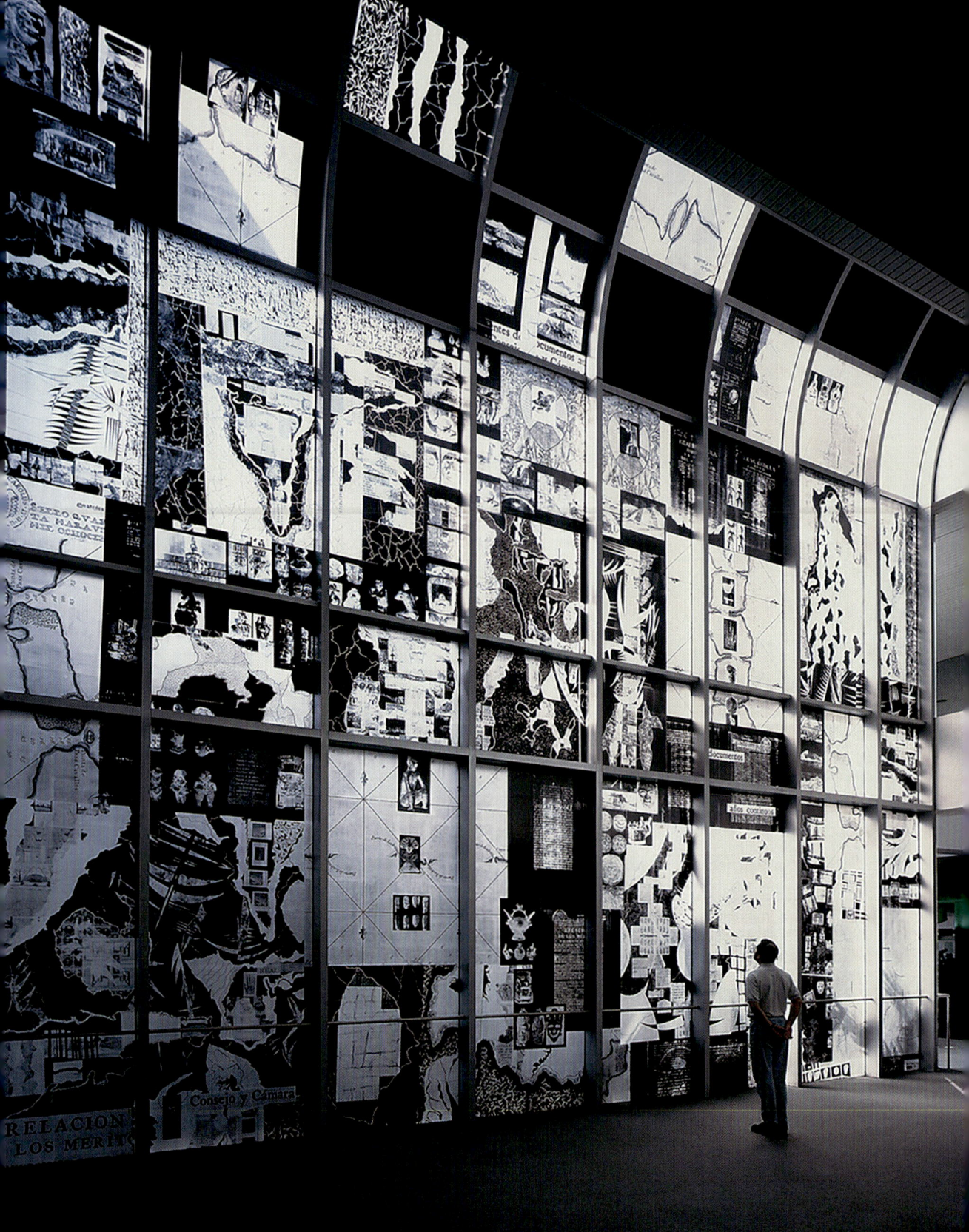

In this retrospective, the video provides a striking encapsulation of the exciting work Martínez-Cañas would produce over the next two decades, during which she would win numerous national and international honors. The video foretells her tightly composed photomontages, with glimpses of vulnerable bodies set amid fluid designs evocative of islands and geometric enclosures inspired by maps of colonial Cuba, maps she studied in Spain in 1986 on a Fulbright-Hays grant.

She has gone on from those early days to establish herself as a nationally prominent photographic artist whose work resides in the permanent collections of such museums as New York's Museum of Modern Art, the Whitney Museum of American Art, and the International Center of Photography, as well as the San Francisco Museum of Modern Art, the Los Angeles County Museum of Art, and the Smithsonian American Art Museum.

Martínez-Cañas the student was not unique in exploring the nebulous fate of mercurial self-portraits, and one could argue that this video is a self-conscious effort from an MFA candidate. Formally, however, it's much more than an obligatory rehash of topical, identity-conscious art by the likes of Cindy Sherman and Ana Mendieta.

And Martínez-Cañas was grappling with her own feelings of being uprooted.

Born the youngest of three daughters in Cuba in 1960, she was barely three months old when her family fled Fidel Castro's regime for Miami before eventually settling in Puerto Rico. It was there that the artist was raised, learning of her homeland from an art-laced pastiche of family memories.

LATIN CULTURE

"She likes to say she is a Cuban-born, Puerto Rican–raised American citizen," says her father, José Martínez-Cañas, a Coral Gables art dealer. "I think she

FIGURE 25. María Martínez-Cañas, *Años Continuos*, 1995–2023. Miami International Airport. Image Carlos Domenech, courtesy of the artist and Fredric Snitzer Gallery, Miami. This work was deaccessioned in 2023 from Miami-Dade County Department of Cultural Affairs, Art in Public Places Trust collection.

really loved hearing the old stories of Cuba. And she grew up, like all my kids, surrounded by Latin American culture. We had writers and musicians in our home. Our friends were artists."

When his daughter moved to Miami in 1986, those memories stayed vivid. In her Bakehouse studio, she kept a snapshot of herself as a chubby-cheeked 8-year-old at a San Juan restaurant with her family and Cuban painter Cundo Bermúdez.

It was also at the age of eight, her father remembers, that his youngest daughter began begging to use his Nikon or her mother's old Rolleiflex. Then her parents gave her a Polaroid Swinger, which she used to shoot things such as colonial archways and patterns in the barks of trees.

"She wanted us to go every weekend to photograph in Old San Juan or at El Dorado Beach," he says. "She had a sense of form from the very beginning."

A formalist spirit with sensuous imagery and echoes of an exile's fragmented past still mingles in her work. Nearly four years ago, while remodeling the studio in her Little Havana home, she temporarily set up shop in a former cigar factory on Calle Ocho amid boxes of dried tobacco leaves that had been left behind—the smell of which brought back memories of a cigar-smoking grandfather.

PHOTOGRAMS

Along with sprays of bougainvillea and other plants, the tobacco leaves became subjects for a stunning new series of semiabstract photograms, produced without a lens by shining light on plants scattered across photosensitive paper the color of lapis lazuli.

"There was something magical and incredible about the whole process," remembers Martínez-Cañas, a petite woman with an intense gaze and tightly curled black hair.

Such combinations in Martínez-Cañas's work have long intrigued Andy Grundberg, a Washington-based independent critic and curator who chose the artist's 1991 work *Quince Sellos Cubanos* (*Fifteen Cuban stamps*) for *Points of Entry*, a nationally traveling 1995 show exploring art and identity.

This stamp series presents intricate, collage-like photographs that arise from a singular technical process and riff on paintings by artists such as Amelia Peláez and other scenes featured on Cuban stamps. As telling documents of travel and cultural icons, the stamps, Martínez-Cañas said then, "became an essential element in coming closer to my Cubanness."

What's amazing in her art, Grundberg explains, "is that she combines this experimental attitude to the medium of photography, and at the same time, the content is really personal, speaking to her cultural experience and to issues of dislocation. I'd put her in a league with Lorna Simpson and Carrie Mae Weems in the sense that she uses photography to evoke the complexities of personal experience."

PHOTOS, VIDEOS

Only five examples from the stamp series made it into the Fort Lauderdale retrospective, but curator Jorge Hilker Santis has included more than 100 works, chiefly photographs and a few videos. It's a dazzling overview, from 1980 to the present, that includes the photographs she used in building her largest image to date, *Años Continuos* (*Continuous years*), a 10-foot-square wall of sandblasted glass for Concourse D at Miami International Airport. In some ways, this 1995 public commission, with majestic layering of maps and landmarks for travelers on real and imaginary journeys, marked a glorious artistic cul-de-sac. Soon after, she realized she needed to move on.

"I felt very tired about the work," she says. "I felt it was time for me to drop anything that had to do with Cuba because, if not, I would start repeating myself. My work was about so much more than the issue of Cuba."

So she became more spontaneous, producing, for example, the unique plant-leaf photograms.

"In a way, I am allowing myself to fail and not thinking so much what is going to happen," she says. "Chance is very much there."

That year Martínez-Cañas also nursed a close friend until his death from a long illness. It was a profound experience that led her to make work memorializing life's transience, such as the eerie, exquisite *Flight (Hospital Bed)* on linen. In this photo, a ghostly, blurred figure—actually the artist—struggles to rise from a quilt-like pattern of botanical prints.

A RENEWAL

"The last few years have been some of the most exciting," she says. And the energy she felt early in her career, when she was making imagery patterned after maps of colonial Cuba, has returned.

One highlight came last September, when she and other artists included in *Arte Latino: Treasures from the Smithsonian American Art Museum*, were invited to meet First Lady Laura Bush and Marta Sahagún, wife of Mexican president Vicente Fox, at a reception in Chicago, where the traveling show was on view.

"For Latino artists to be there was an honor, it was a validation," she says. The prospect of chatting with Laura Bush, however, was unnerving.

"I was shaking," Martínez-Cañas remembers. But their conversation in English and Spanish went smoothly.

"She understands Spanish. They made you feel very comfortable," Martínez-Cañas says. "Some of us have grown up in this country, we feel very American, but we have come from different parts. It was an experience I will never forget."

In memoriam: Cundo Bermúdez, 1914–2008

CUTTING-EDGE ART WILL LEAVE YOU FLARBBERGASTED

August 21, 2002

Flarb.

It sounds a bit like a game, probably something loose and short on picky rules. Noun or verb, it could be a variation on *flab* or *flub* with a fat dash of artful eccentricity or maybe a staccato burst of cheeky energy, as in *flarb this!*

But don't go running to the dictionary just yet. The word has no literal meaning, says Elizabeth Hall, organizer of FLARB2, a showcase of experimental media by more than 20 artists from Florida, Boston, and New York that will run Friday evening and Saturday at the Aqua Hotel on 1520 Collins Avenue, Miami Beach.

"Flarb could also mean Florida Art Bureau," she suggests.

But for Hall, the name's playful oddness suggests the breaking of new ground, even "the intersection of high intellect and free-flowing creativity."

She's hoping to orchestrate such an intersection this weekend with FLARB2, the fifth and by far most ambitious event among a series of smaller video and film screenings she's held since January at the Wolfsonian-Florida International University and the Hotel Astor. They're produced by The Experimental Show, a forum Hall founded on a shoestring budget to showcase new art forms.

"Generally, it's been pretty stimulating," says Charles Recher, a veteran Miami video artist and filmmaker who took part in one screening. "She has a good eye. I've always been very strong about people taking control of your own community [to create] avenues that allow less commercial work."

For the Aqua event, the DropBox Performance Group and award-winning electronic music composer Michael DeMurga have taken *Alphaville*, a 1965 noirish film by influential director Jean-Luc Godard, and run it through their laptop, reconfiguring it into a live performance with computer-generated imagery.

Elizabeth Knowles will create a collage-like installation based partly on her interest in DNA patterns, while Gustavo Matamoros, a sound artist and director of the edgy South Florida Subtropics Festival, will perform *Small Sounds for Sale* in a penthouse suite set up like a casino, using the venue to address notions such as consumerism and desire.

There are few places in South Florida where you can regularly experience and exchange ideas about such emerging forms of new media as video projections, virtual reality, and performance art that engage technology. That prompted Hall, an artist and former art professor at FIU, to action. And the casual, noninstitutional air of a hotel proved an appealing site.

"If we want to raise the level of discourse, and if art is to have an enduring dialogue with science and technology, then we need to talk to more people," she says. "We have to open it up. Art should speak for itself, and I think artists are really striving to say as much as possible. The reason

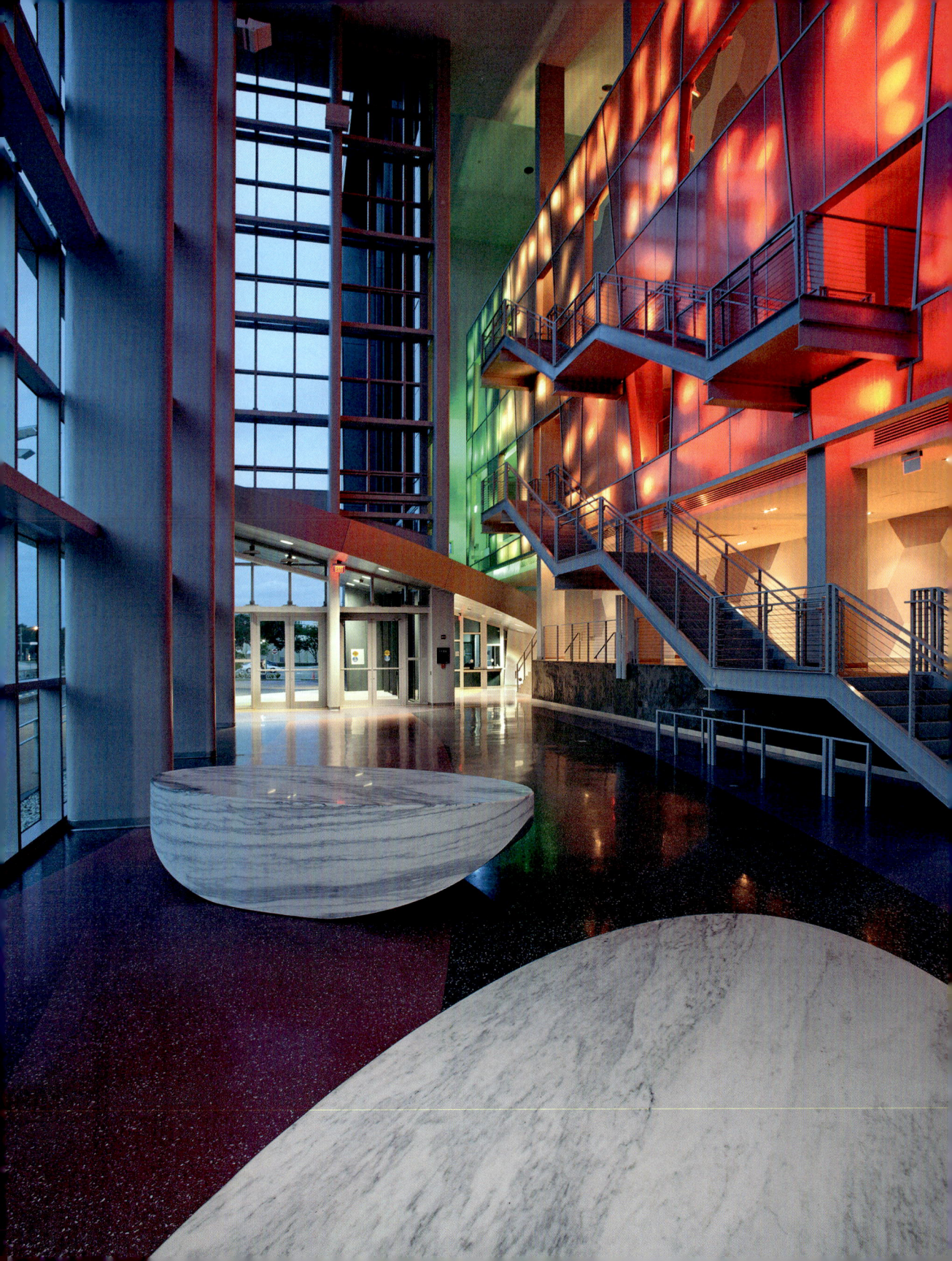

we're seeing new media is that artists are yearning to say more and speak to different levels."

FLARB2 follows in the vein of two of the most promising trends in Miami's evolving art scene—artists cultivating their own inventive venues to push the boundaries of contemporary art and South Beach hotels becoming a place to have informal encounters with such work, such as the start-up fair FAST FWD: MIAMI held at the Nash Hotel last December.

"The idea of taking art out of the white cube of a gallery space is very intriguing," says Jennifer Gray, director of the Wolfson Gallery at Miami-Dade Community College, Wolfson Campus. "There need to be more outlets for artists to show their work, and joining South Beach tourism with the art scene here is really smart."

In memoriam: Charles Recher, 1950–2017

ROBERT CHAMBERS

Sculpting a Moment

September 1, 2002

The bone-white flamingo with the red eyes isn't barking, and a man standing outside John Martin's restaurant wants Robert Chambers to get its bark back.

And Chambers, a Miami-based artist known for richly peculiar sculpture that melds science, art, and sound, is only too happy to oblige. So as rush hour jams Coral Gables's Miracle Mile, Chambers pulls a raft of tools from his black backpack, and within minutes, the flamingo has not only its bark back but also the flash in its beady eyeballs.

FIGURE 26. Robert Chambers, *Light Field and Orbitals 1 & 2*, 2010. Architecture LED lighting, marble. Dennis C. Moss Cultural Arts Center. Image Robin Hill, courtesy of Miami-Dade County Department of Cultural Affairs, Art in Public Places Trust.

"I put a microwave sensor in it, so when you get close, a tiny laser disc plays back the sound of two attack dogs barking, and the eyes glow an angry red," Chambers explains. "It gets a big jump from everybody."

Even the bird's color—or rather, its lack of color—draws attention.

"The flamingo came to me white, and I gave it back white," he continues. "It's like the antiflamingo. They said, 'You forgot to do anything with it.'"

While Chambers's antiflamingo is an eccentric breed apart from the more colorfully predictable plastic birds around town, bringing things to life with unpredictable flair is the artist's maverick MO.

He has not only constructed art from unlikely materials such as hair gel; he has also been an unusually generous catalyst on the local art scene. Last year he curated two attention-getting shows, emphasizing the distinctive work of young and youngish Miami-based artists at The House and the Bass Museum of Art.

This month he has orchestrated several shows to raise awareness—and money—for SAVE Dade, an organization urging a "no" note on the September 10 referendum to remove the phrase "sexual orientation" from Miami-Dade County's Human Rights Ordinance. The shows will take place at Fredric Snitzer and Bernice Steinbaum galleries and at the home of artist Eugenia Vargas and will include performances in the newly minted El Solar Arts House in Coral Gables.

"I like to create a happening that creates awareness either of artists or a cause," Chambers says. And this cause, he says, "reminds us that everyone's human rights can be threatened. People in the arts have always been at the forefront of alerting people about human rights."

Adds Daniel Arsham, who grew up in South Florida and is now an art student in New York, "It's kind of our job. The arts community is a place where there's more openness."

Arsham is among the 200 artists, including Paul Stoppi, Vickie Pierre, and Naomi Fisher, contributing works to the *NO-Show*, which opens Tuesday at Fredric Snitzer Gallery. On that night, all sales of the moderately priced—nothing over $500—artwork will benefit SAVE Dade.

"Obviously, the issue is critical," Snitzer says. "It's good that we are having a stake in this campaign and saying, 'No, this can't fly.'"

Vargas came to mind because, in the past few years, she has organized a lively series of *Home Shows* in which artists have installed works in her home. Besides, Chambers says, "if you don't have your human rights, it's like not having a home"—which inspired the name of the *NO-Home Show*, a one-night event on September 9 at Vargas's home that will include art by Pablo Cano, María Brito, and David Rohn.

OUTSIDE THE BOX

Momentum among artists to support SAVE Dade started nearly two years ago but really raced forward this summer as Election Day neared. Chambers exchanged so many emails and calls with artists that, by late August, the memory card in his cell phone reached its limit.

Such rallying en masse is "something artists should do," insists Vargas. "I really think the Miami arts community is impassive; artists are kind of removed if anything is political."

With a slight smile, Arsham describes the variety of events as adding up to "a normal Robert affair. He thinks completely differently from anyone else who organizes things."

The Miami household in which Chambers grew up in the 1960s seems to have been one that nurtured out-of-the-box thinking. Chambers's great-grandmother was a pioneering midwife on a farm near the Oregon coast, while his father, Edward L. Chambers, taught biology at the University of Miami. Now a professor emeritus at UM, his research there included fertilizing sea urchin eggs. With his own father, who was the artist's grandfather, Edward L. Chambers coauthored the textbook *Explorations into the Nature of the Living Cell*, published by Harvard University Press.

No surprise, then, that the artist's mother, Elenora S. Chambers, is an abstract painter whose lilting canvases have sometimes resembled interlacing cellular forms. While his father would be conducting research in the Marquesas or on the Massachusetts coast, Chambers remembers how his mother brought along huge rolls of canvas that she tacked up to work on.

"My parents led exciting lives," Chambers says. "They were always traveling. They went everywhere from Cuba to remote areas in France, and my father traveled around Tunisia. Some trips I went along with them, and my mother just loved the diversity of all these places and meeting new people. That's how she met my father. She was discussing existentialism with several scientists and she caught my father's ear and eye in Portland, Oregon."

TWIN PASSIONS

So it was natural that art and science would become passions for the couple's son. His parents frequently took him to art museums, and he also developed a talent for making horrific messes in his father's lab, stopping up sinks to create floods. At home, a family heirloom, a charming 19th-century wind-up bird that chirped arias from *La Boheme*, was one of many objects Chambers relentlessly took apart and reassembled.

A burly man with a loping gait, black hair that explodes into ringlets in the summer humidity, and the demeanor of an intelligently manic Peter Pan, Chambers celebrated his 44th birthday in August on his great-grandmother's farm with his wife and fellow artist Mette Tommerup.

"I wish I was stuck at 24," he says. "Then my brain would be matching my body."

Not that the considerable variety of his art—which has been featured in solo shows at the Miami Art Museum and the Museum of Contemporary Art in North Miami, as well as in galleries in New York, London, and Rome—ever suggests sluggishness. Instead, it tweaks the machine-like sculpture of Jean Tinguely with bravura invention and humor. Over his career, he has moved from noisemaking pieces made of castoff industrial parts scavenged from Miami River junkyards to installations oozing with fluorescent chemicals once used to trace water pollutants and reconfigured to suggest bubbling abstract paintings run amok.

Many pieces invite watchful observation or participation, such as the silkily inflating and deflating *Capes* in MOCA's permanent collection or the luminous *Ballship*, a vast fiberglass globe that echoes and distorts ambient sounds, transforming viewers' speech into unearthly music.

"He's very inventive in doing things with different materials," Jeanette Ingberman, codirector of Exit Art, a nonprofit venue in Manhattan, says of

Chambers. "We did a show called *Danger*, which suited him because a lot of his pieces imply danger."

Chambers's piece featured "a huge kind of rotating blade that was quite difficult to turn and made an excruciating noise," Ingberman remembers. "As dangerous as it seemed, it was also quite inviting to use. He's created wonderful machines, and many of them are participatory, so he's creating in his art a situation that you can get involved in just as he does with his curatorial work."

"Not every artist is as generous as a person," she continues, noting that Chambers has frequently recommended artists for Exit Art shows. "Not only does he come up with ideas for the shows, but he comes out with a truck to pick up the artwork."

CREATING BY CURATING

With his free-flowing, unpredictable curatorial projects, including one planned to coincide with December's Art Basel Miami Beach, Chambers is moving into a new phase, an extension of the interactive style he adopted while teaching art from 1993 to 1998 at the University of Miami. Then he took students to New York and introduced them to artists and other contacts he developed while doing graduate work and teaching at New York University in the late 1980s and early '90s.

"I always made sure my students would stay with artists and curators all throughout New York and New Jersey," he says. "We would be spread out all over the place, and then we would meet together at a deli on Second Avenue. I was always mixing it up, so the faculty regarded me nervously."

Now operating in a less institutional framework, Chambers is generating an infectious energy that has been embraced by young artists here such as Jason Ferguson, Christian Curiel, and Brandon Opalka, who call themselves "FeCuOp." At Chambers' insistence, FeCuOp developed the *NO to Discrimination* banner, another work in the SAVE Dade campaign, now hanging outside the Bernice Steinbaum Gallery in the Design District.

"Robert is a little frazzled sometimes," Ferguson says, "but he's really pushed us and helped us get our bearings. He's like a mad scientist."

Mad scientist. Impassioned maverick. Those are just some of the names he's been called by friends and associates.

"He's a total original," adds Miami Art Museum director Suzanne Delehanty. "It is always an inspiration to be around him."

In memoriam: Edward L. Chambers, 1917–2008
Jeanette Ingberman, 1952–2011
Elenora S. Chambers, 1921–2020

MIAMI COLLECTORS COMMISSION ART

November 3, 2002

It can lead to spectacular success and bitter failure. Idealistic art students may shun it as pandering compromise. Some seasoned artists say it leads to mediocre sellouts. Yet others are finding ways to make it flourish. In South Florida, several artists and collectors are getting surprising results by embracing an at times controversial practice: privately commissioning artwork.

An installation by Karen Rifas of oak leaves stitched in strands, for example, playfully interacts with outdoor views in an office building lobby at 1428 Brickell Avenue, Miami. Delicately drawn cityscapes by Glexis Novoa have been commissioned for homes and the lobby of a new South Beach condominium, at once plumbing a vivid present and quietly looking to a colorful past.

The gamut of this genre is vast and fascinating, full of cautionary tales that still apply today.

At its most remarkable, think of Michelangelo's frescoes gloriously illuminating the ceiling of the Sistine Chapel, commissioned by Pope Julius II in 1508. Yet while the Sistine frescoes became one of the most ambitious works of the Renaissance, another grandly conceived fresco became synonymous with one of the 20th century's most notorious art scandals.

After adding a portrait of Lenin to his mural for New York's Rockefeller Center in 1933, Diego Rivera ran afoul of his seriously capitalist patron, John R. Todd, who headed the corporation managing the Rockefeller Center development. Todd had the mural hacked to bits, sparking a huge protest and effectively ending Rivera's career as a muralist in this country.

On view at the Wolfsonian-Florida International University is the result of another run-in between artist and patron—this time governmental—but saved for posterity. In 1926, the Irish Free State commissioned Harry Clarke to design stained-glass windows as its gift to a League of Nations building in Geneva.

Choosing scenes from the best of modern Irish literature, Clarke horrified bureaucrats by portraying a "too virile" young man in snug breeches and a woman in a "too diaphanous" gown, as well as a barely tolerated bottle of Guinness. Implications of sex and drinking didn't fit the image of Irish culture the state wanted to project, and eventually, Clarke's widow bought back his luminous stained-glass panels.

The result was Ireland's loss and South Florida's gain when Wolfsonian founder Mitchell "Micky" Wolfson Jr. purchased these windows that sparkle with more insight into Irish culture than Clarke ever imagined.

SEEKING ARTISTS

Other collectors here are trying to avoid the second-guessing and major misunderstandings—and spinelessness—often at the root of such controversies.

They've sought artists whose work they already know and admire in order to enhance a problematic space, complement a gorgeous view, or satisfy a desire for art to provoke thought and nourish the soul. Some talk with the artist about their hopes for the space and may approve a maquette or drawings, but then the key to a successful commission, they say, is to let the artist work unimpeded.

"I can see only regrets later if you get involved," says collector Richard Shack. "Artists know what they are doing."

When neurologist Jeff Gelblum bought one of Novoa's drawings on canvas, it involved Gelblum choosing a wall in his Miami Beach apartment on which Novoa would draw extensions of his cityscape.

Yet, he says, "I didn't know what he would do, and I would never tell an artist what to do. You either love their work or you don't. I left the keys downstairs and said, 'Glexis, let yourself in and do what you want.' It's a surprise to walk in and see something beautiful."

Novoa's canvas and wall drawing hover above an entryway table, the sort over which many people hang a mirror. For Gelblum, the piece, called *Días despues* (*Days since*), is a poetic mirror of the Western urbanized world's precarious condition. The artist has limned an intricate version of the New York skyline, with the World Trade Center towers encased in a glass dome. Like invaders, mysterious podlike creatures linger above the skyline and swirl in the water.

"We live in vulnerable times," Gelblum says, explaining the work's appeal, which is anything but what he calls "paint-by-numbers for rich people." "We've got this marvelous, sophisticated world called urban civilization, and yet it's still very fragile. To me, art has to pull stuff out of your soul, now more than ever."

Novoa, who swears he drew it shortly before 9/11, says he accepts suggestions from collectors before he begins a piece and studies the size of the space, "but after I have the idea, it would be difficult for me to accept modifications. If it's possible, I like to work with the real view from the site of the drawing and do an interpretation."

ROOM WITH A VIEW

Magnificent views of the Miami River and the bay beyond, seen from his firm's offices on the 34th floor of the downtown Miami Center, were the impetus for José Bedia's paintings that attorney Milton Ferrell Jr. commissioned. They were meant to suggest the diverse realms of North and South America and the firm's far-flung business.

As imaginative scenes presenting a Northern figure and car rushing through a stark gray corridor and a Southern canvas of birds clustered throughout a leafy canopy, they play a bit with clichés about North Americans' obsession with time and Latin Americans' more relaxed pace.

"I can't imagine the space without them," says Ferrell. "You look at one and think you're late, you have too much to do, and the other one is very soothing."

Commissioned artwork by Carlos Betancourt in one of the firm's conference rooms responds more directly to views of the city's skyline. It's a blending of body and building, city and individual. It shows photographic scenes on paper superimposed with the artist's hand and inscribed with his distinctive reverse writing.

Before starting on this piece, Betancourt showed Ferrell catalogs of his work. "He pointed out the kind of work he liked, so I moved toward that. He was extremely open to ideas, and he took his time seeing the sketches I had done. It's important to do a very clear presentation of the artist's intentions and have that approved. Then you are ready."

All of these works arose from long talks with the artists, says Ferrell, about his views on how particular spaces in the firm are used. But a starting point is his respect for their work, and in this case, for "art of the moment, you have to have a good relationship with the artist. What you are getting is the next work the artist is doing."

Talks with Rubén Torres Llorca about a larger conference room yielded a mesmerizing tour de force, *Make Me a Mask*, a series of 42 strikingly carved masks mounted on the wall next to captions that speak to the layers of behavior present in a room where divergent parties meet. "To lie," "To look around," "To confess" read some of the captions.

"I explained to Rubén that I really wanted art that would bring people out," says Ferrell. "People come into this room like projectiles with a point of view they want to keep pounding on."

The title, Torres Llorca explains, comes from a poem by Dylan Thomas. "He mentioned to me that Thomas was one of his favorite poets, and the line came to me right away. I am always interested in other functions of art, not just aesthetic, and he told me how he wanted to motivate people to be open and to discuss."

Longtime collectors Ruth and Richard Shack had long puzzled over a narrow, horizontal section of wall space just above their two-story windows overlooking the bay and the bridge to Key Biscayne. Jutting hardware for the window's hurricane shutters made the space especially problematic.

They had asked many artists for suggestions, but it was Karen Rifas's proposal for the space that won them over. After showing them a precisely made maquette, she spent hours on a scaffold installing multiple strings of oak leaves that float above the window and, in a magical bit of rhyming, re-create the contours of the bridge and islands below.

"I like to do things that are site specific, that bounce off an environment," says Rifas, who stitches leaves together on a 30-year-old Singer. "In a home I have to be aware of what's around, if there's a dog, if there are air currents, and I do have to be considerate of [the collectors'] thoughts."

The Shacks say they wanted something they could live with, but that would also show the artist's work at its best. "It looks effortless and ephemeral, but we are never going to take it down."

In memoriam: Milton Ferrell Jr., d. 2008
Richard Shack, 1926–2012

BHAKTI BAXTER

A Portrait of Nature's Elegance and Intricacy

November 5, 2002

An intriguing, if not altogether cohesive, installation at the Museum of Contemporary Art in North Miami makes up the first solo museum show for Miami-based artist Bhakti Baxter. It gives a richer expression to Baxter's take on the interlacing, rhythmic forms in nature, developing in more detail the fascination with organic growth that he has shown in earlier work, as in *That Place*, a group exhibit in the Design District this summer, and in a group show at MOCA last year.

In the museum's Pavilion Gallery, the artist has constructed a quietly meditative, chapel-like space with individual "stations" for viewers to contemplate. Music with an electronic, new wave cast by Stereolab plays pulsing and lyrical sounds in the background.

While there are no overt references to any specific religions, the piece conveys an almost spiritual reverence for the mathematical elegance of nature and the serendipitous dangling together of things such as leaves and spider webs.

A trio of small photographs on one wall evokes chance encounters with earthy, ephemeral beauty and change, while on the opposite wall, a delicate drawing in blue aspires to cosmic significance. It limns a crystalline star and its radiant points of light, the artist suggests, extending throughout the far corners of the universe.

These images gently seep into your peripheral vision as you enter the gallery. What is most immediately striking is a series of concentric circles of plaster spheres partly embedded in the wall opposite the gallery's entrance. A bit like the vast, circular rose window of stained glass in a Gothic cathedral, these spheres acquire an ethereal presence.

Opposite the radiating spheres is a pedestal balancing a spotlit vessel of water containing the tightly curled green fist of a hybrid vegetable called a broccoflower. It's almost absurdly simple but curiously right for this context. It echoes with imperfect rhythms the formation of spheres, offering a vulnerable, flawed geometry.

This piece seems to be about treasuring essential forms in nature, coupled with emblems of a microcosm and macrocosm that show the world in all its tiny idiosyncracies and in its grand hugeness. Some of these notions may also be at the root of a strange video flickering in a corridor tucked at the back of the gallery.

The video shows colorful morphing spheres in an almost mesmerizing abstract pattern, but it still seems more like the draft for a substantial work than anything that really engages the viewer or adds to the rest of the installation.

The distilled simplicity of this piece is both its weakness and its strength. Baxter relies on a less-is-more aesthetic to evoke a portrait of a universe woven with miraculous intricacy and design, but the spareness of the video and other elements don't always carry the symbolic weight the artist demands of them.

TERESITA FERNÁNDEZ

A Natural Woman

December 1, 2002

You get the sense Teresita Fernández wants to rescue rainbows from the dustbin of visual clichés, from the marketing machinery that equates this confluence of light and water with goofy good cheer suitable for Hallmark.

Still, not even she is immune from that marketing curse that says rainbows are risky subjects for serious artists. "I thought, 'Oh my God, I am making a rainbow,'" she says about a recent installation, a delicate constellation of acrylic cubes shimmering with color and attached to a white wall.

There's no familiar arc in sight to drive the piece into the dustbin, and yet it distills the essence of looking at rainbows.

"We come to regard something in a certain way based on all the information we know about it except the thing itself," says this Miami-raised Brooklyn resident with amused exasperation, sipping an iced coffee at Starbucks in South Miami earlier this month, after her solo show opened at the Miami Art Museum.

"I always think that merits going back to the source itself, like a rainbow, and thinking about what it really is, which is individual drops of water that are reflecting light and color," she explains. "That's all. There's nothing clichéd about it, but we always think of a rainbow not as an event but as an icon."

Rainbows, clouds, pools—and, perhaps most of all, intricately landscaped gardens and the secretive architectural spaces such pools and gardens suggest—are the sorts of "events" that Fernández, 34, ponders these days.

She uses their mix of natural forms and artifice to create spare interiors that viewers can walk through, spurring eventful trips in the imagination.

It's possible to meander among the few clouds and pools fashioned from plastic cubes and glass beads at MAM, for example, and their subtle contours may flicker into more robust landscapes in the mind's eye.

"The viewer is an integral part of the experience, almost like a circuit that completes the work," Fernández told *ARTnews* last year about her work. "What I make doesn't function very well outside of that witnessing."

GAINING POPULARITY

Since graduating from Florida International University in 1990 and earning an MFA two years later from Virginia Commonwealth University, she has also witnessed a rapidly increasing presence in the art world.

In 1996, while she was still living in Miami, her installation suggesting an indoor swimming pool and inspired by modernist designs Adolph Loos created but never built for Jazz Age dancer Josephine Baker was part of *Defining the Nineties*, the inaugural exhibit for the new building of North Miami's Museum of Contemporary Art.

That year she was also tapped for a group show at New York's New Museum of Contemporary Art. Later came shows in Europe, as well as an installation attached to the vast window overlooking the garden of New York's Museum of Modern Art. During the summer of 2000, she took part in *Wonderland* at the St. Louis Museum of Art, joining art stars like Ernesto Neto and Olafur Eliasson to create unusual environments for visitors to explore, supporting the show's claim that "to wander is to wonder."

Travels abroad, including an artist's residency in Japan and a fellowship at the American Academy in Rome, have fed Fernández's own sense of wonder, as well as a wanderlust to cast a wide net. "I like to do this blanket research. I'll spend months researching an idea and knowing a lot about something and still not know how I can make a piece out of it," says Fernández, who lives in Brooklyn with her husband, artist Tom Downs, and their toddler son.

A trip to the art event *Documenta* in Kassel, Germany, led to a visit to the city's baroque mountaintop garden and its man-made cascading waterfall.

Though she's loath to say much about sources, last month she exhibited a waterfall of her own, a minimalist curve rippling with white and blue plastic. It was shown at her New York gallery Lehmann Maupin, which will be bringing her works to Art Basel Miami Beach.

JAPANESE INFLUENCE

In Japan, the intimate *shakkei*, or "borrowed garden," caught her eye. It's a tradition swept away by Tokyo's urban sprawl but found in quieter temples and tea gardens. To explain, she picks up pad and pen and deftly sketches what resembles a tiny theater, a boxy room with one wall covered floor to ceiling with a landscape painting.

The painting is actually a window onto a real vista that has been "borrowed" from nature. "You are in this darkened space. It's more like a glowing film projection," she says. "Everything is real—plants, sky, light—and yet it looks very composed and artificial. It has to do with how you are seeing it."

Researching these gardens, and formal European ones, led to a vibrant installation created at the ArtPace residency program in San Antonio. More ambitious than her MAM work, it's called *Borrowed Landscape*. Pencil-drawn plans for formal gardens are placed on the floors of five cube-shaped tents made from translucent veils in yellow and aqua. Visitors walk among and peer through these harem-like tents, finding vistas changing with each step.

"I was very attracted to the rigor of her work, and yet it appeals to the senses, and that's how it hooks you," says Peter Boswell, MAM's senior curator and curator of her show here. He met Fernández in Rome at the American Academy, when she'd been looking hard at gardens in Tivoli and mosaic floors in Roman churches.

"She talked about how space unfolds," he recalls. "Here was this very young artist who wasn't necessarily looking at art but at a lot of man-made phenomena."

And what about studying such artfully controlled environments after growing up in a place of rampant flora? "She did say something about living down here in nature that has to be hacked at continuously to be kept in place, but I don't know how much that really influenced her."

Nor does Fernández, though she jokes about the fake banyans recently crowding the entrance to a South Miami mall. "It's kind of funny. Here in South Florida, where anything will grow. I knew they wouldn't last."

But looking at gardens and rainbows is the kind of lasting obsession to keep her going, even if clichés do surface.

"That's one of the hardest parts of being an artist—being fascinated by an idea, and yet there's this step in the middle with no rules. You try something, you throw it out, and you edit. You just do it, and it happens," she says, her voice softening, "and that surprise keeps you wanting to make art. It's a very short charge, and you're on to the next thing."

BUNNY YEAGER

'50s Photos Capture Beauty and the Beach

February 9, 2003

In the sweet and cheesy world of 1950s pinup beauties, Bunny Yeager had it both ways. She was the gorgeous girl in front of the camera and the photographer snapping the picture.

A busy professional in a prefeminist era known more for housewives wearing faux pearl necklaces while whipping up tuna casseroles than for career women bearing briefcases, this former Miami model and beauty queen found success in the man's world of pre-*Hustler* girlie magazines.

Yeager made a name for herself by whipping up skimpy swimsuits for models posed in sunny locales, like the leopard-skin numbers in her teasing black-and-white photos of Bettie Page, a 1950s cult icon of sex-kitten kitsch.

They're featured in the current show at Javogue & Ingalls Fine Art in North Miami. In these photographs, Page flaunts her stuff among driftwood on the beach in Key Biscayne; dangles from a mango tree and spears fish like a vixen-ish "you Tarzan, me Jane" TV character; and preens topless among cheetahs in Africa USA, a now-defunct theme park in Boca Raton.

They're typical of Yeager's offbeat ingenuity, celebrating the exotic possibilities of Florida and defining glamour in new ways.

OFFBEAT STYLE

Working out of her studio in Miami Shores in the 1950s and 1960s, Yeager sold beauty and the beach with a catchy sense of style, playful and daring. It did not seem vulgar or pornographic and was devoid of chains and leather.

"Pornography is explicitness of nudity. I think bondage only invites rape and murder if you have a deranged mind," says Yeager, who continues to photograph models and actors. "My girls were beautiful in a nice way."

Yeager saw the market for her work dwindle in the 1970s. But today, there's a steady demand for her vintage photos and books about those years since the 1994 release of the coffee table book *Bunny's Honeys: Bunny Yeager, Queen of Pin-Up Photography* (Taschen America).

"She has a very developed European following and a large audience on the West Coast," says gallery director Chris Ingalls. "I think her recognition is wider than we locals realize. People like the fresh quality of photographs that are now almost 50 years old. It's not campy or jaded."

Eisenhower-era department stores would never have carried the sexy attire of Yeager's models. Instead, they stocked corset-like swimwear fitted out with starchy skirts and industrial-strength zippers.

Yeager's suits, cut high on the leg and low on the breast, or sometimes simply fashioned from strategically taped-on orchids and oleander blossoms, were never meant to be immersed in water.

"These beautiful little outfits," says Yeager, flipping through pages in her book *Bunny Yeager's Pin-Up Girls of the 1950s*, published in 2002. "They were so cute and coy. [Models had] better not swim in my suits," she laughs. "They were for pictures only!"

Now a grandmother of four and a recent widow, Yeager still relishes girlish pink lipstick. Despite her platinum-tinted hair, she's no longer the svelte creature who posed for brochures promoting Miami Beach or the one who carted cameras into the surf when she captured a winsome but alluring kind of beauty for long-vanished magazines with titles like *Flirt* and *Frolic*.

But her enthusiasm remains genuine. She's untroubled by feminist protests about objectifying women and celebrating only a certain kind of full-breasted figure.

"The world revolves around sex," she cheerfully insists. "Man, woman, no matter how you deny it."

And to be a woman photographing beautiful women has always been a pleasurable challenge, a way to do something the men couldn't.

"Because I had the ability to see the potential in a girl by her facial bone structure and the shape of her body in clothes," she explains, "I was able to discover girls who might be overlooked by other, male photographers. Young girls felt more comfortable posing for me than for a man. That's my style, to make women look good, to hide their faults."

In memoriam: Bunny Yeager, 1929–2014

CUNDO BERMÚDEZ

A Life in Color

April 20, 2003

He is a reluctant master. With a self-deprecating smile, Cundo Bermúdez brushes aside attempts by University of Miami students to call him maestro as they film a documentary about his decades of painting impressions of Cuba, turning the island into a place aswirl with baroque opulence and brilliant light.

Dressed in the wintry colors of gray pants and dark blue shirt and walking with a cane and the shuffling gait to be expected for his 88 years, Cundo is the opposite of masterful opulence. These days he can look like a frail and faded heir to the fevered praise he earned as a Latin American art star of the 1940s.

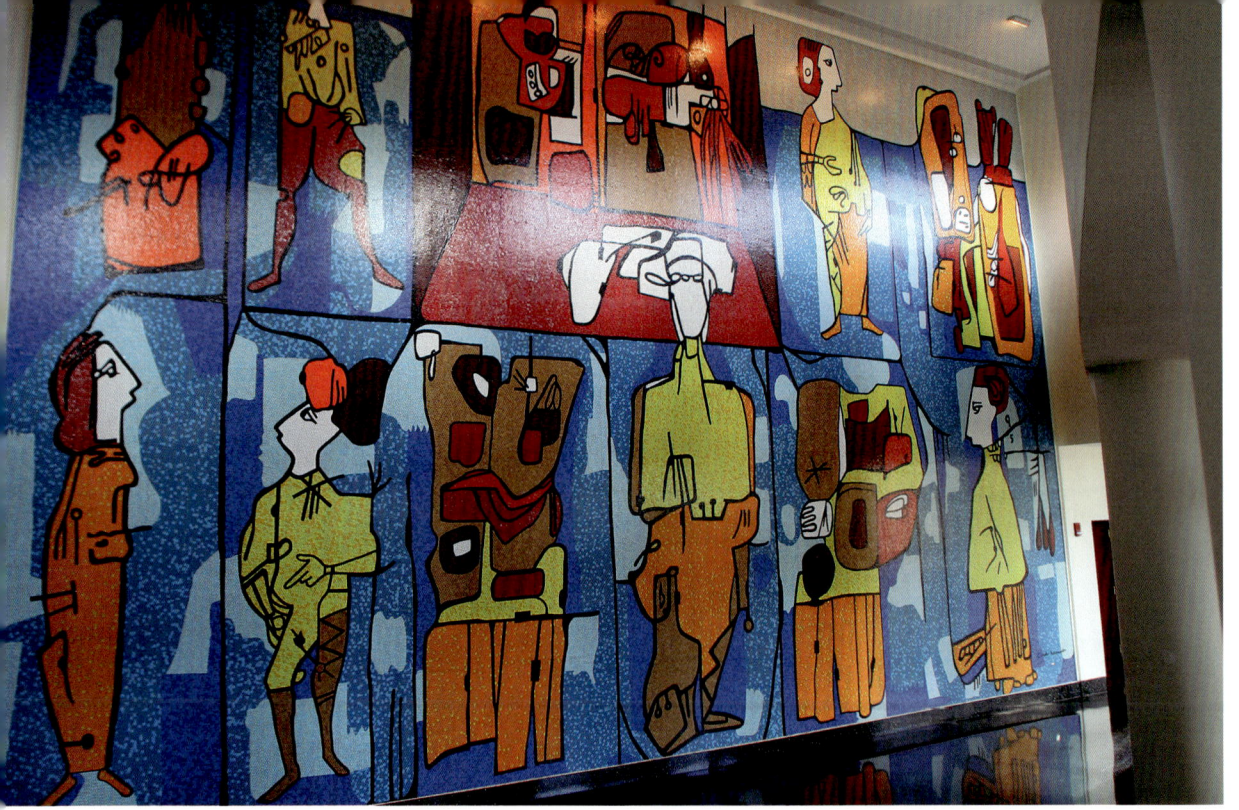

FIGURE 27. Cundo Bermúdez, *Ways of Performing*, 2006. Glass mosaic tile mural. Adrienne Arsht Center, Ziff Ballet Opera House, Black Box theater. Courtesy of Miami-Dade County Department of Cultural Affairs, Art in Public Places Trust.

That's when he "set on fire the peaceful scenes of Cuban interiors," as a New York art critic enthused in 1944 when nine of his paintings were shown in the landmark *Modern Cuban Painting* at New York's Museum of Modern Art.

So striking was his art that MOMA snapped up one of the standouts from that show, *La Barbería* (*The barbershop*), for its permanent collection, along with *El Balcón* (*The balcony*), at a time when the museum was spearheading recognition of Latin American art in the United States, packing curators off to Mexico, the Caribbean, and Brazil.

Never shown before in Miami, these two MOMA acquisitions will be part of *Cundo Bermúdez: A Life in Art*, which opens with a reception Tuesday at the Lowe Art Museum, University of Miami, and covers work from the 1940s through the present.

Cundo, as he's known by friends and scholars alike, is one of the last living links to a golden age in Cuban art. "I can never be anything but Cuban," he says, even though he has spent nearly half his adult life in exile, having left Havana in the mid-1960s when he was 53, settling in Puerto Rico until moving to Miami seven years ago to be closer to relatives.

And despite his often fragile demeanor, he can launch into almost gleeful personal recollections of the place that still feeds his imagination. He deftly describes a girl with perfect posture named Alicia Alonso, on her way to becoming a famed ballerina, who walked past his family's home in Havana every day to dance class. Perhaps she was also a model for the uniquely graceful women in lavish costumes he has painted so many times.

He confides with a laugh, "She told me painters were lazy."

HUMOR AND HAVANA

In these moments, it's not so hard to see why legendary MOMA director Alfred Barr praised his "humorously archaic painting, both vigorous and original."

Some of that humor starts to surface when he recalls the essence of Havana, though tinged with a Proustian quality he'll never find in Miami. "It's the smell that brings you back to a certain place," he says, "the smell of the ocean in Havana, and not just the pleasant smelling things like perfume, but everything else."

He has outlasted compatriots like the painters Mario Carreño and René Portocarrero. They all belonged to a generation that drew accolades in the 1940s for adapting strains of European modernism, from Matissean hues to fractured cubist space, into work that eschewed picturesque clichés and pulsed with a sense of Cuban identity.

And they expanded on innovations by their fabled immediate predecessors like Amelia Peláez and Wifredo Lam, who first fused the language of modernism with the culture of Cuba.

Cundo "played an important role in the 1940s. He was one of those who began to explore the Spanish heritage in Cuban identity," says Florida International University art historian Juan Martínez.

This direction, Martínez adds, "was a reaction to the 1930s, when there was a movement of Afro-Cubanisma in painting, literature, and music. I don't think they were anti-African altogether, but they thought the emphasis should be on the Spanish, the most dominant part of their heritage. There's always been a tension between those two aspects of Cuban identity."

Cundo's generation was enthralled by a sensual aesthetic of "too much is never too much." They enhanced their paintings with the baroque generosity of colonial architecture, the scintillating colors of fan-shaped stained-glass windows, and the exuberant arabesques curling their way through patterned ceramic tile and wrought iron balconies.

The gliding rhythms and repetition of music also figured into his playful scenes of musicians. Such details enliven a painting like his *El Balcón*, with its window opening onto a serenely blue Havana Bay and its couple lounging in rocking chairs, the woman partly nude in a flowing pink gown.

These works from the 1940s remain the most coveted of his art—a 1942 painting of musicians fetched $486,500 at auction in 1999, while later works have sold for five-figure sums.

POST-CUBA PERIOD

The Lowe's show presents a full range of his art, including paintings that are uncharacteristically muted and bleak, from a series called the *Gusanitas*. These are interiors from the early 1960s, no longer filled with light or color but showing languid women surrounded by household treasures. They are solitary keepers of the family wealth for exiles—the worms, or *gusanos*, as Fidel Castro called them—who left after Castro came to power; by 1967 Cundo had left as well.

In Puerto Rico, much of the old exuberance returned to his art, but in a shimmering and labyrinthine way that made fewer references to a specific place. Now he encased mysterious, stylized figures in narrow chambers, connected by surreally curving stair steps. Sometimes these strange interiors allowed for an elusive glimpse of sky through a window or balcony, sometimes not.

In these paintings, echoes of architecture often melt away into a satiny web of ribbons. Festive ribbons drape his figures in costumes that undulate into an entire flamboyant environment, fantastic and remote from reality.

Some art historians, like Martínez and Alejandro Anreus, who's writing a book on Cuban American artists, see a falling off, an increasing sense of decoration for its own decadent sake in these later paintings. Yet the jury's still out on what will endure from Cundo's legacy.

Cundo doesn't seem to care what his critics say about his enthralled dedication to ornament and decoration.

A lifelong lover of the theater and symphonic concerts, he seems perpetually charmed by theatrical artifice. It's fitting that what will probably be his final work for Miami is a 28- by 40-foot glass mosaic mural for the Performing Arts Center.

In this mural, more ambitious than his first, which was created almost 50 years ago for the Havana Hilton, yellow costumed figures pose in glinting chambers of red and blue.

It's called *Ways of Performing*.

It shows, he says, "the machines that create costumes in theater, they create snow, they create rain, whatever you want."

The figures are both actors and stagehands, full partners in the invention of illusions. Says Cundo, "I am always inventing something."

In memoriam: Cundo Bermúdez, 1914–2008

ROBERTO BEHAR AND ROSARIO MARQUARDT

Card Sharks

April 27, 2003

It's as if Miami has become these visionary artists' playroom, a big city that deserves big toys and dreams to match. Their latest living-large toy is a festive house of cards—perhaps about to collapse, but perhaps not—built for the Miami Art Museum and presented in the museum's *New Work* series.

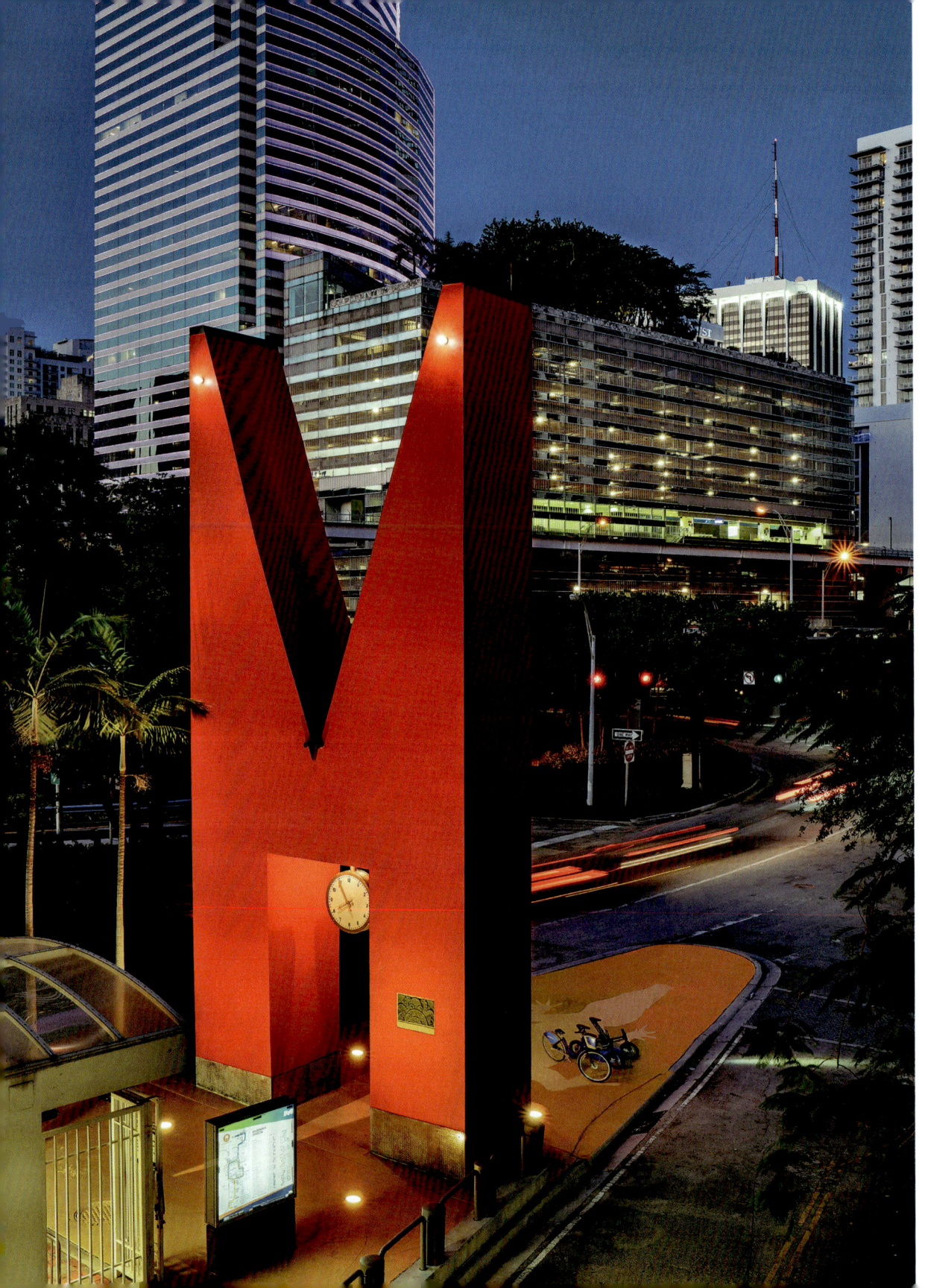

Working in their trademark and moderately gigantic mode, the artists Roberto Behar and Rosario Marquardt have already caused a child's peppermint-red block of the letter M to tower four stories high near the Miami River. It's known as the "M" outdoor sculpture, marking the Riverwalk Metromover station in downtown Miami.

They are also responsible for the stunning urban *Living Room*, with its soaring 40-foot wall of pink and mango wallpaper, scaled with the wide-open charm of a huge doll's house and furnished with a fuschia sofa and white lamps on a street corner in the Design District.

KIDS! is their merry antimonumental pair of girl-and-boy action figures that greet kids at the nearby Design and Architecture Senior High School.

And as if for a rainy day, they've brought indoors the emerald luxuriance of a tropical forest teeming with blossoms and the occasional wary, yellow-eyed creature. You'll find this forest inside the *Paradise Room*, one of their less daring projects, and a 2002 Art in Public Places commission of painted murals lining the Visitors' Center ballroom at Fairchild Tropical Garden.

In a puckish inversion of public and personal space, indoors and outdoors, these Miami-based artists are making rooms in our city where most everyone can come out to play. (Unfortunately, the second-floor *Paradise Room* is not regularly open to visitors.) But this husband-and-wife team has also set out on a serious adventure, seeking sidewalks to places more inviting and communal than the ugly isolation of urban sprawl.

FIRST SIGNS

They've been pointing us in this direction for some time. In 1999, they exhibited *Los Pasos Perdidos* (*The lost steps*), a whimsical tableau in which urban planning meets Alice in a tropical Wonderland. It's a road map for artwork they've made and for other pieces that might one day come to pass.

Constructed like an architectural model of a city plaza, this tableau is

FIGURE 28. R&R Studios, *Red M*, 1996/2021. Architecture, concrete, block concrete, stucco, painting, lighting. Riverwalk Metro Rail Station. Image Zachary Balber, courtesy of Miami-Dade County Department of Cultural Affairs, Art in Public Places Trust.

vibrant with miniature cha-cha dancers, sofas, a paper boat folded from a map, a costumed devil, and yes, a red "M" and a house of cards.

At MAM, their house of cards has become a 12-foot-high mansion of make-believe, built with cards that are 2.5 feet tall. Surrounding it is a wooden scaffold, suggesting we've encountered a place that's not yet taken its final shape.

The one disappointing note in this new work is the *Wheel of Fortune*, a would-be roulette wheel that visitors can spin, pointing them in various directions. Located in a short dark hallway veiled by a curtain of plastic streamers, this "game" is a gratingly obvious device to suggest that viewers arrive in South Florida from a welter of geographic locations.

The House of Cards is part of the installation here called *A Place in the World*. This airy structure is sparingly lit with the colored lights of a street carnival. They bathe everything in a disorienting, pinkish half-light resembling both dusk and dawn.

In this pretend plaza from a twilight zone, a cluster of barely two-feet-tall figures gather around the house of cards, one scaling it with a ladder and another stretched out in dreamy sleep. Tiny star-shaped glitter sparkles on the floor forming upside-down constellations.

Recorded sounds from a speaker slice abruptly into the reflective mood of this work. There's the screech and whine of planes landing and taking off, the distant barking of dogs, and other jangled residues of traffic departing and arriving.

So much of Behar and Marquardt's work is this kind of accessible child's play and fashioned for a young city with lots of arrivals from all over the map. Like the house of cards, their public and personal art is often scaled too big or too small for grown-ups. It is, however, sized just right for minds open to shared memories and multiple possibilities in new, evolving places.

YOUNG AT HEART

"This is about excavating our own memories, and we find that we do indeed have things in common, and they take the form of games and toys," says Behar.

Both he and his wife, Marquardt, who arrived here in the mid-1980s, were trained as architects in their native Argentina, and he speaks English with a swiftly musical Italian lilt, reflective of Spanish spoken in a country settled by many Italian immigrants.

"Who hasn't attempted as a kid to build a house of cards?" he asks. But even if you didn't shuffle a deck to play architect as a child, this piece recalls the kind of game in which success or failure was just one good or bad move away. Charged memories nestle within this classic house of cards. Cunning and precarious, the cards re-create a risky venture for any age that's in the process of either standing firm or toppling down.

In the case of collapse, "we say, 'let's try again,'" he adds. "Now it's realized. So it *was* possible."

EUGENIA VARGAS

A Dream Made Real

May 25, 2003

Miami's Eugenia Vargas was shocked to learn how much certain people knew about her in her native Chile. Especially when curators there chose Vargas to represent the country in the prestigious Venice Biennale next month.

Her nomadic artistic career started to unfold a lifetime ago. It was 1975 when she and her brother—both blacklisted—fled Chile following the brutal coup that toppled President Salvador Allende's Socialist government.

Yet last summer when she entered the Santiago office of Luisa Ulibarri Lorenzini, a prominent curator, she saw a tall stack of papers on Ulibarri Lorenzini's desk, all about Vargas and her art. "It was like the FBI," Vargas laughs. "They had this file on me. I always thought nobody there knew my work."

After all, when she left Chile, she became a twentysomething student of photography at the University of Montana, and then moved on to Puerto Rico, and by 1985 was in Mexico City.

In Mexico she crafted spare, melancholic performance art, like the one within a niche of an abandoned monastery. It played off the grandiose excesses of church architecture and was prompted partly by her memories of the overbearing cathedral to which German nuns shepherded her as a schoolgirl.

Vargas also began photographing herself in an allegorical style etched with personal and historical memory. The images showed her body obscured and ornamented with other materials, from a hazy fog to a handcrafted child's saddle like those from Chile.

"I think every experience we live has an imprint on the body," says Vargas.

Her art struck chords. When Carla Stellweg, a New York–based independent dealer and curator, first saw this work, she remembered thinking, "My, this is as powerful as some of the better-known artists from the mainstream that I'd been looking at, like Ana Mendieta. It's a lot of fantasy, but real life is a part of it."

COMING TO FLORIDA

Six years ago, Vargas moved again, this time to Miami. Along the way, she has exhibited in Europe, the United States, Mexico, and Venezuela, but not in Chile.

Even though Vargas hadn't shown in Chile, Ulibarri Lorenzini says she has been following her career since first seeing her work in a group show at the Venice Biennale in 1993. When it was time for Ulibarri Lorenzini, as cultural affairs director for Chile's Ministry of Foreign Affairs, to oversee the choice of an artist to represent Chile at the 50th Venice Biennale this June, she thought of two expatriates, Vargas and Alfredo Jaar.

The better-known Jaar, whose art chronicles tragedies like ethnic cleansing, wanted to put off taking part until the next biennale. Vargas emerged as the better choice for this 50th Biennale, titled *Dreams and Conflicts: The Viewer's Dictatorship* says Lorenzini, though she admits, "There are some noises here because they don't know her work."

Still, Vargas's work is absolutely right for this biennale, continues the curator in a phone interview from Santiago. "It's about fantasy and dreams and the body."

The global and gondola-driven mother of all art exhibitions, "Venice," as the biennale is familiarly known, offers the chosen unprecedented prestige. It may also say something about Miami's growing art scene, now that an artist working here, for the first time in recent memory and perhaps the first time ever, has been tapped for a solo show in Venice.

And for this occasion, Vargas has been dreaming big . . . and no longer photographing herself.

"Everything I had to say with my body I have already said," explains the artist, a private woman with inky-black hair cropped short.

In her Miami living room, an almost minimalist installation itself of white walls and sofa, Vargas doesn't care to discuss her age or her country's traumatic past for the record. "My work doesn't talk about specific political issues in Chile," she says.

But her Venice project, featuring photographs of dolls playing with toy horses and a performance of sorts by Santiago street photographer Luis Maldonado, is tightly woven from her own past and Latin America's complex past of comings and goings.

PLAZA PLANS

This piece goes back to one of the artist's most pleasurable childhood memories, riding horses bareback on her parents' farm in southern Chile. It also promises to be inflected with sweet but pointed commentary, invoking myths and clichés about girls on horses and set against the souvenir-mongering in the fabled theme park that is Venice.

Just arranging for her solo show, to be located within a biscotti's throw of pigeons and espresso-swilling tourists in Saint Mark's Plaza, has been a work of dreams.

At first she thought of flying in Chilean horses to give tourists rides in this square famously lorded over by its own bronze steeds. Another idea involved rides in a hot air balloon over the plaza to show a rooftop video.

Costs and complicated permits felled these audacious proposals. But her actual project forges links between the plazas of Venice, Italy, and Santiago, Chile.

In a strange way, Vargas's art will travel thousands of miles from Chile in order to come home again in Venice.

She's fashioned her new work with ties to Italy, beginning with Juan Mochi, a 19th-century Italian painter transplanted to Chile who passed his rigid European style on to Chilean painter Ernesto Molina. His *A View of Venice* pleased well-heeled Chileans enthralled by all things European.

Today, Vargas works with street photographer Luis Maldonado, who plies his populist art by making family portraits in Santiago's Plaza de Armas. Working-class families have bought such portraits for decades in Chile. Maldonado's version uses a 19th-century German pinhole camera handed down from his grandfather. Though faster competitors use Polaroids, children still sit for him on a traditional handcrafted model horse.

At the biennale's opening, tourists in Saint Mark's Plaza can pose for Maldonado for free, with the little horse against a backdrop reproducing Molina's painting of Venice.

In a gallery by the plaza, Vargas will show her bittersweet photographs of dolls appearing to control (or be controlled by) toy horses from the series *The Longest Year*. It's a sequel to another series about damaged toys that nearly sold out when she exhibited them a year ago at Ambrosino Gallery in North Miami.

SLY STORIES

Such vignettes release sly stories of love and loss, of physical damage and power plays . . . all very adult themes saddled onto props from a faraway childhood. In Venice, they will be framed by casual but history-laden encounters between photographer and subject.

"It's all about memory, about recording a moment in the time of your life," she says of Maldonado's craft and her project. "I wanted him to be part of my work. I want to blur that line between high culture and everyday life."

ROCKET PROJECTS

Out of This World

June 1, 2003

Tiny spikes of plaster dust hover in the air and sting the eyes at Rocket Projects on North Miami Avenue, where construction drones on at what will be one of Miami's newest galleries. But at this point, the fireworks of liftoff still seem far away.

To get a really good look at the place, to take in the pristine white walls and suitably scuffed cement floor requisite for a venue of contemporary art, you have to squint and rub your eyes.

"Visine, anyone?," quips Nina Arias, one of the gallery's two codirectors, as she swivels on a stylish retro office chair of Lucite that glistens despite the surrounding pallor of dust.

She and codirector Nick Cindric have kept a soothing stash of eye drops for any workers, artists, and visitors who have stopped by for a very early preview. Yet Arias and Cindric, both wearing T-shirts printed with a comic book–style drawing of a rocket blasting off, are betting on this: when the air clears for the gallery's first show of work by Miami artists like the FeCuOp group on Saturday, no one will need any assistance to see their art and high-flying ambitions.

Arias, 27, is the relatively new kid on the art block, with connections to a youthful crowd of artists and out-of-town dealers. She made a splash earlier this year with a smartly curated show, *Drawing Conclusions*, by pulling together work by artists from here and elsewhere in a space donated by Design District developer Craig Robins. A veteran of galleries in Santa Fe, Boca Raton, and Fort Lauderdale, Cindric, 42, is the older hand at dealing art.

"I know how to put on Tom Wesselmann shows and David Hockney shows. I'm tired of that," he says. "Now it's time to do something with a bit more bite. I'd like this to be a place where new ideas are created."

"We want to launch young artists' careers," says Arias. "It's not just one show and that's it. We're going to be taking artists to the -scope art fair and to other cities," she adds, ticking off Los Angeles, San Francisco, and New York. (This contemporary art fair is now named SCOPE Art Show and presents art from international, emerging, and less-established galleries.)

Speaking of Rocket Projects, Miami artist Annie Wharton says, "It has potential here, I like their aesthetic and the way they treat their artists."

WEATHER OR NOT

Arias, showing abstract paintings by Rocket Projects artists Emilio Perez and Brandon Opalka, debuted in New York in March as one of 40 international dealers at -scope, the new fair for cutting-edge art launched about two years ago at hotels in New York and Los Angeles and this past December in Miami Beach at the Townhouse. Art at this fair ranges from the "experimental to embarrassing," opined the New York Times, but it offers a fresh view of the grassroots art scene that is "available nowhere else."

And as a purveyor of the fresh, Alex Hubshman, one of the New York–based -scope fair directors, has his eye on what Arias and Cindric are planning for Rocket Projects. He first met Arias when she was working the fair with Kevin Bruk Gallery of Miami.

"She knows the business, and she has a great eye," says Hubshman. "She's not just doing this as a glam thing; she has an agenda. She wants to show strong young artists to an international audience."

It would be easy, he adds, to turn away Arias for next December's -scope fair in Miami for a bigger, higher-paying gallery, but "we want to have her there." From his vantage point, Rocket Projects is "going to be the hot gallery down there."

Yet launching a gallery in the summer here would have been virtually unthinkable a few years ago, when traditionally, tourists and many arts supporters flee the humidity.

"The weather is not a deterrent, and I think that the sooner the better," says Bernice Steinbaum, whose gallery, focused on established mid-career artists, is a few blocks north in the Design District.

"The fact that Rocket Projects is opening in the summer demonstrates that Miami is becoming more of a city and less of a tourist destination that is only oriented toward the tourist season," says Robins. "I think Nina's one of the people who really has a solid and young vision about the art scene here."

FORT LAUDERDALE

Arias has ties to art in Miami that promise to give the gallery an energetic, if occasionally wet-behind-the-ears, zest. She comes to her new position with a background that speaks of wanderlust as well as creativity.

The daughter of an interior designer, she grew up on Key Biscayne, and when her parents decided to return to their home in Colombia, she finished high school while living with relatives in California. Then came backpacking around Latin America and studies at the Art Institute of Fort Lauderdale. At 19 she signed on for a three-year stint as a flight attendant for Laker Airways.

"My main focus for getting that job was seeing museums all over the world," Arias says. "I traveled everywhere—Malaysia, Brazil, South Africa, Europe. That inspired me like crazy."

By 2000, she'd finished college at Lynn University, was working with Kevin Bruk, and in her off hours had started an underground gallery, LaLush, in her Fort Lauderdale loft apartment. Last June the city closed it down for lack of business permits after word got out about crowds of several hundred showing up for openings with young artists and old-school jazz musicians.

One of those openings is where Cindric and Arias met, leading to talks about working together. LaLush, he says, "created a bit of a scene, but Fort Lauderdale wasn't ready for it."

CHANGING EXHIBITS

When the aboveground Rocket Projects opens on Saturday, visitors will see *Customized*, a group show with sculptural projects and architectural references by Miami-based artists Daniel Arsham, Martin Oppel, David Rohn, and George Sánchez-Calderón. A project room will also show a new installation based on the paintings of Dutch master Vermeer by a trio of artists—Christian Curiel, Brandon Opalka, and Jason Ferguson—who call themselves "FeCuOp" when they work together.

Curiel, who's leaving in July to enter Yale's MFA program, says their new piece will be a "big bang" before a pause in their collaborative efforts. "It's made all of us better artists individually because we just feed off each other. We're not going to stop collaborating."

In addition to Rocket Projects's various changing and guest-curated exhibits, a smaller room will feature a hefty bank of flat files, filing cases for storing such art as drawings, works on paper, and photography, which will represent about 30 artists from Miami, New York, Los Angeles, and Latin America.

"We're not going to just put out all these projects and hope for the best," says Cindric. "This is a business venture, but we do want to expand the things that are available here."

EUGENIA VARGAS

Slice of Latin American Spirit Spices Up Jaded Venice Crowd

June 29, 2003

For one sultry week this month, a little bit of old Santiago, Chile, met up with a bit of old Venice. This unlikely date transpired within a new performance piece by Miami-based artist Eugenia Vargas.

Nostalgia mingled with a poignant take on the cutting edge, and an almost childish glee cut through jaded looks from crowds inspecting Vargas's work and others by Latin American artists during the crush of opening events at the 50th Venice Biennale.

Vargas's performance piece and her compelling suite of related photographs about toy dolls and horses are part of *An Archipelago of Images*, a series of solo shows by artists from nine Latin American countries, organized by the Italian–Latin American Institute in Rome and overseen by curator Irma Arestizábal.

The exhibits are presented in the renovated Convent of Santi Cosma and Damiano on the Venetian island of Giudecca, about a 20-minute boat trip from the heart of Venice in San Marco Piazza.

The artist's performance unfolded in the convent's courtyard, on a lawn that's slightly gone to seed. She'd arranged for Chilean street photographer Luis Maldonado to come to Venice with his prized 19th-century European pinhole camera and his photographer's prop of a quaintly crafted wooden horse on which his subjects—traditionally children with their families—playfully mount.

As he has done for years in Santiago's main plaza, Maldonado snapped pictures of smiling subjects sitting on the toy horse. This time, however, their backdrop was not a real cityscape. It was a large banner reproducing a turn-of-the-century painting of strollers along a picturesque Venetian waterfront; the painting was by Chilean artist Juan Molina, who was trained by a conservative Italian painter transplanted to Chile.

The setting drew "100 percent" more curiosity and excitement than Maldonado receives in Santiago, he says, where he's usually ignored by city residents and only tourists ask for portraits.

PRADA POSING

"Brilliant!" laughed one young British woman in Venice as she posed provocatively on horseback. For the photo she was surrounded by a bevy of fashionista girlfriends, a group clad in flirty lace dresses and red chiffon scarves who called themselves the "Prada-Meinhoff Gang."

The spectacle intrigued observers like Mirta Demare, a Rotterdam art dealer who grew up in Argentina. Photographers like Maldonado, she said, are part of Latin America's cultural iconography. "When I was a girl, there were photographers like him in our parks, but now they are gone," she says.

She liked the way his work intersected with Vargas's photographs inside, with their tension between the real and the fake, between the sense of sweetness and loss that informs their carefully staged versions of childhood memories. The work is "a very funny kind of fake," she says. "It's a fairy tale in a modern box."

Other pieces in the show ranged in quality, with bland paintings by Rosella Matamoros from Costa Rica, but among the strong works was a starkly landscaped video by Charly Nijensohn of Argentina and a room of floating webs of starfish by María Fernanda Cardoso of Colombia, another arresting example of her work's focus on mortality.

PROTESTS

Despite the strength of some of the works in *Archipelago of Images*, they remain part of a troubling aspect of the representation of Latin American art in the biennale. At the biennale in 2001, artists chosen for exhibits organized by the Italian–Latin American Institute staged a protest at the opening, vociferously complaining that their shows were too far away—at least an hour away in Treviso—for anyone to see.

This time around, Venezuelan artist Pedro Morales was shut out of his country's pavilion in the biennale's main venue of the Giardini, a hilly park on the eastern tip of Venice—when the Venezuelan government officials censored his work at the last minute because they felt it criticized the current regime. Morales came to Venice anyway and staged a protest as well.

Although she says it's a "sin" for Venezuela to squander such resources, Arestizábal says the protests don't cast a shadow on the representation of Latin American art and points to the diversity of work by artists from the region showcased throughout the biennale.

Still, the protests are "emblematic of the enmeshment of art and politics in Latin America," says Victor Zamudio-Taylor, a curator who focuses on Latin American art and is involved with the newly established exhibition space Miami Art Central. "As long as art institutions are linked to political regimes, they are not going to have an autonomous status."

The protests are part of a larger problem for some who would like to see changes in the way this region is represented. They argue that grouping such diverse artists as the institute does is counterproductive.

"Asia isn't treated as a lump sum of countries, so why should Latin America be treated that way?" says curator Silvia Karmen Cubiñá, who moved to Miami last year from Puerto Rico and directs the Moore Space in the Design District.

"If you look at the artists [the institute] has featured over a period of time, 90 percent would not have been considered established or up and coming," says Zamudio-Taylor, who thinks an emphasis on national representation may be obsolete. "I think if you have a show on contemporary Latin American art, put together with maybe three curators, and with a theme, it would have more impact."

In memoriam: Victor Zamudio-Taylor, 1956–2013

LUIS GISPERT

These Cheerleaders Root for Their Own Team

July 20, 2003

Not even a cheerleader squad worth triple its weight in gold charm bracelets could compete with the brassily buoyant squad Luis Gispert has assembled.

Wearing cheerleaders' cute short skirts and midriff tops, the young women in his expertly staged video and photographs, which won national exposure when this Miami-raised artist was chosen for the 2002 Biennial at the Whitney Museum of American Art in New York, are tough and tattooed.

Thanks to assists from invisible suspension wires, they can jump really high, though they couldn't land further afield from the airhead suburban royalty of some of your parents' high school yearbooks. In poses more suited to kung-fu flicks, rap videos, or old master paintings, Gispert's cheerleaders strut their considerable stuff in the artist's current solo show at the Kendall Campus Art Gallery of Miami Dade College.

Gispert, who now lives in Brooklyn, has draped the models for his video and photography in jangling pounds of hip-hop jewelry. Their accessories range from clunky bamboo earrings to necklaces flashing with the ominous gold charm of a Tek-9, a cheap automatic pistol.

The series is a winsome and wicked riff on the aesthetics of a pop culture that deifies and demeans women of all colors. Here, inner-city street smarts, spiced with pornographic rap lyrics, match wits with WASPy fantasies of blond virgins pumping and jumping on the sidelines while they cheer for the guys to score.

In Gispert's photographs, cheerleaders instead float aloft with their eyes shut in angelic serenity as their teeth flicker with gold caps and their acrylic nails jab the air like knives. No sweaty gym for these girls. Their background is an ether of Kelly green, where shadows and a sense of place are vague. It invites viewers to fill in background details from their own imagination, just as special effects filmmakers project images around actors shot against similar green backdrops.

Yet the color, as Roni Feinstein points out in her catalog essay, does summon up the pleasures of freshly mowed lawns, allowing it to contrast slyly with the standard-issue lustful clichés that cheerleaders also summon. Gispert's green space spirits this icon-busting squad onto a whole new playing field.

JIM COUPER, BILL BURKE

Of Land and Sky

July 27, 2003

There's a dizzying shift between the enormous acreage of earth and sky and the infinitesimal tiny web of bird and frog arteries that fills paintings and sculptures now at the Art Museum at Florida International University. But whether the subject is acres or arteries, the locale is mainly South Florida in these portraits of flora and fauna by FIU professors Jim Couper and Bill Burke.

FIGURE 29. William Burke, *Landscape*, 1978. Glazed ceramic tile. Naranja Park Recreation Center, exterior 14101 SW 264 St., Naranja, FL, 33032. Image Yusimy Lara, courtesy of Miami-Dade County Department of Cultural Affairs, Art in Public Places Trust.

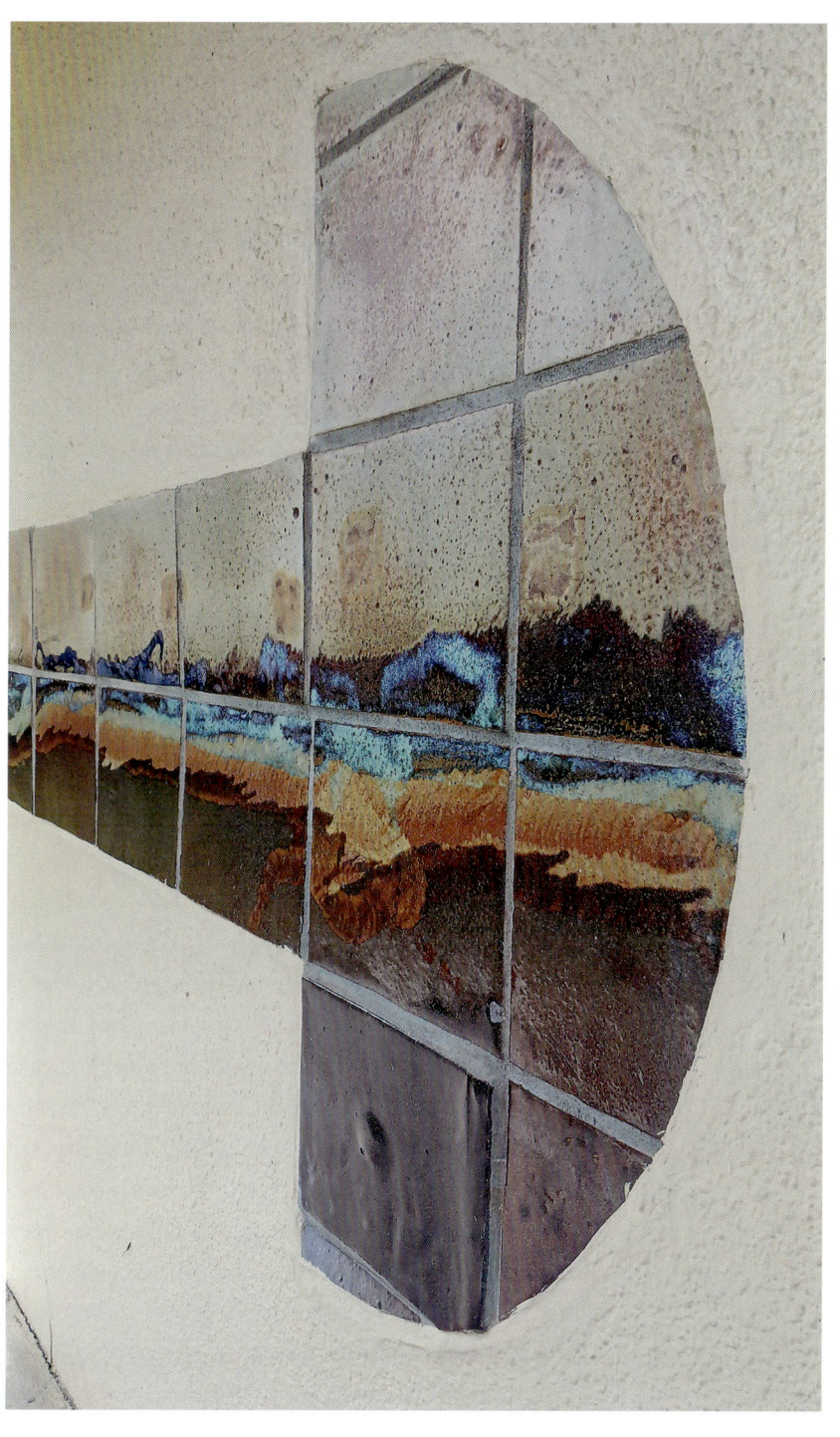

Couper is a prominent painter of the Everglades' mysterious and imperiled panorama, rendering its River of Grass with flecks and strokes of color in which shades of amber sidle up with mauves, pinks, and greens. He uncovers a radiant realm of glorious color and light within this harsh, flat landscape of stormy cumulus clouds and mosquito-infested reeds blazing in the sun. His most interesting paintings celebrate not only this land's unique ecosystem but the painter's eye that reveals its fleeting and unpredictably colored treasures.

Burke is a sculptor with a similar naturalist's bent. His eyes, however, are trained on the tiny traces of life left behind in the once blood-doused skeletons of birds, snakes, and lizards and in the microscopic labyrinth of veined hibiscus petals left to dry in the sun.

For his show, he has accumulated plates of glass and lead that are imprinted with organic relics and fossils of life. They are cool and desiccated memorials, some arranged on gallery shelves in casual clusters. They're almost like stacks of dead specimens still too numerous for their owner to study and interpret. So in the two solo faculty shows the Art Museum is presenting this month, you find yourself slipping between earth and sky, viewed from either a micro or macro perspective. There's no comfortable in-between, no safe middle ground.

HIGH GROUND

Couper's paintings take the high ground, and in this group more than ever he seems anxious to suggest the vastness of his subject yawning way past the four corners of his canvas. But his experiments here with spatial generosity and shaped canvases don't always yield the undulating brilliance of prismatic color that characterizes his strongest paintings. His efforts to shape canvases and suggest the breadth of celestial space with a trio of night and day vistas hung in close quarters prove that Couper is no sculptor.

He's much better at bringing to life the curvaceous rivulets of light and shadow that carve textures within the broad vistas he favors, from the grassy plains of the Everglades to the milky swirls of stars and planets in the night skies over the Atacama Desert in northwest Chile, the subject of one of the few non-Florida scenes in this exhibit.

In paintings like his 1998 *Evening Sky, Everglades*, Couper is really at his best when he shows us the gorgeously abstract tissue and pulse of places we only think we've seen before. *Feels Good*, a series of 30 children's T-shirts hung on the wall to occupy the rectangular mass of a painting, is a gruesome departure from Couper's landscapes.

As an installation, *Feels Good* is oddly connected with the organic narratives of mortality that Burke has sculpted in his objects of lead and glass in this exhibit. The title of Couper's installation comes from an informal, pugilistic comment President George W. Bush made after his public announcement in March that the US-led invasion of Iraq had begun. The piece is dedicated to Ali Ismail Abbas, a 12-year-old Iraqi boy who lost both his arms and his family in a US bombing raid and who swiftly became an international symbol of Iraqi suffering.

DECAY AND LOSS

Printed on the soft cotton T-shirts are graphic color photos of burned and damaged children as terrible souvenirs of feelings that are anything but good.

Bill Burke has long been intrigued by recording the ephemeral process of organic decay, and his art tries to halt rot with a funereal elegance that's casual and strange.

In this show, he has encased the skeletal fragments of small animals and ghostly accumulations of leaves within thin, bubbly sheets of pale-green tinted glass. Their bones, arteries, stems, and shattered bits of tissue don't always form a recognizable relic, but they do become tiny constellations of dissolving memory, like fingerprints gently scavenged from a universal life cycle.

These brittle, translucent shards of corpses possess a surprising visual heft that's missing from the large, imposing imprints of the artist's body that Burke has layered into slate-gray sheets of lead. These leaden sheets hang within rich frames. They offer clouded and spooky portraits of a human form posed with the undignified frankness that the artist finds in his frog and bird specimens.

Still, they make their points about mortality with an enervating, emaciated grimness that falls short when compared to the translucent abundance of Burke's fine, glassy objects.

In memoriam: James (Jim) Couper, 1937–2023

KERRY STUART COPPIN

Diaspora and Destiny

August 31, 2003

Kerry Stuart Coppin swears he was 30 before he realized that *The Wizard of Oz* changes into color after Dorothy leaves Kansas. The movie had simply lived in his memory as the one he'd seen as a kid, eyes trained on a small black-and-white set in his family's apartment in a tough South Bronx neighborhood.

Coppin himself later spent time in Kansas, an outsider hailing from an Oz of a grittier sort who photographed the corn-bred and tornado-prone plains that nearly engulf the state.

"Sometimes it was clear to me I was the first Black person to stumble across these towns in Kansas," he recalls.

On other occasions, during a stint teaching at Kansas State University in the mid-'90s, he trained his lens on small Black communities clustered in urban centers like Manhattan, Kansas, where he shot grinning teens in silky band uniforms gathered to celebrate the end of slavery in Juneteenth festivities.

When he left the Midwest for a job in the art department at the University of Miami in 1999, he was ushered into an immensely varied world of color, though not in the yellow-brick-road shades that Depression-era Hollywood filmmakers had in mind when they spoke of the word *color*.

Miami has been the jumping-off place for a new stage in his career. For the past four years, Coppin, 50, has developed quietly gripping photographs

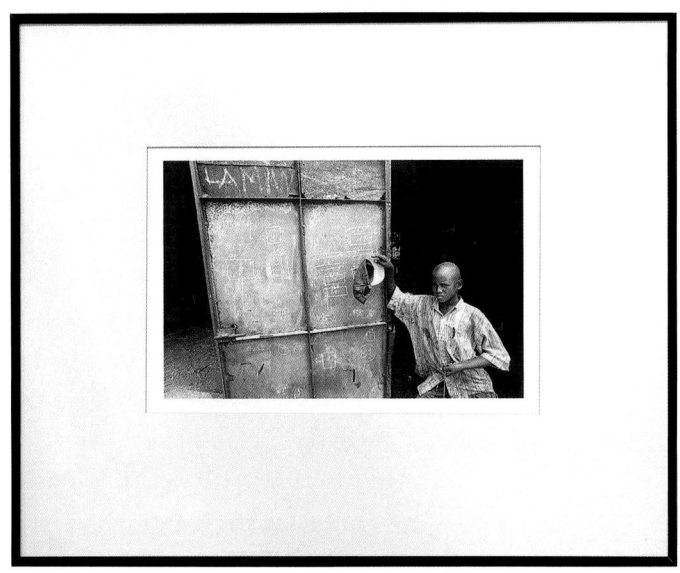

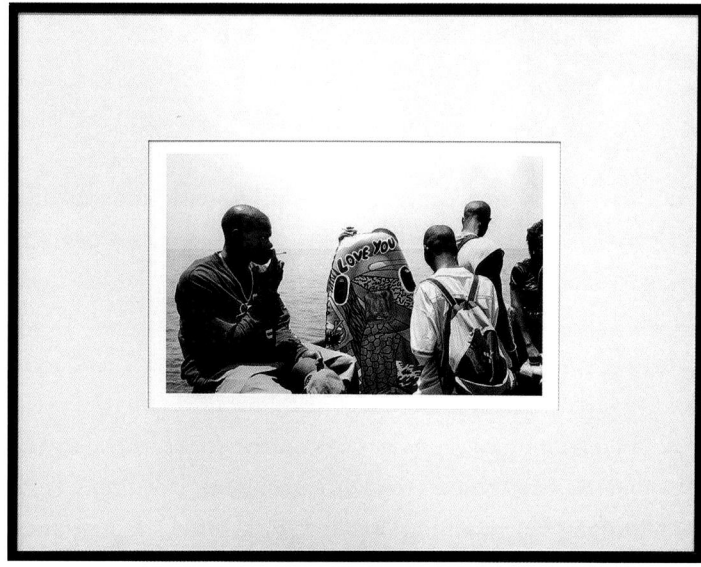

of people of color living in the African diaspora in the Caribbean and North America, from Little Haiti to Havana. He's also traveled to West Africa to document links between the not-so-new world on this side of the Atlantic and the urban, Westernized cities in West Africa.

In his current show of 75 photographs at UM's Lowe Art Museum, a woman in Islamic veils sells shampoo and makeup from her one-room shop in Dakar, Senegal, while her teenage sister in a miniskirt looks on as a flood of sunlight illuminates well-stocked shelves and the owner's gauzily encompassing dress. Older boys in Nike shorts and shoes hang out on a street corner in Dakar. Or they stride about in flamboyant face paint in a stadium in Barbados to stage a "Crop Over" parade, a recently revived tourist attraction that harkens back to slave celebrations at the end of the sugarcane harvest.

These images are tinged with finely nuanced sepia shades of tea and coffee. The colors mine a certain nostalgia. Sepia briefly takes us back to another time—to 19th-century ethnographic photographs documenting exotic customs in jungly locales miles from colonial centers of population.

MODERN TIMES

But the modern reality in his shots of sights like hip-hop fashions and hubcaps for sale in Dakar brings us up short. In some ways, Coppin is catching a diaspora coming and going.

"I'm interested in the idea of Africans born in the Western world, and even if you go to Senegal, it's a Western country. Dakar is a modern city. Yes, it's in decay the same way Havana is in decay, but it was built by the French," he says.

Someone described his photographs of boys on the street in Dakar as a tribal image, but he rejects that completely. "There's no sense of a rural environment in that photograph. Everything's been manufactured," he continues.

"When North Americans think of Africa, there are particular images that come to mind that are rather romantic," says Courtney Reid-Easton, exhibitions coordinator at Duke University's Center for Documentary Studies. "They have an overlay of antiquity. You imagine people wrapped in traditional cloth, babies slung on backs, but Kerry is showing us this wave, this tide-in, tide-out of cultural exchanges."

The center will exhibit many of Coppin's photographs now at the Lowe in an exhibit that opens October 22, pairing his show with one devoted to Walker Evans's classic scenes of the rural South.

It will be Coppin's 11th solo show this year, part of a packed schedule that includes a solo show at the Museo Casa de Africa in Havana and a group exhibit at the Art Institute of Chicago. His work is in the Art Institute's permanent collection, as well as those of the Brooklyn Museum of Art, the Smithsonian's American Art Museum, and the Bibliothèque Nationale de France in Paris.

For Reid-Easton, Coppin's work transcends the literal punch of most documentary photography. "His images are also beautiful. I think he's a photographer whose work is rooted in documentary, but he's also pretty expressive and interpretive," she says. "I'm really drawn to his street images of signage and murals."

There's a captivating mix of the immediate, personal, and painterly gesture and the concrete ordinariness of commercial sidewalks in his shots of murals and graffiti on both sides of the Atlantic. They become pictures larger than the sum of their parts. In one scene from Dakar, you notice a mathematical grid of geometric symbols, washed-out lettering that could have spelled out "Grande Mosque," and an intricate array of hubcaps lined up with dense abstract patterns that approach the ornate tiles in Islamic designs.

Another shows a serpentine wave of eyes coursing over a wall in Havana, where Santería ceremonies are regularly performed for tourists, while an image from Little Haiti captures the illustrative details of that neighborhood's distinctive commercial signage.

In memoriam: Kerry Stuart Coppin, 1953–2023

ART AND CULTURE CENTER / HOLLYWOOD

Bringing Electronic Art to Light

October 5, 2003

Leaning over a light box in his studio, where finicky grade-school-era film projectors share space with 1940s *Life* magazines and thousands of old slides and photo transparencies gleaned from garage and going-out-of-business sales, Kevin Arrow lays strips of gray plastic film in fanciful patterns across photographs of boring office equipment.

He fits together bits of dirt-gray film on bone-gray film. They form a mosaic for the color-blind—or maybe a craftsy collage appealing to only the most geeky and demented of office cubicle hermits.

And yet this small photo collage stands out as inspired and anachronistic wit, especially when compared to the far more technologically advanced videos and laptop-powered installations that surround it in *Plugged In: New and Electronic Art*, a new show at the Art and Culture Center/Hollywood. Arrow's piece even slyly reminds us of the obsolescence that awaits technology spotlighted in *Plugged In*.

Though South Florida museums have presented riveting shows by nationally and internationally known artists pushing the limits of video, DVD, and other electronic media, this exhibit is one of too few to take an extended look at the diverse talent here in this field.

The ambitious *Plugged In* focuses on mostly South Florida artists who haven't always gotten the attention they merit—like Michael Betancourt, Dimitry Saïd Chamy, Edward Bobb, and Elizabeth Hall. It also includes *Dynamic Ribbon Device* by Chicago-based artist Siebren Versteeg, which uses an internet connection to meld live news feed with a video mimicking the Coke logo.

Better known for his experimental music, Bobb has choreographed *Gesture No. 4 (Multiple Peady)*. In this cartoon, an impish troupe of plant and phallic forms cavort to electronic sounds, generated in part by thousands of simple drawings he sketched with his fingertips on a mouse pad.

One of the largest pieces in the show, Hall's chimerical video installation shows a woman who seems part bride and part extraterrestrial ephemera breaking into a prismatic strata of frantic computer graphics. An emblem of information overload, it shimmers in a room swathed in pink tulle.

There's also a faux boardroom displaying a satiric motivational video skewering the art market and late-night infomercials. It's by a sassy group of anonymous, chiefly twentysomething South Florida performance artists who call themselves MSG—or "Multi-national Sales Group," explains one of the group's members, who calls himself Kenneth Cohen but lets slip he also goes by Jorge.

ANACHRONISMS

And then there's the experimentally anachronistic Arrow.

"I think of myself as using old media for early 21st-century art," Arrow muses in his garage studio in Miami Beach, holding a well-read copy of the book *New Media in Late 20th Century Art.*

"Kevin was the antithesis of everything else in the show I was interested in, in the ideas of technology and how technology brings new tools to artists," explains Samantha Salzinger, the curator of *Plugged In.*

But from the day last February she began visiting studios to find art for this show, Salzinger wanted to include Arrow. "There's something so retro and intelligent and thoughtful about what he's doing," she says.

It's also a quixotic ode to 1950s TV Land that may suggest a bridge to more hectic and high-tech pieces in the show.

"When I started curating, I didn't realize how unapproachable art can be to some people," says Salzinger, an artist with an MFA from Yale. "Video is hands down the most difficult for people to understand. I think it's because it's so much a part of our everyday life. Everyone watches TV. We think of this media as entertainment, and yet a lot of video art has no narrative— you can't watch it like TV. You have to be more open. A lot of the pieces are abstract, about evoking emotion."

There's no real story in Arrow's animated collage either, except what you project.

It shows a dated hulk of photo lab machinery, originally captured in a photo transparency with all the yawn-inducing sterility of a trade catalog, but now draped in mystery. In this altered picture, fat vines curl up walls and latch onto machinery controls. Slick and weird, these collaged vines recall the people-crunching flora in the fantasy flick *Jumanji*.

The plastic strips are actually 1950s relics used to make early animation. When you look at them through a rotating plastic Polaroid filter Arrow rigged up for a vintage film projector in his piece for *Plugged In*, the strips make this boxy machine gyrate with vivid stripes. Projected by a beam of light on the wall, this image becomes a crazy optical delight on the cheap. Think of a time machine whirring manically in an old cartoon.

Accompanied by a spoofy text claiming the piece involves declassified FBI documents, Arrow's work is called *Untitled (Hell)*. It takes a cue from the machine's brand name of Hell, which is also German for "light," but doesn't totally avoid hints of a fiery apocalypse fueled by runaway technology.

Says Arrow, "I just love creating these small intricate things that you can project on a large scale with light."

UNDERGROUND QUALITY

He's not alone. Others in the show have wrought a flickering network of intricate details that unfold over time, like Chamy's dream sequence of pillows bathed in blue rainfall, but they are fashioned electronically on a computer screen with pixels rather than on a light box with hand-cut slivers of plastic.

Betancourt's films are a mercurial flow of mesmerizing geometric designs. They're built up with a complex process that plays glitches deep inside computers against technology for recording outer space phenomena like sun flares. One work unfurls lush abstractions; another reinvents a travelogue of India.

Hall also works with glitches to push the language of video. And as a well-traveled curator who has staged innovative one-night festivals of video and electronic art around town, she maintains a website for fostering new art.

Such work could be much more visible in South Florida, says Hall. She'd like to see artists here have affordable access to the kind of costly technology video and electronic work requires, like facilities in Boston and New York that charge a fraction of some of Miami's rates of $1,000 a day.

But the underground quality of this art is also a plus. When there aren't a lot of commercial galleries bent on showing and selling high-resolution videos and DVDs, she said, it's easier to avoid highly polished paths. "The good thing about Miami is that there is a lot of freedom to experiment," she explains, "and not conform to what a gallery would want."

MIAMI ART CENTRAL

New Space—and Its Artists—Has a Lot of Potential

November 30, 2003

Three weeks before the start of Art Basel Miami Beach, the ambitious new Miami Art Central still looked like construction site central. Workers on a forklift tried for the third time to install the building's freight elevator; the parking lot was piled high with lumber awaiting its final resting place on a rooftop deck.

But inside, the contours of a dramatic exhibition space were taking shape, heralding more changes for Miami's evolving art scene. Miami Art Central— MAC—expects to showcase a diverse program of art, music, and film. Its 33,000 square feet of galleries spell bold potential, with its inaugural exhibition, *10 Floridians*, opening Tuesday.

"We want to be a catalyst for working together in the arts," says philanthropist and collector Ella Cisneros, founder of MAC, who also is a trustee of the Miami Art Museum and a patron of the Miami City Ballet. "We haven't called it a museum. We want it to be a meeting place."

She has in mind a unique South Florida meeting place for visual arts lovers, where artists of Latin American heritage will be granted yearlong residencies.

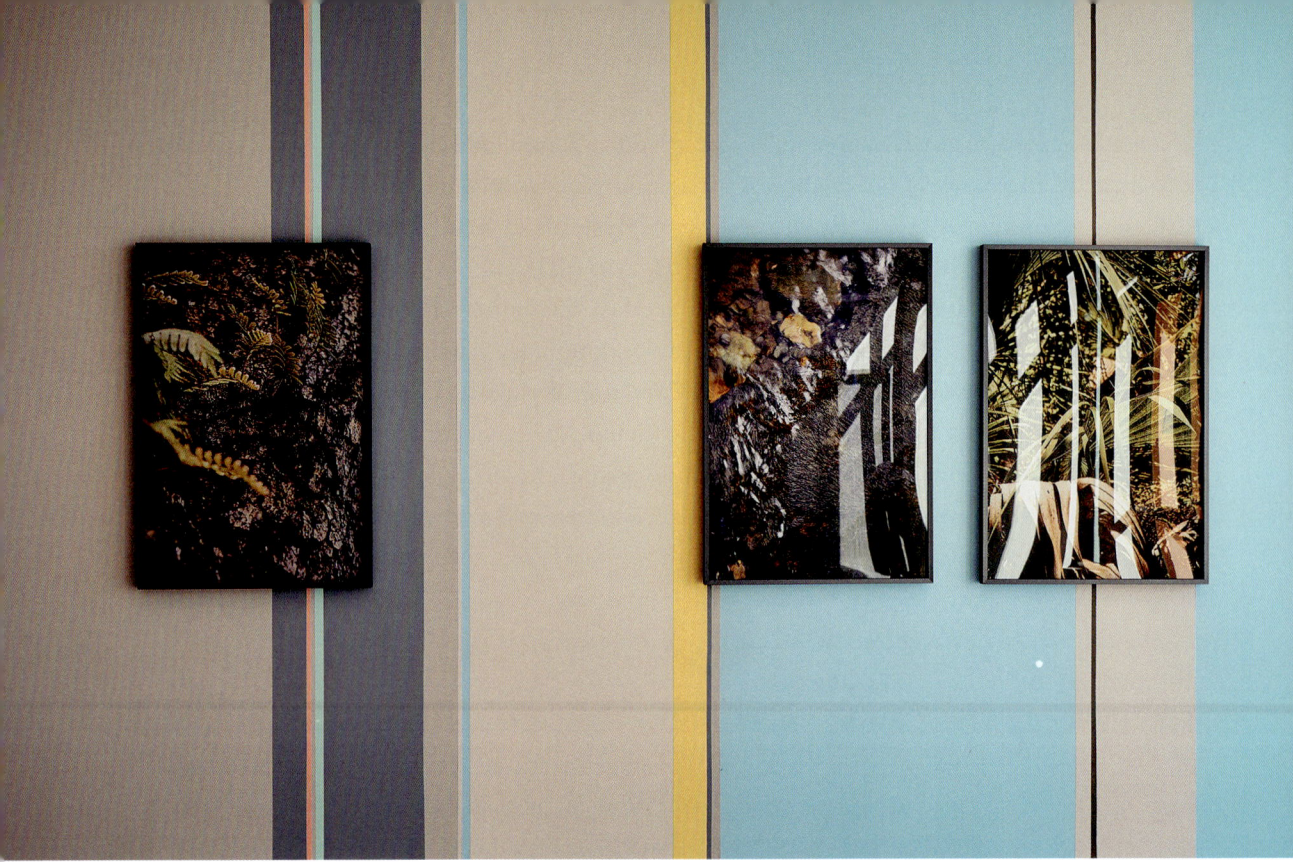

FIGURE 32. Adler Guerrier, *Wall Paintings (Diurnal Heptad plus SW7028) and six photographs—deploy as an occurrence of tones and elements from the nearby commons, compel these articulated points of relation into form—a community room*, 2021. Acrylic paint on wall, archival prints on Hahnemühle paper. Smathers Plaza, 1025 SW 30th Ave., interior first floor. Courtesy of the artist and Miami-Dade County Department of Cultural Affairs, Art in Public Places Trust.

"We're trying to make people more aware of Latin American art history, which isn't the biggest forte in this area," she says.

Manuel Gonzalez, her well-connected right-hand man for the project, says he has put together a group of art professionals, including New York's New Museum of Contemporary Art director Lisa Phillips, to help bring future programs to MAC.

With the first show just days away, drills rattled eardrums and powdery dust swirled at eye level as Cisneros surveyed the progress with an air of controlled calm. Gonzalez gestured in the air, showing artist Jacin Giordano where the walls would go to display his paintings.

Giordano is one of eight Miami-based artists in the show, but one of the few painters included, and was chosen by curator Ivo Mesquita along with Gean Moreno. Both cultivate a handcrafted touch without getting sappy; Giordano stitches knotty bursts of thread to his canvases, while Moreno devises collages from plastic streamers. The two are tantalizing "silent intruders," wrote the curator in a catalog essay, in an exhibit that covers lots of ground, but especially film, video, and installation art.

The only other paintings are by José Bedia, bearing the timeliness of war. In this suite of marine battle scenes, modern warships run disastrously counter to Afro-Cuban symbols of primal wisdom.

No one else is as grimly topical, though a spiraling installation of Glexis Novoa's drawings depicts fantastic and foreboding cityscapes. Luis Gispert, a rising star who lives in Brooklyn, returned to his family's home in Miami to make photographs for a unique family album of sorts. He captures relatives posed in the baroque glitz of hip-hop bling.

Dara Friedman and Mark Handforth experiment with effects of light. Friedman's best known for her film and video, but she'll be showing her first piece in stained glass. Just back from working on several shows in France, Handforth molds sculptural variations on discarded industrial lighting.

Though there's no real theme in the show, Sergio Vega, who lives in Gainesville, and Adler Guerrier are each lured by idyllic dreams of landscapes. Guerrier's new photographs explore parks and backyards; Vega's photographs and installations are based on his travels around Latin America searching for a latter-day paradise.

The techie wizard Robert Chambers has created a new piece, *A Group of Objects Assembled to Suggest a Kinesthetic Experience*. It should be another example of his effortlessly daring penchant for twisting science and art to unimagined ends, at once entertaining and thoughtful.

PATRICIA VAN DALEN

Seeing's Not Believing at Fairchild Field

January 11, 2004

It's a botanical mystery: thousands of tulips have sprouted in the tropics.

South Florida's wintry bout with tulip mania is a panorama of artful illusion, simple and majestic. At Fairchild Tropical Garden in Coral Gables, what looks to be a field of dazzling pink, orange, and pomegranate-red flowers is really a lawn jabbed with 100,000 small plastic flags, the sort of mundane marking devices used on construction sites.

This garden illusion is thanks to a temporary site-specific installation, *Flower Square* by Venezuelan artist Patricia Van Dalen, which Fairchild recently commissioned. There's also a selection of her acrylic paintings and collages in a nearby gallery as part of Van Dalen's current solo show, *Luminous Gardens*, at Fairchild.

As angled labyrinths that flash with color, Van Dalen's paintings are unremarkable when compared with the bold strokes of *Flower Square*. Individually, the paintings are lively compositions, but as a group, their expression and ideas are limited, stuck in a kind of splashy, expressive restatement of abstract geometric art from the 1960s.

When Van Dalen leaves the gallery for the garden, however, her ideas and sumptuous sense of color shift into much higher gear. The modest simplicity of her materials, repeated 100,000 times over in a spectacularly verdant setting, makes for a bodily encounter with beautiful art.

You can walk among *Flower Square*'s rows of pink and orange and red and feel immersed in a vast painting—or a deftly minimalist flag or quilt—that undulates whenever a stiff breeze sweeps through the Lowlands, as this field is called at Fairchild.

Look to your left and right, and you see swerving, splotchy patterns made with these three colors. In one section, a circling line of pink seems to suggest eyeglasses framing a pair of red eyes—a coincidence, since the artist provides 3D glasses to look at the piece, making it seem like a huge hologram.

Surrounded by another colorful patch of flags, you can even briefly feel as if your body has become a speck within a rosy impressionist painting of clouds at sunset.

This piece of public art is not quite on the order of Christo's magnitude, but it is plenty big. It resembles a giant striped flag in the grass, creating 14 stripes that are 250 feet wide and 10 feet long. They combine with strips of grass to form a 62,500-square-foot square.

Like the traditional compass rose on a map, *Flower Square* is something of a navigational tool, neatly aligned with points north and south, and slyly nudging the midpoint curve of Fairchild's Pandanus Lake.

It's both geographical and mathematical, which is why conceptually this environmental piece is stronger than the artist's paintings. This artwork is delineated with the rules of geometry to form a strict pattern of boundary lines and markers, but in the execution, *Flower Square* becomes a porous, organic tissue of earth, air, and flickering man-made color.

At a time when the world is especially divisive and dangerous, this piece uses flags to become the antithesis of a territorial marker. You can just as easily bypass or pass through the plot of land occupied by *Flower Square*. And from many perspectives, as you gaze across this piece, its sweeping stripes lose their formal status as borders. The marvel is that they seem to melt into each other and then seep into the surrounding earth and water.

AMAZING JOURNEY

Naomi Fisher, Hernan Bas Connect in Life and Art

January 19, 2004

They are blood relatives via their shared DNA for art and fashion, Miami style.

She's the warrior maiden who collects machetes and British designer miniskirts. He's the skinny boy searching for the perfect cameo pin to wear with his Jill Stuart for Puma shoes.

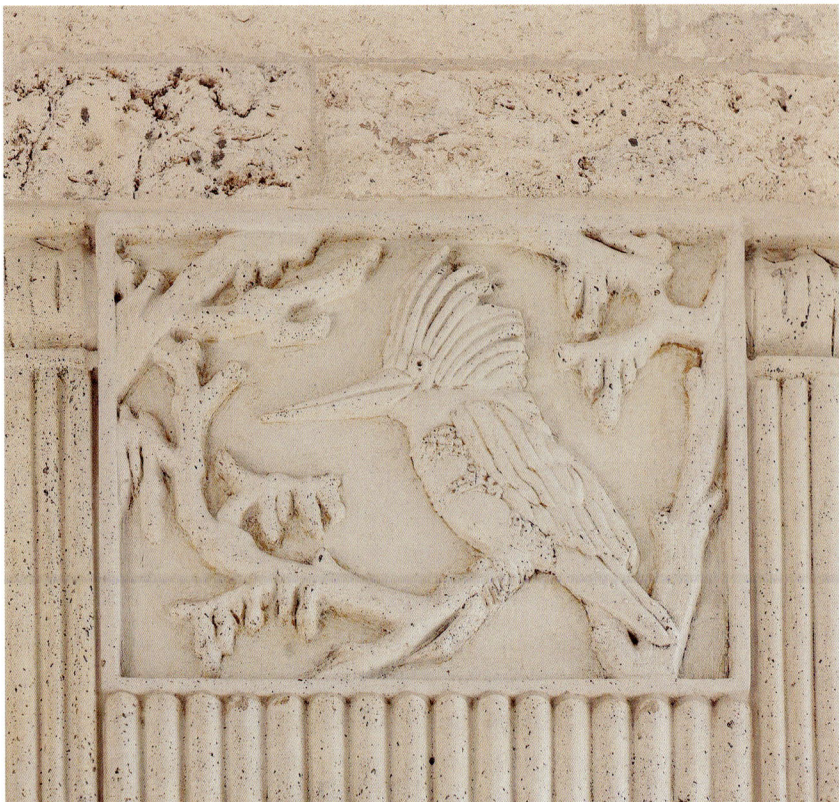

FIGURE 33. Naomi Fisher, *The Frieze Project*, 2014. Cast Portland cement. Fairchild Tropical Garden. Image Gesi Schilling, courtesy of Miami-Dade County Department of Cultural Affairs, Art in Public Places Trust.

And as close friends and classmates trained in exceptional art programs at Miami-Dade County Public Schools, both Naomi Fisher and Hernan Bas are climbing the charts at a red-hot pace, winning praise and purchases from prestigious tastemakers around the art world.

Fisher's fiercely beguiling, blood-colored drawings of women were tapped for the inaugural show in 2002 at the Palais de Tokyo, the new contemporary art museum in Paris, and were just purchased for a prominent foundation in Essen, Germany.

Bas will show his delicate, shadowy paintings of waifish boys on risky adventures later this year at London's cutting-edge Victoria Miro gallery and at the 2004 Biennial at New York's Whitney Museum of American Art.

During the past Art Basel Miami Beach, their Miami dealer, Fred Snitzer, sold out his stock of paintings and drawings by both artists as well as Fisher's photographs—which are all priced between $1,500 and $6,500—to a competitive flock of international collectors.

In South Florida, the precociously gifted pair have already been shown at the Museum of Contemporary Art in North Miami, Fisher had a solo show at the Miami Art Museum, and their art is part of world-class collections owned by Donald and Mera Rubell and Rosa and Carlos de la Cruz.

FRIENDS FOREVER

She is 27. He is 25. They met in a high school creative writing class at the New World School of the Arts; both worked for a time at the Rubell Family Collection and now share a studio in Miami's Design District.

Sharing a studio is not just a matter of convenience. In conversation, though Fisher is the more talkative, they seem like artistic soul mates. Working together in close quarters, she says, "is great because you challenge each other, you inspire each other, so you don't become stagnant and think you can just get away with things."

They ask each other if their drawings are finished and continue to ask if they disagree. They don't mind listening to the same CDs "over and over and over," Bas says. They know what feeds the other's creativity. They recommend old movies to each other.

"Oh, Naomi will like this," Bas says he thought when he stayed up late one night to watch *Alucarda*, a shrieky, blood-drenched horror cult flick from the 1970s set in a Mexican convent. He was right. It played right into the gory battles with meat hooks and poisonous thorns that Fisher had been recording in her dream diaries, dreams that have often seeped in strange ways into the violent conflict and beauty of her drawings and photographs.

They know each other so well they often become involved in each other's art.

Regarding her photographs of young women variously embraced and smothered by gorgeous tropical vegetation, she says, "If I'm in it, there's a good chance he clicked the shutter. He used to joke that he knows how to take a Naomi photo," but Bas protests. "I would do, like, a Hernan Naomi photo."

Such a hybrid thing, they agree, would be more crowded, more like a snapshot, and would lack the dramatically spare and centered composition of, for example, her *You Know That It's Real If You Feel That It's Real.* Bas clicked the shutter on this photograph that Fisher staged in her backyard a few months ago. In it, she's wearing black underwear and lifting a machete triumphantly toward a throbbing red sunset.

"It's a wild moment of total triumph, for a total war cry," she explains, as Bas nods.

"I was just saying the other day, we're like 'emo' artists. Emo is this brand of emotional music. A little on the cheeseball," he adds.

"Psychodrama," she says.

"Soap opera," he corrects her. "That's more me, the narrative."

EARLY SUCCESSES

But there is a narrative of early success they do share. "They have been connected at the hip and have gone through the same amazing journey," says MAM curator Lorie Mertes. "Not so long ago they were in school, and here they are in collections and having shows in museums before a lot more seasoned artists have had. To me, that's the epitome of what's so exciting about Miami now, that this is possible."

Some of their supporters were surprised when art by Bas, but not Fisher, was chosen for the coming Whitney Biennial, the show that's the ever-controversial but widely watched bellwether for trends in contemporary art.

Even Whitney curator Debra Singer seems at a loss by the turn of events. "I don't have a perfect answer for why Naomi will not be in this biennial," she said by phone last week from New York. "I am sure there will be a future biennial that she will be in, absolutely. Naomi's an outstanding artist, and we all love her. She has this really wonderfully aggressive imagination that is very poignantly explored in her photographic work and also in her drawings."

Bas, she said, was chosen because his work is a striking example of the current interest in drawing, painting, and portraiture. "It's so highly personal and fantastical at the same time," she says of his drawings, paintings on paper, and installation art.

They evolve from the artist's fascination with low-brow culture, sentimental longings, and grand mythic journeys. Bas weaves storytelling images that spin from *Moby-Dick*-styled adventures, Hardy Boys mysteries, and the homoerotic appeal of slim male fashion models.

OUTSIDE INFLUENCES

Fashion figures in both their art making. You can tell from the Prada ads of male models that Bas, who is gay, has posted on their studio walls or from Fisher's paintings in progress of women enmeshed in baroque gowns of bows that stream with red vines and are sometimes accessorized with arrow-shaped earrings and machetes.

But the machetes usually stay in their studio. When they go out, "they are both amazing dressers, super stylists," says Anna Maria Diaz-Balart.

Diaz-Balart grew up with Bas and Fisher. She attended Design and Architecture Senior High School, while her chums were at New World. With her business partner, Maria Barraco, she owns M-80, a trendsetting shop for vintage fashion and styles by independent designers. They rent studio space to Bas and Fisher in the back.

"When we were all in high school, I was studying fashion, and they were studying art. The schools were amazing," Diaz-Balart remembers. "No one knew what the future held for us. Many of the kids we graduated with went on to New York, but the fact that we're here speaks to the potential and promise of Miami."

WAY OUTSIDE THE GALLERIES

February 29, 2004

As stiff breezes whipped through a cool December evening in Miami Beach, the dapper Swiss impresario Samuel Keller took a break from exclusive SoBe parties to pocket an orange served up from a jet ski trailer parked in front of the Free Spirits Sports Café, a deliciously seedy hole in the wall in Miami Beach that had become an impromptu art salon.

"Wonderful, we'll get a lot of vitamins thanks to you," said Keller, Art Basel's director, to artist Raymond Saá, who had tossed him the orange, gratis. With his former New World School of the Arts classmate Michael Loveland, Saá had retrofitted an old trailer to make a street cart for pushing fruit and art during the week of Art Basel Miami Beach. The Free Spirits Bar was a natural destination for their vividly decked-out vehicle.

Grapefruit and oranges sold for $1 apiece. Paintings and collages by Saá and Loveland cost hundreds of dollars.

Keller had come to this street cart and corner bar to find a tonic even stronger than vitamins. He wanted something to counter the Swiss penchant for impeccable organization, something unexpectedly creative, something unscripted.

He easily found that something within the particularly ingenious, can-do qualities of Miami's art scene. These continue to be on display this month and next near downtown. The venues make up a loose network of artist-run spaces in the Design District, Wynwood, and Edgewater neighborhoods—The House and Placemaker Gallery, World Arts Building, and the Food-CultureMuseum, as well as yet another space opened earlier this month, Art on the Walls @ Light Box, featuring projects curated by Miami artist Diego Singh.

A partially arts-driven boom in real estate now looms over the availability of some such spaces, but ingenuity is stepping in for artists like Loveland and Saá, who upended their fruit cart to concoct *Urban Recipes*. This is an ambitious, collaborative project with fellow artist and Miami native Joshua Levine at Rocket Projects gallery in Wynwood.

In December, while settling into the cheesy, citrus-colored cushions adorning the artists' fruit cart, almost a minisalon itself, fair director Keller explained how the casually un-Swiss but so-Miami project at this corner bar had come to pass. "The rules are very little budget, no planning in advance," Keller said.

He recounted how he and Basel architect Jens Henrik had called up Miami artist and famously adventurous curator Robert Chambers less than a week before the fair. They brainstormed ways to give artists, especially those not affiliated with galleries at the fair, more access to Basel crowds—and how to tempt those crowds with a zesty alternative to the fair's luxurious VIP Lounge in the Miami Beach Convention Center.

The result: The Free Spirits Artists' Lounge. With the blessing of bar owner Tim Wilcox, several dozen artists installed an eclectic range of photography, painting, and sculpture, such as Julie Kahn's photographs of Central Florida hunters, presented on the bar's greenish countertop like images inside an oversized lightbox. "It was very productive," recalls Chambers. "The Basel people really enjoyed hanging out. They weren't slumming; they were having a chance to chat with local artists in a way they normally wouldn't get to do."

Chambers fielded inquiries from fairgoers from France, Germany, and Japan. "I don't know how many times I gave out artists' names and numbers and email addresses to curators. Things really started up after midnight." Miami Art Museum curator Cheryl Hartup was among those who stopped by. "To me what was so amazing was that it came together in a very short time," she says. "It was spontaneous, and the variety of projects and how they used the space had a great energy. It seemed very homegrown and genuine."

And it was a revealing example, she says, of the interconnected, rapid-response resources of the local arts scene, in which "people really rise to the occasion and make a wonderful happening."

At the same time, "these smaller groups are networking with other groups and having exchanges with other cities. It makes a place really interesting when you're inviting people to have a dialogue with people working here."

WORM-HOLE

Another homegrown space that debuted during the fair just completed its run on Saturday—Worm-Hole Laboratory, generally located in the modest Edgewater apartment of its founder, independent curator José Carlos Diaz. He moved here last September from San Francisco and works in MAM's education department.

"The idea of Worm-Hole is not about a specific location. It's fluid and nomadic, a laboratory where interesting things can happen. I don't want to be confused with a gallery," said Diaz, walking this month through his apartment, where an eerie group of sculpture, murals, and photography from *Haunted*, his first show, still dominate the kitchen and living room.

Stuffed animals and green snakes collided with a colander and other kitchen implements in a sly, violent installation by Pepe Mar, while Jen Denike's coolly staged photographs of young suburban vampire victims gave bland interiors a gothic bite. Elsewhere were Cristina Lei Rodriguez's resin and plastic model of crazily aberrant but slimily seductive landscape architecture and sparkling murals of ghostly, psychedelic creatures by Diego Singh.

On February 13, Diaz held a reception for new work by San Francisco artist Shane Aslan Selzer and a project by Miami artist Aja Albertson, organized by Mar. Selzer's work is particularly apt, inspired by the history of the Carolyn Apartments, where Diaz lives, a lonely remnant of Miami's 1920s real estate boom on a block recently transformed by high-rise condominiums.

DIRTY SOUTH!

A loosely focused look at Southern takes on urban pop culture (think skateboards, rappers, tacky road signs) in art made in Miami and New Orleans, *Dirty South!* is another show Diaz put together as part of his Worm-Hole Laboratory projects. This one is at the World Arts Building in Wynwood, where artist Charo Oquet has also helped organize a series of projects for Miami artists, including Jay Oré, Eugenio Espinosa, and herself. Unlike the intimate scale of the Carolyn, this rambling, multistoried building invites encounters with fleeting but thoughtfully designed art projects both large and small.

Dirty South! is especially strong, with a sense of wrecked Walmart ornament in works on paper by Chris Jahncke and Michelle Weinberg. You can also find here one of Oquet's poetically meandering altar pieces draped in fabric and heaped with packets of discarded dolls, as well as Oré's provocative series of low-tech Polaroids mimicking images relayed from outer space.

Oquet puts together shows under Edge Zones, an organization she set up to create more opportunities for artists and curators. Spanish curator Antonio Zaya tapped Edge Zones artists Oquet, Carlos Betancourt, and

Carlos de Villasante to exhibit earlier this month at ARCO, the international art fair in Madrid.

"I am very much a believer of do-it-yourself," says Oquet, who busily prepared a dish of green bananas with cilantro to serve at a recent brunch at the World Arts Building. At ARCO, she invited an independent French curator to bring a show of very portable art to Miami.

"Then in turn we can send a suitcase show of Miami artists to Paris," she proposes. "There's a real need for this to happen. It's important to keep Miami growing."

A few doors away from the World Arts Building is a low-key gem of a warehouse, painted in the blues of lapis lazuli and topaz and usually open only by appointment but freighted with succulent visual surprises. This is TransEAT/FoodCultureMuseum Miami, where artist Antoni Miralda and his wife, chef Montse Guillén, display their astonishing collection of art and artifacts spiced with the richly interactive seasonings of food and culture and occasionally showcase related works by Miami artists like Oquet and Betancourt.

In vitrines resembling a grocer's frozen food display, you'll find some of the museum's collection assembled around a host of themes, like the gender-rich assortment that includes a pink Easter egg adorned with Barbie, cheese marketed with a *Mona Lisa* smile, and a can for chocolatey "Menopausitive" soft drinks.

A visual feast is also the theme of *Urban Recipes* at Rocket Projects. It's a short drive away in Wynwood, though while Miralda and Guillén travel all over the map for inspiration, the artists of *Urban Recipes* kept their focus local, absorbing the sights, signage, sounds (even cackling chickens on opening night), and flavors of Wynwood.

The gallery becomes a vibrant walk-in mural and streetscape, with walls striped in citrus greens, yellows, and hot pinks in a Caribbean palette similar to the paint job on the Cerro Supermarket down the street and the fruit cart re-created by Saá and Loveland. Shopping carts, fruit drink dispensers, Saá's shadowy cascades of tropical foliage, appropriated ads for jerk chicken, and Levine's surveillance cameras speak of a place with an entrenched neighborhood character, but one also inevitably becoming more self-conscious, more closely connected to art galleries, studios, and rising real estate values.

At The House in Edgewater, a similar sign of the times is evident in *Kiss Me Quick before I Change My Mind* by the artists' group called SALT, which devised an intricate installation aimed to dissect the commercial hoopla of international fairs. Miami artist Daniel Arsham says this will probably be the final show at The House, the enterprising alternative space and artist collective that also creates shows for Placemaker Gallery in the Design District.

"We do have a lease until August," says Arsham about The House. "But we are the only ones left on the block, which is making it an unpleasant experience. There are people breaking into the houses around us, so we could leave as early as the next month."

Other artists who lived nearby, like Naomi Fisher and Hernan Bas, have already left, even though, he says, developers are touting Edgewater as an arts neighborhood.

"But we're not going to stop doing things like 'SALT' even if it does become more difficult."

In memoriam: Antonio Zaya, 1954–2007
Montse Guillén, 1946–2025

MICHELE OKA DONER

Nature's Stunning Beauty Is Her Wand

April 22, 2004

Michele Oka Doner's seventh-floor, soaring bird–level Miami Beach apartment has enchanting ocean views, both inside and out. At night she sees the moon and a silken stretch of sand scoured by the surf.

Then there's the indoor beach nestled on the apartment's shelves and window sills—hundreds of artfully displayed treasures that Oka Doner found while beachcombing: seed pods, egg cases, bony bits of bleached coral that look like skulls, feet, even nascent alphabets. A tiny round buckle fallen from a bikini strap nudges a spiraling shard of conch shell.

"All of these are moments. They are about the beauty of the dry things that are left," says well-known artist Oka Doner. She's a tall woman with the firm stride you'd expect from her muscular size-10 feet, which she once re-created in gilded bronze soles, an energetically pedestrian self-portrait.

The apartment is a time-out retreat for the Miami Beach native, who has lived for years with her family in a studio loft in Manhattan's SoHo.

"It makes me smile every time I come inside. It allows me the luxury of dreaming in my own language," she says.

No grocery lists clutter the refrigerator door. Romantic lighting at night comes from 16 white candles on the bronze candelabra she cast from a bristling bush blown onto a friend's doorstep after an ocean storm. As the candles burn, slender ribbons of melted white wax drip into a bed of sand below, encircled by orchid roots.

"I love the wax droppings," she says. "You see the process, the remains of evenings past."

On every surface, the apartment is textured with the sense that art and design and the designs of the natural world are all one piece.

Another prominent collection, displayed with the grace of a slightly musty shrine, is her archive about Florida plant and marine life. There are yellowed journals with titles like *Strange Sea Shells and Their Stories* and *Florida Honey and Its Hundred Uses*.

Oka Doner, who has 21 public art projects around the country, will be talking about the shared bloodlines of art, design, and nature tonight at the Wolfsonian-Florida International University in Miami Beach.

WORKS AT MIA

In Miami, Oka Doner is especially known for *A Walk on the Beach*, the splendid, seemingly endless concourse floor of midnight-black terrazzo embedded

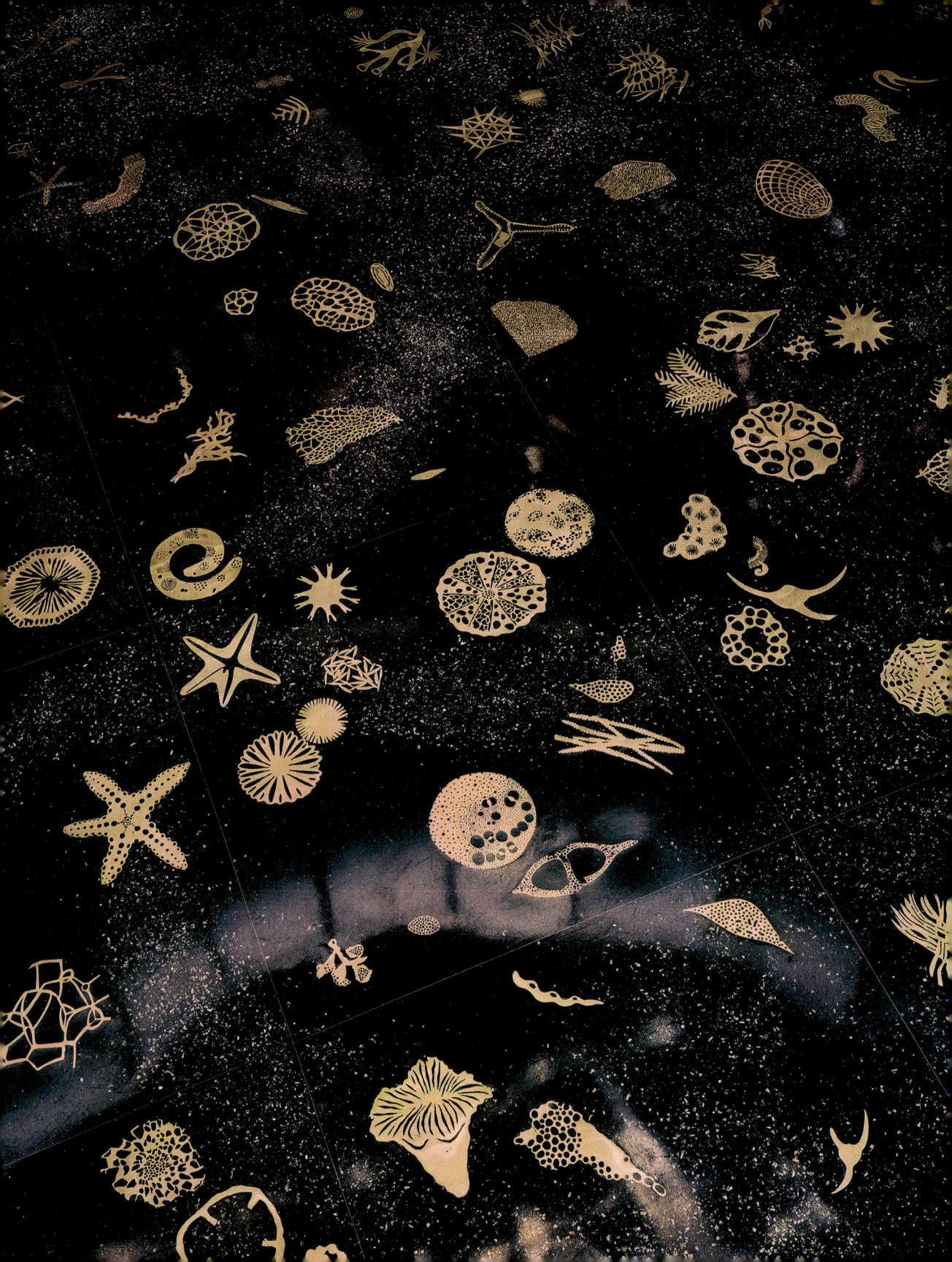

with organic bronze shapes at Miami International Airport. She's currently working on an even longer extension of the concourse in white terrazzo.

In addition to her public art projects and recent series of sculptures of the human figure, figures so embedded with the shapes of coral reefs that only the feet are truly unfettered, she's also created celebrated designs to embellish home and body.

A thorny-legged table she cast in bronze belongs to Chicago's Art Institute. New York's Museum of Arts and Design owns her gold shoulder pin resembling a root system.

She has cast pleated, wedge-shaped palm fronds into vases for Christofle, the luxury silversmith. Her made-to-order jewelry includes a cuff cast in bronze from a knobby clump of grape stems and ornamented with freshwater pearls that cap its small branches like bubbles.

Designs for objects like jewelry and vases, along with her public art and sculpture, are featured in a new book, *Michele Oka Doner: Natural Seduction* (Hudson Hills Press). The book is ranked number 8 in the May/June *Metropolitan Home* magazine's annual list of top 100 designs. In the magazine, Michael Lassell calls the book "an homage to the metal magician whose jewelry, tableware, and public spaces are rooted in the nuances of nature."

TABOO IGNORED

For years, Oka Doner has walked the other way when many in the art world set up a wall between art and design.

"When I was in grad school, it was taboo if something functioned, because then it wasn't art, and I thought, what are they talking about? You had Isamu Noguchi and Alexander Calder making sculpture and hair ornaments and tables," she says. "The issue is how beautiful is something, how exuberant, how creative is it?"

FIGURE 34. Michele Oka Doner, *A Walk on the Beach*, 1995-1999. Epoxy terrazzo, bronze, mother-of-pearl (black). Miami International Airport, North Terminal Concourse D. Image Nick Merrick, courtesy of Miami-Dade County Department of Cultural Affairs, Art in Public Places Trust.

Now more than ever, she seems to be hitting her stride in straddling art and design. After seeing her candelabra in the National Design Triennial at the Cooper Hewitt National Design Museum, Smithsonian Institution, in New York last year, representatives of Steuben Glass are talking with her about creating a table in glass.

In the past year, she's been showing at New York's blue-chip Marlborough Gallery. Designs continue to evolve for the white terrazzo floor at MIA, the extension of *A Walk on the Beach* and perhaps her most ambitious public art commission to date.

It's so fitting that she chose the soles of her feet to be a stand-in for a self-portrait, or that so many of her public artworks are made for walking.

They are earthbound in the most uplifting way. In a 1997 essay published in the recent book about her, the famed architect Morris Lapidus confided that *A Walk on the Beach* made him forget to use his wheelchair.

"One look at the beauty of more than a half-mile of Oka Doner's creation so astounded me that all I wanted to do was to walk along and study it," he wrote. "The splendor of this great work wrought a miracle only an artist can understand."

MARK HANDFORTH
AND DARA FRIEDMAN

April 25, 2004

Mark Handforth and Dara Friedman are members of a rarefied club: Married Couples Who've Shown in the Whitney Biennial as Individual Artists.

It's such an exclusive club that even New York's Whitney Museum of American Art—where Handforth's sculpture is part of the current biennial and where Friedman, who works in film and video, showed four years ago—can't say who else might belong.

Probably just as well. Making art isn't exactly about seeing eye to eye, even

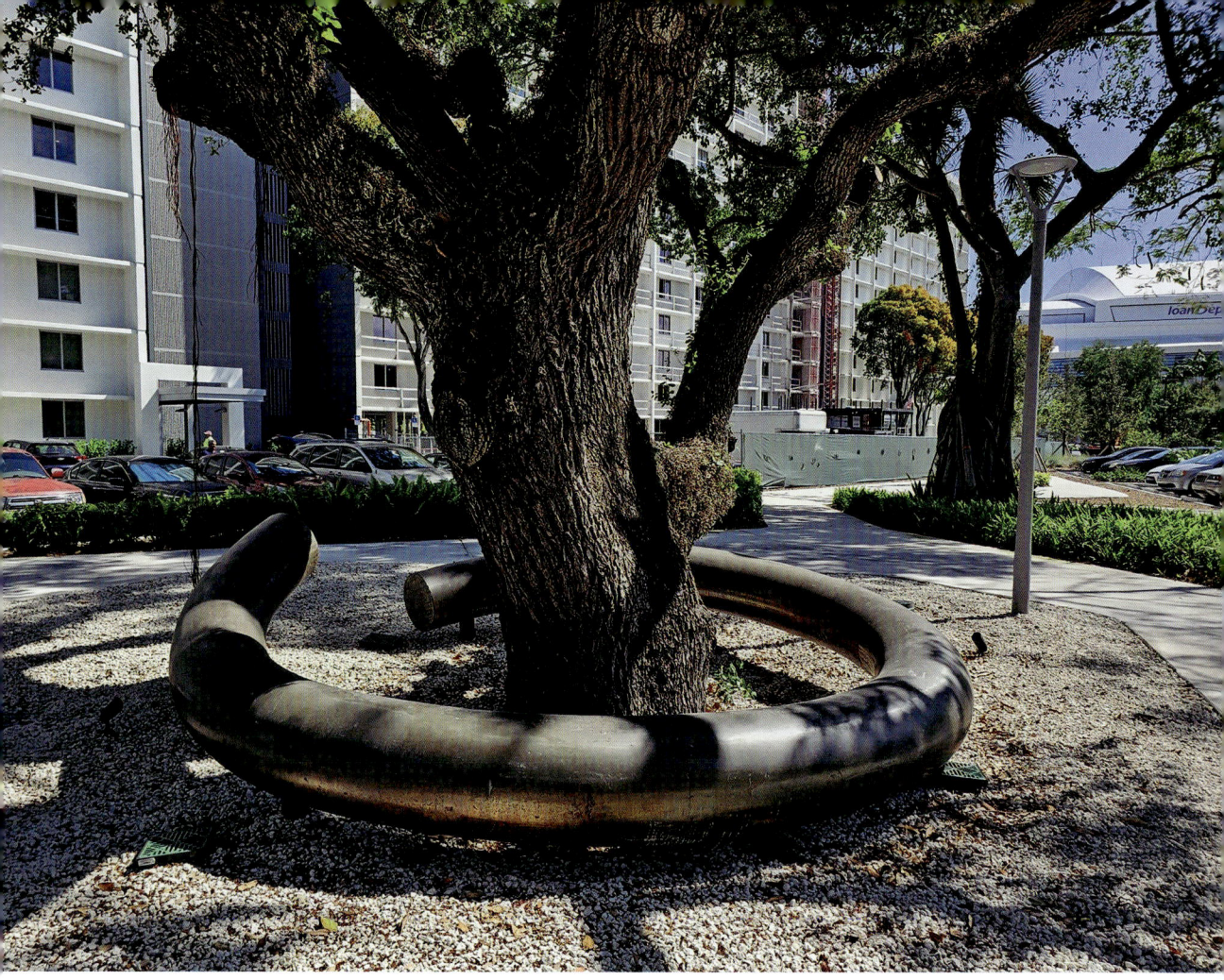

FIGURE 35. Mark Handforth, *Broken River Ring*, 2023. Cast bronze, landscape, site-specific sculpture. Gallery at River Parc, 1355 NW 7th St., Miami, 33125. Image Stefania Barigelli, courtesy of Miami-Dade County Department of Cultural Affairs, Art in Public Places Trust.

if you are a couple. And chitchat about who's married to whom isn't supposed to seep into serious art talk. (After combing his memory for a couple of minutes, Handforth says that the few couples he can think of who might have been fellow club members aren't together anymore.)

Despite what they share—their art, two daughters, and 11 years of marriage—they still see their own ways. What amazes one will often be completely missed by the other, who's busy being captivated by something else.

Friedman, barefoot in a button-down shirt and skirt, explains how this

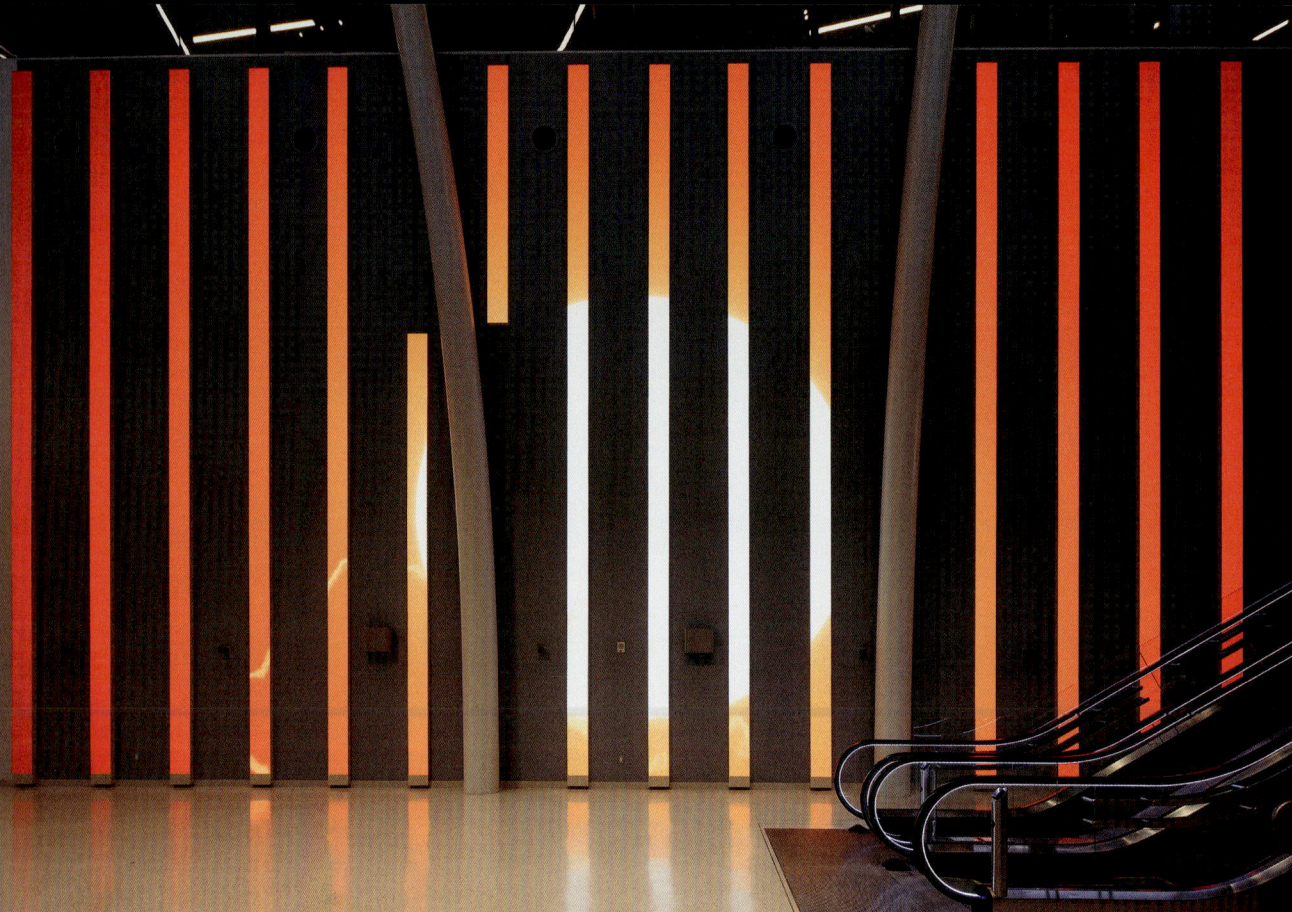

FIGURE 36. Dara Friedman, *Sunday*, 2022. 35mm cinema transferred to 6.5 video, conformed to LED, neutral 7 paint. PortMiami–Terminal V, First Floor Entrance, Virgin Voyages. Image Robin Hill, courtesy of Miami-Dade County Department of Cultural Affairs, Art in Public Places Trust.

works, ruminating in the thoughtful way that will lead to one of her favorite topics, the importance of artists sharing what they know with younger, aspiring artists.

She's relaxing on a sofa in their Miami Beach apartment with Handforth, a leggy London native wearing faded, frayed jeans and a white T-shirt. Their apartment, on the upper floor of an art deco building, is airy and uncluttered, furnished in a way that says, "Artists live here."

Over the fireplace is a film still of a couple kissing in a blurry close-up twist on the standard movie-screen smooch. They're one of dozens of anonymous couples Friedman filmed making out outdoors for *Romance* during the year she won a coveted fellowship at the American Academy in Rome. Soon after, *Romance* was shown at the Miami Art Museum in 2001; it was also screened at the Museum of Contemporary Art in Los Angeles.

On the coffee table is a scrap of metal, a model for one of Handforth's sculptures now at the Whitney, a piece that resembles a huge sign on I-95, all the way down to its white fluorescent vinyl letters. It reads "No Exit"—but upside down, as if this improbable sign had made its own exit by falling over and warping in the process.

"They normally don't have really huge No Exit signs," Handforth says, smiling, his British accent softened to a slight drawl. He sees the piece as a kind of pop art ready-made, with echoes of Ed Ruscha's surreal pop paintings of imaginary signage, but there's also a timely darkness to the sculpture that jives with daily news of war and terrorism.

Lighter notes in the apartment are trim brown op-art Marimekko pillows, a small baroque Venetian chandelier looped with pastel glass flowers, and generously splotchy drawings by daughter Violet in the bathroom. Her drawings are saturated with an indigo that would make the crazy-for-blue French painter and provocateur Yves Klein do a double take.

About their own double takes on the world: "Mark will be like, 'Oh my God, did you just see that?' He'll be talking about the corner of a building," says Friedman, who, like her husband, is 35. "So we were really looking in opposite directions. I'll say, 'I can't believe you missed that face, it's so outrageous.' And Mark is looking at grilles or something."

PATH TO MIAMI

It was a similar case of bifurcated vision that led them to Miami in 1992.

They were students in London, having met in art school in Germany, and had driven out one snowy day to see Stonehenge.

Handforth has always been fascinated by monumental objects, but particularly by those damaged by time and catastrophe, like the lampposts he saw overturned in a riot in London's Trafalgar Square in the late 1980s (Whitney curator Debra Singer calls Handforth's sculpture "a phantasm of beloved ruins.").

Friedman didn't see the same stones as Handforth. She saw an enormous bird. "I had this extraordinary vision of this blue parrot as big as a jet plane, and I said, 'What we have to do is go to Miami.'"

By the following August, the couple was setting up home and studio in Miami Beach. Then, says Handforth, "Hurricane Andrew happened, and everything was trashed. . . . Lampposts falling in the street. Cars were all puckered with these little holes."

Still, they were stunned by South Florida's fertile, chaotic energies. The ex-pat Brit marveled that each day brought the possibility of finding a baboon snacking in your garden.

"Animals could escape from the zoo and live quite happily because we were in the tropics," he says.

Keeping a home base in Miami and returning to Germany in the summer and fall to live in the family villa in which Friedman grew up, the couple nurtured their separate visions as their careers developed.

"They were a key component in that sort of sea change that happened in Miami," recalls MAM curator Lorie Mertes, speaking of the mid-1990s when the city started to show more support for contemporary art. "Their enthusiasm and, I think, their success helped to buoy Miami's own perception of itself."

Louis Grachos, director of the Albright-Knox Art Gallery in Buffalo, New York, has been following their careers ever since he was a curator at the Center for the Fine Arts (now Miami Art Museum) from 1991 to 1994.

"Art is completely integrated into how they live and think, and I suspect they are probably each other's best critics," he says.

Grachos gave Friedman one of her important shows outside Miami. In 2001, he curated a solo exhibit of her film and video at SITE SANTA FE, a well-known contemporary arts organization in New Mexico.

"Her work is rooted in some of the great conceptual work of the 1970s," Grachos says. "But what I love about it is that it has an edge of humor and seduction to it."

RUBELL LINK

Around 1996, Handforth landed the job as the Rubell Family Collection's first director, in its early stages as a lone outpost for art in Wynwood. "It seemed like such a crazy idea, the whole idea of moving to Wynwood at the time," says contemporary art collector Mera Rubell. "But [Handforth] was part of formulating the vision. When you are about to take an adventure, you need to surround yourself with people who believe in the journey."

Mertes appeared in Friedman's 1998 film *Untitled* as one of several newscaster-styled talking heads. "You felt that whatever her vision was, you wanted to please and be what she was seeing," Mertes says. "She's always drawn people to her."

A year later, *Untitled* was shown at the Museum of Contemporary Art in North Miami in an exhibit spotlighting annual winners of the South Florida Cultural Consortium fellowships, which included both Handforth and Friedman. The fellowships gave each artist $15,000. The couple sunk nearly all of it into making work for their first show at Gavin Brown's enterprise, their hip New York gallery.

"It was a nightmare," recalls Handforth. "We had massive debt, and we didn't sell anything."

ON TO INDIA

So with the $5,000 or so they had left, they left town—for India.

"When we first arrived in Mysore, the cows were painted fluorescent yellow and pink and they had red-tipped horns—like a Warhol cow walking across the street," he says.

At a friend's just-opened gallery in Delhi, Handforth showed a recent photograph in a big light box, spotlighting a vast tree draped in fluorescent light bulbs. Locals asked if the photos were taken in Miami. "I'm, like, it's India, it's just down the street," he says, shocked that no one recognized a homegrown sight.

For Friedman, who tried to film an April festival in India in which revelers throw colorful, powdery pigments in the air, contemporary art seemed almost beside the point in a country so rich in spectacle. "Like, why?" she wondered. "You have fluorescent cows in India wandering down the street, and the last thing you need is contemporary art."

Today, Friedman has set her sights on giving back. She waxes enthusiastically about her first formal teaching job two years ago as a visiting assistant professor at UCLA, part of a program that encourages contemporary artists to teach.

Talking about how to make art, she says, "is something that I know. You're getting to a certain age where you find your voice and you have things to say."

A place where young artists can learn from a fluid roster of more established ones is something Miami desperately needs, she argues. "Otherwise there won't be any lasting resonance after the joie de vivre and excitement of Art Basel has come and gone. The spotlight will inevitably shift away from Miami—it always shifts if there isn't an anchoring, a foundation-laying, a school by the time the shift happens. The heat happened and stayed in a place like Los Angeles because it was anchored."

A school, she offers, could even be tied to the Miami Art Museum in its proposed new building. "It's kind of a classic thing, to tie a school to a museum, but then it becomes a really strong web, a foundation," she says. And Miami, she adds, "is such a new place, like everybody knows, but it's time to lay some roots."

CREATING PUBLIC TREASURES

May 2, 2004

It was not a performance, really, though it felt like one. In a black double-breasted suit, the elderly man with a maestro demeanor stood on a bare stage looking up at a balcony filled with waving, camera-clicking admirers. They were saluting a new work by Cundo Bermúdez that may very well be his swan song.

Octogenarian Cuban painter Cundo, as he is known to scholars, family, and friends, is the first of five artists scheduled to complete public art projects commissioned by Miami-Dade Art in Public Places for the Performing Arts

Center of Greater Miami, now set to open in 2006. The artworks were commissioned nearly seven years ago; they'll cost approximately $4.2 million.

At a mid-April reception, his 28-by-40-foot mural was unveiled in the still raw, concrete-and-girder canyon of the PAC's Studio Theater.

It's a boldly colored glass mosaic mural, a cubist-inspired view of the choreographed movements of actors and stagehands as they go about their art backstage. Its title is fitting: *Ways of Performing*.

The stage is presented as a distant, red-framed shadow box. It takes a back seat to a larger cast of assorted figures merging with semiabstract forms that seem to delineate curtains, scenery, and costumes.

In part a lush, streamlined recollection of a historical moment in Cuban culture, *Ways of Performing* carries the style of acclaimed modernist paintings that Cundo began producing in 1940s Havana, paintings that were shown in a seminal 1944 exhibit at New York's Museum of Modern Art. His best-known works often feature statuesque women in baroque hats gliding among interlocking spaces saturated with ripe colors. Some may be modeled after a ballerina-to-be named Alicia Alonso; Cundo used to see her walking to dance class.

SPANISH HERITAGE

As a pivotal figure in the 1940s who was less interested in Afro-Cuban culture than was the older, better-known Wifredo Lam, Cundo "began to explore the Spanish heritage of Cuban identity," Florida International University art historian Juan Martínez said last year, when the Lowe Art Museum mounted a 50-year survey of the artist's work.

At the PAC last month, sunlight glanced off the mural's glass mosaic tiles while workers gingerly laid them out in sections on a concrete floor. Then, with officials like the PAC's president and CEO Michael Hardy watching, Cundo stepped slowly across the tiles. Flickering in graduated shades of blues and yellows, they gently nod to a period 1950s look, though their shine was subdued by a protective coating.

This was the artist's first time to see his mosaic in one piece.

"We're going to ask God for his help and permission so that I can see it when everything is finished, because I am 89," he said.

And then the artist, whose paintings have also featured musicians, shyly added that he would also love to hear one of his favorite arias performed, "Casta Diva" from Bellini's opera *Norma*, at the completed PAC.

He is looking at about a two-year wait. Plagued by several years of delays and millions in cost overruns, the $255 million César Pelli–designed center is now set to open by May 31, 2006. Near that time, *Ways of Performing* will be installed in its permanent site, the Studio Theater's lobby of the PAC's Delores and Sanford Ziff Ballet Opera House. Facing a glass exterior wall, the mural will be visible to passersby on the corner of Biscayne Boulevard between Northeast 13th and Northeast 14th streets.

OTHER ARTISTS

But Cundo's mural is the only art ready now to be glimpsed in total. In February, New York–based painter Robert Rahway Zakanitch was in town to present a mock-up of his painted velour *Hibiscus Curtain*, a work that will recall South Florida's vivacious flora, for the Sanford and Delores Ziff Ballet Opera House.

In about six weeks, said Art in Public Places director Ivan Rodriguez, there will be a sneak peek at some of the projects by José Bedia, a Cuban-born artist who moved here in 1990 and has built an international reputation based on his intimate knowledge of Afro-Cuban lore and ritual. Bedia is creating etched-glass balcony railings and terrazzo floor murals for the lobbies of the Ballet Opera House and the Carnival Symphony Hall.

"This is the good news about the center," said Rodriguez, acknowledging ongoing criticism of the building's costly delays. His office has had to postpone the artists' work so that their site-specific projects can mesh with the construction schedule. "Obviously, the artists are anxious and eager. It's a little frustrating that it's taking so long, but it's a huge project, and I understand the intricacies."

A recent dusty, hard-hat tour of the site underscored that frustration but also opened up thrilling possibilities of the kind of visual art that will be running 24/7 at the completed center—particularly the generous, sweeping curve of the lobby floors and the railings that promise to be animated by Bedia's theatrical sense of line.

On the concert hall's lobby floors, there will be the broad silhouette of the palm of a beckoning hand flanked by stars and flying birds, an emblem of applause, unity, and welcome.

Translated into glass and terrazzo and inspired by both music and Miami, Bedia's line drawings should offer a gifted articulation of space. For visitors looking upward from the lobby, his transparent railings etched in gold and silver will reveal concertgoers as they move across tiered balconies.

CHANGING PROJECTS

Works by Bedia and Cundo have not evolved much from their initial proposals. But other projects have undergone more change, says Rodriguez.

Plans for sculptural elements by California artist Anna Valentina Murch to enhance the pedestrian bridge crossing Biscayne Boulevard, linking the Ballet Opera House and the Symphony Hall, were scrapped because of safety issues with trucks going under it, says Roberto J. Espejo, senior associate for Cesar Pelli's architectural firm.

Murch's contribution, rendered in stone and travertine marble, will involve curvilinear benches in the PAC's oval-shaped Plaza for the Arts and a fountain of water flowing down a nearby wall softly textured with wavelike patterns.

Funds that would have been spent for her work on the bridge will go to a new piece by Zakanitch, a semitransparent scrim that will veil the organ for the 2,200-seat Carnival Symphony Hall.

The project for a 6,400-square-foot plaza by Miami-based artist Gary Moore seems to have metamorphosed the most. Called *Pharoah's Dance* after a 1965 composition by Miles Davis, it's located in the Sanford and Delores Ziff Ballet Opera House Plaza at Northeast 2nd Avenue and 13th Street and will look toward Overtown.

HISTORIC FOCUS

"Originally it was a very tightly constructed project, more historically focused," recalls Moore, who had proposed creating cast stone medallions dedicated to specific songs by Black composers.

His new approach, in colorful terrazzo, will be more true to the improvisational spirit of jazz. "It sort of freed me up, because I realize that public art on some level is a performance," he says. He plans benches, a large disk-shaped sculpture lit in pink and purple neon for showcasing outdoor performances, and a planter of dark, purplish-colored bamboo reeds that will whistle in the wind.

"As the area grows more commercial, I'm thinking the plaza could be used by people on lunch breaks, by students from New World School of the Arts," he adds.

But the traffic here will be significantly different from that of other AIPP projects sited in locations like the Miami International Airport, the Port of Miami, and the Metrorail stations.

Those are in practical and functional settings, says Rodriguez. "The PAC is a fusion of all the arts coming together—architecture, performing arts, and visual arts. It's an excellent opportunity to make an impact on the culture of the community, because it all comes together here."

In memoriam: Cundo Bermúdez, 1914–2008
Anna Valentina Murch, 1948–2014
César Pelli, 1926–2019
Juan Martínez, 1951–2020
Ivan Rodriguez, 1947–2024

MIAMI-DADE COUNTY MAIN LIBRARY

The Colors of Haiti

May 9, 2004

Secured with one blink-sized stitch after another, the thousands of sequins in Haitian Vodou flags flash a heritage of sumptuous splendor and heart-crushing sorrow.

That heritage is spotlighted in a show at the Main Library of the Miami-Dade County Public Library System devoted to these flags, *Haitian Inspiration: Sequins and Beads Speak of Spirits*. Perhaps no other art from Haiti marks such an interplay between religion and the military—and, in recent years, the art market. This raucous chorus of spirit and soldier adds a tragic, profound resilience to their glorious shimmer.

In Port-au-Prince in March, Miami-based artist Edouard Duval-Carrié saw sequined flags of his work, resembling large paintings and depicting critical moments in the violent history of his native Haiti, destroyed. They were torched by military forces opposed to former president Jean-Bertrand Aristide in the bloody aftermath of Aristide's departure February 29.

These works had been commissioned by Haiti's Ministry of Culture in honor of the country's bicentennial and installed a week before in the capital's presidential compound.

"After Aristide left, the military went back and claimed the building. Since most of my works were very critical of them, they had them burned," said Duval-Carrié. "I was very upset, but what can you do? They're gone."

He has commissioned new flag paintings of his work, which will be shown in October in his solo show at the UCLA Fowler Museum of Cultural History in Los Angeles.

Revolt and religion are part and parcel of Haitian flags.

About a decade ago, Boston art historian Anna Wexler sat with Vodou priest and artist Clotaire Bazile, touched by the spiritual power of the flags. She wanted to learn the secrets of making them.

"Everything must be done with great concentration. It's really meditative—the repetitive motion, the sequins reflecting the changing light of the day. In Haiti when you work on them, people are singing or talking about the dreams they have, and you are right in the environment of the religion," Wexler recalled.

STAINED GLASS

Gleaming like stained glass, the flags are used in religious Vodou ceremonies in Haiti and sought by collectors drawn simply to the flags' beauty.

Some younger flagmakers, like Mireille Delice, are moving away from classic ceremonial images of Vodou motifs and spirits. Delice, with her whirling portrait of the serpent Dambala, a spirit linked to water and wisdom, and others are spinning more painterly compositions.

Duval-Carrié commissioned his painting-like flags from a Port-au-Prince Vodou artist and priest known simply as Edgar. The notion came to Duval-Carrié after friends told him how Port-au-Prince artist Myrlande Constant had rendered one of his paintings into a flag, complete with his signature.

The Main Library exhibit sheds light on the flags' fluid, fascinating tradition. Presenting loans from South Florida collector, curator, and writer Candice Russell, the show brings together 50 examples of Haitian flags created since the mid-1980s.

They are fashioned from silky rectangles of cloth. Many are ornamented with mermaids, serpents, and saints drawn from the Vodou pantheon, but others are notable departures, like one of a soldier by Salana and another of a secret nocturnal society by Wagler Vital.

On every square inch, the flags glitter with latter-day Byzantine brilliance, hand-stitched mosaics for modern times. Originally made without so much market-driven glitter, the flags spring from traditions observed for over two centuries in temples honoring Haitian Vodou.

SACRED PRACTICES

As the nation's much-maligned folk religion, Vodou combines a host of New World influences imaginatively, resiliently forged from the legacy of enslaved Africans. In its sacred practices and art objects, West African spiritual beliefs mingle almost seamlessly with the ritual-rich French colonial exports of Roman Catholicism and Masonic Lodges.

At the beginning of Vodou ceremonies, worshippers carry the flags to salute and entice the religion's spirits, hoisting the flags in sparkling movements. Glittering light is essential. "You have to remember that there's no electricity in the countryside," says Duval-Carrié. "The beauty is realized when you have candles, and the flags create a magical feeling. In the squalor of these temples, you have these shimmering things."

Scholars link the flags' ornate patterns to brocaded Roman Catholic vestments and their choreographed presentation to military exercises.

Military troops, both foreign and domestic, mark an especially vivid legacy in the flags—something that surfaced with bitter irony in the story of Duval-Carrié's destroyed artworks, including his imagery of a puppet-like brigade of Haitian soldiers in the Republican Army of St. Domingue, a reference to the colonial name of Haiti.

In the Main Library exhibit, many flags display dynamic geometric borders, with squares bisected to create a parade of multicolored triangles. It's a style with echoes of 18th-century French military flags carried by Haitian forces enlisted by Napoleon to quell revolts but who defected to fight for their country's independence.

It's only been in the last 20 or 30 years that Haitian Vodou flags have been ornamented with such brilliant surfaces and acquired a wide commercial market. An early 1970s book about busy painters and bustling galleries in Port-au-Prince never mentions the glistening flags.

GARMENT FACTORIES

But that was also the decade that garment assembly factories began to spring up in Haiti, says art historian Anna Wexler, who teaches Afro-Caribbean culture and art at Springhill College in Boston. (With the Haitian economy in such dire straits, artists now often import beads, sometimes with the help of collectors.)

Those earlier factories, many US owned, made wedding gowns and party dresses for posh events far from Haiti. At such affairs, women never suspected that scraps from their dresses had been recycled into a stunning Caribbean mosaic by residents of one of the world's poorest nations.

"People who worked in the factories would sweep up sequins on the floor afterward and would sell them. That's how Clotaire started," says Wexler. Encouraged by French collectors, Bazile was the first to systematically adorn flags for the art market, she said. Known for his immaculate flags in classic Vodou designs, Bazile is represented in the exhibit by a dazzling pink and orange flag dedicated to goddess of love Erzulie Fréda Dahomey.

His example led priests and artists into a style of ornamenting fabric with a fabulous sparkle that's unparalleled in the world. "You do see it on textiles in Southeast Asia and India," Wexler says. "But in terms of sequins totally saturating the fabric, no. The reflective aspect of sequins is considered to be spiritually powerful. As Clotaire explained to me, the spirits love light and are drawn to light. Beauty draws the spirits."

Not all Haitian flags are so reflective. Some still look like flags made before the party dress factories touched off a new era in Haitian art. "The flags that are circulating in the market are not typical of the vast areas in the countryside," she says. "In remote areas, they are painted or embroidered."

The impulse to shine, however, is long-standing. Today there are resourceful gleams from flags in poor Vodou temples. "People use what they can. They are very efficient," says collector Russell. One artist used transparent sequins and painted them with pink nail polish. "I know this because they started chipping," Russell says.

Russell has nearly completed a book on Haitian flags, to be published by Schiffer. Over the course of many trips to Haiti since the middle 1980s, she said, one of her most spectacular moments was walking into the studio of Jean Baptiste Jean Joseph in a town east of Port-au-Prince.

FLOOR TO CEILING

"His studio is like a shotgun house with four rooms," she recalls "The walls are crammed floor to ceiling with Vodou flags, Vodou bottles, vests, eyeglass cases, beaded decorations for Christmas trees. I thought I had died and gone to heaven. I had never seen so many things in one place. And here was this flagmaker, this unassuming man in Nautica shorts, hovering over teenage boys working there seven days a week on these beautiful designs."

While Joseph's studio is typical, in which perhaps a dozen people labor over the nearly 20,000 beads sewn into a single flag, his flags are not. Russell considers him among the most imaginative Haitian artists working in the medium. Several of his creations are in the Main Library exhibit, including a slender golden banner of Adam and Eve and another in which Agoue, the

Vodou god of the sea, is portrayed as a luminous fish, though this deity is usually represented as a ship.

The designs on Haiti's lavish flags have crossed over to decorate numerous items. Pink and red vèvès, the intricate drawings that evoke Vodou spirits, dance across a $90 beaded purse at an exclusive boutique selling Dolce & Gabbana in South Miami.

"I have seen the flags in fancy stores in Paris and London, in a booth at a jazz festival in New Orleans," says Duval-Carrié. "You have things from $20 to $10,000. I am sure one day you will have Vodou flags on Tiananmen Square. Why not?"

Before her travels to Haiti in the early 1990s, Wexler was skeptical of the way Haiti's traditional art forms were being marketed. Then she realized that because of the nation's poverty, "flagmakers would openly admit they tailored their work to customer demand, some more than others," she says.

That's not so different from the 1940s, when American collectors gave temple priests materials to make paintings. "Artists then took up a new medium and explored it. Even though they were exploited—their work was sold here for a lot more than it was sold for there—they were able to survive in terms of their resources," Wexler said. "Haiti is so amazing, people will be creative in the most desperate circumstances. Whatever they do, they make it their own."

KAREN RIFAS AT STEINBAUM, RALPH PROVISERO AT DORSCH

Sculptors Give New Shape to Old Materials

May 17, 2004

So many sculptors have dispensed with the weighty seriousness of bronze and marble that unusual materials enjoy the status of art-as-usual. Still, two

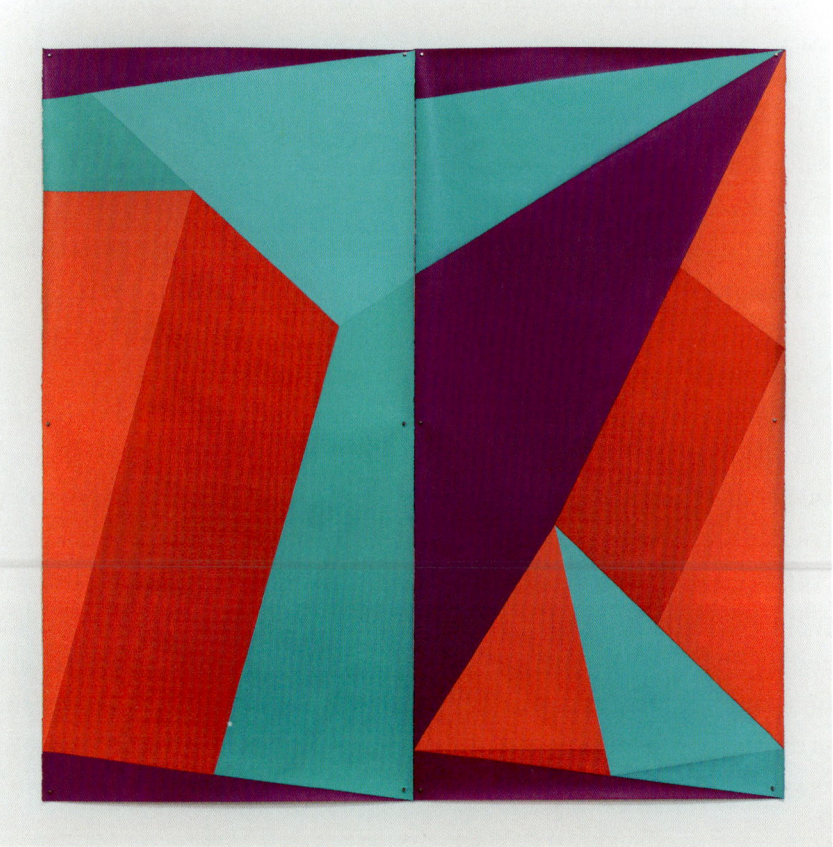

FIGURE 37. Karen Rifas, *Bass*, 2018. Acrylic painting on paper. Image Frank Casale, courtesy of Miami-Dade County Department of Cultural Affairs, Art in Public Places Trust.

current gallery exhibits show how South Florida artists are giving solid minimalist significance to materials that exceed the mainstream's taste for eccentricity-as-usual: oak leaves and battered maple wood tabletops from a middle school shop class.

At Bernice Steinbaum Gallery in the Design District is *This Ain't No Retrospective (I'm Too Young)*, a gathering of sculptural objects by Karen Rifas, who surely knows more than anyone else in the world about how to use a vintage sewing machine to stitch together expansive sculptures from oak leaves.

Rifas's gift is for carving space with large, airy strokes. In a work at the gallery like *Between the Lines*, she turns these strings of variously sized oak leaves into three-dimensional line drawings, akin to Sol LeWitt's murals of sleek geometric mazes.

NATURAL VARIATIONS

While LeWitt evoked an optical texture and depth through a dazzling interplay of colored lines, Rifas tweaks the flatness of her stitched lines with a nod to the natural world's infinite variations. Creating innumerable combinations in number and size, she builds up lines of lightly suspended oak leaves, working with assorted groupings of leaves that are fat, thin, and in between. You probably never knew the humble dried brown live oak leaf came in so many different body types.

The strings of leaves in *Between the Lines* carve out two wide rectangular planes tilted diagonally, in sly opposition to Richard Serra's heavy minimalist abstract sculptures. These rectangles are juxtaposed by a pair of soaring columns of leaves that, viewed from different points, can stand apart or melt into the mass of horizontal lines.

Standing out or melting into a larger form is a theme Rifas plays out in many of her smaller sculptures here, which are often whimsical combinations of women's work objects plucked from sewing baskets, toy chests, kitchen drawers, and the vanity table.

Vegetable steamers, sieves, and colanders are commandeered into becoming quirky creatures and charming lanterns but retain their humble-tool identities as well; groupings of round makeup mirrors take on the ominous look of watching eyes.

In this context, *Between the Lines* isn't just a title about formal considerations. Reading between the lines is an idea that spills into her lineup of brooms in the *Clean Sweep* series. They suggest saucy extras from the animated version of *Sorcerer's Apprentice* but coyly bear un-Disney-esque names like *Hidden Agenda*. The brooms are clever, but they're one-liner art.

Then there's another oak-leaf piece, *The Present Absent*, which contrasts neat rows of spools with dangling miniature daggers known as needles. Reading between the lines, you see in Rifas's best art an effort to reweave those cautionary myths about never-good-enough girls—like Sleeping Beauty, for instance, who paid for her curiosity with a long coma.

A LIGHTNESS

New Work: Ralph Provisero at Dorsch Gallery offers a promising interplay between Provisero's swift drawings and his steel and wood sculptures. The sculptures convey an unexpected lightness of being and are handsomely displayed in Dorsch's big space. *Maleducati* (*Maleducated*) shows steel rods grasping tilting wooden planes of maple tabletops, battered from years of service in a middle school shop class. The artist recovered these tables from his former school, according to dealer Brook Dorsch, after shop classes were phased out.

Like Rifas, Provisero knows the minimalist drill of spare geometric forms. He has used that language to suggest pared-down machine parts, propellers, assembly lines. His work suggests a bare-bones ode to a hands-on manufacturing economy replaced by a service economy, recalling machinery's formal integrity even when productivity has fled.

END OF AN ERA

The House Artists Gather before the Wrecking Ball Hits

June 11, 2004

The House in Edgewater, a ramshackle structure that once boasted an airy porch and an open-minded atmosphere, is closed up and going down for the count. Its last hurrah is tonight, with a one-night-only exhibit in which several hundred artists have been invited to participate.

Since opening in 2000 as a spirited venue run by its live-in artists to showcase themselves and other artists, The House has been a catalyst for Miami's youthfully expansive art scene.

"We're asking people to leave the work, and all of that will go down with The House," says current tenant Daniel Arsham, who's already moved out. For the moment, The House is a two-story 1930s Edward Hopperesque survivor on a weedy block giving way to brisk development. It's slated for demolition once the lease Arsham shares with artists Bhakti Baxter, Martin Oppel, and Tao Rey expires on Tuesday, Arsham says.

For tonight's exhibit, he envisions ephemeral artwork placed inside and outside The House, even drawn on or carved into its walls, as offerings to the energy it has generated. "It's been an easy place to show and to make things happen in," Arsham adds.

In the past four years, this surprising shoestring venue has exhibited some 350 artists from here and elsewhere, won positive notices in the local press and in the *New York Times*, and drew attention from curators including Edsel Williams, who chose work by House artists for the Four Seasons Hotel in Miami.

In 2001, Bonnie Clearwater, Museum of Contemporary Art director and chief curator, tapped artists associated with The House to present a group show at MOCA in North Miami. It was a grand recognition for these twentysomethings.

"There are other people who have done similar things, but what's special is their sensitivity to the art while upholding high standards and their general philosophy about the relationship between art and the viewer," says Clearwater. "The camaraderie they've built helped in a great way to create an artists' community here that expands beyond Miami because of the way they've reached out to artists in New York."

The imminent wrecking ball is part of a too-familiar cycle. "It always happens when artists move into areas prior to development. Real estate can change very quickly. But I think their beliefs can carry on in their programming at Placemaker," she continues, referring to the Design District gallery that The House artists operate.

On Saturday, Placemaker will open *Obituary*, a group show running through July 17 and highlighting art exhibited at The House. Others making new works for *Obituary* are Hernan Bas, Naomi Fisher, Cooper, David Rohn, Robert Chambers, and Adler Guerrier.

Guerrier will show his drawings of the DuPont Plaza, where in the late 1990s, he and fellow New World School of the Arts student Martin Oppel organized experimental shows. In those projects, he said, "there was a spirit of do-it-yourself, and that was something Martin took to The House, which was a total success as far as young artists taking control and not necessarily waiting for the blessings of the art world."

Such control isn't always a match for rising real estate values. "I feel that developers in this town don't have any sense of artists' studios and the reality of their presence in any neighborhood," said Guerrier. "It's tough. We have to work somewhere, so I guess eventually we'll find the next cheap place that's close in, because we can't all move to Miramar."

332

Part III

PART IV

GLOBAL
ART
LOCALLY,
2005–2007

During hectic days now known as Miami Art Week, Miami's art community steadily built on enthusiasm for contemporary art generated by Art Basel Miami Beach and its satellite fairs. Changes occurred with far-reaching consequences. The community became more mindful of its recent past. This section includes reviews and profiles of artists Clyde Butcher, Teresa Diehl, Francie Bishop Good, Antoni Miralda, and Glexis Novoa.

Part 4 begins with "Global Art Locally: Rubells Collect 10 Miami Artists" from June 2005. Pervading this gathering of art was an eminently Miami-styled, dreamy sense of wanderlust and fantasy fused with imagery of out-of-control vegetation titled *At This Time*. It represented a significant recognition for these artists on their home turf by international collectors Don and Mera Rubell of Miami, who launched the Rubell Family Museum in 1993 in a retrofitted Drug Enforcement Administration (DEA) warehouse in Miami's Wynwood neighborhood.

Don and Mera Rubell acknowledged that this show of Miami artists was something of an accident. "It was not our intent to put together Miami artists," Don Rubell said. "They put themselves together."

How did that accident happen? A traveling show based on work they'd collected by artists in Leipzig, Germany, encouraged them to look closely at Miami artists they'd collected over the years.

"In order for a city to function, you have to have energy coming in from the outside. That was something we learned in the Leipzig show," said Don. "For us, it's important that when we hang a show, it teaches us. It's not a pedantic exercise," Mera said.

For Miami artists, "The concerns are not local but global," said Don. "Not all of them have found their voice in an equal fashion, but they are all on their way."

The artists in *At This Time* were Hernan Bas, José Bedia, Cooper, Naomi Fisher, Mark Handforth, Jiae Hwang, Norberto (Bert) Rodriguez, Cristina Lei Rodriguez, and Purvis Young. The show was curated by collection director Mark Coetzee. As part of this exhibit, two performance pieces by Pablo Cano, *Animated Altarpieces* and *The Pursuit of Love*, were staged in the private museum's sculpture garden when this show opened in mid-May.

Art by Purvis Young would later be featured in the wide-ranging exhibit *Purvis Young*, which opened December 2018 at the Rubell Family Collection during Miami Art Week. For that exhibit, a hardcover catalog documenting over 200 works was published. It includes a 2005 interview by Hans Ulrich Obrist with the artist. There are also essays by Rashid Johnson, Gean Moreno, Franklin Sirmans, César Trasobares, and Barbara Young. The exhibit and catalog assured Young's prominence in Miami art history. In 2019, the Rubell Family Collection moved to a new location with a new name.

Just as the arrival of the Rubell Family Museum in Wynwood in 1993 set in motion a dramatic transformation of Wynwood—from an edgy arts neighborhood to a hip retail neighborhood with rising rents and property values causing art galleries to move to more affordable spaces—so history is surely repeating itself after the Rubell private museum relocated to Allapattah in 2019. In that gentrifying neighborhood, it is now joined by commercial galleries and private collections.

And in 2019 during Miami Art Week, there was another major addition to Miami's cultural ecosystem. That was the arrival in Allapattah of El Espacio 23, a 28,000-square-foot contemporary art space established in a repurposed warehouse by collector and philanthropist Jorge M. Pérez. Open to the public with free admission, it provides opportunities for artists and curators with artist residencies and changing exhibitions.

The years 2005 to 2007 marked the end of an era in the art community. Consequential changes inevitably left space for new developments. A major change was the departure of art services supervisor Barbara Young, recounted in "Barbara Young: Art Mobile Librarian Hits the Road." In July 2005, after almost 30 years of nurturing Miami artists and the community at large, she retired. Her successor was Denise Delgado. With the final exhibits Young curated, she reached the end of her to-do list but not the end of a generous legacy she began as the county's first Art Mobile librarian. That legacy continues to inform the present, documented by the Vasari Project and Women Artists Archives Miami (WAAM).

Young's first library job involved planning shows for the Art Mobile, a van covered on the exterior with wild zebra stripes and luscious tropical flowers painted by Lowell Nesbitt. With a small staff, she took the Art Mobile to schools, shopping centers, and branch libraries. In its busiest year, she had 60,000 visitors. It was in operation through the early 1990s, thanks to the efforts of Southeast Banking Corporation and the Miami-Dade County Public Library System.

One of her final shows was a selection of hand-beaded "paintings" stretched on vinyl by Gerald Winter. "I have always wanted to show Winter's work," she said. "His beaded pieces are mind-boggling."

"Every now and then I run into people who were his students," she said of Winter, an artist who retired from the University of Miami in 2002, two decades and one year before his death in 2023. One of Winter's students was Michael Spring, now director emeritus of the Miami-Dade County Department of Cultural Affairs. Spring is quoted in Winter's online Artwork Archive profile by Julia Muench. Muench's archive, created following Winter's death, documents the span of his career and his extravagantly colored, minutely detailed beaded canvases.

In 2006, conceived as an outlier's audacious sequel to the 1998 *Grandma's Recipes—Miami Bureau* at the Miami Art Museum, Antoni Miralda and his collaborators brought *Tastes & Tongues/Sabores y Lenguas* to Miami. That year may have been the last time that one of Miami's more unorthodox art venues, TransEAT/FoodCulture, was open to visitors. Located in a Little Haiti warehouse, it stored hundreds of food-related items that Miralda and his partner and chef Montse Guillén had gathered.

Now closed, it exists online at https://www.foodcultura.org/about/ as a radical kind of "anti-museum" dedicated to the cultural concept of food. The FoodCultura concept, as the website explains, sees food and rituals for consuming food as "vehicles" that convey or subvert contemporary social traditions. In July 2006, "Miralda: Tasty Exhibit a Delightful Mix of Food and Culture" reviewed his latest project investigating the art of food. At that time with stops in Miami and Coral Gables, Miralda and his collaborators were almost halfway through the cosmopolitan progressive dinner that was *Tastes/Sabores*. Miami was the sixth stop on a tour beginning in Caracas and was intended to wind up in Barcelona, Miralda's hometown.

Much more than a far-fetched foodie extravaganza, *Tastes/Sabores* was an evolving artwork, with photographic, culinary portraits of each city.

They were populist and participatory. It was shown in museums in Caracas and Bogotá and was invited to important international art festivals in Latin America, including the Havana Biennial in June. After its appearance in Miami, *Tastes/Sabores* was scheduled to travel to the São Paulo Biennial.

Miralda sighed when asked to explain the art of the exhibit. "It's always difficult, because there is not a product that people can take home as a piece of art. So they take home more a memory, and an image, or an experience." For him, art happens at the nexus of food, history, and anthropology. He prefers poking around supermarkets in Paris to galleries at the Louvre.

"I always feel an artist needs to be crossing barriers," he said. In a remark that seems a radical rebuke to the art market, he added, "[Artists] need to go through the refrigerators. They need to walk with people."

The project, he said, offered an "urban culinary topography" deeply rooted in daily life. In each city, *Tastes/Sabores* became part festival, part imaginary dinner party, with giant tongue-shaped photo collages, a video, and dozens of unique objects created by inhabitants of that city. They documented daily examples, mostly humble but disarming, of how food and creativity mesh.

In perhaps the most consequential change of all, the board of the Knight Ridder newspaper chain, which owned the *Miami Herald*, approved in 2006 a sale to the much smaller McClatchy newspaper company for $4.5 billion in cash and stock. It was a humbling blow for the vaunted Knight Ridder newspaper chain, which had chalked up 85 Pulitzers won by its 32 newspapers.

This momentous event was consistent with the precipitous, ongoing slide in local news coverage nationally. Still, new business models have been devised and philanthropists have dedicated $500 million to support local news. As of this writing, Amanda Rosa covers all the arts, not strictly visual arts, for the *Miami Herald*. Her work is funded through the Jorge M. Pérez Family Foundation CreArte grant program.

In addition to the *Miami Herald* arts coverage, ArtburstMiami.com is a local nonprofit media source for the arts featuring original stories by writers who specialize in theater, dance, visual arts, film, and music. The *Miami Herald* and other news outlets can republish these stories at no cost.

The community became more mindful of its past even as new voices appeared. In October 2005, as observed in "Museum of Contemporary

Art: Made in Miami," the Museum of Contemporary Art in North Miami (MOCA) launched its 10th anniversary season. Over the years, MOCA and its predecessor, the much smaller COCA, North Miami's Center for Contemporary Art, heightened Miami's presence in art. By the museum's count, MOCA had shown over 50 Miami artists in 2005. "When we showed them, nobody cared. Most of them didn't even have galleries," said director Bonnie Clearwater. The museum has also provided opportunities for local artists to interact with nationally and internationally known artists it exhibited.

In 2013, Clearwater left her position as director of MOCA to become the director and chief curator of NSU Art Museum Fort Lauderdale. The following year, the new Institute of Contemporary Art (ICA Miami) was founded in Miami's Design District. A dispute erupted among battling board members of ICA Miami and MOCA in North Miami regarding the proper home of MOCA's permanent collection. In 2014, prominent former MOCA board members decamped to the new ICA Miami temporarily established in the Moore Building in the Miami Design District. In 2017, ICA Miami opened the doors of its striking three-story building and sculpture garden. Admission to ICA Miami is free. Following the death of leading Miami collector Rosa de la Cruz in 2024 and the subsequent permanent closure of the next-door de la Cruz Collection, ICA Miami purchased the building once housing the collection for $25 million. It allowed the museum to expand by an impressive 30,000 square feet, no doubt adding to the role Miami can play in the contemporary art world.

Since that time of turmoil for MOCA in 2014, the museum now has a new website and has created more community-focused programming. It's currently led by Chana Budgazad Sheldon. The first show under her direction was AFRICOBRA: *Messages to the People*, curated by Jeffreen M. Hayes; after its MOCA premiere in 2018, the exhibit traveled to the 2019 Venice Biennale. That was the first time, Sheldon noted in a 2022 interview with online publication Curator, that a Florida museum had organized an exhibit chosen for the Venice Biennale.

For the September 2006 column "José Carlos Diaz, Claire Breukel, Carolina García: Young at Art," art professionals in the early stages of their careers spoke about working here. The progress each has made in their careers is a testament to how Miami has become a critical stepping-stone for many in the visual arts. "Miami should be a destination for young people, whether you are a young curator or a young artist in college," said José Carlos Diaz, assistant director of Diana Lowenstein Fine Arts Gallery in Wynwood. Diaz, who was born in Miami, moved back to Miami in 2001 from San Francisco. A three-month internship in early 2003 at the Rubell Family Collection gave him an intensive course in curating and contemporary art. During Art Basel Miami Beach in 2003, he introduced a curatorial project called Worm-Hole Laboratory in his modest apartment near downtown Miami. He later became a curator at the Bass Museum in Miami Beach before his career moved ahead to other cities. Currently, Diaz is the Susan Brotman Deputy Director for Art of the Seattle Art Museum. He's held previous positions at the Andy Warhol Museum and Tate Liverpool.

In 2006, the executive director of the nonprofit Locust Projects, South African–born Claire Breukel, articulated the good and bad effects wrought by Art Basel Miami Beach. The good? "Art is being bought. Artists are able to work as professionals and make a living." The bad? "I would like to see less emphasis on the commercialization of art [so that] people will look again at the quality and not just the market value. The commercial aspects may be taking over a little too much and becoming very trend based." Breukel heads the Zeitz Museum of Contemporary Art Africa's international patron program, which includes American Friends of Zeitz Museum of Contemporary Art Africa (AFOZM). As an art professional, she is also a curator and writer.

Lawyer Carolina García in 2006 directed LegalArt, a nonprofit organization providing artists access to affordable legal services and seminars for professional development. She came to Miami because the University of Miami School of Law ran a clinical program for fostering economic redevelopment. "The first year of Art Basel Miami Beach was my first year of law school," she said. "The impact of Basel on the art community is why LegalArt grew at such a huge pace," she added. In 2016, she was appointed CEO of the National Young Arts Foundation, a prominent arts organization in Miami recognized for cultivating young teenage artists. She is now Carolina García Jayaram. As founding CEO of the Elevate the Prize Foundation, she has significantly expanded efforts to create a nonprofit organization with international reach. But her ties to Miami's art community remain strong. She codirects the University of Miami School of Law's Master of Laws Program in Sports, Arts, + Entertainment Law.

In 2007, I interviewed art collector Howard Farber for "Howard Farber: The Eye of the Collector." He was a relatively new face in Miami but committed to the contemporary art of Cuba. That year the University Press of Florida published *Cuba Avant-Garde: Contemporary Cuban Art from the Farber Collection*, coinciding with an exhibit of the Farber collection at University of Florida's Harn Museum of Art.

The first time Farber set foot in Cuba was in 2001. It was an odd introduction to the island. Stepping off the plane in Havana, he and wife Patricia carried shopping bags nearly bursting with foot powder from a Walgreens pharmacy in Manhattan. Patricia, a New York City patron of ballet, was bringing much-needed supplies for the foot-sore ballet dancers of Cuba.

Farber at the time was a collector of American modernist art and contemporary art from China. Although the couple went to Havana for a tour of Cuban art and architecture organized by the Metropolitan Museum of Art in New York, Farber insisted on that trip, "No art. I am not buying any art. I am totally involved with Chinese art." That attitude quickly changed as the hardcore art collector discovered adventurous art in Cuba. He wondered how contemporary works came to not only exist but thrive in the communist nation.

A natural-born raconteur, Farber told of his change of heart while sitting at the dining table in his Miami Beach apartment, where he and Patricia were living part time.

Farber's zealous devotion to Cuban art led to the creation of a valuable online resource. The Howard and Patricia Farber Foundation established Cuban Art News, a free database of some 850 stories with photos, videos, and interviews. In 2020, the Farbers announced the conclusion of Cuban Art News, although its archives can be found online at https://cubanartnewsarchive.org/category/for-collectors/.

In 2022, *Barron's* reported that the Farber collection of Cuban art would be sold at Christie's auction of Latin American art. "The Farbers have been on a mission to assemble a world-class collection devoted to recent art from

Cuba from the mid-1980s through present," Marysol Nieves, a specialist in Latin American art at Christie's, said in a statement. "The results rival those of any museum collection and are evident in this amazing group of works that will be offered."

From 2005 to 2007, local recognition came to internationally known artists with deep ties to Miami. Félix González-Torres and Nam June Paik spent their final days in nearby locations, but 10 years apart.

In 2006, I wrote a *Miami Herald* obituary for Paik, "Nam June Paik: Video Artist Found Refuge in South Florida," to provide local context to the abundant coverage his death received. Paik, hailed as the inventor of video art, died at age 73 in Miami Beach, where he'd kept a part-time residence for years, in addition to his home and studio in New York. His health had been failing following a stroke in 1996.

His legacy is vast: work in museums the world over and countless mentions in history books on 20th- and 21st-century art discussing his innovative, multifaceted legacy as a video and performance artist and composer. Not covered in many history books, however, are Paik's ties to the South Florida arts community.

In the late 1980s, Paik began coming to his Ocean Drive apartment in Miami Beach as a respite from Manhattan and his international travel, said artist César Trasobares and developer Craig Robins. South Beach hadn't yet evolved into a glamorous destination. Both men got to know him then.

"He had this amazing sharpness and clarity about what he was doing," Robins said. "I think that in many ways his work was a self-portrait of his mind," he continued. "Nam June was always operating on many circuits."

In 1988, Paik began work on projects that the county's Art in Public Places had commissioned for Miami International Airport (MIA).

Paik's MIAMI, 74 monitors stacked to spell "Miami," was created for the greeter's lobby of Concourse E; WING, created for the greeter's lobby of Concourse B. Both were installed in 1990 at MIA. The combined cost of both works was $195,000. (In 2006, neither was still working nor installed.)

For MIAMI, Paik "developed images he had taken of Miami," said Trasobares. "He composed them in his characteristic style of fast cuts and blinking images. He had his own effects—he would do images, dissolves, and an image would turn around and then disappear."

Recently, those unavailable works have been rescued from obscurity. They were part of *Nam June Paik: The Miami Years* at the Bass Museum of Art from October 4, 2023, to August 11, 2024.

This exhibit followed the Bass's recent acquisition of Paik's TV *Cello* (2003). *Nam June Paik: The Miami Years* provided an illuminating look at the artist's close ties to Miami, revealing the often obscure history of the artist's time in Miami Beach while examining his pioneering adaptation of media technologies for his art.

My June 2007 column "Félix González-Torres: A Posthumous Honor for Cuban-born Artist" looked at the Miami response when Félix González-Torres was chosen to represent the United States in the 2007 Venice Biennale.

While some in New York complained that this competitive honor went to a dead artist, in Miami there was a nearly euphoric feeling that the acclaimed Félix González-Torres, who died in Miami in 1996, was finally getting his due.

"This is a Cuban American artist representing the United States. It is a rare honor and speaks volumes about the work," said art collector and Miami Art Museum trustee Peter Menéndez, who was a close friend of the artist. "His museum exhibits are enormously popular because they connect with the public in a very quick fashion."

González-Torres was a conceptual artist who created visual poetry and gently provocative public art like billboards of simple photographs resonant with a sense of loss. He created art from strings of 15-watt light bulbs, such as *Untitled (America)*, which greeted visitors as they entered his Venice exhibit. These defiantly low-tech pieces evoke the simplicity of light and humble gatherings of friends in a diverse, divisive world.

In Venice, 12 billboards by González-Torres were scattered throughout the city as a part of his Biennale show. Miami collectors Rosa and Carlos de la Cruz, major collectors of his work, loaned their billboard of a lone bird. "Venice is a perfect city for that. It's surrounded by water, and Félix's work deals a lot with the sky and sea," said Rosa de la Cruz.

Art by González-Torres was regularly on view at the de la Cruz Collection, the private museum the de la Cruz collectors founded in Miami's Design District in 2009, until it closed permanently after Rosa's death at age 81 in February 2024. The closing sparked debate in Miami about the legacy of private museums and their place in the city's cultural ecosystem. In May

2024, an auction at Christie's of 25 works from the collection sold for $34 million, setting an auction record for González-Torres. Fetching $13 million was his *Untitled (America #3)*, a string of 15-watt bulbs and an edition of the original piece displayed in 2007 in Venice.

It is truly unfortunate that apparently there were no funds available to purchase the artist's iconic *Untitled (America #3)* in order to keep this piece in Miami, considering its historic connections to his posthumous recognition at the 2007 Venice Biennale as well as his rich legacy for artists in Miami, the Caribbean, and Latin America. In 2020, the Bass Museum acknowledged that legacy by commemorating the 25th anniversary of González-Torres's death in Miami with talks by art professionals who admired his work and the exhibit *What Remains*.

The final review in this book, "Richard Blanco and John Bailly: Poetry and Painting Combine for a Beautiful Show" in 2007, documents an inspired collaboration bringing together two exile sensibilities.

Place of Mind was a memorable collaborative show at the downtown Main Library of the Miami-Dade County Public Library System. It combined Richard Blanco's poetry with John Bailly's paintings and artworks on paper.

"It's our journey, sharing this sense of not belonging anywhere and feeling that we could belong anywhere," said Bailly.

Imagery by Bailly evoked maps of vaguely familiar coastlines and bodies of water but resisted clear nomenclature. Poetry by Blanco described a ferry cleaving the water of Boston Harbor as a metaphor for travel to uncertain destinations.

For Blanco and Bailly, those contradictory feelings that home can be anywhere and nowhere arise from their very Miami, very multicultural backgrounds. Bailly was born in England and grew up in France. "When I came to the US, I could only read and write 'cat' in English. With my French family, I've always been the American. With my American family, I'm always French, never fitting in anywhere."

Blanco's personal experience echoed Bailly's. "I'm a mutt like him," the poet said. His mother left Cuba for Spain when she was several months pregnant. Blanco was born in Madrid. After barely a month, his family moved to New York and later to Miami. "I was five years old when I came to Miami." He added, "I don't feel Cuban, I don't feel European, I don't feel American."

Their talents continue to shape Miami's cultural life with national and international impact.

Chosen by President Barack Obama to be the fifth Presidential Inaugural Poet in 2013, Blanco was the youngest as well as the first Latinx, immigrant, and gay person in that position. In 2023, President Joe Biden awarded him the National Humanities Medal from the National Endowment for the Humanities. In 2022, he became the first Poet Laureate of Miami-Dade County.

Bailly is a French American artist and Faculty Fellow of the Honors College at Florida International University. As the inaugural McCormick Art Fellow, he spent four years as a resident artist at the Deering Estate. That residency culminated in the 2022 exhibit *In Situ*, a series of paintings and drawings inspired by the estate's natural and Indigenous history, curated by Melissa Diaz. Since 2006, the Deering Estate has presented imaginative arts programs, a further example of Greater Miami's increased cultural offerings following the arrival of Art Basel Miami Beach in 2002. Among those offerings at the Deering Estate are historical and contemporary art exhibits, concerts, and an on-site artist residency.

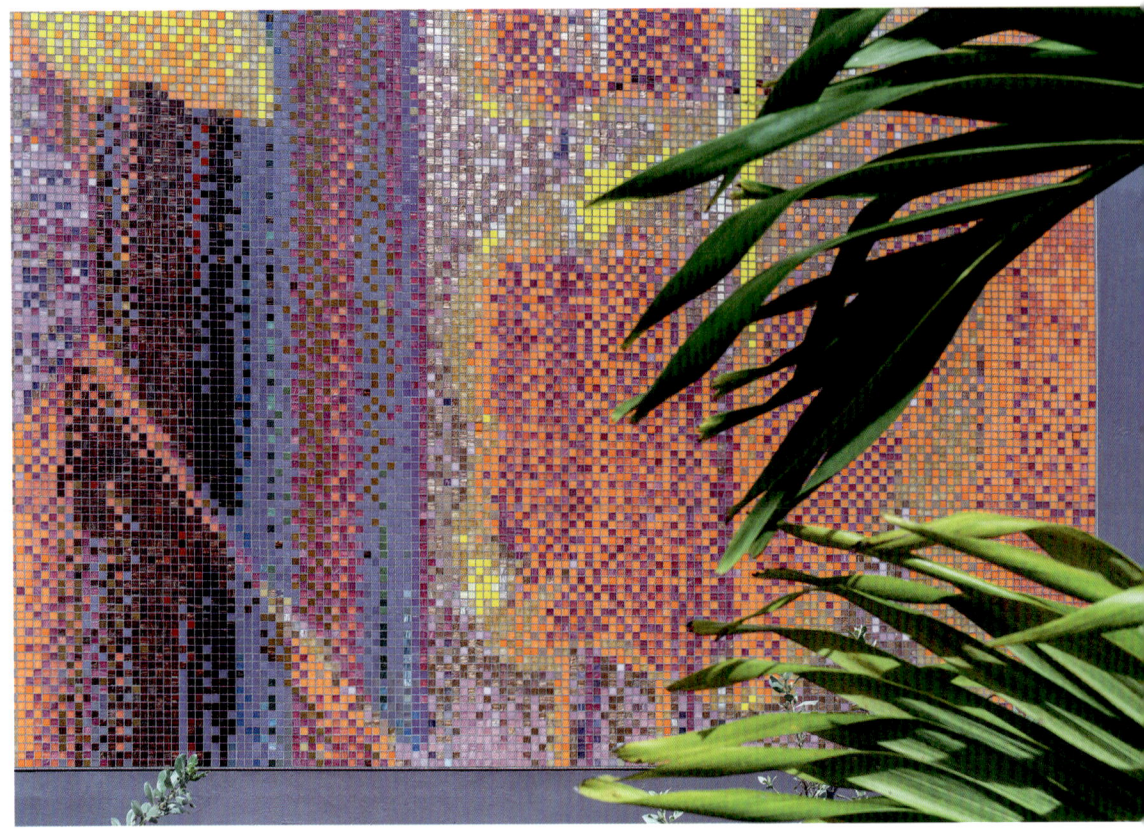

FIGURE 38. Cristina Lei Rodriguez, *Homegrown*, 2022. Vitreous glass mosaic tile. Westchester Cultural Arts Center, exterior facade, 7930 SW 40th St. Image Zachary Balber, courtesy of Miami-Dade County Department of Cultural Affairs, Art in Public Places Trust.

GLOBAL ART LOCALLY

Rubells Collect 10 Miami Artists

June 26, 2005

A dreamy sense of wanderlust and fantasy fused with out-of-control plant life pervades *At This Time: 10 Miami Artists* from the Rubell Family Collection.

Chiefly installed in the second-floor galleries of the handsomely expanded Rubell Family Collection in Wynwood, this inventive if hardly comprehensive mix of memorable art made in Miami rubs shoulders with the international group of contemporary artists that the Rubell family collects.

In an interview one morning last week, longtime collectors Don and Mera Rubell acknowledged that the current show of Miami artists was something of an accident. But it was, it seems, an accident waiting to happen.

"It was not our intent to put together Miami artists," Don Rubell said. "They put themselves together."

As they speak, the couple is sitting in the collection's new library, where a formidable collection of 30,000 books and exhibition catalogs on 20th- and 21st-century art line the shelves. And they are musing about how the accident of this Miami show happened.

A previous show based on work from their collection, *Life after Death: New Paintings from the Rubell Family Collection* that's now at the Massachusetts Museum of Contemporary Art, provided some of the impetus to look at the Miami artists they've collected over the years. *Life after Death* examines work made by a group of artists working in Leipzig, Germany. These relatively young artists have amassed extraordinary attention.

Critic Gregory Volk, writing in the June/July issue of *Art in America*, acknowledges that their attention could partly be explained by the excessive hype the art world now heaps on young artists but believes that in this case, that hype is deserved. He finds their art "fresh" and full of "meaningful" innovations.

"In order for a city to function [as a place that nurtures a group of artists], you have to have energy coming in from the outside. That was something we learned in the Leipzig show," said Don.

"For us, it's important that when we hang a show, it teaches us. It's not a pedantic exercise," Mera said.

The Rubells see Miami as a "petri dish."

"The concerns [of Miami artists] are not local but global," said Don. "Not all of them have found their voice in an equal fashion, but they are all on their way."

The artists in *At This Time* are Hernan Bas, José Bedia, Cooper, Naomi Fisher, Mark Handforth, Jiae Hwang, Norberto (Bert) Rodriguez, Cristina Lei Rodriguez, and Purvis Young. The show is curated by collection director Mark Coetzee. As part of this exhibit, two performance pieces by Pablo Cano, *Animated Altarpieces* and *The Pursuit of Love*, composed of about a dozen sculptural elements, were staged in the private museum's sculpture garden when this show opened in mid-May.

Bedia's *Naufragios* (*Shipwrecked*) is an impressively detailed installation greeting visitors in the first gallery on their left when they enter the building. It's art that makes you stop in your tracks. As you look at the gallery it occupies before walking inside this room, you puzzle over Bedia's dramatic murals of black antelope-like creatures on two of the three walls. They recall the painted animal hides of the Plains Native Americans that have long fascinated the artist. Bedia's black-on-white wall paintings blend his signature jut-jawed male figure with long-limbed animals that bristle with actual horns.

The installation should be seen in one dramatic look all at once and then explored as you investigate its small nuances bit by bit. It becomes an ever-expanding altar to the cross-cultural Afro-Cuban spirits and ceremonies that have played such a major role in Bedia's art.

It is also an ode to lives lost at sea making the dangerous ocean crossing from Cuba to the United States, and in the back of the installation, there's a tiny altar, with the classic offering of a glass of water. The installation is made with the remains of a rafter-less raft, full of faded long-sleeved jackets, that the artist found washed ashore here. This piece recalls a time when stories about ill-fated crossings were almost daily news.

First installed here in 1996, *Naufragios* constructs various forms of transportation, evoking a passage both physical and spiritual.

There's a plane bombarded with arrows, a black-painted model steamboat, and a kayak. With its tough reminders of loss and change, this is a fluid, even fierce, meditation on travel and immigration at various times and at various places. For this reinstallation, Coetzee says he often finds small offerings, like wrapped candies, that visitors have left behind.

The rest of *At This Time* continues upstairs. There are over a dozen works by Bas and Fisher each, as well as a small gallery dedicated to Young. Highlights from the exhibit:

Purvis Young: With a floor-to-ceiling presentation of his paintings on splintered wood and found objects, the works depict a claustrophobic universe of figures with large and luminous heads, the profile of a very pregnant woman, rows of chunky trucks, and the squiggles of color that almost always roil their way into rearing stallions—symbols, Young once suggested, of defiant opposition to Miami's decayed neighborhoods.

Mark Handforth: An altarpiece of a more secular sort is represented in *Honda*. It shows a Honda motorscooter laid on its side, as if suddenly abandoned, and streaming with dripping residues of candle wax in blue, orange, yellow, and other bright colors. Lighted candles continue to add to tumbling ribbons of candle wax. It makes for a bizarre juxtaposition—a found vehicle of zippy modern speed nearly smothered by the remains of time-honored devices linked to light and spiritual sustenance.

Hernan Bas: There's a huge representation here, from his works on paper and canvas to two installations each given their own gallery. Not to be missed is his *Fragile Moments*, an installation with two DVD projections that flashes by affecting black-and-white scenes of running children, the tattered windblown sails of a boat-shaped kite, and lethargic young men swimming and swooning. It's accompanied by strains of "Sunrise, Sunset" as if played on a music box.

With its unexpected jostle from image to image, the piece manages to turn back the tide of sentimentality that threatens to wash over it. In his romantic way of depicting boyish same-sex lovers, Bas exploits an excessively sweet tendency only to give it a curious new edge, danger, and beauty. *The Swan*

Prince is a lavish, deliberately over-the-top painting, oddly replete with fairy tale fantasy and joy as well as the ominous threats lurking in travel by water.

Naomi Fisher: Fisher's photographs look good with the charged sensuality of Bas's work, and they also go with the two sculptures by Cristina Lei Rodriguez that are included in this show. Fisher's forte is showing us flesh entangled—either outrageously adorned, as in her *Assy Flora Suite*, or trampled and nearly strangled, as in the series *You Can't Fight Mutha Nature*—with over-the-top excesses of tropical flora.

Cristina Lei Rodriguez: The sculptor's distinctive work is a hectic mix of plastic and sparkly lights. They convulse together in streams of acid yellow and fake cacti, tropical vegetation, and artificial birds. In *Experimental Garden (Desert)*, these forms collide in a white plastic trough, like fabulous residues clogging a rain gutter saturated with summer's torrential rains. Both Fisher and Lei Rodriguez seem to be pointing out a tropical tendency for dazzle and destruction.

Art by Jiae Hwang, Norberto (Bert) Rodriguez, and Cooper seems less fixated on Miami's glamour. Rodriguez's series of the same photo of the artist talking on a cell phone, neatly packaged in identical plastic-wrapped frames, shows a cool guy, but turned into a mass-produced sample that is not cool at all.

Cooper: The installation is as difficult as its paragraph-long title, beginning with a cot, large tubes, videos and medical devices and supplies, it explores a visceral journey, apparently through the digestive tract, but the mythic resonances here are cloudy.

Jiae Hwang: Blithe pencil drawings on blue graph paper from her series *I Am the Real Princess of the Magical Land* deftly show simple drawings, wrought with a wistful but knowing determination, that speak of more sophistication than the schoolgirlish airs they only seem to assume.

In memoriam: Purvis Young, 1943–2010
Mark Coetzee, d. 2022

BARBARA YOUNG

Art Mobile Librarian Hits the Road

July 27, 2005

After almost 30 years of nurturing and championing Miami's visual arts community, Barbara Young has reached the end of her to-do list, but not the end of a rich and generous legacy she started in 1976 as the county's first Art Mobile librarian.

Young, 62, retires on Friday as art services supervisor of the Miami-Dade Public Library System. About a week before, she walked a visitor through the three current exhibits she has organized for the Main Library at 101 W. Flagler Street, the last of many, many library exhibits that she has organized since the late 1970s.

The variety of these current exhibits reflects her open-minded spirit: *Tools and Shrouds*, a show of achingly direct black-and-white photographs by recent Fulbright fellow and Barry University art professor Stephen Althouse, a gathering of vintage toy robots from the collection of Miami gallery owner Fred Snitzer, and a selection of six vibrantly hand-beaded "paintings" stretched on vinyl in *Gerald Winter: Homemade Fantasies, Paintings, and Other Things*.

"I have always wanted to show Winter's work," she says. "This is one of the last things on my to-do list. His beaded pieces are mind-boggling."

Her depth of knowledge about the art scene here is mind-boggling too. "Every now and then I run into people who were his students," she says of Winter, an artist who retired from the University of Miami several years ago. And she casually mentions that one of Winter's students was Michael Spring, now director of the Miami-Dade County Department of Cultural Affairs.

"She has always been there as the most incredible cheerleader for the artists," says Miami-based artist Carol Brown. "I have to appreciate her genuine attempts at bringing art to literally everybody and to make it more accessible."

"Barbara's exposed us to art we wouldn't have seen," adds Raymond Santiago, director of the Miami-Dade County Public Library System. "She's been instrumental in bringing exhibitions here, recently from Italy and Latin America."

Though Young had always vowed not to follow in her mother's footsteps and become a librarian, she began working here after attending library school. She already had a degree in art history. Her first library job involved planning shows for the just-acquired Art Mobile, a hard-to-miss van covered with wild zebra stripes and luscious tropical flowers. With a small staff, she took the Art Mobile to schools, shopping centers, and branch libraries. In its busiest year, she had 60,000 visitors.

"The interior looked like a little gallery. There weren't so many museums here then," she recalls. "We would talk with the kids, let them ask questions. We always carried original work.... The Christos [artists Christo and Jeanne-Claude, whom Young befriended when they created *Surrounded Islands* in Biscayne Bay in 1983] did a show with us."

When Young started, one of the very few places Miami artists could show their work was the library. She helped Purvis Young (no relation). One Purvis Young show predated the current Main Library building, which opened to the public in 1985. "We had Purvis do a huge painting all over the walls of [the] auditorium," she says.

She also curated special thematic shows, encouraging artists to submit and even create new work on a certain subject. "In experimenting for those shows, I did something I would probably not have done otherwise," says Brown.

Among Young's favorite shows: *Boat Images from South Florida Collections* and *Becalmed in Miami* in 1995 and *All God's Children Got Shoes* in 1999.

During her tenure, Young also developed the library's art collection—now around 2,000 works—and its extensive files on Miami's growing art scene.

"She is so sensitive to artists and to everything about the creative process," says retired *Herald* art critic Helen L. Kohen. "I don't think anybody is unaware of the library and its backing of artists.... She's opened the eyes of other curators in town because of it."

In her retirement, Young plans to do lots of reading—something she thought she would do when she first started at the library. She and her husband, artist Robert Huff, will divide their time between Miami and a home in rural western Virginia. Her successor is library curator Denise Delgado.

In memoriam:
Purvis Young, 1943–2010
Robert Huff, 1945–2014
Helen Kohen, 1931–2015
Jeanne-Claude, 1935–2009
Christo, 1935–2020
Gerald Winter, 1933–2023

TERESA DIEHL

Exploring Allure, Gray Areas of Fleeting Childhood Memory

October 2, 2005

Teresa Diehl's new installation at Bernice Steinbaum Gallery pulls the viewer into the sweet, sharp seductions of childhood memories.

In her video and photos, you see the rich emotional and tactile spectrum of our formative years as human beings, from babies nursing and bathing to children consuming sweets and giggling at party games. Diehl's telling sense of composition, which pairs intense close-ups of fleshy encounters with an abrupt sense of narrative, keeps this work from lapsing into the cloying and obvious.

As they unfold in the six DVDs in this exhibit, *The Return of Pleasure, a Video, Sound, and Photo Installation*, most of her images slowly swim into focus. Or not.

The show "is based on reconstructed and fictional memories," the Miami artist says. "There are certain moments that we think happened. We have seen that moment somewhere. Is it my moment, or did somebody else put it in there for me? In that sense, memory is a kind of game."

Diehl drew closely on her memories of growing up in Venezuela. In

Daydreams, a series of three DVDs projected on three screens in the middle of the gallery, there are glimpses of a girl playing games with other children. The games include "Blind Chicken," which Diehl says was a common game played in Latin America when she was growing up. A child is blindfolded, spun around to become disoriented, then feels the faces of the other children to try to identify them.

"If you identify the person, you win the game. The crazy thing is that for winning, you often get a little baby chick," she says. "The minute you went home, the little chick died, and you were crying. It was a total contradiction. We work for things and then they are taken away. It's that little line between the innocence and darkness that I am so intrigued with," she adds.

Diehl immerses her audience in negotiating these precarious spaces.

Take *Giggle Balls*, a set of spheres covered with soft white synthetic fur and suspended from the ceiling in a darkened corridor in front of the gallery's desk. To see the rest of the show, you must walk through them. As you walk through them, they emit odd sounds of childish laughter and bounce awkwardly off your face and body.

Grouped in another corner are her *Merengue Balls*, playful but slightly disconcerting spheres covered with vanilla-colored silicone. They could be thorns or perhaps luscious drips of sugared icing.

That sense of discomforting beauty is memorably captured in *Cream*. Its strange undercurrent of sexuality appears in a photograph of a finger nearly smothered by a river of white icing as a tongue moves close to lick it.

Childhood and its parties end, but in this show, their memories may unsettle for years.

MUSEUM OF CONTEMPORARY ART

Made in Miami

October 9, 2005

What a difference a decade makes.

With MOCA *and Miami*, the Museum of Contemporary Art in North Miami launches its 10th anniversary season. MOCA's elegant building designed by Charles Gwathmey with Jose Gelabert-Navia, with high-ceilinged galleries that can contract or expand to accommodate the diverse needs of contemporary art, actually opened to the public just shy of a decade ago, in February 1996.

Over the years, the area's art scene has undergone its own dramatic expansion in that decade, particularly since the first Art Basel Miami Beach in 2002.

A few years before the acclaimed international art fair set down its first roots outside of Basel, Switzerland, however, there were excited stirrings of a solid interest in contemporary art in this community. MOCA contributed in large measure to that interest.

"Obviously, Miami is a hot scene," Lowery Sims told the *Herald* in January 1999, when the then-curator with New York's Metropolitan Museum of Art was here for Art Miami.

"We are in a crossover time, and Miami is a crossover place," Samuel Keller told the *Herald*, also in January 1999. Keller, who now directs Art Basel Miami Beach, was here as an Art Basel spokesman to check out Miami Beach as a site for a future art fair.

Beginning with the late 1990s, more talented artists were starting to work here. A few of them took the area's meager exhibition opportunities into their own hands. Eugenia Vargas, who represented her native Chile at the Venice Biennale in 2003, occasionally hosted *Home Shows*, inviting artists to transform every corner of her home into an impromptu gallery. Some artists also set up edgy exhibition spaces in low-rent neighborhoods north of downtown.

Internationally admired art collectors Don and Mera Rubell bought a former DEA warehouse in Miami's Wynwood neighborhood to house their remarkable collection of contemporary art. The Rubell Family Collection opened to the public in 1996. Soon after, important Wynwood pioneers Dorsch Gallery and Locust Projects set up shop. In December 2002, the Margulies Collection at the Warehouse, a Wynwood warehouse showing the significant holdings of collector Martin Z. Margulies, began holding public hours.

MOCA and its predecessor, the much smaller COCA, North Miami's Center for Contemporary Art, helped foster this community's interest in the art of our time and our place. With its distinctive building opening in 1996, MOCA could do much more in that arena, and it has.

By the museum's count, it has shown over 50 Miami artists. "When we showed them, nobody cared. Most of them didn't even have galleries," says MOCA director Bonnie Clearwater. The museum has organized eight solo shows of Miami artists and commissioned eight annual productions with the startling marionette sculptures of Miami's Pablo Cano, whose work is included in this show. MOCA has also provided important opportunities for artists here to interact with nationally and internationally known artists it exhibits.

MOCA *and Miami*, featuring 29 artists, is a show to reflect upon the astonishing leaps in quality and quantity that we've witnessed in this town's visual arts community. The catalog for this exhibit, with an essay by Clearwater, records critical developments in the art scene during this past decade and in the 1990s.

In the early 1990s, Miami was the new home for several '80s generation Cuban artists, like José Bedia, who had received international attention while in Cuba for their spirited art. In the late 1990s, however, artists trained in Miami, like Naomi Fisher, began to emerge.

"Miami is no longer a New York outpost. A lot of people still believe that, but it has matured into its own," Peter Doroshenko told the *Herald* in July 2000, when he was here to speak at MOCA about projects developed by an international team of curators.

Doroshenko then directed the Institute of Visual Art (INOVA) at the University of Wisconsin-Milwaukee. Later that year, INOVA gave Fisher her first museum solo show.

MOCA *and Miami* is the third major show organized by this museum to give us a sweeping look at art produced here. The first was *Defining the Nineties: Consensus-Making in New York, Miami, and Los Angeles*, the museum's inaugural exhibit in February 1996. The second was *Making Art in Miami: Travels in Hyperreality* in December 2000.

Sixteen artists from *Making Art in Miami* are shown in MOCA. The show, says Clearwater, is limited to artists whose works are in MOCA's collection. The show includes artists who had their first museum solo show at MOCA. One of these is Hernan Bas, who showed an installation and drawings at MOCA in 2002. Demand for his work skyrocketed after he was tapped for the 2004 Biennial at New York's Whitney Museum of American Art. In the show is Bas's painting *The Sea Nymphs*, a lush example of his richly textured, gender-bending work that spins fantasy narratives, often based on watery journeys.

MOCA *and Miami* is an embarrassment of riches. There is thoughtful, challenging, disappointing, and defiant work being made in Miami. You can find much of it—but by no means all of it—in the current exhibit.

Two installations begin this show. One is *Standing Still While Moving across Land*, a mixed-media installation with ultraviolet light, by John Espinosa. It shows a flock of garishly colored birds connected by thin rods that resemble neon tubes but are actually coated with fluorescent paint. The piece somehow pulses with frozen energy.

The second is *Cargo Cult* by Bedia. It shows two adjacent walls painted to evoke the gray hulk of a battleship at sea. One wall is punctuated with nautical flags bearing abstract, painterly splashes of blue, perhaps a bemused comment on the purely formal art Bedia avoids. It incorporates an altar linked to Afro-Cuban rituals and beliefs that have long inspired Bedia's art, which has also reflected Native American lore and primal, non-Western rituals found across the globe. The piece is about problematic exchanges between developed and developing countries, when ancient spiritual beliefs intersect in odd ways with Western capitalism.

It's strong and affecting work but does fall short of the passionate vigor animating *Naufragios* from 1996 at the Rubell Family Collection and *Mi Coballende*, made for the Art Museum at Florida International University in 1999.

You'll find video and film here, especially works that show women in

357

Global Art
Locally,
2005–2007

aggressive roles, such as Dara Friedman's luminous *Bim Bam* and *Friend or Foe* by Beatriz Monteavaro, based on her reinvented action figures. The video *Not My Mama* by Ali Prosch smartly uses B-movie styles to reshape Earth Mother myths.

Painting and sculpture are here in good measure. Drawings, especially, stand out. There's an untitled portrait, rough and gorgeous, in red ink on Mylar by Fisher. Daniel Arsham's series of gouaches on Mylar, such as *Blueprint for a City in Ruin 1*, are finely imagined meditations on decay and surviving remnants.

We'll be watching for the next chapter in the saga of MOCA *and Miami* when the museum opens its annex at the Goldman Warehouse in Wynwood on December 1.

NAM JUNE PAIK

Video Artist Found Refuge in South Florida

February 5, 2006

Last week Nam June Paik, hailed as the inventor of video art, died at age 73 in Miami Beach, where he'd kept a part-time residence for years, in addition to his home and studio in New York. His health had been failing following a stroke in 1996.

His legacy is vast: work in museums the world over and countless mentions in history books on 20th- and 21st-century art discussing his innovative, multifaceted legacy as a video and performance artist and composer. Not covered in many history books, however, are Paik's ties to the South Florida arts community.

"Even though [Paik] was in many respects a superstar, he never had a superstar kind of attitude," says developer Craig Robins, who came to know Paik in the late '80s and early '90s. "He had a genuine affection for the energy [in Miami]."

One of Paik's distinctively startling works, with its flashing use of video and vintage television sets, is now on view at MOCA at Goldman Warehouse, a Wynwood satellite of the Museum of Contemporary Art in North Miami.

Burn Calories, Not Octane, a 1993 robot-like sculpture with digital laser discs, is part of the museum's ongoing show of selections from its permanent collection.

"It's a fantastic piece, among people's favorites," said MOCA director Bonnie Clearwater. "*Burn Calories, Not Octane* makes so much sense with our collection and exhibition history. Next year we're doing a major retrospective of Merce Cunningham's collaboration with visual artists," she says. "This work has stacks of old radios and televisions, and some of the images flashing constantly are of John Cage and Merce Cunningham. He worked with both those artists."

In the late 1980s, Paik began coming to his Ocean Drive apartment in Miami Beach as a respite from Manhattan and his international travel, says artist César Trasobares and developer Craig Robins. South Beach hadn't yet evolved into a glamorous destination. Both men got to know him then.

"He had this amazing sharpness and clarity about what he was doing," Robins says. "[But] you never knew where he was coming from. There was a process of deciphering what he would say. Order and disorder. I think that in many ways his work was a self-portrait of his mind," he continues. "Nam June was always operating on many circuits."

In 1988, Paik began work on projects that the county's Art in Public Places had commissioned for Miami International Airport, while Trasobares was executive director of the Art in Public Places program. Robins served on the program's board in the late '80s and early '90s.

Paik's MIAMI—74 monitors stacked to spell "Miami"—was created for the greeter's lobby of Concourse E and WING for the greeter's lobby of Concourse B. Both were installed in 1990 at Miami International Airport. The combined cost of both works was $195,000. (Neither is still working nor installed.)

For MIAMI, Paik "developed images he had taken of Miami," says Trasobares. "He composed them in his characteristic style of fast cuts and blinking images. He had his own effects—he would do images, dissolves, and an image would turn around and then disappear." The piece "was always meant to be played at the exit from Customs, so as people would arrive, they would encounter this work with images of Miami."

Miami-based artist Ali Prosch—whose video, photography, and drawings were shown recently at Wynwood's Rocket Projects—says that Paik remains an important figure to young artists who regularly study him in art school. "I was just looking online at some work he did with these laser things, and I thought, 'Man, he's really on point.' He definitely still influences artists. I've been thinking about him a lot, as I think of new projects with installation and video."

In memoriam: Nam June Paik, 1932–2006

WITH 65 ARTISTS, THE BAKEHOUSE IS COOKING

May 1, 2006

In its two-decade history, the Bakehouse Art Complex in Wynwood has survived sea salt corroding the concrete pillars in its sprawling 1920s building and the perils of a decaying neighborhood beset by crime and now by startling earmarks of gentrification: quaint coral rock bungalows chockablock with art galleries, vintage warehouses, museums, and traffic-snarling construction.

Now the Bakehouse enjoys a run in popularity with South Florida artists. All space is spoken for among the dozens of affordable art studios lining its 33,000-square-foot building located on 2½ acres on Northwest 32nd Street.

"We are experiencing 100 percent occupancy for the last year and a half, which is something we did not experience too often prior to that," says Doris Meltzer, executive director of the Bakehouse.

Currently, 65 artists rent studios in the Bakehouse. Studios start at $200 a month, she says, and their size ranges from 250 to 900 square feet.

Artists and their art are all over this aging, retrofitted bakery. It is a unique and vital cultural resource. Yet few members of the public find their way to its studios and gallery, which was renovated in the fall of 2005. The expanded, approximately 4,500-square-foot Bakehouse exhibition space—the size of a small museum gallery—now boasts handsome new lighting.

Lights shine on the current unusual and historically reflective show. It is the visual arts portion of a two-part exhibit *"And you thought you brought it with you . . .": Art and Culture in Miami Before 1980*. A smaller gallery space nearby highlights playbills, costumes, photographs, museum catalogs, gallery announcements, and other items recording the city's early cultural life in music, opera, theater, dance, and the visual arts. The scope of this gathering, curated by board president Robert Apfel, astonishes.

The opening reception for the exhibit in early April "was like seeing old friends. It brought back a lot of memories," says Coral Gables dealer Virginia Miller, who's had a gallery here since 1974. Other veteran dealers attending the opening, she said, were Barbara Gillman and Gloria Luria, as well as artists in the show like Bob Huff, Louis Ullman, and Jim Couper. Notices in this smaller exhibit document important early shows in these early galleries as well as those of Dorothy Blau.

During the December influx of art-loving visitors, when Miami was crawling with high-profile collectors and museum curators in town for Art Basel Miami Beach 2005 and its satellite art fairs, the Bakehouse stayed relatively quiet. Meltzer draws a blank when asked to name an out-of-town museum group that has toured the Bakehouse in the past six months.

"I think usually when out-of-towners come in, they want to see what's hot, of the moment. The Bakehouse has had a long history of maintaining itself and providing space for artists. It has never sprung up on the radar as something that's hot, that you've got to see," says Westen Charles, a cofounder of Locust Projects, the well-regarded and edgy artist-run alternative art space in Wynwood since 1998.

"Are curators coming to the Bakehouse to look for artists? Not as frequently as we'd like," says Meltzer. That's one of the reasons for the current two-part exhibit.

It has generated sales for the artists, she says. To see both shows, you walk past studios whose outer walls display artwork, much of it paintings, some interesting and others bland and derivative.

Meltzer would like more visitors. "We do not get the attention that we feel is deserving of an institution that has been in the community for 20 years, that has managed to keep its head above water, no matter what the situation was with funding for the arts," she says. "We wanted to do something that would bring people out who have not been coming out."

The effort is in some ways sadly ironic. To call attention to its artists and their work, the Bakehouse has put together a show about the Miami art scene that predates the Bakehouse.

As a collection of affordable art studios, the Bakehouse Art Complex held an open house in May 1986 while renovations continued on the building, a former bakery standing vacant in the early 1980s; it was fully open in February 1987, according to *Miami Herald* archives. Visionaries Helene Pancoast and Faith Atlass found the finances to make it happen.

SURPRISING EXHIBIT

The current art show, curated by Meltzer, is strong. It will surprise some visitors. It includes a loan from the Norton Museum of Art—*The Understanding*—an oil painting by Jill Cannady, who worked here for years before relocating to Deland. Cannady's ultrarealistic rendering of satiny fabric falling in folds from a woman's lacy gown briefly recalls John Singer Sargent's lush turn-of-the-20th-century portraits of society women.

From this exhibit, you see that Miami was not a hotbed for experimental work—for exciting innovations in the once-spanking-new media of manipulated photography, video, and installation art—but for years there have been solid, professional artists at work here in painting, sculpture, and printmaking. In painting, you could find realism by Louis Ullman and abstraction by Robert McKnight.

Around 1980, the late Enrique Castro-Cid was a pioneer in computer graphics. Few photographers are represented. Black-and-white photography prevails, as it did at the time. There's the geometric, elegant 1950s *Palm Frond* by little-known Klara Farkas and a portrait of Orson Welles with cigar by the established Timothy Greenfield-Sanders, on loan from veteran Miami collectors Ruth and Richard Shack.

Not all artists here are represented by their signature work. Couper is known for painterly views of glinting light in the Everglades. Yet here we see a self-portrait of Couper, with handlebar mustache, in his intimate painting *Family Portrait* of 1978.

Humberto Calzada, who has since churned out kitschy nostalgic views of Cuban colonial architecture layered with watery reflections of itself, is represented by a mercifully less tortured painting, *Mampara*, depicting colorful fan-shaped windows.

20 YEARS

The visual arts portion of the show comes with a lavishly illustrated catalog. It contains a fascinating timeline of culture in Miami, beginning in 1896, when the city was founded. An essay by Dorothy Jenkins Fields tells of African American culture in Miami before the civil rights movement. Essays by retired *Miami Herald* art critic Helen L. Kohen, consultant to the Vasari Project at Miami-Dade County Public Library System, and by Lilia Fontana focus on Miami art history.

This is a valuable historical document. It does have a major error: it reproduces the show's playful silk-screened print, *Rainbow City*, a semiabstract composition of clouds and curvy stripes, by Robert Huff, who is incorrectly listed as dead since 1971. Huff, one of some 50 artists in this show, continues to exhibit in Miami. He produces far more weighty sculptures, on exhibit this April at Edge Zones in Wynwood.

For its 10th anniversary, the Bakehouse suffered grim finances. "We could definitely go belly-up," Bakehouse artist Matt Zbornik told the *Miami Herald* in 1998. With the help of the Miami-Dade County Cultural Affairs Council, board members and artists rallied the institution.

"We are and have been for three years totally in the black," says Meltzer. The annual budget is close to $300,000. Soon to come: a capital campaign for at least $1 million to fund major renovations to the building.

Previously, board president Apfel had spoken to the *Herald* of ideas for making the Bakehouse a more vibrant, active member of the arts community engaged with its surroundings. One idea was to have local collectors sponsor Bakehouse residencies for out-of-town artists they collect.

Those residencies haven't happened. The Bakehouse remains somewhat removed from the percolating art scene in Miami that's gaining more international attention. It takes money and energy just to keep this unique art complex running.

"It isn't that we wouldn't like to maybe do a residency . . . but what we have been able to do is cater to a very large scope of artists in many different facilities," Meltzer says. She notes that the Bakehouse has "up-and-running" facilities for artists working in ceramics, metal, and glass. "We are vast in what we cater to in the world of art."

In memoriam: Dorothy Blau, 1917–2014
Enrique Castro-Cid, 1938–1992
Robert Huff, 1945–2014
Gloria Luria, 1925–2023
James (Jim) Couper, 1937–2023

CLYDE BUTCHER

Lensman's Lyrical Trip in Cuban Countryside

March 16, 2006

Orchestrating shades that range from velvet black to silvery pewter to egret-feather white, Florida photographer Clyde Butcher bucks the bias for color photography by shooting grand views in black and white.

His current show at Art + Gallery, *Florida and the Cuban Expeditions*, takes us back to the days of superb black-and-white landscape photography by Ansel Adams in the 1930s and 1940s. Adams is revered for his majestic scenes of wilderness in the American West.

Both photographers are known for their environmental concerns. Butcher has applied Adams's illustrious example to his own well-known scenes of Florida's endangered natural landscape, especially the Everglades.

He shows us scenes of glinting wetlands, lacy stretches of cypress strands, and cottony mountains of cumulus clouds. Sometimes he treads too close to his famous predecessor.

In the show at Art +, it's not hard to see Butcher's *Moonrise, Big Cypress National Preserve* as a rip-off of Adams's *Moonrise, Hernandez, New Mexico* of 1941. The artist may argue that this work is really a homage to Adams, but I remain unconvinced. Still, the heart of this show are photographs that give us many views of rural Cuba in images that aren't as well known as his scenes of Florida. These show us forests, rivers, fields, and mountains of Cuba's countryside. It's a view of Cuba that takes us miles beyond clichéd shots of vintage American cars crowding streets in Old Havana.

These are images of a Cuban landscape that Butcher shot in 2002 and 2003. At that time, he was asked to photograph Cuba by the country's UN ambassador, Luis Gomez-Echeverri, and Naples businessman John Parke Wright IV. The request coincided with the United Nations declaring 2002 as the International Year of Mountains.

Butcher attended an environmental conference on mountainous habitats, held in the Sierra Maestra mountains of eastern Cuba. It was a meeting to draw conservationists from the Americas and the Caribbean.

Just as Adams helped people understand the raw beauty of the American West, so Butcher gives us a lyrical view of Cuba's natural treasures. He captures the silvery, silken stream of plunging waterfalls in Salto el Rocio. In *Caballete de Casa (A House Easel)* he shows a panorama of mountains rising from fields, dusted with clouds, and seen through a scattering of royal palms' slender trunks.

The filigree of a tree fern becomes a self-conscious, fan-shaped focal point in *Ancient Tree Fern*, a work that shows how the overzealous Butcher can occasionally slip from the grand to grandiose.

GLEXIS NOVOA

Drawing on Architecture

May 7, 2006

Architecture is like an alphabet for Glexis Novoa. He patiently draws the architecture of a city, capturing towers, arches, facades, and even public monuments, spelling out a story of beauty and doom.

He makes his graphite drawings on canvas, marble slabs, and plaster walls. Few people walk his city streets. A chilly silence floods their plazas and urban canyons, as rendered in the 13 works now on view at the University of Miami's Lowe Art Museum in *Glexis Novoa, Visionary Artist*.

Movement can erupt in the form of machines shaped like birds, slicing through space with needle-sharp beaks. They seem to be swift, robotic hummingbirds on a mission of stealth. You see them on their busy rounds in Novoa's *F.L.U.C. TOW (Flying Checkpoint Tower)* at the Lowe. These robotic birds dart among clusters of towers, which are drawn with their own needle-sharp spires that could be architectural ornaments, or more likely "Big Brother" antennas for transmitting messages. Looking at this drawing, as with much of his work, viewers can't help but admire the finesse and precision of these renderings, even as Novoa lures the viewer into asking questions about these imaginary, unsettling places.

Sometimes the cities seem bizarrely familiar. Could that be Seattle's landmark Space Needle in *F.L.U.C. TOW*? And why is that silhouetted figure standing on a tower with his arm raised? Is that a pose of victory or defiance? Is this person wielding a sword or another needle-sharp antenna? Or is the person a statue, balanced through a feat of engineering? Why is a bridge, vaguely reminiscent of the Brooklyn Bridge or of the Golden Gate Bridge, passing through the urban forest of towers on one side of the drawing? What is being bridged, anyway?

Novoa's delicate shading of architectural volumes contrasts with the porous, finely mottled surface of the slightly chipped marble slab on which he's made this drawing, acquired by the Lowe. For the most part, his art commands an ongoing curiosity through the way he's manipulated a delicate sense of texture and shape. Novoa layers architectural beauty with dark, bizarre suggestions of "Big Brother" devices for watching and listening.

In *Illegal Zone*, we see Miami's skyline, perhaps looking through dense vegetation on Key Biscayne. It's a view of Miami's towers shimmering with wealth and power. The viewpoint is from the water, possibly suggesting the view from an immigrant who has just made a dangerous ocean crossing. Tiny devices, like minuscule cameras for listening and watching, are barely perceptible in Novoa's drawings of branches and leaves.

In another ragged view from the water's edge, *Tsunami Day*, danger seems imminent. It's a drawing on a chipped and battered slab of marble. To recall a line from the Irish poet William Butler Yeats, Novoa makes drawings in which "a terrible beauty is born."

"You can discover a beautiful view of the city, but at the same time you feel the fear," says Novoa, talking about his work at the Lowe. "You feel a certain type of paranoia, if you get inside what is happening in the drawing."

Yeats' poetry referred to Ireland's historic Easter rebellion of 1916, a seminal event that set the stage for Irish independence from the British. Even though Yeats's poetry and Novoa's drawings are separated by decades and thousands of miles, grim reminders of war and deadly conflict form unusual links between the two kinds of art. Recalling Yeats's "terrible beauty" is a way to understand the visual contrasts that make up the strength of Novoa's art.

Two strands of ideas reflect the terrible beauty in his visionary drawings. First, Novoa, 41, grew up in totalitarian Cuba. Although a member of the island's admired "Eighties Generation" of artists whose avant-garde careers developed after Fidel Castro came to power, he finally found the island too confining and left Cuba for Mexico in 1992. In 1995, he settled in Miami. At the Lowe, several drawings, such as *La Habana Hoy* of 1998 and the more veiled *Calle 76#29B06* of 1994, do refer to Havana's hailed architecture and its eclectic mixing of colonial styles with more modern ones like art deco.

Of these two, *La Habana Hoy*, produced after Novoa left Cuba, weaves together more direct references to Havana architecture and the country's totalitarian regime. Here, you see tiny figures mysteriously marching in one direction. One figure sprawls on the ground while another tumbles out of a high window to certain death.

The artist says that he owes his fascination with architecture in part to walks he took as a child through Havana with his mother, writer Ivette Vian. As they walked, she would talk to him about the differing building styles. He recalls that once they made a special trip to see the sunrise breaking over the historic, decaying waterfront architecture of Havana's legendary Malecón.

Second, Novoa's art relates to the obsessive paranoia he and many others believe has engulfed this country since the terrorist strikes of 9/11. As the current administration wages war in Iraq, and as the "war on terror" becomes a frequent excuse for eroding civil rights, Novoa's vision is the bleak world of "terrible beauty" described in his drawings.

All but two of the works in this show were made after the strikes of 9/11 in 2001. The show includes *Untitled, New Work Miami*, from November 2001. It's a fragment of a site-specific graphite wall drawing created for his show at the Miami Art Museum. It was part of an installation that included a "panic door" for exiting the museum gallery and a free pay phone for making local and international calls. This wall drawing, with a horizon at eye level, encircled the museum gallery.

At the Lowe, we see the most dramatic part: an island crammed with finely rendered architectural and public landmarks, including an angel-like figure waving a sword. This vengeful figure, the artist explains, was inspired by a prominent patriotic statue in St. Petersburg, representing the Motherland of Russia calling her sons to war. Mysterious flying objects, like balloons or missiles, gather in force around the island. No other works in this show approach the scope and ambition of that installation.

Despite Novoa's great skills as a draftsman, he can become precious and repetitive, as in *Flamingo, FL*. He does stake out new territory in *Landscape of Events (Battering Ram)*. It's the only sculpture in the show. It shows what seems to be an industrial wheeled cart supporting a marble slab the artist purchased at a Wynwood shop. The store owners told him the marble came from the late Gianni Versace's Miami Beach mansion. With the chipped edge of the marble slab positioned at eye level and dabbed with glistening gold leaf, Novoa spells out his vision of collapsing, beautiful cities.

Here, cities crumble at the intersection of flags and weapons. The piece is meant to evoke a battering ram, with a robotic eye at the front casting a wide and terrible gaze. As with much of his work, Novoa's memory of crumbling

Havana and the World Trade Center towers informs this most recent piece, a new experiment in form.

For him, this piece looks to a bleak future and back to a glorious past. The landscape is yet another way to show, he says, "beautiful places, but in the middle of darkness, in the middle of chaos. Cuba is pretty much like this. You can see the history in the architecture [and] its beauty and at the same time you feel sadness."

ANTONI MIRALDA

Tasty Exhibit a Delightful Mix of Food and Culture

July 2, 2006

This dinner party spans 13 cities. So far, with their current stops in Miami and Coral Gables, Antoni Miralda and his collaborators are almost halfway through the cosmopolitan progressive dinner that is *Tastes & Tongues/Sabores y Lenguas*. Miami is the sixth stop on a tour that began in Caracas and will probably wind up in Barcelona, Miralda's hometown.

Much more than a far-fetched foodie extravaganza, *Tastes/Sabores* is an evolving artwork, with photographic, culinary portraits of each city. It's been shown in museums in Caracas and Bogotá and has been invited to important international art festivals in Latin America, including the Havana Biennial in June. The next stop: the São Paulo Biennial in October.

"I am behind the project as artistic director and artist, but it is a project made with all the different people. It is a collective project," says Miralda. The show was preceded by his 1998 exhibit at the Miami Art Museum, *New Work Miralda: Grandma's Recipes*, a warm-up for the more ambitious *Tastes/Sabores*.

He sighs when asked to explain the art of the exhibit. "It's always difficult, because there is not a product that people can take home as a piece of art. So they take home more a memory, and an image, or an experience." For him, art happens at the nexus of food, history, and anthropology. He prefers poking around supermarkets in Paris to galleries at the Louvre.

"CROSSING BARRIERS"

In some ways, at 64, this longtime Miami resident, who wears his thinning salt-and-pepper hair pulled back in a short ponytail, remains a child of the irreverent 1960s. He's not really interested in art with a capital *A*, secured behind velvet ropes. "I always feel an artist needs to be crossing barriers," he says. Artists "need to go through the refrigerators. They need to walk with people."

He spins artistic metaphors about cultural identity from the humble contents of refrigerators and busy street markets. In Miami's Collins Building, he laughs as he looks at the photographic portrait that *Tastes/Sabores* produced of Mexico City. Images of corn and huevos rancheros make bold splashes of red, green, and gold.

Growing up in the lean years of Franco's Spain, Miralda came of age as an artist in 1960s Paris, soaking up the revolutionary tides of the times, the populist spirit of pop art, and the street culture of happenings from that rebellious era. He made an international name for himself by staging baroque festivals that combined the three *P*'s: public art, pop art, and performance. They had almost nothing to do with the art market. In 1977, he took part in the international art festival of Documenta in Kassel, Germany, planning a parade and feast inspired by that city's statue of the mythic figure Leda. In 1992, there was the notable *Honeymoon Project* he staged around the metaphoric marriage of New York's Statue of Liberty and Barcelona's statue of Columbus.

Such art projects are seasoned with stories layering food, culture, and myth. They sparkle with puckish fun. His works have provided grand reasons to turn a traditional festival on its head or to make an old one new again.

Miralda's current project brings a latter-day pop and performance-art twist to his ongoing culinary diary of cities. He says the project offers an "urban culinary topography" deeply rooted in daily life. In each city, *Tastes/Sabores* becomes part festival, part imaginary dinner party, with giant tongue-shaped photo collages, a video, and dozens of unique objects created by inhabitants of that city. They document daily examples, mostly humble but disarming, of how food and creativity mesh.

In the project's video about Miami, on view at the Collins Building, you see a saucy sign, painted on a fish restaurant in Little Haiti, in which a leaping sailfish sports a chef's cap. In the photo collage about Miami, you see a dish of frothy Key lime pie, Publix sushi, takeout packages of Joe's Stone Crab, fried frog legs, a lavish dessert from Cacao in Coral Gables, smoked sausage from Jackson's in Overtown, ropa vieja from Versailles.

Before coming to Miami, *Tastes/Sabores* made stops in Caracas, Lima, Bogotá, Mexico City, and Havana. Next it will go to Managua, Santo Domingo, San Juan, Montevideo, Buenos Aires, and Barcelona.

In each city, Miralda and his assistants photograph the remarkable range of places where food is consumed or sold: markets, grocery stores, restaurants and bars, street corners, banquet halls, and tables in private homes. Miralda and his team have asked about 200 people in each city, many of them artists, to decorate a simple white plate in a way that somehow reflects the cultural taste of their city.

At the Collins Building in Miami's Design District, white plates are laid out on a floor to create a dazzling mosaic in a giant, tongue-shaped design. Not all plates are playful; some are left empty. They might be emblems of want in this city of haves and have-nots. In that vein, artist Duane Brant has sculpted on his plate a misshapen baby out of Wonder Bread toast. It's his riff on the scathing satire about cooking infants for poor families in Jonathan Swift's classic *A Modest Proposal*.

On his plate, artist Pablo Cano has created a rippling tower of merengue, looking like an armless Michelin Man, in homage to the merenguita his Cuban grandmother used to make. Father and daughter team Tom and Claire Austin painted a pinkish-orange wedge of pie crawling with large black ants.

Each previous venue has included a wall, like the one in the Collins Building here, painted with chalkboard paint. Sticks of chalk abound for folks to scribble their thoughts about food and art or whatever. An example here: "Say yes to life, yum!" There's a video section that flickers with photographs shot of Miami scenes, like signs for Mary's Soul Food and one for Chef Creole, the chef-capped sailfish.

VIDEOS, LATIN SONGS

At Centro Cultural Español in Coral Gables, you'll see videos playing photos from the cities *Tastes/Sabores* has already visited. In Lima, butchers hack into fleshy, raw sides of meat; in Havana, a bartender mixes mojitos leafy with mint; in Mexico City, street vendors hawk juicy oranges and pink cotton candy.

The videos flicker with always-changing images; just as you have absorbed most of the detail in a particular image, it fades away and is replaced by yet another image packed with nearly as much color as a child's exploded piñata. As the videos play, you hear a soundtrack of Latin songs about food, some dating back to the 1940s. They're songs that Miralda collects as part of the several thousand items in the archive that he and Montse Guillén, the talented chef who is his partner, are obsessively assembling in their Little Haiti warehouse, TransEAT/FoodCulture Archive. Some food-related items, gathered from local collectors, are on display there now: wooden mortars and pestles from Haiti, children's lunch boxes, vintage shirts printed with coconut palms.

At the Centro Cultural Español, one regrets the lack of contextual information about the food. Without an insider's knowledge of the food common in each city, the video for each city reads as a juicy travelogue of an unknown destination, raising more questions than it answers. Maybe that's the point—to open a dialogue, even a dinner conversation, about what really makes each city unique.

Not all of the links between food and culture have been savory. Blackboard comments in Havana railed against Cubans' meager diet. The comments were not censored, Miralda thinks, because officials were too busy running the biennial. In Caracas, he said he was censored. Officials asked him to remove items from his museum exhibit, products like pasta and milk bearing pro-Chavez slogans. "I showed some of the official products of Chavez. And they thought we were making a joke of that," he says. He agreed to remove the products, but they'll be in the catalog for the complete *Tastes/Sabores*.

In memoriam: Tom Austin, 1955–2022
Montse Guillén, 1946–2025

JOSÉ CARLOS DIAZ, CLAIRE BREUKEL, CAROLINA GARCÍA

Young at Art

September 10, 2006

Miami's emerging visual arts scene draws young professionals from more established cities, yet Miami's fine arts scene has for years suffered from brain drain, with talented artists, musicians, and playwrights moving to New York or elsewhere just when their careers are beginning to take off.

Now the thriving visual arts scene—evidenced by Art Basel Miami Beach and the spectacular growth of galleries and private museums, among other things—is beginning to draw young art professionals from outside South Florida to the area.

"Miami should be a destination for young people, whether you are a young curator or a young artist in college," says José Carlos Diaz, assistant director of Diana Lowenstein Fine Arts Gallery in Wynwood, who moved back to Miami—the city in which he was born—in 2001 from San Francisco.

Diaz is one of a growing number of young art professionals coming from New York, Chicago, and more established cities to learn everything from curating to marketing.

Says Mark Coetzee, director of the Rubell Family Collection in Wynwood, "I don't know of any other city in the world where a young artist or curator will turn their lounge [or living room] into an exhibit and the art community, collectors, and museum people will make the effort to look at what they do at least once."

The following are stories of three young art professionals who are helping bring energy to Miami's evolving art scene.

JOSÉ CARLOS DIAZ

José Carlos Diaz, 28, was born in Miami and raised in California. He moved back from San Francisco in 2001 with a degree in art history from San Francisco State University.

"My parents both love South Florida, so I sort of inherited this interest in South Florida."

When he arrived here, he did not know anything about commercial galleries and had only a passing knowledge of contemporary, cutting-edge art. In college, he says, "you learn things out of books. They don't teach you about the gallery scene."

A three-month internship in early 2003 at the Rubell Family Collection gave him an intensive course in curating and contemporary art. During Art Basel Miami Beach in 2003, he debuted a curatorial project called "Worm-Hole Laboratory" in his modest apartment near downtown Miami.

Diaz came to Miami in part because it was a familiar city but also because he finds the art community here growing and more flexible than in other more established cities.

"In San Francisco, the museums are well established, not going through the growing phases of MAM and MOCA," he says. "No private collections there are open to the public. For someone fresh out of college in San Francisco to decide to be an art curator, the odds are sort of against me. I knew I wanted to move somewhere, not sure I was ready for New York, so I came here."

When he arrived, he didn't really have a sense of what it would take to be an independent curator. "I think Miami gave me a hands-on experience," he says, noting how he got his start as the alternative exhibition spaces The House and Box were also being run by young artists. "When I started the internship [at the Rubell Family Collection], I lived on Biscayne and 22nd Street. I could walk to the galleries and could host an exhibition on an art night and have the community less than a few blocks away. It was easy to invite someone to one of my projects because they were already in the area."

Some of the artists he showed there have moved on to grander venues. The strange botanical extravaganzas of Cristina Lei Rodriguez have since been shown at the Rubell Family Collection, Galerie Emmanuel Perrotin in

Wynwood, and the Astrup Fearnley Museum of Modern Art in Oslo, Norway. Sculptural objects by Pepe Mar resembling goofy stuffed animals have evolved into more sophisticated works shown at David Castillo Modern & Contemporary Art in Wynwood and at Freight & Volume gallery in New York's Chelsea neighborhood.

In his new position with Diana Lowenstein, he'll travel to international art fairs in Cologne and Dubai and curate small shows for the gallery. In November, he's planning to show work by Manny Prieres, no stranger to the boundary-pushing, out-of-the-mainstream places where Diaz got his start. Prieres was one of the artist-founders of Box, an alternative art space that closed in 2004, along with Jose Reyes and Leyden Rodriguez-Casonova.

"I think I have an eye for art," Diaz says. Artists that capture his eye are those who can look beyond their studio "to the art world in general and to what's going on in the world, and how that somehow becomes intertwined with art."

CLAIRE BREUKEL

Claire Breukel, 27, is the executive director of Locust Projects, the alternative art exhibition space in Wynwood recently awarded a $107,000 grant from the Andy Warhol Foundation in New York. Before that, she was the director of exhibitions at the ArtCenter/South Florida on Lincoln Road.

Breukel moved to Miami in late 2003 for an internship at the Rubell Family Collection. After the internship, she returned to work for a year in her native South Africa and then came back to Miami.

Right now she is dealing with how Locust Projects takes a different approach to its audience than she found at the ArtCenter/South Florida.

Locust Projects generally aims for a more informed audience already attuned to the eccentric, experimental nature of contemporary art. The space "allows the artist to experiment, to push the envelope, without any commercial concerns," she says.

She would like to see fewer of those market-driven concerns shaping the art scene here now that Art Basel Miami Beach is established. "The nature of an art fair is primarily a commercial venture," she says. As a result, the fair has had both good and bad effects.

The good? "Art is being bought. Artists are able to work as professionals and make a living." The bad? "I would like to see less emphasis on the commercialization of art [so that] people will look again at the quality and not just the market value. The commercial aspects may be taking over a little too much and becoming very trend based."

CAROLINA GARCÍA

Carolina García, 31, is the director of LegalArt, a not-for-profit organization that gives artists access to affordable legal services and seminars for professional development. She came to Miami because the University of Miami law school ran a clinical program for fostering economic redevelopment that interested her. She always assumed that after law school she would move back to New York. While a law student, she made friends with artists here. "The first year of Art Basel Miami Beach was my first year of law school. The impact of Basel on the art community is why LegalArt grew at such a huge pace," she says.

With the fair, the number of galleries in town increased, and many more collectors were checking out Miami-based artists. Suddenly, she says, the artists' professional needs became more apparent.

"As artists become more sophisticated in their career, their needs grow in grant writing skills and basic business planning," she says. LegalArt's first Emerging Artist Grant of $3,000, awarded in December '05 to Bert Rodriguez, drew 70 applications. In June, the ArtCenter/South Florida exhibited *Native Seeds*, work by the top 10 finalists for that grant. That show included art by Mar, who had shown in Diaz's first curated project in his apartment near downtown Miami.

Miami's growing cultural scene keeps García here.

"I've stayed for all of the opportunities here in general for development," she says. "I've always been around artists. That's always been my social circle; I wasn't a typical law student. I went to law school because I knew that I wanted to have a nonprofit arts organization."

In memoriam: Mark Coetzee, d. 2022

FÉLIX GONZÁLEZ-TORRES

A Posthumous Honor for Cuban-Born Artist

June 3, 2007

When the 2007 Venice Biennale opens a week from today, the United States will be represented by the late Cuban-born artist Félix González-Torres.

His inclusion marks only the second time that a deceased artist has represented the United States in the modern history of the biennale, the art world's most prestigious international showcase. (Robert Smithson received this posthumous honor in 1982.) While some in the New York art world complain that this coveted and competitive distinction is going to a dead artist, in the Miami art world, there's a nearly euphoric feeling that the influential and internationally acclaimed González-Torres, who died in Miami in 1996, is finally getting his due.

His show, *Félix González-Torres: America*, runs through November 21 at the Venice Biennale.

"This is a Cuban American artist representing the United States. It is a rare honor and speaks volumes about the work," says art collector and Miami Art Museum trustee Peter Menéndez, who was a close friend of the artist. "His museum exhibits are enormously popular because they connect with the public in a very quick fashion."

González-Torres was a conceptual artist with a unique gift for creating visual poetry and quietly provocative public art projects: billboards of simple photographs charged with a deep sense of loss, like those with one bird in flight, or an empty bed where someone had recently slept, or stacks of paper or piles of candy functioning as gifts to museumgoers. He created art from strings of 15-watt light bulbs, such as *Untitled (America)*, which greets visitors as they enter his Venice exhibit. These defiantly low-tech pieces evoke the simplicity of light and humble gatherings of friends in a diverse, divisive world. His art reached out beyond museums to people on the street, possibly spurring them to think about social injustices of the era.

In Venice, 12 billboards by González-Torres will be scattered throughout the city as a part of his Biennale show. Miami collectors Rosa and Carlos de la Cruz, major collectors of his work, have loaned their billboard of a lone bird. "Venice is a perfect city for that. It's surrounded by water, and Félix's work deals a lot with the sky and sea," says Rosa de la Cruz.

She is struck by the visual poetry of his imagery evoking an island landscape, surely derived from his childhood memories of the Caribbean. She recalls exchanging recipes for Cuban dishes with him when he visited the couple's Key Biscayne home.

"His work is very connected . . . to this idea of pleasure that food gives. He loved food and talking about cooking."

A year before he died of AIDS-related causes, he was in the running for the Venice honor but was not chosen.

"He was an extraordinary artist," says artist María Martínez-Cañas, who is among the Miami artists, collectors, museum professionals, and art supporters who knew the New York–based González-Torres. She recalls how he seemed at home in Miami Beach, where he kept an apartment. "Miami was very energized at that time. It was the beginning of all the changes that later brought on Art Basel. A lot of artists were coming here to work. That kind of ferment appealed to him."

His ties to the Miami art scene run deep. When the new building for the Museum of Contemporary Art opened in North Miami in February 1996, director Bonnie Clearwater included González-Torres in the inaugural exhibit, *Defining the Nineties: Consensus-Making in New York, Miami, and Los Angeles*.

The artist didn't live to see the MOCA show. He died in early January, a month before *Defining the Nineties* opened with three of his artworks. The following May, the de la Cruzes gave one of the works in the show—a paper stack called *Untitled (Ross in LA)*—to MOCA in memory of González-Torres. (All his works are called *Untitled* followed by a kind of subtitle in parentheses that varies with each artwork; it's a style that suits his subtle and poetic approach.)

His legacy in Miami is burnished by another friend from Puerto Rico, Damian Fernandez, who heads the Cuban Research Institute at Florida International University. Fernandez founded the Félix González-Torres Community Art Project in 2005 at the school. "For him, education was a way of understanding himself and the world and a way of changing people's preconceived notions. His art speaks across cultures. It's basically metaphors. Félix's art is transcendentally revolutionary because people can take many of the pieces with them when they exit the museum."

Each year, the FIU program brings a stellar artist to campus for a week to work with art students and give a public lecture. González-Torres's longtime New York dealer, Andrea Rosen, says the program is in sync with the artist's philosophy: "Félix never wanted to be marginalized. He was proud of being Cuban born, he was a gay activist, but he didn't want to have advantages because he was a minority. When it came to his artwork he wanted to be judged equally, not because he was part of any subset. He considered himself an American equal to anyone else."

Because he charted many new directions for contemporary artists, González-Torres is called an artist's artist. "The idea that art can have a sensuous, enjoyable quality while also being smart and conceptual is how his art has influenced Miami artists," says Clearwater. She notes that art by the collective Friends With You and by Bert Rodriguez and Frances Trombly shows traces of the late artist's ideas. Carlos Betancourt says he's made artworks, including a billboard for the Bass Museum, that pay homage to González-Torres. When Miami artists get together over drinks, he adds, "everybody dissects Félix's work. He has a huge impact."

In memoriam: Félix González-Torres, 1957–1996
Rosa de la Cruz, 1944–2024

HOWARD FARBER

The Eye of the Collector

June 11, 2007

The first and last time Howard Farber, a collector of contemporary Cuban art, set foot in Cuba was in 2001. It was an odd introduction to the island.

Stepping off the plane in Havana, he and wife Patricia lugged shopping bags full of foot powder from a Walgreens pharmacy in Manhattan. Patricia, a New York City patron of the ballet, was bringing much-needed supplies for the foot-sore ballet dancers of Cuba.

Farber at the time was a collector of American modernist art and contemporary art from China. Although the couple went to Havana for a tour of Cuban art and architecture organized by the Metropolitan Museum of Art in New York, Farber insisted on that trip, "No art. I am not buying any art. I am totally involved with Chinese art." For good measure, he added, "My brain can't handle another collection."

That attitude quickly changed as the hardcore art collector discovered adventurous art and wondered how contemporary works came to not only exist but thrive in the communist nation.

A natural-born raconteur, Farber tells of his change of heart while sitting at the dining table in his Miami Beach apartment, where he and Patricia live part time.

As he talks about that fateful trip, Farber's looking through the bilingual catalog for *Cuba Avant-Garde: Contemporary Cuban Art from the Farber Collection*, which is now at the Harn Museum of Art at the University of Florida in Gainesville. It's there until September and then will travel to more museums.

Six months after his visit to Cuba, a museum professional in Cuba emailed Farber to ask about his contemporary Chinese art collection.

"I was fascinated because it was the first time I've ever received an email from Havana," he says. Through that person, whose name he says he can't divulge, Farber's quest to collect Cuban art began.

"In another life I must have been either an art critic or an art historian because to me the history of art is as important as the artwork itself," says Farber, 64.

A trim man of medium height, he says he hates public speaking, but in the quiet of the Miami Beach apartment, furnished with a stylish simplicity that looks almost Asian, he enthusiastically talks on and on about art.

As with each of his collections of American, Chinese, and Cuban art, he notes that he feels like "I have an eye for art, but I have had a lot of help. Someone has to train you." For each of his collections, he found advisers.

To learn more about Cuban art, he trolled the internet, consulted people in Havana, and had lunch with Holly Block, who wrote the book *Art Cuba: The New Generation*. It came out the year that Farber traveled to Havana.

Another critical book in his quest to collect Cuban art was *New Art of Cuba*, which Luis Camnitzer wrote in 1994. Farber calls it his bible. He keeps copies at his homes in Miami Beach and New York. "I go on vacation and I take it with me. I read it on the beach. I could read it 50 times."

Farber used a strategy that served him well in his American and Chinese collections: identify the group show that captured a pivotal moment in the art he pursued.

For Cuban contemporary art, it was *Volumen I*, which opened January 14, 1981, in the Centro de Arte Internacional in Havana. Camnitzer writes in his book that this show "has come to symbolize the emergence of the new art in Cuba for artists and critics alike," and he asserts that the show had a historical impact on Cuban art in the 20th century.

Its impact since seems undiminished: five of the artists from that 1981 show are in the Farber show. They include three who frequently exhibit in South Florida: José Bedia, Tomás Sanchez, and Rubén Torres Llorca.

A second strategy Farber used was to seek out the artists themselves. Some were in Cuba; others were in Miami, Canada, Spain, France, and Australia. He contacted them to ask where he could find the artwork that they thought was the best example of their work.

"What I did was try to find the artists, find their great works, try to collect them, and put them in a show to have these works seen for the first time in many cases," Farber says.

Through what he calls sometimes "nefarious" methods, one painting after another from Cuba reached him in New York. "It was usually rolled up and dirty because it had been sitting for years either in a basement or attic," he says. After he would have a work cleaned and stretched, he says, "there before me was a miraculous work."

Carlos Estévez, who now lives in Miami, was in Paris when Farber emailed him. He benefited from one of Farber's artistic search-and-rescue missions. In the catalog (but not in the show) is *Across the Universe* by Estévez. A large sculpture that weighs more than 200 pounds, it shows a Christlike man with a candle and huge wings.

"He saved that work," says Estévez, who hadn't seen the sculpture since leaving Cuba in 2003. When he saw it again, he became emotional.

Farber says he has been impressed by the deep friendships among Cuban artists: "I never met a group of artists so dedicated to other artists."

He saw an example of that in February at the opening party for Carlos Gonzalez at Chelsea Galleria in Wynwood.

"They are all [there] for support," he says. "They all have a history together. The original dirt on their feet is from Cuba."

Tina Spiro of Chelsea Galleria remembers Farber from that night. He was observant, charming, and curious. Farber doesn't strike her as a collector who likes art as a status symbol.

"He has a personality that is in sync with art. He's in touch with what he's looking at," she says.

Farber says his passion for Cuban art is "only about the art" and doesn't carry any political message.

"I know that in Florida people really get bent out of shape with the history of Cuban art," he says, his voice rising. "People have to realize that not everybody that has the ability to collect Cuban art is involved in politics! It has to be said and I'm not afraid to say it."

In memoriam: Holly Block, 1958–2017

FREDRIC SNITZER GALLERY

Made in Miami

July 22, 2007

Why call an art show about Miami artists a confluence?

It's a word that paints a picture of rivers coming together.

It seems inappropriate for art made in an ocean-front city.

But take a look at the full title of the show at Fredric Snitzer Gallery.

Confluence: A Collaboration, featuring 59 works by more than 50 artists, is all about artists coming together to make art—performance art and video, drawings, sculpture, painting, photography, and even a piece of needlepoint. The artists work with such diverse materials as crayons and wine, a firecracker and bullet.

Says artist Alvaro Pereyra, whose work is in the show, "The only way for an art scene to succeed is through a sense of community and sharing. It creates a good energy."

The one artwork credited to a single artist is a performance about the essence of art by David Rohn. In his *Untitled*, he stood next to a gallery wall for several hours the night of the July 14 opening. A solid black rectangle was painted on the wall behind his head. In slow motion, he smiled, frowned, looked sad and quizzical, and conveyed a range of human experience.

On the checklist for *Confluence*, most artworks are credited to two or three artists. The video *Fomercial* is credited to 11. Created in the collaborative spirit that the TM Sisters have made famous in their art fusing video games with performance art, the hilarious and snappy *Fomercial* is by Tasha López de Victoria and Monica López de Victoria (known as the TM Sisters), Jiae Hwang, Susan Lee-Chun, Karelle Levy, Samantha Kruse, Aja Albertson, Kathleen Hudspeth, Muriel Olivares, Jen Stark, and Ramona Boucher.

Fomercial is a deliciously clever spoof on the infomercials that are the bane of late-night TV addicts: upbeat spots hawking magic elixirs for losing 200 pounds in two weeks, exercise programs that guarantee to triple your muscle mass in three weeks or your money back.

This video opens with Tasha López de Victoria jogging on what seems to be an indoor track. She radiates energy. "Now I'm strong!" she beams in the video.

At the opening, Tasha smiles happily, wearing a black-and-white striped outfit that could have come from an old Jane Fonda exercise video. "Monica and I wanted to do another video like we did for the last collaboration," she says. (This show is a sequel to a group show in 2005 at the Bas Fisher Invitational space in the Design District; Miami artists Bhakti Baxter and Jason Hedges curated the Snitzer and Bas Fisher shows.)

This sequel at Snitzer Gallery allowed the 11 artists in *Fomercial* to bond together, share talent, and make art. "We had fun," Tasha grins, describing how the artists brainstormed together and created a storyline with characters they invented. She adds, "We dressed up in front of the screen and talked about how the product changed our lives."

In one scene, Hwang is garbed in a wig with very pink and very long hair. Her head floats among travel magazine shots, including a scene of the Taj Mahal. "I used to be tired, but now I'm seeing the world," she enthuses dreamily.

Graffiti-like drawings on glossy paper, offering an assortment of creatures and collage, are a mixed-media collaboration by Jon Peck, Kevin Arrow, and Jim Drain. "It's in the genre of free jazz," Peck says. "A lot of this stuff happens synchronistically," adds Arrow, talking about an evening he and Drain met to make art together. The next day, Peck came by and picked up their drawings. "I took them home, cut them apart a bit, and added on sculptures," Peck says with a mischievous smile.

Among the crowds at the opening were Sibel Kocabasi and Alvaro Pereyra, who have curated an upcoming show of 29 Florida artists opening in Istanbul on October 17. The Istanbul show is *Undertow*, and it includes some of the artists in *Confluence*. Coincidentally, both shows have titles with a watery theme, perhaps evoking the rippling effect that Miami artists seem to be making around the globe.

"The thing that's interesting about the Miami scene is that it's very pluralistic," says Pereyra. "There's no major theme. There's all types of art made in all types of media." Adds Kocabasi, an artist of Turkish descent living in Lake Worth, "I think there are a lot of cultures here. I'm seeing a lot of young artists with fresh new attitudes." (She is setting up a website for the Istanbul show.)

One performance that night was highly impromptu. There was a traffic jam of people clustered around a section of the gallery where a drawing of Bert Rodriguez's face was on the wall and, a couple of feet below the drawing, a hole in the wall that looked like an out-of-place birdhouse. People whispered and giggled. Although you couldn't see him, Rodriguez was sealed into a space behind the wall. At different times during the evening, his erect penis emerged from the wall, stayed in place for a few seconds, and then withdrew.

This was a performance provoking hysterical guffaws. It was a visceral asserption of an artist's right to make his own artistic statement no matter what, saying in essence the crudest thing possible to tastemakers and the rapacious art market.

Fred Snitzer says that he and others had ways to signal to Rodriguez so that he didn't "perform" when children were passing by. "It's always tricky territory," he admits. But he loved the daring "who cares?" spirit of the show. Snitzer adds, "If you get a big group of artists from the community you're going to have a lot of raw energy. It felt really good after too long of trying to be curatorial and proper."

BERNICE STEINBAUM GALLERY, CENTRO CULTURAL ESPAÑOL

Two Exhibitions Focus on the Feminist Mystique

September 16, 2007

Feminist art is getting new traction these days in exhibits around the country, and two shows currently in South Florida focus on feminism: *Carly Series*, at Bernice Steinbaum Gallery with digital photographs by Francie Bishop Good; and *face2face*, a show of video and installation art at Centro Cultural Español in Coral Gables.

At Steinbaum, subtle feminism animates a compelling show that tells the story of a girl moving from childhood through adolescence, making lively connections to art in South Florida, like Kelly Flynn's photographs of herself costumed as a cowboy. Good has photographed her niece Carly since she was seven years old; one work in the show is of Carly wearing childish butterfly wings. Good captures Carly when adolescence and adulthood mingle in a girl's life, pairing shots of Carly's face with mature artwork. The beguiling beauty in these images catches you off guard. Many pieces show Good's latest work, which she calls her *Artist Hero* series.

"It's more in your face," she says of one piece that focuses on one section of an artwork combined with a close-up of Carly's face. The sculpture by Louise Bourgeois in *Carly with Bourgeois* came from a photograph Good shot at an art fair. "I thought that Carly's face being out of focus and kind of sculptural would work really well with the piece, and when I put it together, it sang."

Good paired Carly with art by women making strong statements in art history because "it seemed like a perfect marriage," she says. Good often marries art and feminism. This month she donated to the Museum of Art Fort Lauderdale a set of six photographs in the limited edition series *Feminist Art after Photography*. She's excited about Girls' Club, a Fort Lauderdale alternative space showing art by women, including art she collects with husband David Horvitz. It opens in October with *Talking Heads*, a show she curated with Girls' Club director Michelle Weinberg, also an artist.

At Centro Cultural Español, the art in *face2face* gives a woman's perspective on immigration and discrimination. Much of the art promises to be more agenda driven than subtle.

"You get a broad picture of the world through women," says director María del Valle as she watches a video about transsexuals in India by French artist Floy Krouchi. It shows a young man posing in a purple sari. "It makes us think. I was amazed by this video because I'm not familiar with this culture."

RICHARD BLANCO
AND JOHN BAILLY

Poetry and Painting Combine for a Beautiful Show

October 21, 2007

For Miami painter John Bailly and poet Richard Blanco, home is a state of mind, a world packed with wild and wonderful memories, no matter its physical location.

Place of Mind is their haunting and quietly beautiful collaborative show now at the downtown Main Library of the Miami-Dade County Public Library System. It combines Blanco's poetry with Bailly's paintings and artworks on paper. Drinking buddies and friends in Miami for years, they worked together for two years to create this show, which bubbled up from shared bottles of cranberry vodka and spirited conversations about the meaning of home.

"We had a fun time doing this. It's our journey, sharing this sense of not belonging anywhere and feeling that we could belong anywhere," says Bailly.

"I'm still waiting for someone to tell me, 'Richard, your plane is waiting to take you home now.' There's a paradise out there somewhere. Or not," adds Blanco.

Place of Mind is a show to peruse with the mind and eye. Poet and painter invite you to travel with their artistic imagination as a tour guide.

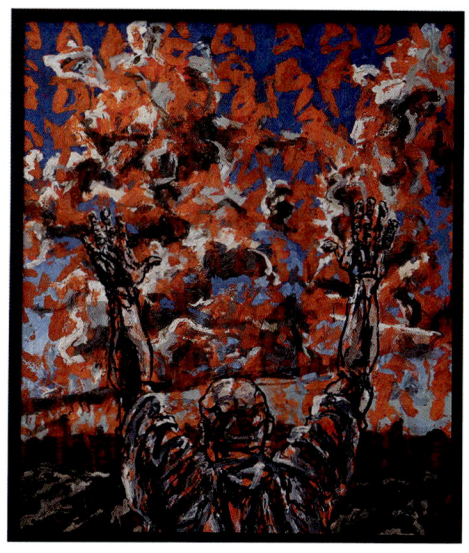

FIGURE 39. John Bailly, *Derrida*, 2000. Oil painting on canvas. Clark. Image Ryan Holloway, courtesy of Miami-Dade County Department of Cultural Affairs, Art in Public Places Trust.

Bailly's artworks on paper often describe bridges, such as in *Guantánamo*. It's not clear what this bridge connects, and shadowy shapes of people and words layer this artwork. They are hard to identify and resist a logical explanation. If you squint, you may make out these futile words in *Guantánamo*: "I've calculated the world with x's and y's"—a statement brimming with false confidence.

Your eye can wander among the interlacing veins of color and maplike shapes in Bailly's mixed-media painting *Los Hermanos Islets*. Stare at this subtle painting long enough and you will find that your memories of world maps begin to merge with what you see in his layers of paint, color, and texture. Shapely reminders of the Mediterranean Sea and the coastal edge of North Africa interrupt a dense network of crisscrossing lines. Red circles stamped with the letter *U* are bold interruptions. The scattered circles create an odd, almost threatening reminder that you're not really looking at a map.

"The *U*'s are a chain reaction of uranium when the atom bomb goes off," says Bailly. "We build up a whole world and then destroy it for some reason."

Like the red circles in *Los Hermanos Islets*, poems by Blanco add another layer of texture and meaning to Bailly's art. *Place of Mind* is about these mutually illuminating connections. Visual art by Bailly gives library visitors another way to "read" Blanco's evocative poems, which are mounted on large placards throughout the exhibit.

Lines in Blanco's poem "Crossing Boston Harbor" reverberate in your mind as you explore this exhibit. He writes, "The ferry's chine makes an incision across the bay, its churned waters bleed a wake of lustrous blue / behind us as we head west, scanning the coastline. So much of my life is spent like this—suspended, moving toward unknown places and names or / returning to those I know, corresponding with / the paradox of crossing, being nowhere yet here."

For Blanco and Bailly, those contradictory feelings that home can be anywhere and nowhere arise from their very Miami, very multicultural backgrounds. Bailly was born in England and grew up in France. "When I came to the US, I could only read and write 'cat' in English. With my French family, I've always been the American. With my American family, I'm always French, never fitting in anywhere."

Blanco's personal experience echoes Bailly's. "I'm a mutt like him," the poet says. His mother left Cuba for Spain when she was several months pregnant. Blanco was born in Madrid, and after barely a month, his family moved to New York and later to Miami.

"So by the time I was 45 days old, I could claim citizenship in three different countries," Blanco laughs. "I was 5 years old when I came to Miami. . . . I don't feel Cuban, I don't feel European, I don't feel American."

The fluid sense of identity shared by poet and painter plays out in the way this exhibit is organized. There isn't a clear-cut relationship between poems and paintings mounted next to each other. "I never wanted to make a painting about one of his poems, and I don't think he wanted to make a poem about one of my paintings," Bailly says.

Blanco concurs. Their collaboration was extremely casual. "It was very refreshing to see it visually and reinterpret the poems," says Blanco.

CONCLUSION

Art Bearing a Miami Postmark

A touchstone for my writing about Miami is a remark the late Yale scholar and author Robert Farris Thompson made in 1999. We spoke during a phone interview about internationally acclaimed Miami-based artist José Bedia, whose art interlaces strands of Caribbean, African, and Native American cultures with resonant power. "Miami is teaching the world what it will be like in the 21st century," Thompson told me. "Bedia's right at the forefront of contemporary art and culture. José is teaching us how to move into this multiethnic situation."

Looking back from the year 2025 on my two decades of art writing for the *Miami Herald*, I find Thompson's observation about the future more revelatory than ever. It's also unexpectedly trenchant for this deep dive into Miami's past. His comments were always floating in the back of my mind as I chose which reviews, profiles, and reported stories to bring together in this book.

When I was writing them, I was too immersed in the dailiness of news-paper deadlines to realize how these stories were painting an intricately faceted portrait of what makes creative Miami truly and essentially Miami. That portrait is much more nuanced than what the world sees in the highly publicized, high-end glamour of those high-flying days in early December called Miami Art Week.

Now I understand how the opening quotation in this book may come close to an exile's universal lament. "It's always going to be with you that you can't go back," Cuban-born Arturo Rodriguez told me for my September 20, 1987, column "Arturo Rodriguez: Spirit of Exile Shines in Painting for Pope." The column reported how Florida International University had commissioned a painting by Rodriguez to give to Pope John Paul II in honor of the 1987 papal visit to campus.

Rodriguez's painting *Exiliados* captures an exiled family's feeling of profound loss. The uprooted family seems to be stranded near a beach, the father hobbled by two left feet, the mother holding a squirming baby. Their surroundings appear bleached by an intense tropical sun. The distant skyline could belong to Miami.

That quotation from Rodriguez as this book begins finds a poignant parallel in the final column 20 years later, "Richard Blanco and John Bailly: Poetry and Painting Combine for a Beautiful Show." For their 2007 collaboration at the downtown library, Bailly and Blanco were inspired by their spirited conversations about the meaning of home.

The collaboration between poet and painter revealed, Bailly told me, "our journey, sharing this sense of not belonging anywhere and feeling that we could belong anywhere."

As I spoke with them both at the library, the poet added, "I'm still waiting for someone to tell me, 'Richard, your plane is waiting to take you home now.' There's a paradise out there somewhere. Or not."

As I have tried to show throughout this book, the culture of Miami springs from many hands and many minds belonging to those who have landed in this ever-evolving cosmopolitan place from points near and distant. Many have left places they once called home. Sometimes there was time to pack bags and make plans for a new life, sometimes not.

This common experience of uprootedness often occurred when homes became hostile and barely recognizable. Or it may have happened when homes were too confining to nurture a Miami-styled restless spirit questing for new challenges. While departures for many can be either panic-stricken or purposeful, artists who choose to leave their country and place of origin for Miami have gathered resources to heighten its cultural spark and diversity over decades. They've cultivated a grand spirit of experimentation and openness to innovation in their adopted home.

Traveling here from across the map, artists have brought thought-provoking traditions and perspectives from their own countries that weave among vivid threads in Miami's unique tapestry. It's one that flickers and flashes into new permutations, pushing back against easy definitions.

This book has sought to spotlight those vivid threads for a community rushing forward so swiftly it could be more mindful of the past making the present possible.

During the years recounted here, national and international recognition came to art bearing a Miami postmark. In the late 1980s, art by Arturo Rodriguez traveled to the Vatican in Rome. Art by María Brito traveled to Seoul, South Korea. In the 1990s, the National Conference of Artists, a national organization of visual artists of African descent, included art by Charles Humes Jr. and Dinizulu Gene Tinnie in a show presented by what is now named the Marshall L. Davis Sr. African Heritage Cultural Arts Center in Miami's Liberty City. The column "*Touched by* AIDS *Honors Pivotal Figures of Miami's Art Scene*" at what is now known as Miami Dade College placed artists lost to AIDS in a national context through its connections with the Los Angeles–based Estate Project for Artists with AIDS. Carlos Alfonzo was represented in the Whitney Biennial in New York City.

And the list goes on. In the aughts, María Martínez-Cañas was included in *Arte Latino: Treasures from the Smithsonian American Art Museum*. Teresita Fernández was awarded the MacArthur Foundation "Genius Grant." Eugenia Vargas represented her native Chile in the 50th Venice Biennale.

In November 2024, notable recognition continued at a branch of the Smithsonian, tellingly on the pressing topic of home. Conceived by Miami artist Cornelius Tulloch, *Ebb + Flow* was an interdisciplinary installation created for the South Florida nonprofit Artists in Residence in Everglades (AIRIE). It was part of *Making Home—Smithsonian Design Triennial* at Cooper Hewitt, Smithsonian Design Museum, which ran through August 10, 2025. Spotlighting local communities, *Ebb + Flow* intended to offer a richly layered, multisensory portrait of the Everglades' imperiled wetlands and preservationists' efforts to conserve its culture, beauty, and history. Collaborating on this installation were architect Germane Barnes and artists Atéha Bailly, Ania Freer, and Christina Pettersson.

At this Smithsonian Design Triennial, art with a Miami postmark was created to be compelling and immersive. It was an audacious, defiant leap of faith to imagine that even a semblance of the watery wildness of the Everglades could be housed within a Gilded Age, Georgian Revival mansion on New York City's Upper East Side, one that's now converted to a museum. But that leap of faith did happen, soaring northward the 1,000-plus miles from Miami and the Everglades to Manhattan.

This momentary second home of sorts for the Everglades brought new urgency to its fragile beauty through a series of sounds, stories, and textures. It dug deep into Everglades history. Enriching *Ebb + Flow* were contributions of Daniel Tommie of the Seminole tribe of Florida and Black Historical Research Project board members Wallis Tinnie and Dinizulu Gene Tinnie. Images printed on curving window seats by Pettersson depicted traditions for making a home in the Everglades, from workers in sugarcane fields to Seminole chickee huts of palmetto thatch over an open-air log frame.

In recent conversations with Pettersson and Tulloch, they shared with me their thoughts about the impact of *Ebb + Flow*. "The show really comes down to humans belonging to the landscape," said Pettersson. "But of course people have been evolving with the landscape forever."

Describing how all the elements of *Ebb + Flow* fit together, Tulloch said that they "created a space of solace for people to relax and take in the stories."

And yet as a truly homegrown concept, *Ebb + Flow* harkens back to a rich tradition of art reinventing what is precious and poignant about making a home in a place balanced precariously on the edge of the Atlantic. That concept arises from a place at once scarred and ennobled by transience, by an inevitably diverse procession of people coming and going, and increasingly a witness to the destructive reach of rising seas in the face of relentless real estate development and drastically changing climate.

Even as a memory, *Ebb + Flow* aims to rescue from erasure the too often overlooked natural treasure and history of South Florida's Everglades. It is perhaps the latest chapter in Miami's art history traveling anew on that classic homeward journey.

ACKNOWLEDGMENTS

First, I must express appreciation to former colleagues at the *Miami Herald*. Their professional dedication for 21 years permitted my art criticism to reach readers of printed pages in the *Miami Herald*. Admirable standards set by my late predecessor art critic Helen Kohen continue to inspire.

I am forever indebted to Alberto Ibargüen, *Miami Herald* publisher when many columns in this book were written. His supportive presence at the *Miami Herald* from 1998 to 2005 made my prolific newspaper career possible. It was quite unusual for an art critic who was an independent contractor to have the opportunities I did. My years at the *Herald* included international assignments to biennials in Havana and Venice; art fairs, museums, and other venues in Basel, Switzerland; and art communities of Port-au-Prince and Jacmel in Haiti. The experiences of such travel inform my art writing in countless ways. As John S. and James L. Knight Foundation CEO and president, Alberto approved a very generous Knight Foundation grant allowing this book to be published.

For their graciously executed accomplishments on behalf of this book, I express profound thanks to Victoria Rogers during her tenure as Knight Foundation vice president of arts; Rosie Gordon-Wallace, lead curator and founder of Diaspora Vibe Culture Arts Incubator; and Nhadya Lawes, arts program officer at the Knight Foundation. At the University Press of Florida, the leadership of director Romi Gutierrez and the guidance of senior acquisitions editor Sian Hunter have been unfailingly valuable.

For steadfast encouragement of the idea for this book and the book itself as it progressed toward publication, I am grateful to former *Miami Herald* publisher David Lawrence Jr.

For their thoughtful insights about ways to strengthen this book before publication, I express sincere thanks to an anonymous peer reader and to peer reader Jeremy Mikolajczak.

For early endorsement of this project, my heartfelt gratitude goes to Michael Spring during his tenure as director of Miami-Dade County Department of Cultural Affairs. Welcome support for the creation of new essays placing my historical writing in a contemporary context came from two sources: a 2023 Creator Award from Oolite Arts and a 2023–24 Miami Individual Artist (MIA) grant approved by Miami-Dade County Board of Commissioners and Mayor Daniella Levine Cava, implemented by Cultural Projects administrator Jane Thayer of Miami-Dade County Department of Cultural Affairs.

I am deeply grateful to Franklin Sirmans, Sandra and Tony Tamer Director of the Pérez Art Museum Miami, for his concise foreword to this book.

To provide color reproductions of art for this book by artists whose work belongs to the Art in Public Places Collection of Miami-Dade County, the Art in Public Places team could not have been more helpful. Abundant thanks go to the director of Miami-Dade County Department of Cultural Affairs Marialaura Leslie; chief of Art in Public Places Patricia Romeu; curator and artist manager of Art in Public Places, Amanda Sanfilippo Long; and APP special coordinator of projects Yusimy Lara. I am grateful to artists Pablo Cano, María Martínez-Cañas, and Arturo Rodriguez for permission to reproduce their art and to Liza and Arturo Mosquera for permission to reproduce art by María Brito from their collection.

For assistance in submitting grant applications related to this book and for her work with Miami-Dade Art in Public Places staff, Pablo Cano, María Martínez-Cañas, Arturo Rodriguez, and collectors Liza and Arturo Mosquera to transmit images of art to the University Press of Florida, I express much appreciation to Amanda Bradley.

I am very appreciative of artist Carlos Betancourt for permission to reproduce his 2009 digitally assembled photo collage *Re-Collections VIII (rojo y azul)* on the cover of this book.

"Milestones in Miami's Coming of Age Saga," a series of condensed columns dated 1999 to 2004 adapted from this book, previously appeared in *Making Miami: The Story of an Art Community* by Vivek and Carolina García Jayaram, published in 2023 by Jayaram and EXILE Books.

When my career at the *Miami Herald* ended in 2007, I realized that since I was never a full-time employee, as an independent contractor I wanted access to all those years of hard work. In March 2009, a dear lawyer friend David Appleby wrote to the then *Miami Herald* publisher and executive editor requesting that I be allowed to obtain a complete catalog of my writing. As a result, I received permission to go to the *Miami Herald* building, regrettably since demolished, and download my writing on my own flash drives from computers in the *Herald* library. Ana Riera of Riera Computer Consulting transferred the "data," as she called it, into searchable archives on my laptop. From those archives I compiled this book. Words cannot express how much I value their early role in this book.

There are many who agreed to comment on parts or all of the manuscript in its early stages. I am immensely thankful for their advice, conveyed over the course of lunches, email correspondence, and phone conversations. They include Rina Carvajal, Sergio Cernuda, Linda Chapin, william cordova, Carol Damian, Suzanne Delehanty, Cathy Leff, Amy Rosenblum-Martín, Donna Ruff, and Barbara Young. My gratitude also goes to these readers: Kathy Martin, one of my first *Miami Herald* editors; Artburst Miami editor and arts journalist Michelle Solomon; and transdisciplinary artist and designer Dimitry Saïd Chamy.

Sources I found especially helpful in researching new material for this book were websites documenting artists' careers as well as websites for Art-Speak of FIU Lee Caplin School of Journalism and Media, Artists in Residence in Everglades, Bakehouse Art Complex, Commissioner.us, Miami-Dade Public Library System and Vasari Project, Wet Heat Project, Women Artists Archive Miami, and Women Photographers International Archive.

Writing this book and preparing it for publication has been an endeavor fueled by joy and determination. A belief that this history deserves to be preserved and shared drove me forward. There are so many stories enfolded in these columns that I think are worthy to be told again in the format of this book. It is my hope that they may inspire the telling of more stories and more attention to art made in Miami. That attention is surely all the more vital now as Miami confronts rapidly accelerating costs of living, affecting the availability of artists' studios, and a degrading environment.

In 2025, those challenges have been intensified by assaults on freedom of the press, civil rights, and funding for revered social and cultural institutions. In these uncertain times, I believe this book pays insistent homage to the persevering creative spirit from which we all stand to gain.

As ideas for this book took shape in my mind and then moved toward publication, it's been a gift to be encouraged by friends, artists, colleagues in the arts, and former *Miami Herald* colleagues. Among them are Marta Barber, Robin Cembalest, Robert Chambers, Lou Anne Colodny, Connie Crowther, Morel Doucet, Margaria Fichtner, Jay Flynn, Lilia Garcia, Maureen Gragg, Elizabeth Hanly, Carol Jazzar, Carl Juste, Mitchell Kaplan, Dennis Leyva, Marika Lynch, Gary Monroe, Paula Musto, Valerie Ricordi, Leyden Rodriguez Casanova, Emily Rosenthal, Dennis Scholl, Onajide Shabaka, Roscoè B. Thické III, Kate Grace Thome, Mette Tommerup, Frances Trombly, Tom Virgin, Bonita Whytehead, Pauline Winick, Wendy Wischer, Morton Wright, Jan Yelen, and Karen Zusman.

I was incredibly lucky to benefit from the unconditional love of my immediate and extended family when producing this writing. There were moments when my deadline anxiety and compulsion to revise "just one more time" intruded into our time together. Years later, when I was working on this book and writing new essays, that anxiety returned. Endless thanks go to my adult children Grant and Margaret Smith, who were quite young when my *Herald* career began. My deepest thanks of all goes to my husband, Eric Smith. His love, support, and patience have been absolutely essential for the writing of this book.

INDEX

Page numbers in *italic* refer to figures.

ELISA TURNER is an award-winning art critic and art journalist in Miami. In 2020, she received the Rabkin Prize for art writers. Other awards include First Place for Arts Commentary & Criticism from Florida's Sunshine State Society of Professional Journalists, the Leadership Award of the Florida Chapter of ArtTable, and the President's Volunteer Service Award from Miami Dade College. She covered the visual arts for the *Miami Herald* from 1986 to 2007, with international assignments to Basel, Haiti, Havana, and Venice. During that time, she was the Miami correspondent for *ARTnews* magazine. She has taught writing and remedial grammar at Miami Dade College, and she holds a BA in English from DePauw University and an MA in comparative literature from the University of North Carolina at Chapel Hill.

FRANKLIN SIRMANS is the Sandra and Tony Tamer Director of the Pérez Art Museum Miami (PAMM). Appointed director in 2015, he has strengthened the PAMM Fund for Black Art and created the museum's International Women's Committee and Latin American and Latinx Art Fund, enabling the museum to acquire over a thousand artworks through donation or purchase. His focus emphasizes the museum's mission to present international modern and contemporary art while underscoring its commitment to Miami and the surrounding region. He recently organized *Hurvin Anderson: Passenger Opportunity* and *Every Sound Is a Shape of Time: Selections from the* PAMM *Collection*. Previously, Sirmans was the department head and curator of contemporary art at Los Angeles County Museum of Art (LACMA) and the head of Modern and Contemporary Art at the Menil Collection, Houston.